Structure, Space and Skin The Work of Nicholas Grimshaw & Partners

Structure, Space and Skin The Work of Nicholas Grimshaw & Partners

Introduced by Kenneth Powell

Edited by Rowan Moore

Contents

Foreword 7

Acknowledgements 8

Introduction
by Kenneth Powell 9

Channel Tunnel
Railway Terminal
at Waterloo, London,
1993

24

Shopping and Leisure
Project, Port East,
London Docklands,
1989

104

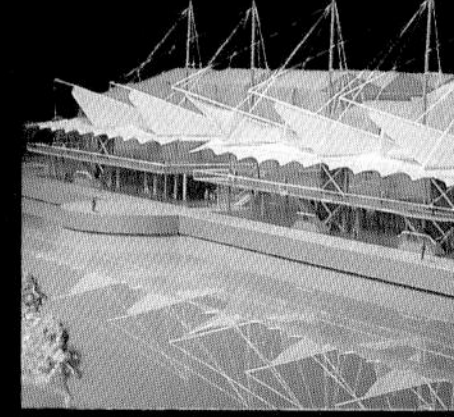

North Woolwich
Pumping Station,
London, 1988

56

Satellite and Piers,
Heathrow Airport,
London, 1993

114

British Pavilion
Expo 92, Seville, 1992

62

Venice Biennale,
1991

134

Operations Centre
for British Rail at
Waterloo, London, 1990

84

Nicholas Grimshaw
& Partners' offices,
London, 1992

146

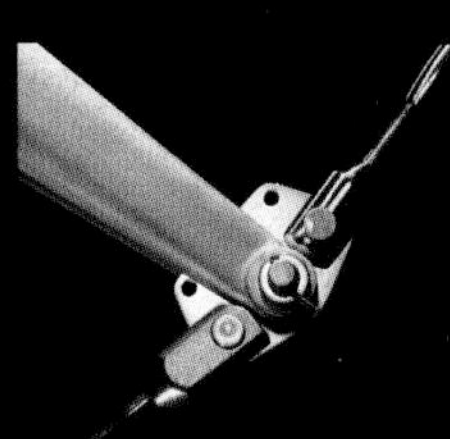

Igus Headquarters and Factory, Cologne, 1992

158

Bibliothèque Nationale de France, Competition, 1989

176

Hartspring Business Park, Watford, 1986–

186

Western Morning News, Plymouth, 1992

194

Berlin Stock Exchange and Communications Centre, 1991–1995

216

Combined Operations Centre for British Airways, London, 1993

228

'Structure, Space and Skin'
A lecture by Nick Grimshaw 236

Interview
Nick Grimshaw and Hugh Pearman 244

Awards 249

Project list 250

Bibliography 252

Project data 254

Nicholas Grimshaw & Partners
The team 1985–1993 256

Phaidon Press Limited
Regent's Wharf
All Saints Street
London N1 9PA

First published 1993
Reprinted 1994
First paperback edition 1995
Reprinted 1997

ISBN
0 7148 2850 5 (hardback)
0 7148 3457 2 (paperback)

A CIP catalogue record for this book is available from the British Library

Printed in Hong Kong

Foreword

This book is the first of a series. It deals with our work from 1988 to 1993, a period which takes in the nearly completed Channel Tunnel Railway Terminal at Waterloo, the completed British Pavilion at Expo 92 in Seville, and the Berlin Stock Exchange and Communications Centre, which has not yet started on site. The book, therefore, is very much a record of work in progress.

Where architecture is concerned, it seems there is never a 'right time' to produce a book. The start of a new commission is always a cause for celebration but the completion of a project often goes unmarked in the turmoil of the client taking occupation. There never seems a right time to record the completion. If a photographer shoots a building unoccupied then the spaces may seem unlived-in and inhuman. If the photographer waits for the client to move in, he or she often cannot find the peace to get the shots that are really wanted.

In a busy office, however, most projects seem to come under the heading of 'in progress'. We have tried hard in this book to record the *process* of achieving a building, from early sketches and models through computer simulations to final, detailed drawings. And from these the making of the components and the joining of them together to form the finished buildings. It is our hope that by attempting to show the entire building process the reader will be given a much greater understanding of our buildings and will be led away from the idea that architecture is merely the formation of facades.

The key preoccupations of our early work – the quality of life in a working environment, the significance of geometry, the importance of structure and flexibility, and questions of detailing and energy conservation – continue to be important themes. However, there now seems to be a new appreciation in society of architecture as one of the fundamental arts that shape contemporary life. The fascinating thing about this is that clients have come to perceive that what is justified in the name of order, economy and geometry is governed also by other forces. We now have clients who expect architecture to be an art and to have creative force behind it. Of course, they also expect buildings to be completed on cost and on time. However, the simple awareness that clients want a landmark – something that will last and be loved – is a marvellous experience.

This feeling of creating something, as well as simply producing, affects the entire design team. The dedication to the project shown by people in my own office is quite extraordinary. I know they see the process of creating a building as of intense importance both to themselves and to the clients. Both sides are drawn into producing the artefact. I am convinced that, if a project is created in this way with mutual enthusiasm and commitment, it will be a success.

We hope that the foundation of economy and good detailing laid down in our early work, when combined with the elements of structure, space and skin, as demonstrated in this volume, will help the other books in this series to demonstrate the sense of continuity that we feel is so important.

Nick Grimshaw
December 1992

Acknowledgements

Photography

Victoria Boyarsky/ Architectural Association *p11*
Dan Branch/Architectural Association *p19*
Richard Bryant/Arcaid *pp21, 63*
Keith Collie and Mick Thomas *Channel Tunnel Railway Terminal and Combined Operations Centre*
Hanya Chlala *Nicholas Grimshaw & Partners' Offices and p256*
Stephane Coutourier/ Arcaid *p15*
Hayes-Davidson *rendering of the Combined Operations Centre and Operations Centre at Waterloo computer models*
Richard Davies *p16*
Joachim Diederichs *Berlin Stock Exchange model*
Michael Dyer Associates *model photography for Bibliothèque Nationale de France, Channel Tunnel Railway Terminal, Berlin Stock Exchange, British Pavilion at Expo 92, Port East, Satellite and Piers at Heathrow Airport*
S. Farmer *p17*
Kyle Stewart *Operations Centre at Waterloo p86*
Anthony Oliver *Channel Tunnel Railway Terminal, and Operations Centre at Waterloo*
Jo Reid & John Peck *pp9, 18, 23, Expo 92 Pavilion, Igus, Western Morning News, Nicholas Grimshaw & Partners' Offices*
Phil Sayer *p3*
G. Shane/Architectural Association *p22*
Ezra Stoller/Esto/Arcaid *pp13, 20*
Peter Strobel *component photographs of Channel Tunnel Railway Terminal and Western Morning News*
Jens Willebrand *Igus interiors, Venice Biennale*

Other contributors

Unit 22 *modelmakers*
Jan Kaplicky *Venice Biennale exhibit*
YRM Anthony Hunt Associates *CAD images for Channel Tunnel Railway Terminal*
Briggs Amasco Curtainwall *glazing drawings for Channel Tunnel Railway Terminal p45*

Introduction

Nicholas Grimshaw's first building was completed over a quarter of a century ago. By the early 1980s, he was recognisably one of the leading figures on the British architectural scene, a radical exponent of the engineering tradition in architecture that, in Britain, has a noble ancestry extending back to Brunel, Paxton and the great industrial architects of the 19th century. He might well have been described, like Jean Prouvé, as a 'constructor'. To this day, fine building and the necessity to do things well matter supremely to him. He has always been an urban architect, with a passion for cities, though his work has never been tailored to accord with established views of urban propriety. Grimshaw, it seemed to some, was too radical, especially in a Britain where mid-Atlantic Post-Modernism seemed to have captured the mood of the times.

Grimshaw, in truth, has emerged as one of the most versatile of the major European architects of the present day. Now in his early 50s, he has achieved a strikingly authoritative maturity – yet he is not content to rest there. Change, development, progress are inherent to the way he looks at architecture. He has advanced steadily, pragmatically (though he is the last architect to despise the role of theory) and self-critically. He retains the enthusiasm, the desire to experiment, of a young man. He heads an office that is a place of innovation, invention and imagination, a place where the atmosphere is more that of a laboratory or a think-tank than of a simple drawing office. The practice has produced a series of projects, built and unbuilt, of dazzling quality and variety. A great railway terminal, airports, city-centre public

Financial Times Print Works,
Tower Hamlets, London, 1988.

Glasgow School of Art
by CR Mackintosh, 1907.

buildings, factories, an exhibition pavilion (a building type always at the leading edge of architectural progress) – all these commissions have produced schemes that are as humane as they are technically advanced. There is an essential continuum in Grimshaw's work. The recent projects develop themes that can be found in his earliest work.

If he is a 'constructor', Grimshaw is equally an architect – a creator of buildings that excel in their wholeness and richness of form and meaning. The details matter to him, but a work of architecture is more than an assembly of details and components. It is as the creator of an architecture of form and space that Nicholas Grimshaw is rapidly emerging as an international leader.

History still matters profoundly to Grimshaw. His vision of history is based in engineering – the family tradition in which he grew up. He reveres Paxton, whose Crystal Palace of 1851 he points out as an example of an initial conceptual sketch carried through almost unaltered into the completed building. 'I say that if you get the concept right then you can create great buildings – if you are determined enough'. Grimshaw admits that he was 'acutely conscious' of the precedent of the Crystal Palace when working on the British Pavilion for Expo 92 in Seville. The palace was prefabricated off site, using established technology, albeit on an unprecedented scale, as was the Grimshaw pavilion. In the case of Seville, everything was shipped in from Britain as a 'kit of parts', except for the concrete substructure. The pavilion has the same seriousness and earnestness as Paxton's masterpiece – it is intended to educate as well as to entertain, and it eschews the pure showmanship and easy kitsch of some of the other Expo buildings. Like the Crystal Palace, the British Pavilion has a disciplined order that gives it a measure of formality.

Grimshaw's view of materials has its roots in history: 'It's not a matter of *which* materials you use, but more about *how* you use them', he argues. 'Rigour is vital, whatever you are using'. The architects of the past whom he really admires – Gunnar Asplund, Charles Rennie Mackintosh, Alvar Aalto – as well as Pierre Chareau at the Maison de Verre and his contemporary, Renzo Piano, have a 'way' with materials. Truth to materials is a tenet of the Modern Movement, but it can be traced back to the 19th century and to AWN Pugin's strictures on 'honest construction', and was certainly central to the philosophy of the Arts and Crafts movement.

Grimshaw's work is clearly and consciously rooted in the tradition of metal and glass architecture that extends back to the Industrial Revolution. But he does not see metal and glass as the *only* materials suitable for building in the modern age. His traditionalism is more subtle than that. 'I love wood and stone', he says, 'properly used, where they are appropriate'. Grimshaw has lavished care on the old barn that he has restored as a weekend retreat, mixing repair of the old fabric with new work of an entirely contemporary character. 'I would be happy to construct new buildings in wood and stone – or thatch, or any other traditional material, for that matter – if it made sense in terms of the brief and the needs of the client and users'. There could be nothing more truly 'functional', he believes, than the vernacular architecture of barns and windmills. They were built using the most up-to-date technology and most durable and economical materials available at the time. Many will regret it – and they too will call themselves traditionalists – but the world has changed and steel, aluminium, glass and concrete are, for the moment at least, the functional materials of today. Good building is Grimshaw's aim. 'I'm a traditional architect, carrying on a British tradition of good detailing, good construction, and serious design', he insists.

Earlier Modern Movement critics looked to Victorian engineering for the antecedents of the 'functional tradition'. Grimshaw realises that there were good reasons why the Victorians ornamented their railway stations, seaside piers and warehouses – the filigreed webs below the great arches of the roof at Paddington Station are structurally efficient as well as decorative, he points out. His architecture makes no pretence of pure Functionalism, any more than does that of Norman Foster, Richard Rogers or the other British architects with whom he is sometimes bracketed. History does not provide an apologia for Functionalism, says Grimshaw. Look at Le Corbusier's Ronchamp – is that 'functional'? Yet it is one of the sublime works of modern architecture. Is the work of Asplund or Aalto, the Stockholm Cemetery chapels or the Helsinki Cultural Centre, say, Functionalist? The mention of Aalto always arouses Grimshaw's enthusiasm. Grimshaw admires the Finnish master as a great creator of form and space, a poetic artist who never descended to the merely arbitrary, who never thought much about 'style'. It is expressive power of the order of Aalto at his best, one suspects, that Grimshaw strives for in his current work. But then Grimshaw has the same view of tradition as Aalto had: it is not about preserving the past or disinterring what is gone, but about building for the future in the wake of the knowledge and achievements of those who have gone before.

Aalto once said that the 'trouble with the Rational style was that the Rationalism didn't go deep enough' – in other words that it could lead to arid superficiality. Grimshaw takes issue with anyone who suggests that he is a super-Rationalist whose solutions to a brief are part of some preconceived programme of design. Responding to places matters to him greatly – he is always anxious to establish the *genius loci*. But it is often difficult to say what the predominant character of a place is. Look at the typical high street in Britain – a collection of frontages of all periods and styles, where no architect or builder has ever paid much heed to the nature of what already existed. Yet vernacular buildings share a universal architectural language while being, of their very essence, the product of the locations in which they stand. So how does a modern architect, who can use any material in existence if he chooses, respect the character of a place? Is not modern architecture essentially alien?

No, says Grimshaw, who believes that modern architecture – using modern technology and materials – is the vernacular style of today, the most obvious, 'natural' way of building. 'Fitting in', Grimshaw once declared, 'is to do with things like scale and height, light and shade, the feeling that a building has at ground level, at people level....It's not to do with just matching the building next door'.

Grimshaw's Port East project for example, in the

Maison de Verre, Paris,
by Pierre Chareau, 1932.

Wichita House by Buckminster Fuller, 1946.

shadow of Canary Wharf, had to relate to a magnificent, grade one-listed group of early 19th century warehouses, the best thing of their kind surviving in London. Preserved ships were to be tied up at the adjacent wharves. The designs were, says Grimshaw, 'definitely nautical', with memories of the many sea journeys he has enjoyed. Walking around under the great masts that supported the structure would have been like being on-board ship. The visitor might have leaned on the hand-rail and simply enjoyed the passing scene. But there was nothing obvious about these references: they were suggestions, memories, not part of a nautical 'styling' exercise. Grimshaw builds naturally, but with the site at the centre of his thinking.

At Waterloo with the Channel Tunnel Railway Terminal, he had to respond to a tight urban context, with a large (if not very distinguished) example of early 20th-century railway engineering abutting the site. At Western Morning News, the site was a beautiful wedge of country, on the edge of the city. Igus had another city-edge site, but one more compromised by recent development. Three sites – and three very different responses.

Regionalism is currently a resurgent force in world architecture. Grimshaw sympathises with the instinct, but is suspicious of some of its consequences. Contrived folksiness annoys him, as does monument-making for its own sake. He likes the straightforward, the reasonable, the natural. This is the essence of his genuine feeling for places and regions. Grimshaw's forthcoming stock exchange and communications centre in Berlin looks set to be a generous and complex response to its location in the centre of the city. His Igus factory, just outside Cologne, might appear to be one in a line of masted structures he has completed. Yet Grimshaw is adamant that it is 'not true to say that it's not specifically for the site – it's an eye catcher'. Igus expresses the tension in Grimshaw's architecture. It is a model factory, 'an elegant working machine', in line with his view of a universal modern architecture, but also another landmark, this time intended for a city-edge location that lacks an obvious sense of place.

None of the pressures working on architects today could be more irresistible than that of what is broadly termed 'green' philosophy. As an architect for whom technology is a way of improving human life, Grimshaw is acutely aware of the dangers inherent in its misuse and of the potential that it holds for good. He still treasures a picture taken in 1967 – in front of his newly completed service tower in Sussex Gardens – showing him with Buckminster Fuller. The building (now demolished) was a straightforward enough piece of work, providing bathrooms for a row of Victorian, terrace houses used as a student hostel. It was simple, ingenious, low-cost; appropriate technology in the Fuller mould. Grimshaw recalls Fuller as a 'staggering philosopher' who highlighted the conservation of scarce resources and the protection of the environment as key issues for modern architects. Few listened at the time – they have had to take notice since – but Grimshaw was impressed. 'Bucky' did not shape the look of his buildings, he says, but he was an inspiration to a man still in his 20s. There is a seriousness, a moral and social dimension to Grimshaw's architecture, which derives in part from the great Victorians and the

Modern Movement but was certainly reinforced by the example of Fuller.

Buckminster Fuller talked of 'the intellectual productive ability of science and technology which displaces the individual as a productive slave'. The words ring true in many of today's working environments. Grimshaw realises that highly serviced, artificially lit buildings are not 'natural', that there is more to feeling content with a space than just being warm in winter and cool in summer. The Seville pavilion commission provided Grimshaw with a marvellous opportunity to explore climatic and environmental issues – it was effectively a testbed for projects of the future and pushed forward his thinking about the servicing of buildings and their relationship to site and region. He looked at the way traditional Spanish buildings cope with summer heat, but sought to adapt the lessons learned to a new technology. This is typical of the man: study and learn from history, but use all the means available to an architect working in the 1990s. Grimshaw, of course, came to maturity as an architect in the 1970s – the decade of the energy crisis – and the over-optimism of some of his predecessors has never affected him. He sees the limits of purely technical progress.

Grimshaw also places enormous importance on working with clients to develop the detailed brief that underlies any successful building. Every project is, for him, a new adventure. Since he sees architecture always in its human context, he cannot conceive of a building as a perfect, finite work of art. Perfection is not a word Grimshaw likes to use. Much as he admires the work of Mies van der Rohe, for example, and the Seagram building in particular, Mies is not his exemplar. Continuous formal refinement is not his aim. He is forever rethinking, exploring. The development of a detailed client brief is fundamental to his methodology.

Grimshaw says that the jobs he finds most satisfying are those where the client has a clear vision of the completed building, so that architect and end-user can work together to develop the scheme. In the 19th century, the architect had the job of applying architecture to an essentially functional building – hence mills that look like Venetian palazzi or medieval fortresses. Today the architecture and the industrial process are inseparable. Traditional factories grew by accretion: more bits were simply tacked on when they got too small. Grimshaw sees industrial buildings as pieces of machinery in their own right. He has pushed the definition of flexibility and adaptability very wide and nowhere more so than at Igus, Cologne, for example.

The degree to which the entire interior space at Igus can be moved around and rearranged as the company progresses, with office floors quickly dismantled and reassembled elsewhere, is in the tradition of Prouvé's Maison du Peuple. Grimshaw has realised, to a remarkable degree, the Modern Movement ideal of the building as machine. If that ideal once had rather inhuman connotations, Grimshaw has given it a human dimension as part of his philosophy of making buildings that respond to people's needs. 'A working machine that has elegance' is his aim. He contrasts his buildings with 'the status quo of monolithic brick and concrete, of immovable, inflexible extensions to the earth's crust' – his

Seagram Building, New York,
by Mies van der Rohe, 1957.

Herman Miller Central Distribution Centre, Chippenham, 1982.

architectural language and his social ideals are closely interlinked. Flexible buildings allow people to shape their own surroundings. Grimshaw takes what was even 30 years ago a futuristic flight of fancy and makes it real and appealing through his practical approach – a way of doing things that attracts industrial and commercial innovators who are successful because they know how to balance common sense and sheer daring. The first Industrial Revolution was conducted against the background of a *laissez-faire* society, where the entrepreneur was encouraged to 'get on with the job', regardless of the consequences. The results were the industrial cities of the 19th century. Industrial buildings today must be environmentally clean, aesthetically pleasing, socially benign. The demands of society are increasing; Grimshaw is one of the few architects who is keeping ahead of them.

When a new commission comes to Grimshaw, he immerses himself in the job, visiting the site, walking around it at all times of day, feeling the terrain, experiencing the light, observing the local scene. With his team – and the Grimshaw office is full of enthusiasts who share his approach – he talks: to the client, the potential users, the engineers, the makers and suppliers of components. A Grimshaw building is not ordered 'off the shelf' but developed in discussion with everybody involved. If architecture is not made this way, Grimshaw argues, it risks degenerating into a service industry. There is nothing of the 'star' mentality about Grimshaw. Few front-rank architects today are as prepared to credit the teamwork involved in any big building project and the contribution of the other professionals. Grimshaw does not work *for* clients, but *with* them, in a 'fruitful collaboration' that produces high performance, durable buildings. He finds the American notion of 'signature' buildings distasteful, though he is now eminent enough to be asked to create some. Good, 'real' architecture, with substance, not surface, is his forte. All buildings should aspire to that quality, he says. The division of architecture into 'good' or 'serious' and 'commercial' is distressing to him. He believes that his work is both good and commercial, in the sense that it is good value and designed with a close eye to functional requirements.

Grimshaw relishes the challenge that each new job brings. He is convinced that he can do things better now than he could 10 years ago. He always stresses that architects must never stop learning as they have to work in a world of continual change. Looking at a typical Grimshaw project of the last few years and comparing it with something similar from his earlier years of practice – Igus, say, with Herman Miller, Bath, or Western Morning News with the Financial Times Print Works – there are always persistent themes and ideas. But there is equally so much that is new. 'It can't all be there from the beginning', Grimshaw stresses. 'Everyone has to strive really hard to get it right'. The earlier projects inform and enrich the later ones. But Grimshaw is not interested in simply repeating past achievements.

His work in the late Eighties and early Nineties has demonstrated a growing willingness on his part to be boldly expressive. The Venice Biennale project was highly sculptural. Yet there is no artifice about it, nothing 'arbitrary'. The form (to quote the old Modernist saw) follows the function, but via the medium of architecture, not through some mysterious, deterministic process.

So intense (and well known) is Grimshaw's interest in structure and construction that it is too easy to underestimate his concern for what happens inside buildings: ' I do care very much about piecing spaces together', he says. Aalto once wrote that the dominance of the structure in modern architecture threatened to create an 'architectural vacuum' at the centre of a building. Aalto also defended the role of the imagination: 'pure and playful forms', which began by being aesthetically pleasing, could end up being highly practical. The architect should not allow pure logic to imprison him.

The poetic expressiveness in Grimshaw's architecture has been bubbling under the surface for years – look at the wavy roofs in his Vitra factory at Weil-am-Rhein (completed in 1981). Now, at last, he is allowing it a free rein. The great spaces below the train shed at Waterloo are likely to be a revelation for those who perceive Grimshaw as someone for whom interiors are almost incidental. Interiors are very definitely not, for Grimshaw, a matter of chance. He wants to have a firm control over interior design, right down to the furniture – he is never content to leave any detail to other hands.

Grimshaw, in fact, far from being indifferent to internal space, loves to manipulate it. In this matter, as elsewhere, his rejection of pure Functionalism is made clear. But, ultimately, his interiors are always the product of functional necessity. Stagey effects are not for him. If the Igus factory has a noble interior, it is because it is this sort of space that flows from the client's requirements. 'We like to think that our buildings work because we get close to people and embody their ideas in the designs', says Grimshaw. Perhaps for this reason, Grimshaw has something of a reputation for creating buildings that are enjoyed rather than endured. The Berlin project, one suspects, could be a milestone in this direction, with its interweaving of public and private space. If factories and offices are to be communities, as Grimshaw believes they should be, they must reflect that character in their interior architecture. From Herman Miller onwards, Grimshaw has acquired a reputation for humanising the industrial environment.

Space in a Grimshaw building is space for people. Grandiloquence is not in his nature, but he admires real grandeur like that of Foster's HongKong and Shanghai Bank or Rogers' Lloyd's, buildings that combine cathedral-like space with attention to detail. It is, perhaps, unfortunate that Grimshaw was not given the chance to build on this scale until the Waterloo terminal commission. He now looks increasingly to the more measured spaces of classic Modernism and, in particular, to the later work of Le Corbusier and the Scandinavian masters. His avowed aim in Berlin to 'respond organically to the constraints of the site' and create 'an open democratic feel' could have been echoed by Corb or Aalto. Grimshaw is a profoundly democratic architect. The point of his great glazed screen wall at the Financial Times Print Works was as much to let the printers see out as for the public to see in. Grimshaw knew well that they had spent their working lives sealed up in a building without views or daylight. He has repeated the

Chapel of Notre Dame at Ronchamp by Le Corbusier, 1954.

Bracken House, London,
by Michael Hopkins and Partners, 1992.

operation for Western Morning News in Plymouth, where the views are rather better. He gets as much satisfaction from providing vastly improved accommodation for railway staff at Waterloo Station – where his British Rail operations centre slots almost unnoticed into the old trainshed – as from more glamorous and costly projects. And he gives the work the same degree of close attention to detail.

The 'democratic' inspiration is working too in his designs for the Berlin Stock Exchange, where he sees the language and materials of the new building as symbolic of the new Berlin, a contrast to the heaviness and pomposity of the old. Undeniably organic in feel, 'alive and very light', it promises to be one of Grimshaw's most subtle and expressive buildings. The local press has already compared it to a reptile. The architect accepts the simile (as he concedes that the Plymouth building is, in a sense, a ship) but restates his conviction that forms in architecture cannot be arbitrary – hence his disagreement with the Post-Modernist and Deconstructivist schools. Berlin is a landmark in the development of a new language of modern architecture. But it is an architecture rooted in realities – functional, social, constructional – not the arbitrary form touted, with the assistance of much bogus philosophy, in the more fashionable journals as the way forward for world architecture. Although Grimshaw has allowed his architecture greater freedom in recent years, there is no sense of indiscipline or showmanship. The 'rigour' is always there – perhaps the engineering roots hold him back from ever building for pure effect. 'My architecture is a balancing act, I suppose', he says, 'on the tightrope between structural engineering and art'.

Engineering will always matter for Grimshaw, as it has from the beginnings of his career. It is his anchor. When he produces a building where primary and secondary structure, cladding and other components cannot be clearly read, when his buildings cease to be flexible and non-finite, then an era will have ended. But his architecture is unlikely to turn in this direction. Grimshaw has stuck by his convictions for 25 years in practice and they have been largely vindicated as transient fashions have waxed and waned. The technical craft of building well is one he mastered long ago, but it never ceases to fascinate him. It is the pure art of form that he is exploring to ever better effect. It is no accident that this coincides with a growing emphasis on environmental and ecological issues. Architects cannot stand apart from a global concern about the destruction of the natural world and the brutalisation of urban life and an ever-increasing movement to 'get back to nature'. The expressive new architecture of Coop Himmelblau, Future Systems, Frank Gehry and Daniel Libeskind is full of organic power. For some architects, however, the deterioration of the human condition is the cue for buildings that express – even celebrate – confusion, disjunction, disorder. This is not a viewpoint with which Grimshaw has much sympathy. His view of architecture is essentially constructive.

Grimshaw sees himself as a 'doer, as well as a philosopher'. He is someone who not only thinks a lot about his work but also believes that research is a vital activity for an architect today. From research comes learning. 'Some people think I talk too much about learning', he says, 'but I believe that you can't just stand still'.

Grimshaw enjoys practice above all else. He loves 'engaging' his mind in a practical problem. He is actively involved to some degree in everything his office does. He guides his colleagues, pushes them forward, debates with them, learns from them and teaches them. He does the same with clients. 'He seemed to get to grips with the job the first day we met', says his client at Igus, Cologne. 'It was quite a performance'. Talking to the employees of Western Morning News as he worked on the scheme for the company's new building, he felt, he says, 'like an itinerant psychiatrist'.

To foreigners, Grimshaw probably seems a very British architect. There is nothing insular or nationalistic about him, but his work has been moulded in the Britain of the last quarter of a century. British High-Tech was one of the dynamic forces in world architecture in the Seventies but Grimshaw was never really a High-Tech architect. His earlier works do not so much 'celebrate' technology as make use of it in an efficient, honest way. There is a continuum in Grimshaw's work that flows from his early restraint. He has never changed his 'style' because he never had one – he has a way of building, which is still evolving. How different is the case of a contemporary whom Grimshaw respects – Michael Hopkins. It is hard to see an obvious continuity between Hopkins' earlier works (the Schlumberger laboratories or the Greene King bottling plant, say) and his recent essays in a modified historicist mode. Grimshaw is unlikely to make such a change in direction. Rather he is like his contemporary Renzo Piano, an undogmatic advocate of progressive technology. He is a few years younger than Piano, but he does not disguise his admiration for his work. Piano's versatility with materials intrigues Grimshaw, who responds to his deep humanity. Will Grimshaw explore a wider range of materials in the next few years? Only, one suspects, if the exercise were justified on grounds of practical benefits and cost: he is not someone who cultivates the middle ground.

Grimshaw is unafraid to offend the critics or to bewilder his supporters. He pursues his course logically, calmly but with a very great deal of thought at every turn. He agonises, one senses, at times, and feels every decision deeply. Nicholas Grimshaw's position in British architecture has nothing to do with compromise, and there is no reason to believe that he has moved from a hard-edged Modernism to a soft contextualism. It is the world that has moved – and Grimshaw has recognised the fact. He has seen the rise of fashions that have faded and found them wanting. More to the point, he has held his ground and seen his consistency vindicated.

All these themes are present, in varying degrees, in the key schemes that have confirmed Grimshaw's position amongst the leaders of the British architectural scene.

London Heathrow is a far remove from the sort of airport Nicholas Grimshaw would like to create. Nearly half a century of piecemeal growth has produced a confusing agglomeration, a complex of buildings and spaces, like a badly planned town, where the inherent excitement of air travel is almost totally lost from sight. While Heathrow awaits major surgery to fit it for its role as a gateway to Europe, Grimshaw has been working

Ircam School of Music, Paris, by Richard Rogers and Renzo Piano, 1987.

Xerox Research Engineering Centre, Welwyn Garden City, 1988.

there, seeking to instil rationality, clarity and comfort into an environment under stress.

Heathrow's Terminal One was the starting point for an exploration, in the autumn of 1992, of some of Grimshaw's most recent, and most accomplished, buildings. The main terminal building is a product of the 1960s. Internally, it entirely lacks drama or any sense of movement. The character of the place is a rather anonymous blandness but its once spacious interior now feels distinctly under pressure as passenger numbers continue to grow. Terminal One is a place to pass through quickly – yet air travel is not always so straightforward. On a bad day, with flights delayed by bad weather, the terminal has a weary air of desperation. The fact is that it is bursting at the seams.

The solution was a new main pier and subsidiary piers, with nine gates, waiting areas, a baggage hall and some facilities for eating, drinking and shopping. It sounds simple, but was fiendishly complicated. The site could hardly have been more difficult. The new pier had to be built across busy service roads. with the business of moving passengers going on around it.

Along the way, Grimshaw had to face cost restraints and economies but his Heathrow revolution has survived intact. The key to the success of the satellite and pier project lies in the logic of the plan, achieved only after intense discussion with the client. As a result, passengers move easily through the building. There is no confusion, no clutter. There is space – and light. Natural light is a precious commodity in a place like this, yet airport authorities seem reluctant – for security reasons, perhaps – to allow passengers a view out. Grimshaw slips in windows and skylights, allowing them a glimpse of the weather, of the reality beyond the building. His Heathrow interiors are cool, calm but not undramatic. There is something of the movement of travel in them. They provide a civilised environment for air travel. The passenger feels like a person with dignity and choice, not part of some mechanical process.

I went to the new satellite and piers as they were nearing completion. Parts were fully in commission. The domestic gates and baggage hall were still in the final stages of fitting out but there was enough there to see that the scheme had within it the embryo of a Grimshaw airport, the major airport he has yet to build but that he previewed in his celebrated contribution to the Venice Biennale.

The link between the Biennale project and Heathrow is, of course, obvious. The Venice exhibit was based on Grimshaw's proposals for Terminal Five, on which he had worked long and hard and was not inclined to consign to oblivion. For some, the Biennale model, huge in scale and with 3,000 model people populating its interior, was a revelation. It seemed to presage a more fluid, expressive architecture than that normally associated with Grimshaw.The project marked a logical progression from his earlier work, along with a recognition of the opportunities for a dramatic but entirely functional design. The scheme was everything that the existing Heathrow is not.

Grimshaw has, on many occasions in the last couple of years, taken the route I took from Terminal One. He must surely enjoy the flight, in a propeller-driven Dash 7 aircraft, across southern England to Plymouth. The airport is in the old mould – just a small terminal building and a runway. The plane lands briefly – and then flies on westwards. A short cab ride from the airport, on the edge of the city, is a building that has transformed the prospects for modern architecture in this part of the country.

The centre of Plymouth was badly ravaged by wartime bombs and extensively rebuilt to a plan that combines Beaux-Arts urbanism with low-voltage Fifties' architecture. The premises of the *Western Morning News*, one of the great cultural and social institutions of the west country, came as a relief in the aridity of its surroundings. The paper's offices were housed in a pre-war survivor, a polite, not inelegant 1920s' neo-Georgian block. Around the back, facing on to a blank back street, was the printing works, recognisably an industrial building and with a well-worn griminess that inevitably recalled the great days of Fleet Street.

Grimshaw's new building for the *Western Morning News* represents as great a break with tradition as the move of the *Financial Times* from Bracken House in the City of London, which produced Grimshaw's famous printing plant. The advantages of new technology are now beyond challenge and Grimshaw's Plymouth building is designed to accommodate leading-edge methods of producing newspapers.

But the key to the building is that it is not, like the new generation of newspaper buildings in London, just an office block or simply a printing plant. In line with tradition, it is an integrated newspaper factory but, in a clear break with tradition, everyone who works here will enter and leave by the same door. The copy is written here, the pages made up and the paper printed and distributed, all from the same building.

The job has been intensely satisfying for Grimshaw. He was given the chance to work with a strong-minded, positive, highly demanding client who had a clear vision of what was wanted. This is Grimshaw's ideal and, in this instance, seems to have worked exceptionally well. Jerry Ramsden, *Western Morning News*' managing director, wanted a building that was not only functionally efficient – a 21st-century home for an old institution – but which expressed the character of the paper. As far as was possible, the building was to be one for the community – nobody ever imagined that visitors, especially the young, would ever be anything but welcome there.

I arrived at the building on a brilliant autumn day, when the views out to Dartmoor and Plymouth Sound from the very top of it can be properly appreciated. The setting is not so much suburban as city-edge – and Plymouth is small enough to lack the depressing sprawl that surrounds larger towns. The neighbours are nothing special – a military depot, an evangelical meeting house and a residential home for the elderly – an odd mix. But there is a small and beautiful valley below the site of the new building, a green surround that Grimshaw and his clients have done everything possible to protect and enhance.

The building was in the final stages of fitting out, a time when everything seems to be happening at once. In the printing plant the newly installed presses were being run and production engineers were scrutinising the colour pages of the paper as they appeared. Elsewhere, office partitions were going up, toilets were being fitted, a staircase was going in and the building's distinctive prow was emerging from a

Stockholm Crematorium,
by Gunnar Asplund, 1939.

Johnson Wax complex, Racine, by Frank Lloyd Wright, 1936.

shroud of protective sheeting. I climbed the stair to the boardroom, set in the conning tower that sits on top of the building, which provides the really spectacular views out. But should this be described as a 'conning tower'? Or a 'bridge'?

Grimshaw finds the public image of the building as a great beached ship, a tribute to Plymouth's many centuries of naval history, understandable but slightly exaggerated. One cannot go to Plymouth without being aware of the sea and ships, he admits, but the nautical reference is an oblique one. It is gratifying for any architect to find that his building has a public image at all – and Western Morning News seems to have made its mark in Plymouth – but Grimshaw feels that the characteristics that the building shares with one of the modern warships seen in the Sound are more than visual. Like them, it is a bold, purposeful thing, finely engineered and with nothing that is superfluous, no 'trimmings'.

A visit to the building underlines the degree to which its form is anything but arbitrary or contrived. The site is steep, even dramatic – a contrast to the East India Dock Road, where Grimshaw's earlier newspaper building is located. The plan comes out of the marked contours of the site. At the same time, it reflects the client's desire to create a building for the community, welcoming outsiders and creating a sense of community for those who work there. Even in the throes of fitting out, the interior exuded the determination of a progressive employer of the present day to follow in the tradition of those who commissioned Wright's Larkin Building or his complex for Johnson Wax. It is the dynamism of the space and the quality of light that will make the completed building an exceptional place to work. The typical journalist, designer or printer may not pay much heed to the superb quality of the detailing but everyone will benefit from the sheer good sense of the plan.

Good sense is not the sum of what one expects from a Grimshaw building. The great concave wall of glass is the necessary result of the architect's quest for transparency without reflection. It is probably more important, for architect and client, that the printers can see out than that the public can see in – but both matter. The building has an expressive power that instantly impresses, but I soon realised that there is nothing in it that is there for effect. One might exclude, I suppose, the top floor boardroom. It is a luxury. Grimshaw feared it might be cut to save money but it survived. It is the touch of sheer pleasure in design that seals the triumphant success of this building.

Another morning departure from Terminal One took me to Cologne, where the first phase of the Igus factory provides a further insight into the client / architect relationship that is one of the foundations of Grimshaw's success. Igus is a family concern, founded in 1964 by Günter Blase, who still runs it – though his sons are increasingly to the fore in its management. The firm makes machine parts of high quality plastics, a very competitive business where its success has been international. Blase's son, Frank, in charge of marketing, explained that the company had moved twice in its relatively short history, most recently (1976) to the present premises, a converted textile mill of late 19th-century vintage. The buildings are typical of those colonised by growing industrial companies – well-built, adaptable and quite modest in purchase cost. However, Igus has clearly outgrown its old site and the problems of using a multi-storey block intended for a quite different form of manufacturing have become pressing.

A walk around the factory highlighted the contrast between the process and its setting. Frank Blase explained the background to the Grimshaw commission. His father had always been interested in architecture and considered a number of names for the job. Eventually, it was a choice between Grimshaw and a German architect. There was little doubt that Grimshaw was the man: 'he seemed to have thought exactly along our lines – he saw the need for a highly flexible modern building, but one which embodied the ideals behind the company', said Blase. The German architect proposed a separate office block, divided by a pool from the factory. 'We could not believe it', says Blase, 'having offices and factory together was virtually our most vital requirement'. Igus is 'very unhierarchic' – everyone, from Günter Blase to the youngest apprentice on the shop floor, has always eaten in the same canteen. Innovative manufacturing depends on a close relationship between employers and employed. The new factory embodies all this. 'It's like a cruise liner – all one class. We are trying to live up to an ideal of co-operation'.

I met Günter Blase at the new factory. The first phase was complete and the first machines were being installed. Blase was preoccupied with the job of getting the building into operation. He stressed that he had never seen the new factory as a landmark in the obvious sense – 'we want a flexible, functional building' – but the quality of the building matters when it comes to capitalising on people's abilities. Inside, the scale is deceptive. There is a clear floor-to-ceiling height of over 7m and the structure provides clear spans of over 33m. Everything is bathed in the clear light from the roof domes. The structure can be read clearly – the building is a cathedral to rational modern industry. I long to see it at work.

By contrast, I first saw Grimshaw's Expo 92 pavilion early in 1992, before the Expo opened and before the summer heat of Andalusia began to test its innovative climatic engineering. Given Grimshaw's great interest in the 19th-century, British engineering tradition and in Joseph Paxton's Crystal Palace in particular, it was fascinating to see the pavilion complete – all the more so in the context of the 'pluralism' of the Expo's architecture. Grimshaw did not disappoint: the building was clearly part of a tradition, but it was equally radical and novel. Grimshaw had taken the bold decision to attempt an exercise in climatic control that allowed a modern building to make use of, rather than ignore, the Spanish sun. The great wall of water, designed in collaboration with the sculptor William Pye, impressed instantly and unforgettably.

But it was the interior, a great room defined by a lightweight, steel structure, that confirmed the thorough-going quality of the pavilion: it was majestic. Paxton did not have escalators or travelators but his late 20th-century successor made full use of these modern means of conveyance to make the building a place of movement, actual and metaphorical. The basic structure of the pavilion, however, would have been thoroughly intelligible to Paxton, though it makes use of manufacturing techniques unavailable in the

Menil Collection Museum, Houston, by Renzo Piano, 1986.

Paimio Sanatorium
by Alvar Aalto, 1932.

Victorian period. The pavilion provides one of Grimshaw's most memorable interiors – one that will hopefully survive in some form. It seems clear that the building will now remain where it is, though it was designed to be demountable, recyclable, and there were, at one point, proposals for it to be brought back to Britain. It was designed for Spain and that is surely where it should stay.

If the Victorian engineering tradition came inevitably to mind in Seville, thoughts of the 19th century can hardly be avoided at the Grimshaw railway terminal at Waterloo. It is the finest railway station to be built in Britain this century and a worthy successor to London's King's Cross and St Pancras, and the equally splendid stations at York and Newcastle-upon-Tyne. Yet Grimshaw's Waterloo has a role of which the Victorians dreamed but never realised. It is the terminal for through-trains from the Continent via the Channel Tunnel.

The terminal is slotted into a narrow, curving strip of land alongside the great spread of the existing Waterloo, a vast, not especially distinguished terminal of the early 20th century. Grimshaw, a great admirer of the Victorian terminals, had to ask himself how relevant their model was for travellers in the 21st century.

He saw the Channel Tunnel Railway Terminal from the start as the equivalent of an airport terminal at the centre of London. But it is unmistakably a railway station, with the trains on top of a great viaduct, displayed within a shed of striking transparency. The nature of the site meant that everything apart from the platforms themselves had to be at a lower level, from where passengers would go up to board their trains.

Grimshaw's train shed, often seen as an organic design but more readily intelligible as a direct response to the site, is one of the new sights of London. It is a marvellous and rather reassuring structure – proof that the international railway renaissance has not bypassed the country that invented railways. Oddly enough, walking about inside the shed, its relatively low height, in comparison with the Victorian terminals, gives it an even more striking sense of movement and direction, while the lightness of the structure avoids any sense of enclosure.

A tour of the nine-tenths of the new Waterloo that lies below ground demonstrated that the train shed, for all its visible splendour, is just the most public element. Passengers will be drawn from a daylit concourse and booking hall into a progression of waiting areas before they emerge again into the daylight on the platforms. These spaces could easily be oppressive, but they can be seen, in the event, as being analogous to the undercroft of a fine Gothic church – a preparation for what is above. A great deal of care has gone into this area of the terminal, with Grimshaw and his colleagues looking for real grandeur, even if of a different sort to that of the shed. The process of boarding a train here should be quite exciting, with the announcement of a departure and passengers taking escalators and travelators up to platform level.

I expected to find the spaces below the tracks at Waterloo somewhat oppressive. Anticipating an artificially-lit area, I found daylight streaming in along the western flank of the building, where an arrivals' lounge overlooks the main road approach and passengers can descend to a taxi rank or to be collected by car.

With work on staff accommodation in the existing station continuing, and likely to be extended to link up with the new terminal, Grimshaw is transforming Waterloo into one of Europe's most efficient modern stations. Approaching the new shed, as I did, through the grandiloquent 1920s' Victory Arch, and gazing along its silvery length, it would be a cynic who doubted the future of cross-Europe rail travel. By the end of the century, this will be a hub of London, extending its influence into the revitalisation of the entire South Bank area. It is Grimshaw's supreme achievement to date. More than anything else he has done, it epitomises his approach to architecture: rooted in history, guided by humanity, optimistic, well-made and inspired by a feeling for form, which is that of a master.

Grimshaw's position in British architecture has nothing to do with compromise. His philosophy of design has not changed in its essentials; he remains a modern architect. But the world *has* changed in the 25 years since he completed his first building and he realises that architects cannot and must not ignore the fact. He has seen the rise of architectural fashions that have since faded and found them wanting. More to the point, he has held his ground and seen his consistency vindicated. But concern for the natural environment, for social harmony, for the needs of people – these are not passing fashions but the issues that are changing the outlook of mankind. Grimshaw has done more than respond. He has thought deeply, researched, experimented, worked hard to develop a humane modern architecture for the 21st century. His architecture is reaching a new maturity, characterised by a richness of expression that is as much a part of the new age as a reflection of Grimshaw's respect for the classic era of modern architecture. The work presented here is striking in its scale, diversity of form and consistent quality. It is the product of a remarkably fruitful period for Grimshaw and his team. One waits eagerly for what he will be doing in the second half of the Nineties.

Kenneth Powell

Grand Union Walk, Camden, London, 1988.

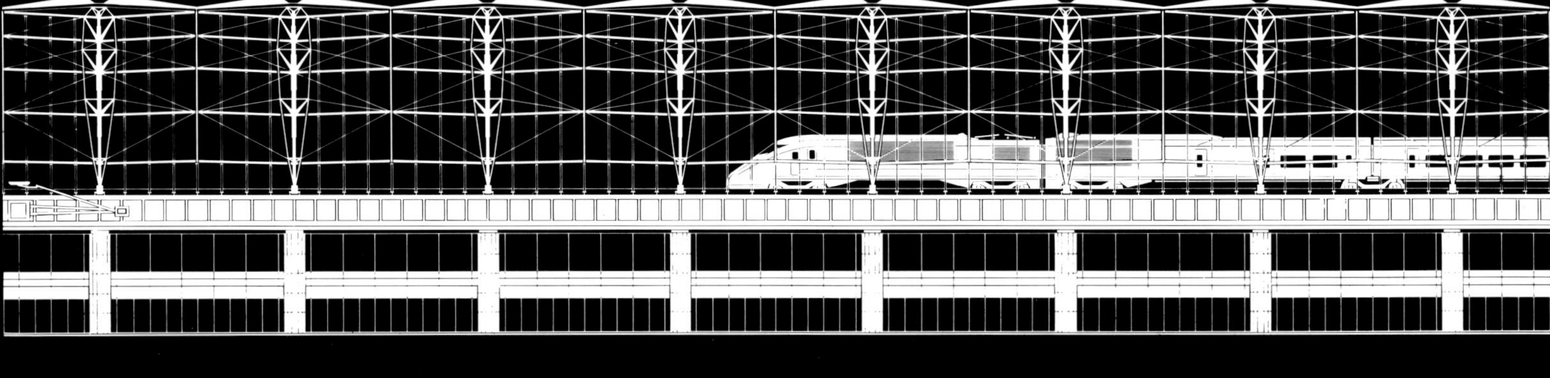

Channel Tunnel Railway Terminal at Waterloo, London, 1993

'The letter inviting 10 firms of architects to submit details of their firms to British Rail stated: "This must be one of the most exciting commissions in Europe today". I think this has certainly been the case for us. It has been a major project occupying a third of the people in the office for five years. Nothing about it has been simple.

'I hope the creative energy and the hundreds of thousands of hours that have gone into this building show. I hope the care that has been lavished on the castings and all the other details shows. Above all, I hope that everyone entering the station will be as exhilarated by looking at it as we were by doing it. Certainly none of us will walk into a station or climb on a train ever again

Previous page
Interior view looking west through overlapping roof glazing. The cast stainless-steel bracket assemblies allow glazing to adjust to the changing geometry.

Above and right: two aerial photomontage views of the 400m-long terminal roof in relation to the surrounding cityscape.

Nicholas Grimshaw views the Channel Tunnel Railway Terminal at Waterloo as a 'heroic railway station with the same function as a 21st century airport'. It is in direct competition with air travel, as the place from which eventually it will be possible to reach Paris in three hours, and it has most of the accoutrements of an airport – immigration and customs' controls, security checks, extensive subsidiary spaces. It has the capacity to handle 15 million passengers a year, or up to 1500 in four minutes. At the same time it remains a railway station, a heroic building on a constrained urban site, less than 10 minutes' walk from Trafalgar Square, and has a taxi drop-off only 15m from the ticket barrier.

The site both complicates the project and gives it the potency and significance which Heathrow, say, lacks. It is only just wide enough for both the terminal's structure and its five tracks. The site is limited down one side by live electric rails, underneath by shallow London Underground tunnels and overhead by a proposal – eventually abandoned – to build an office block above the terminal. In spite of this, the terminal has been inserted into Europe's busiest railway station without any disruption of services.

The station is a symbolic and actual threshold between Britain and the Continent, and the first monument of a new railway age, when high-speed trains will compete with aeroplanes as the most effective form of travel within Europe. British Rail, aware of the terminal's significance, wanted a great railway station in the tradition of Brunel and his peers, an updated Paddington or St Pancras. Grimshaw wanted 'to create a sense of wonderment', and talks of 'the excitement of departure and the exhilaration

of arrival'. Given the practical considerations, wonderment could never come from an architecture forced onto a merely functional solution. It had to grow from a constant attentiveness to the richness of the problem, and a sustained will to find elegant solutions.

The focus of both technical skill and architectural spectacle is the roof. Although it does not have to contend with steam and smoke, and can therefore be lower and flatter, it is a clear descendant of Victorian train sheds. It is not, however, a copy but a response to its own circumstance: its tapering span (from 50m to 35m), and its narrow, sinuous plan, are determined by the site and the track layout. Its most striking quality, the asymmetry of the trusses, derives from the

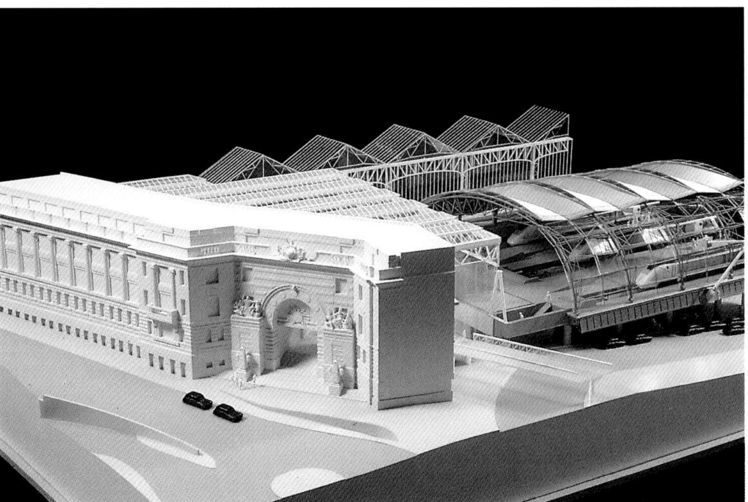

A model of the project showing three views of the north end of the terminal where it abuts the existing Waterloo Station.

Left, top: passengers are treated to spectacular views of the international trains as they enter Waterloo Station, thereby orientating themselves before proceeding down to the departures' concourse and then below the trains to the departures' lounge.

Left, bottom: the trains are separated from the concourse by a glass wall and a completely unobstructed space – in effect an international frontier. The old and new roofs have been kept separate, with the new roof following its own geometric laws.

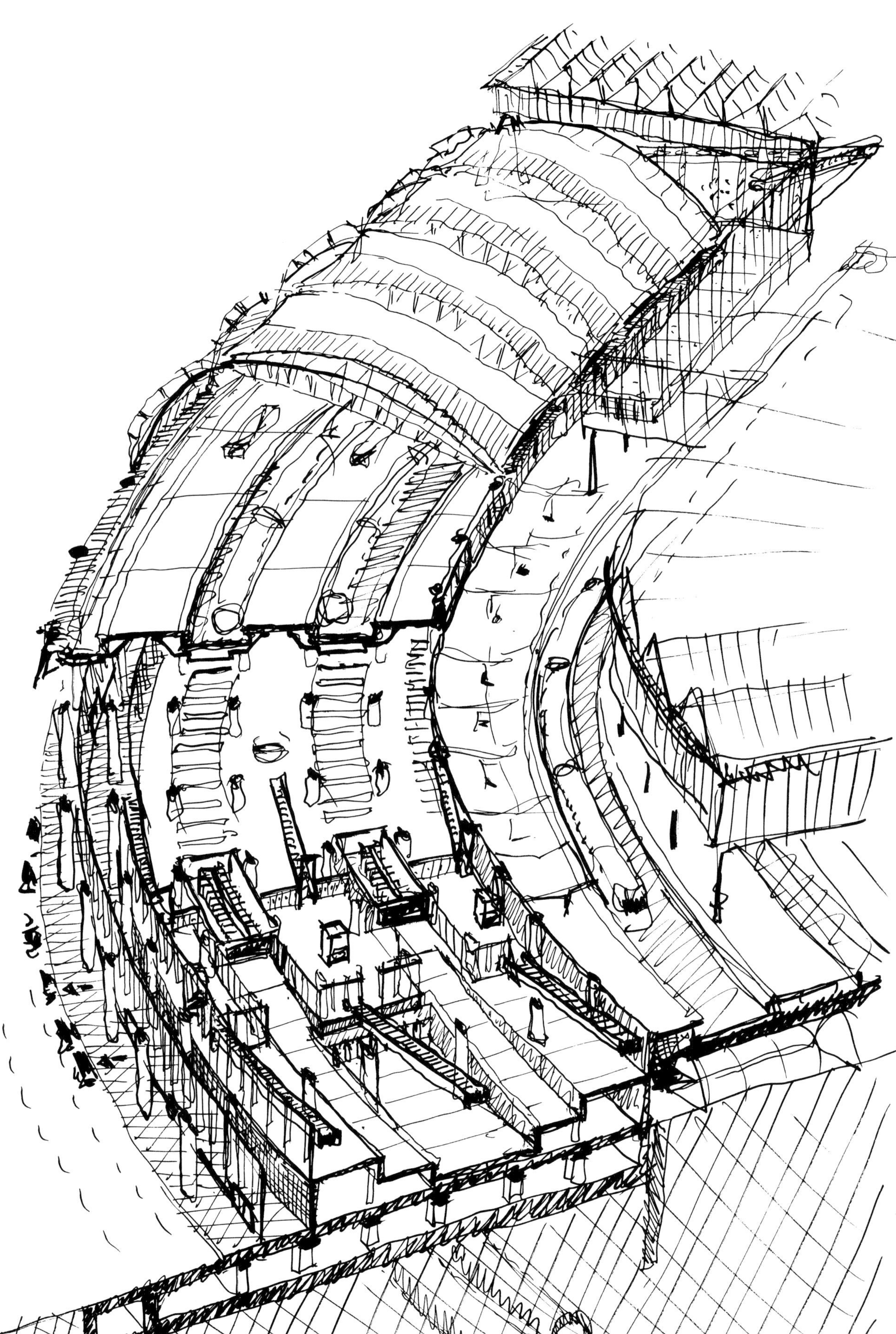

30 A sketch by Neven Sidor of the building as a five-layer sandwich comprising roof, platforms, departures' level, arrivals' level and basement car park. The western wall, where taxis drop off and pick up passengers, is completely glazed, while the eastern wall is solid. This sketch also shows the three passenger-control lobbies, which separate arrivals from departures, and which allow the doubling up of escalators and conveyors in both modes.

Computer-generated views of the arrivals' concourse, and (below) of the arrivals' ramps leading to the customs' hall.

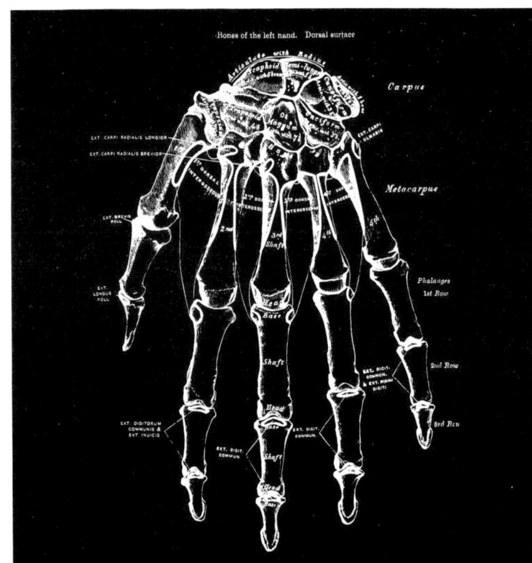

Annotated drawing of the bones of the left hand.

position of a single track tight onto the western edge of the site, and the resulting need for the structure to rise more steeply at this point, to clear the trains. Since this is the side from which the terminal is approached, Grimshaw's team have taken the opportunity to run the structure on the outside of the cladding, which here is entirely of glass. The western side becomes a public showcase for the trains, and allows arriving passengers to glimpse Westminster and the River Thames.

The trusses derive their elegance partly from this inversion of structure and skin (and of tension and compression members) as they pass from east to west, but also from the tapering of their members, created out of telescoping circular sections. This allows the members to respond, with economy of material, to the distribution of forces in each truss.

If the irregular site presented difficulties for the structure, it raised the nightmarish possibility of cladding made largely of one-off panels, with the associated production costs, and the prospect of co-ordinating a 400m-long jigsaw puzzle on a rapid programme. The solution devised by Grimshaw's team is a cross between the scales of a reptile, a simple tiled roof and the articulation between train carriages. Since the production processes of heat-soaked toughened glass mean that non-orthogonal glass has to be finished by hand, all the glass sheets are rectangular, and they overlap at top and bottom, like roof tiles. They are joined at their sides by concertina-shaped neoprene gaskets, which can flex and expand to accommodate turns and varying widths. A rhythm of troughs and crests (which help throw off rainwater)

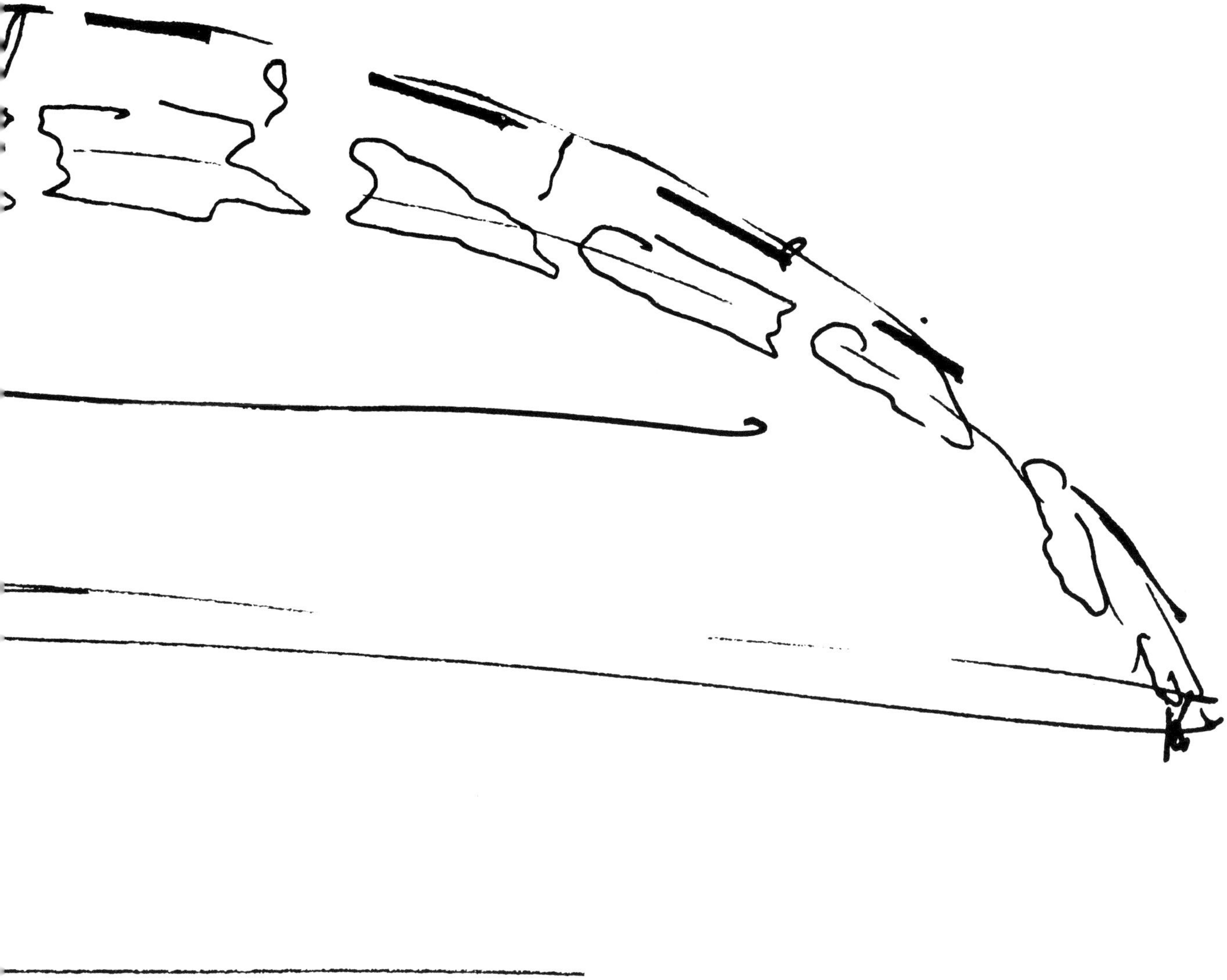

An early sketch by Nick Grimshaw indicating the asymmetry of the design from its earliest stages.

Exploration of a junction capable of containing the forces of a variety of loads from different directions.

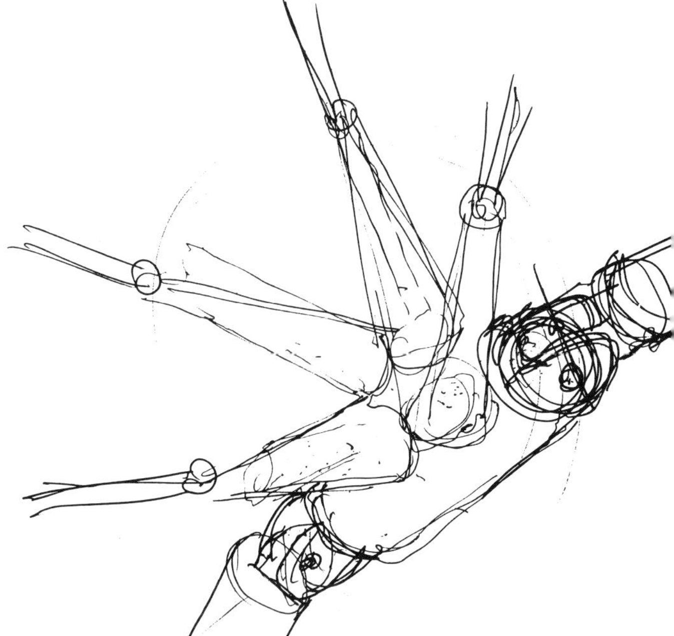

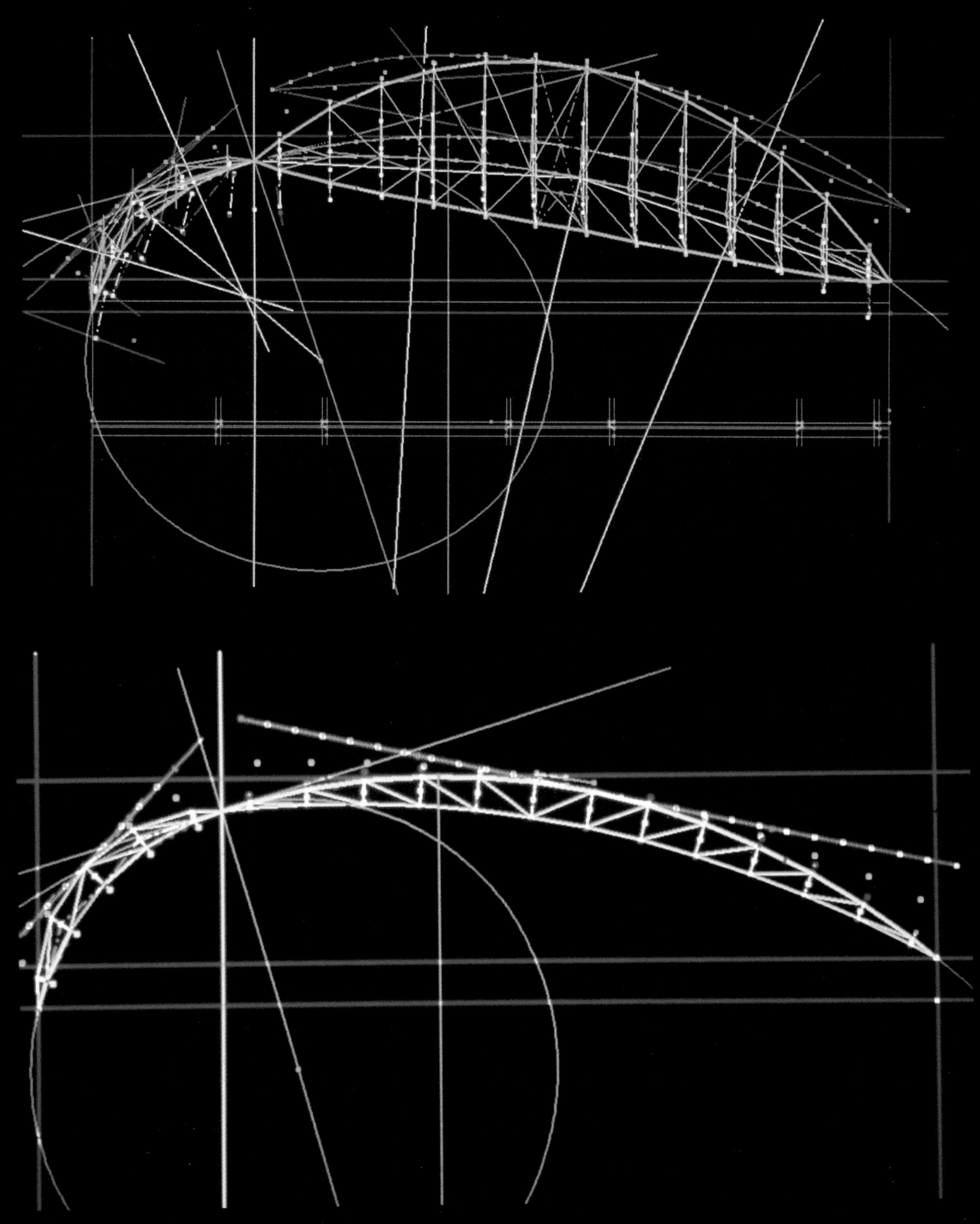

The final roof form – a three-pin arch with its central pin displaced to one side – reflects the assymetrical configuration of five tracks and three platforms. The tension cord is on the inside of the major truss, and then on the outside of the minor truss, flipping over at the point of contraflexure. The complex geometry of the roof structure was mastered using computer-assisted design.

A brass maquette of one roof bay, made by the office.

Overleaf
An external view from the west showing the minor truss and the roof glazing.

causes the whole structure to undulate and, although the concept is simple, it gives the effect of something supple and alive.

The roof is the most spectacular part of the project, but it accounts for only 10 per cent of the cost. Perhaps more vital to the performance of the terminal are the reused vaults under the existing station, some of which house the catering and support services, and others through which large crowds are guided, efficiently but pleasurably, through the spaces beneath the tracks.

This architectural clarity has a practical role in directing passengers, and the design continually orientates them with views of trains and the roof, through simple planning, and through following the geometry of the tracks. Departing passengers will see the noses of their trains from the station concourse, and then pass through a linear progression of ticket, security and passport checks to the waiting area, from where they will rise by one of two escalators or a travelator to the point nearest their seat place. For arriving passengers, the direction of the travelator and one of the escalators is reversed, taking passengers down to a further ramp and on to a ground-floor arrivals' concourse, which opens directly on to the road outside.

In all this, the quality of the internal environment has been upheld by high standards of artificial lighting, by admitting natural light through the glazed western wall and by hollowing generous spaces out of the confined section. Services and shops are concentrated under the deep structures that carry the tracks, leaving the more generous spaces under the platforms for circulation. A double-height space along the western

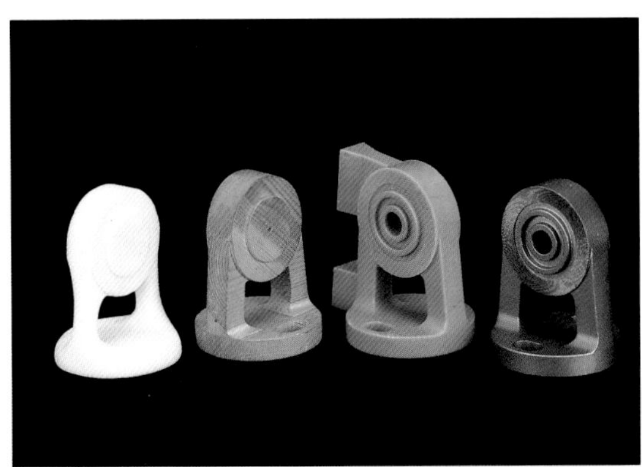

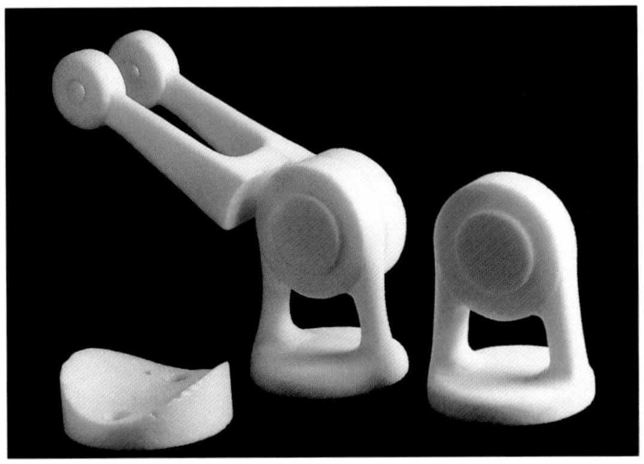

Owing to the curvature of the Waterloo Viaduct and the spread of the track alignment, the roof geometry would have required 2000 sizes of glass. For ease of construction the glass was standardised and the discrepancies were accommodated at overlapping joints.
Above: various stages of patterns for the lost-wax casting process used for the rotating arms of the overlapping junctions.

Stainless-steel rotating arms seen on the floor of the machine workshop.

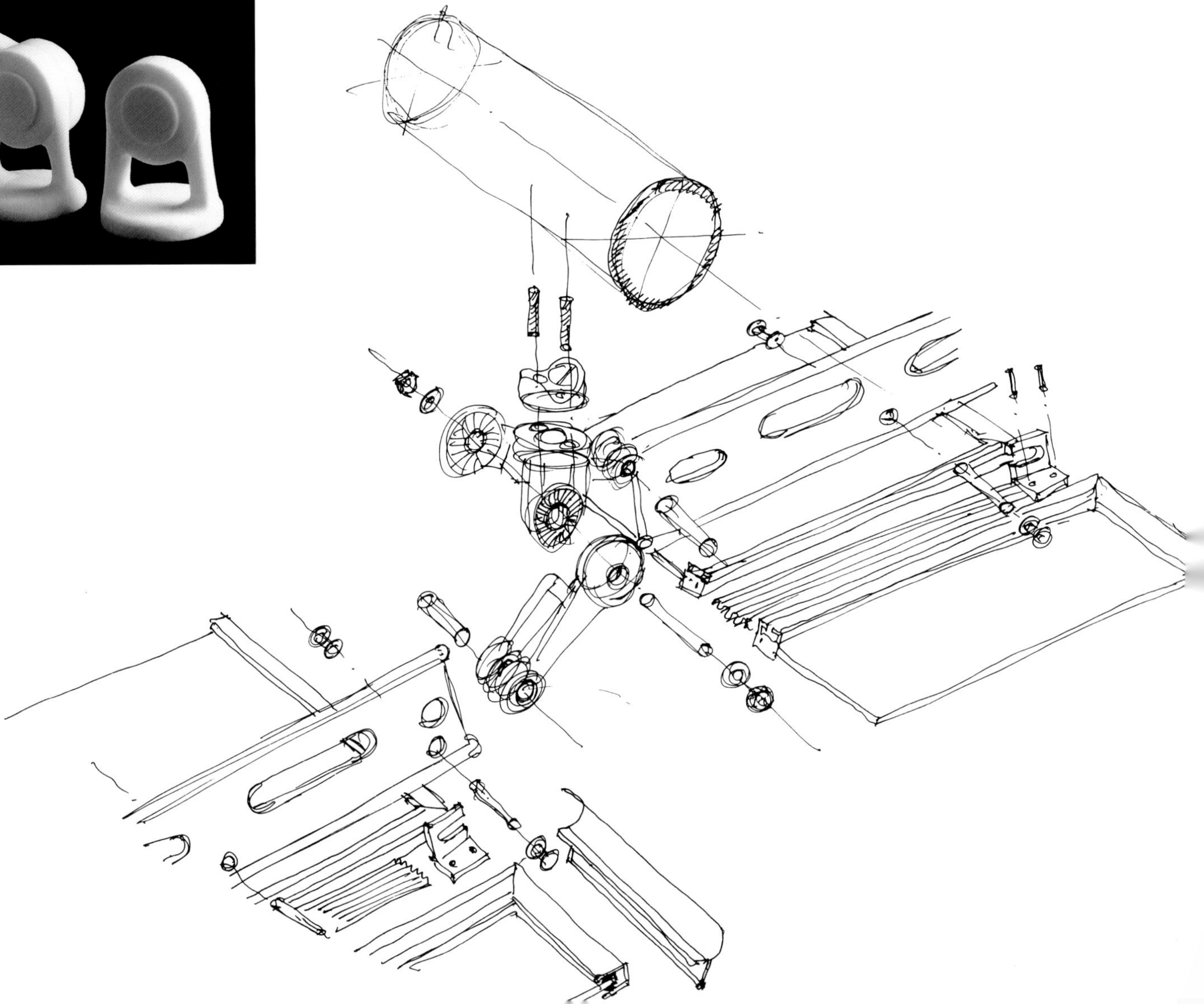

An exploded component sketch by David Kirkland of the assembly, which allows for the degree of flexibility required in the glass roof.

Detail of the rotating arms featured on the previous page.They were cast using the lost-wax process, which achieves high precision (the components are shown twice actual size).

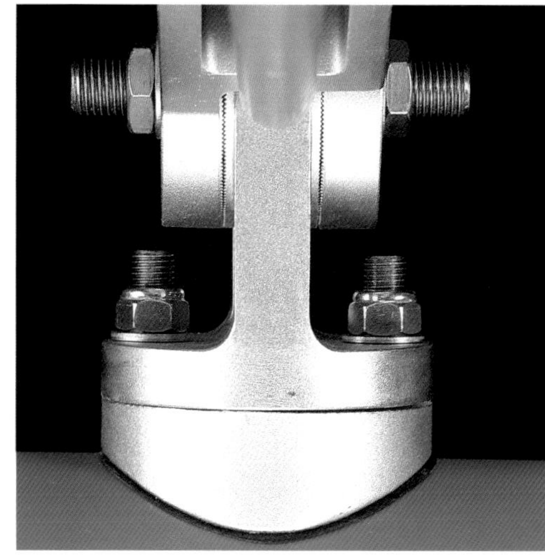

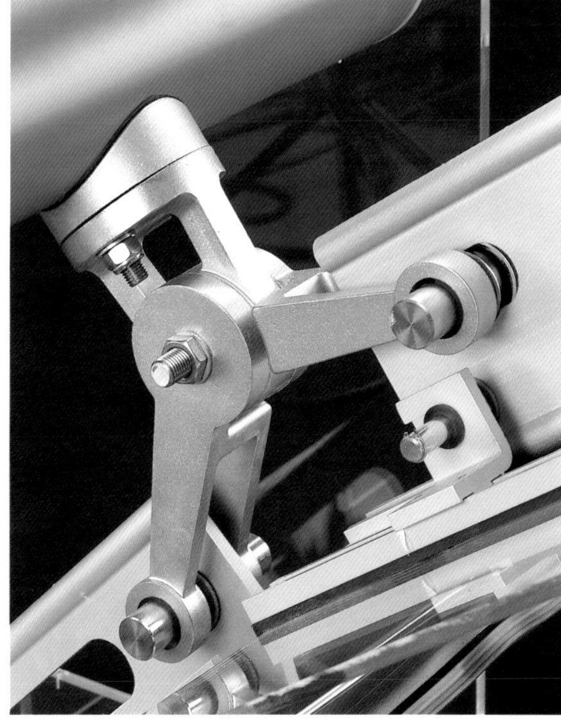

Views of prototype assembly of the stainless-steel rotating arms for the glazing structure.

side forms a spatial link between arrivals and departures.

To achieve civilised spaces within a railway viaduct is not easy. In particular the glass western wall has to form a weatherproof barrier while accommodating civil engineering tolerances, and deflections of up to 6mm caused by moving trains. Its panels are held together by the most sophisticated of the stainless-steel castings which, with variants at the Financial Times Print Works, Western Morning News and elsewhere, are becoming a Grimshaw trademark. The Waterloo version has to allow for substantial movement in all three dimensions.

The casting is a microcosm of the terminal. It is a lucid reflection of its purpose and an intriguing object, but one that could not have been pre-ordained. Like the trusses, the cladding and the building's organisation, it is the final stage of a lengthy process, and one informed by an openness to circumstance and a desire to solve problems with grace.

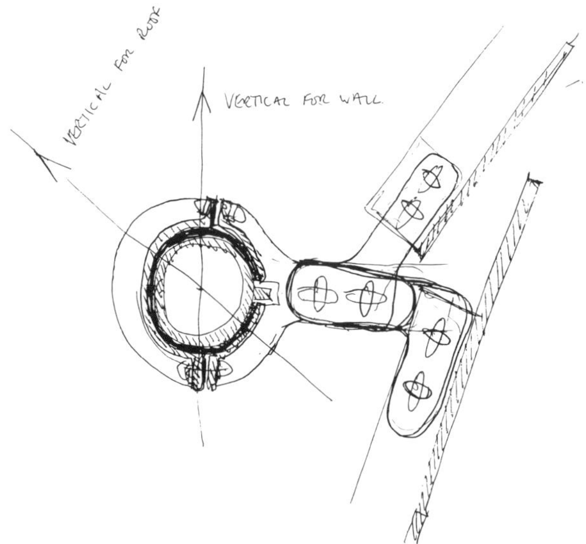

Early Nick Grimshaw sketch of the glazing overlap detail.

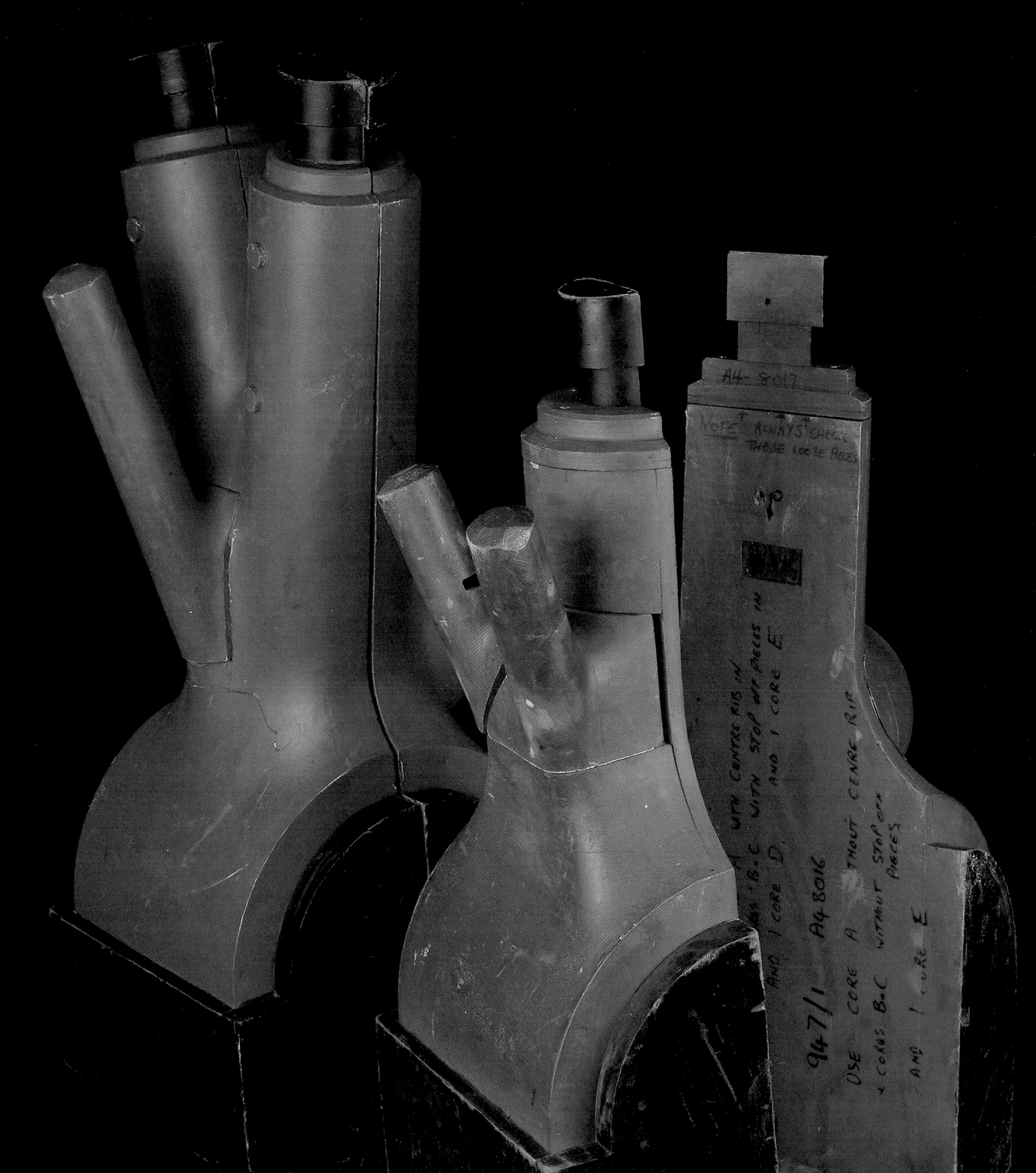
A4-8017
ALWAYS
THESE LOOSE PIECES
WITH CENTRE RIB IN
WITH STOP OFF PIECES IN
AND 1 CORE D. AND 1 CORE E
947/1 A4 8016
USE CORE A THOUT CENRE RIB
+ CORES B-C WITHOUT STOP OFF PIECES
AND 1 CORE E

Mild-steel sand castings, used as part of the steel frame, made complex connnections simple.

Left, two of the patterns for the pin joints at either end of the roof structure.

Far left: the foundry where the mild-steel pin joints were cast.
Left: detail showing how the castings fit together.

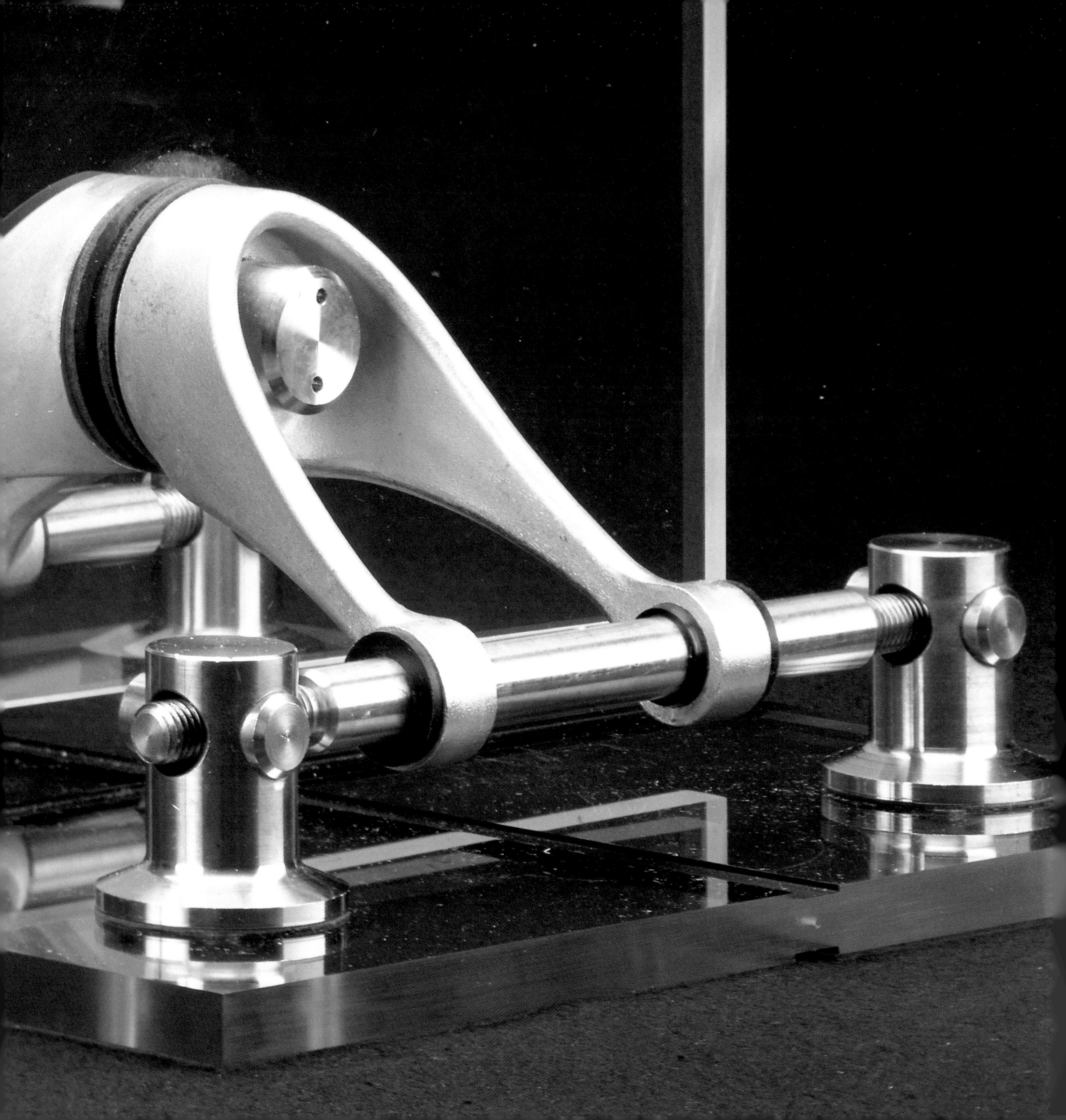

The glazed wall on the west elevation hangs below the platform and track bed slab and, as trains enter the station, the slab moves by up to 80mm horizontally and vertically by up to 6mm.

Left: detail of a stainless-steel bracket.

Below: vertical, glass fins restrain the glazed wall from the inside and stainless-steel brackets secure the glass panels.

Conceptual sketch by Andrew Whalley, exploring the form of the glazing bracket.

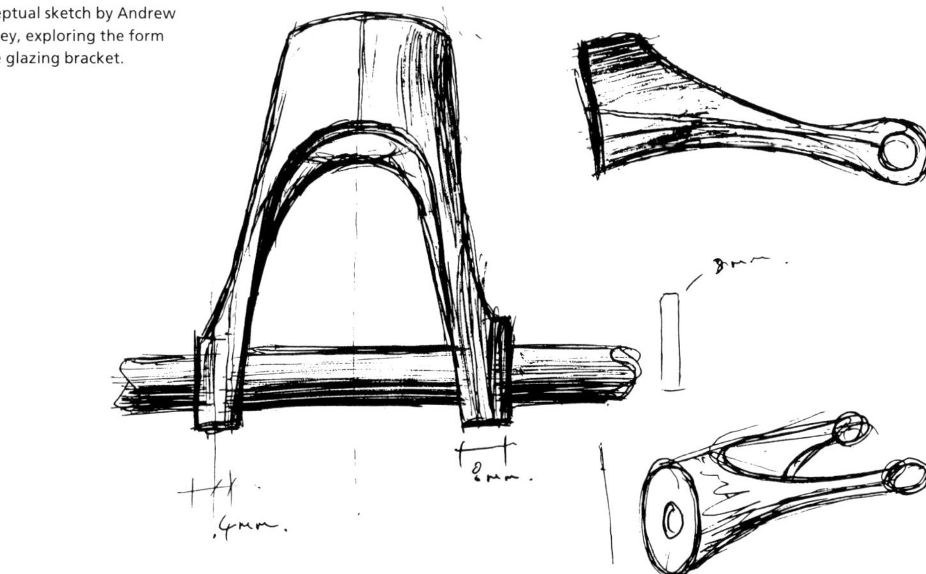

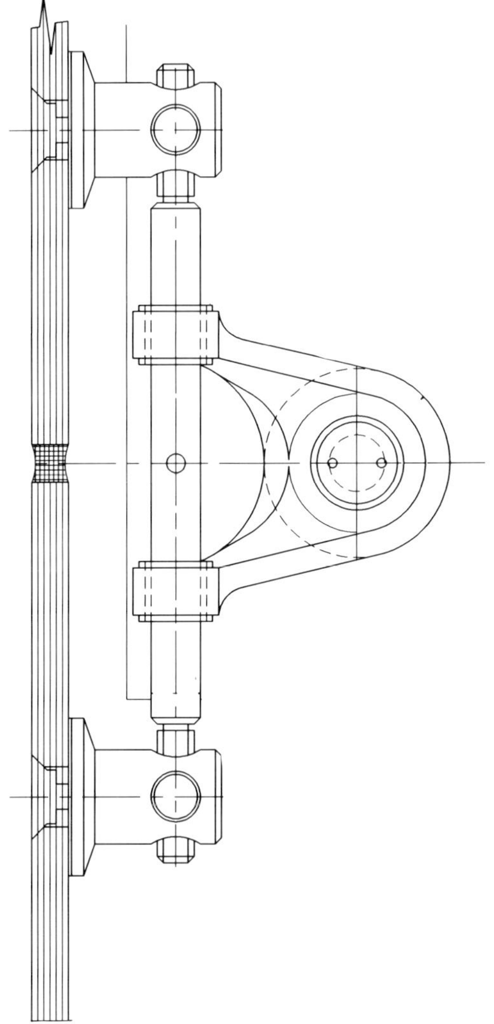

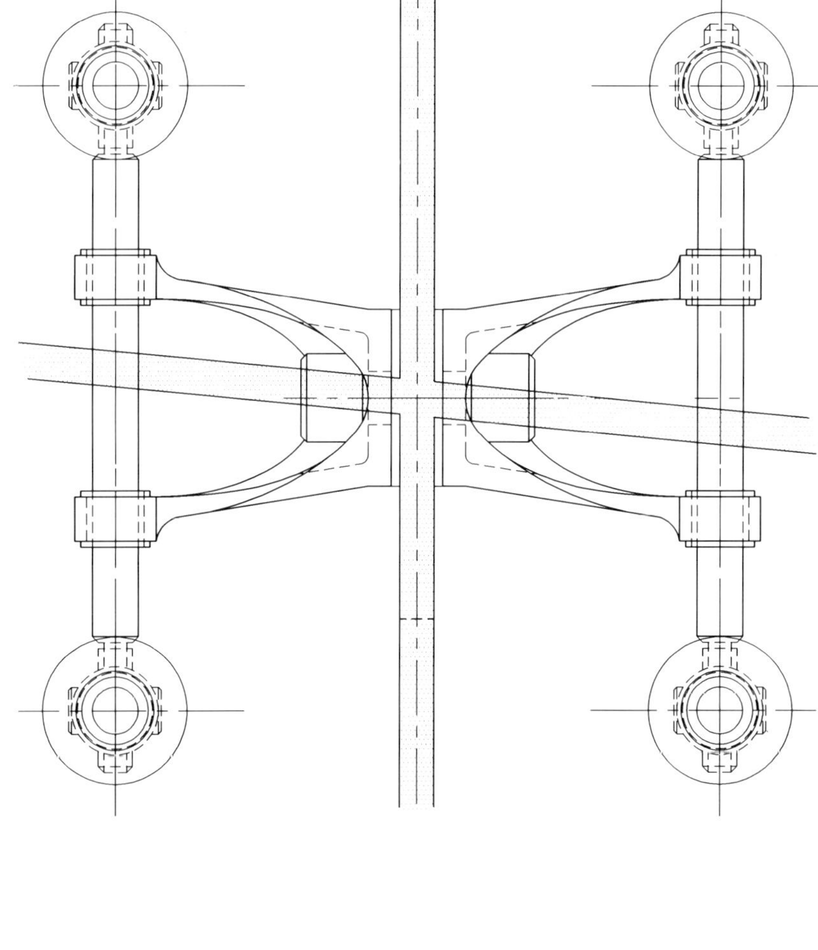

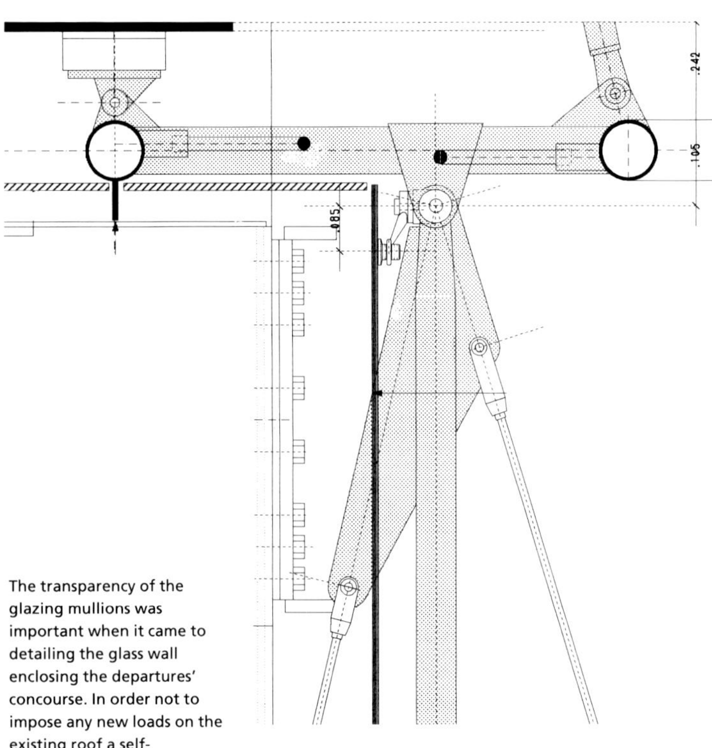

46 The transparency of the glazing mullions was important when it came to detailing the glass wall enclosing the departures' concourse. In order not to impose any new loads on the existing roof a self-supporting, bow-string system was devised.

Right: detailed sections through top and bottom of bow-string system.

Far right: section through glass wall.

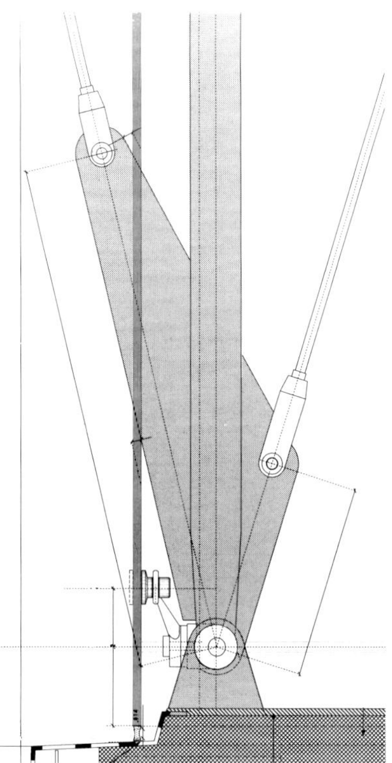

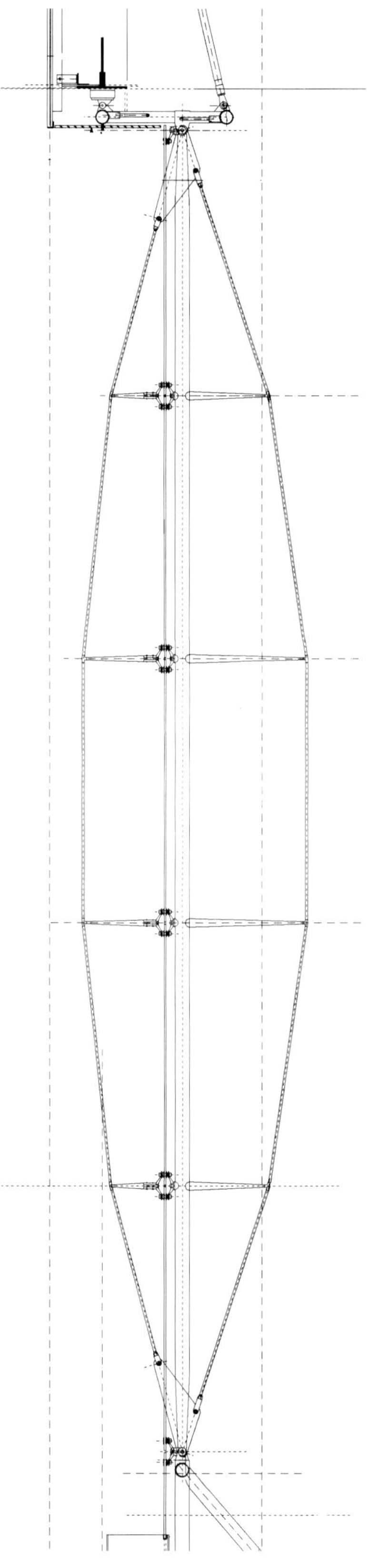

Detail of a prototype for a mid-junction of the bow-string system.

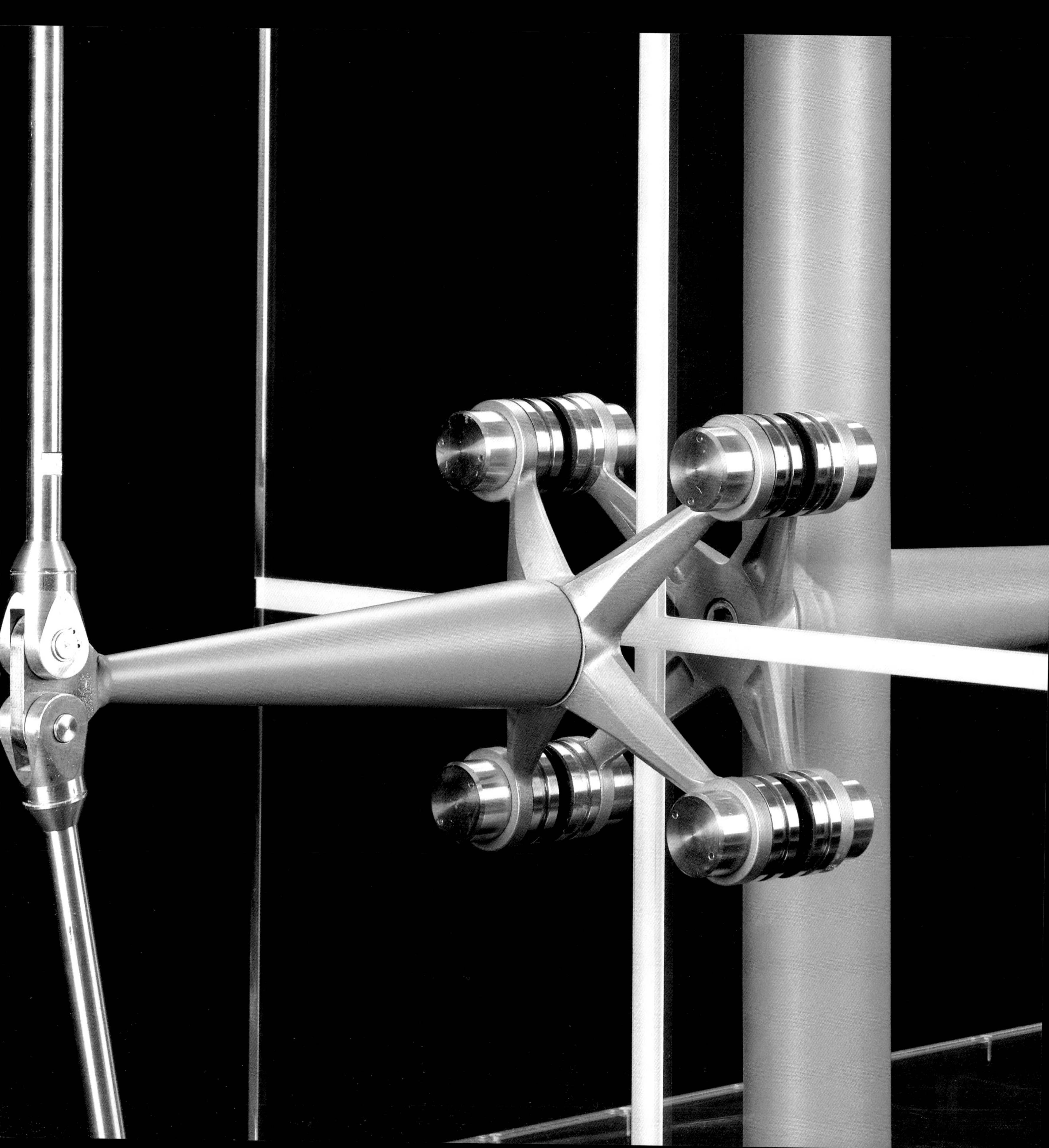

One entire bay of the roof, complete with glazing and cladding, was erected at Weatherby, Yorkshire. The exercise proved invaluable as a means of validating the design and as a learning tool for erection crews, as well as a pretext for an office outing.

Compression booms within the trusses are composed of interlocking sequences of stepped, tube sections whose telescoping properties allow these members to stay in proportion within the overall span, whether this is 48m or 35m.

Left: view of a major truss in the workshop and members of the design team.

Right: the tapered tubes that resolve the difference in overall diameter from the main boom to the tension rods.

Overleaf
Site photograph during construction looking along the tracks and platforms from the concourse end of the development.

Bovis
Fire Exit
O'ROURKE

Departures' plan

1 departures' concourse
2 ticket sales area
3 escalator up from the London Underground
4 lifts down from Network SouthEast
5 escalator to and from Network SouthEast
6 taxi drop-off area
7 ticket check-in
8 security check
9 staff security check
10 temporary passport check
11 ramp to/from catering suite in arches
12 departures' lounge
13 internal ramp linking departures and arrivals (external paving and taxi road follow these levels)
14 void over arrivals' concourse
15 passenger-control lobby
16 ramp to arrivals

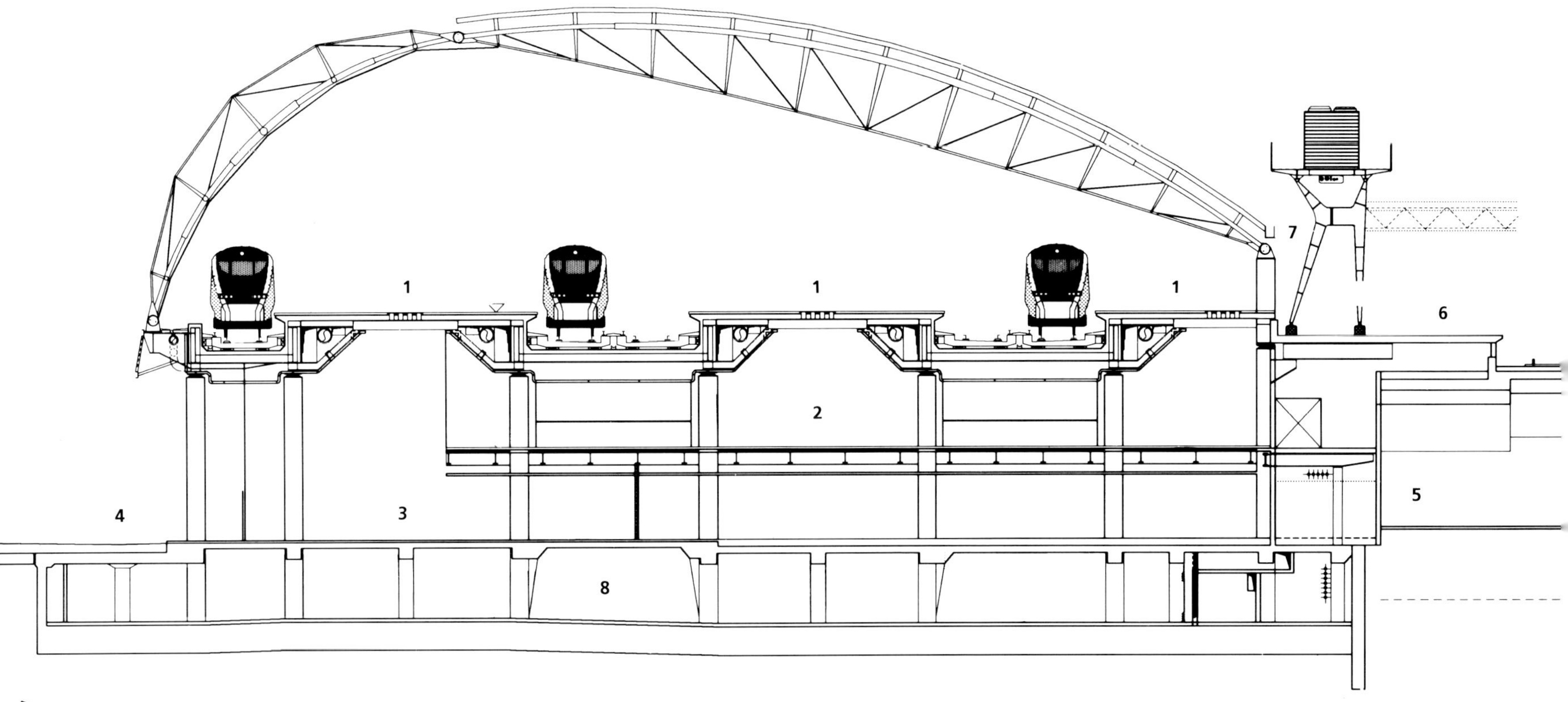

Cross section

1 international platforms
2 departures' lounge
3 arrivals' concourse
4 taxi drop-off/pick-up point
5 existing Network SouthEast arches used for ancillary international functions such as catering
6 Network SouthEast platform 19
7 international frontier
8 car park

Channel Tunnel Railway Terminal

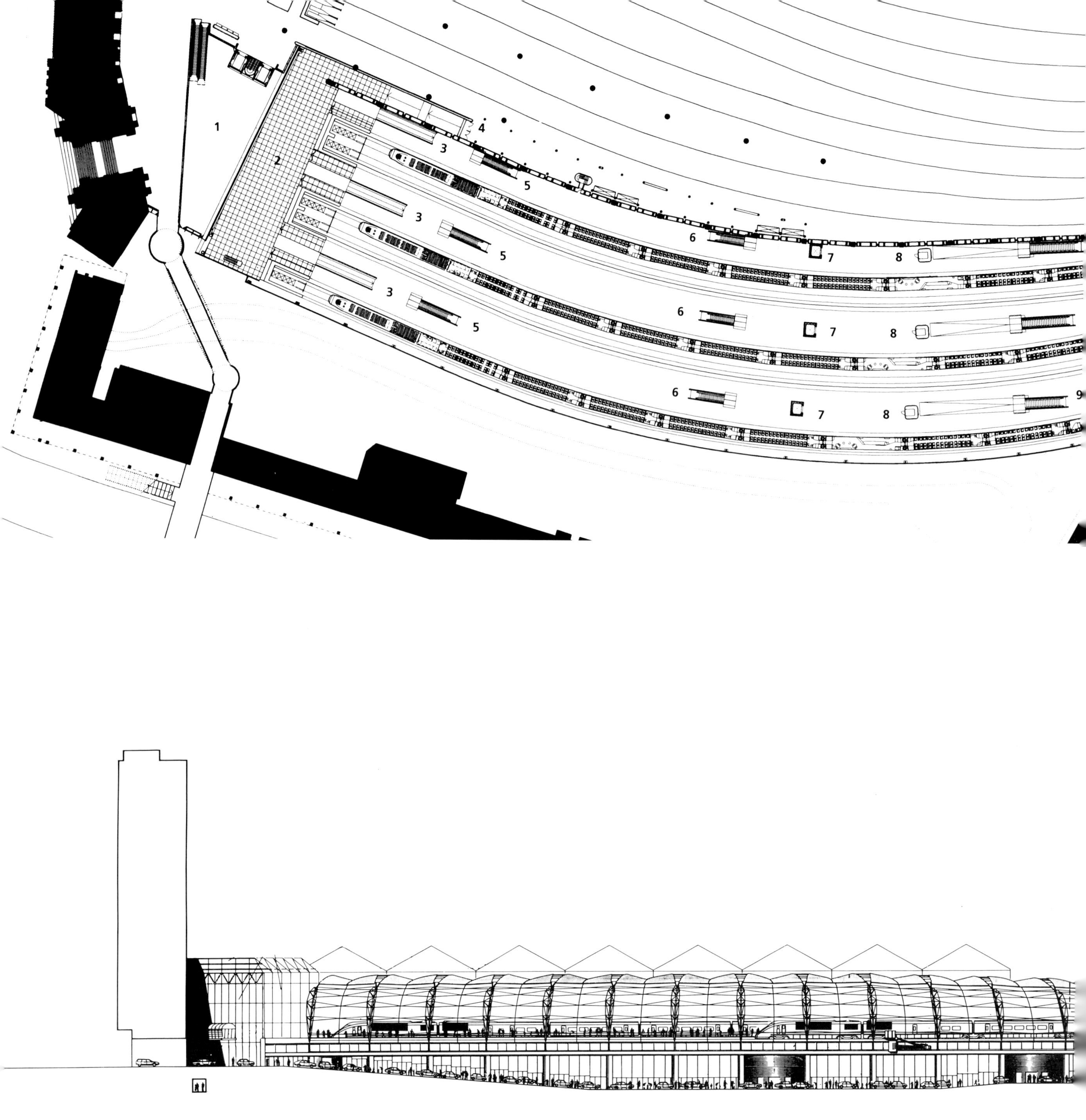

1
2
3
4
3
5
3
5
6
7
8
5
6
7
8
6
7
8
9

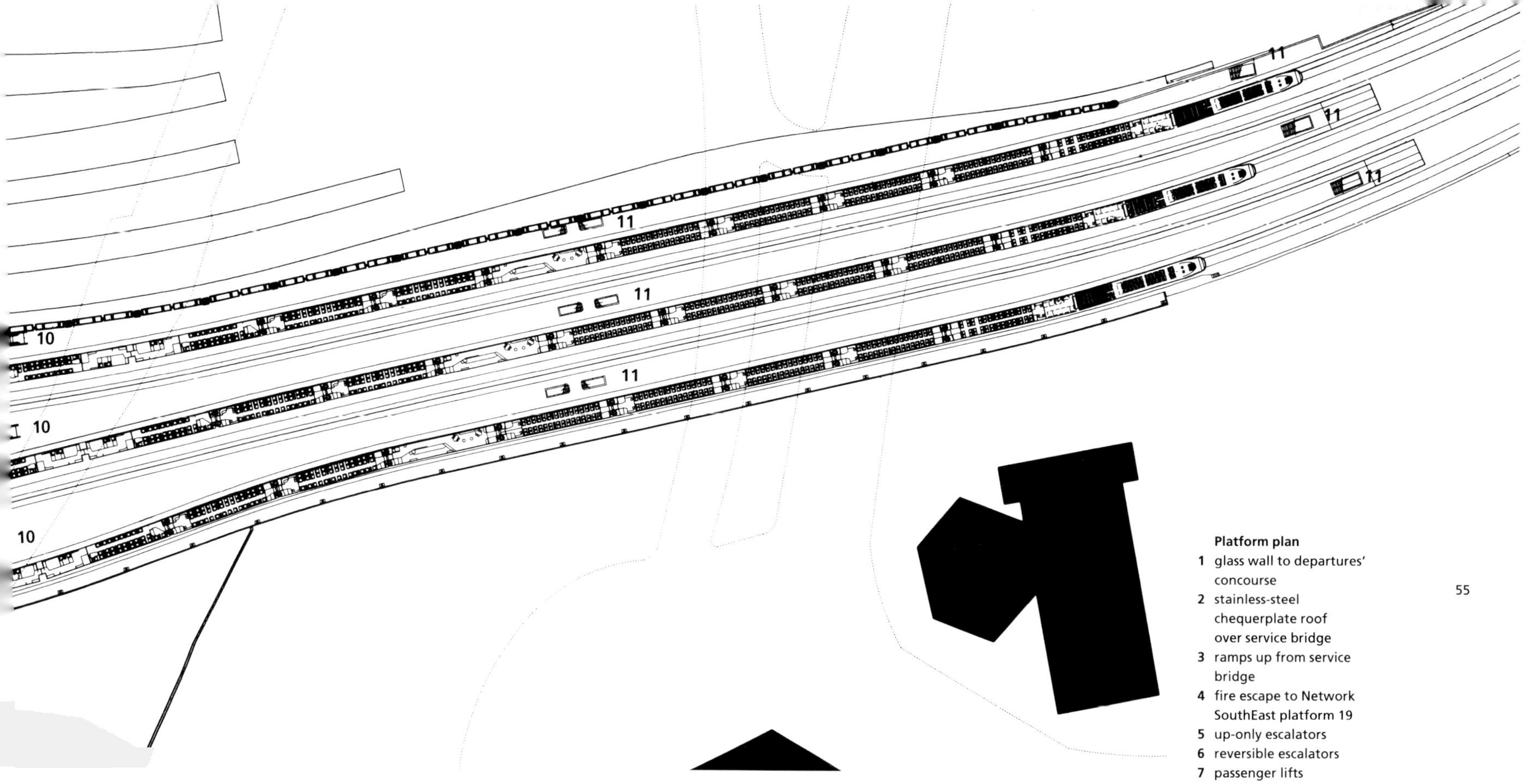

10
10
10
11
11
11
11
11
11

Platform plan

1 glass wall to departures' concourse
2 stainless-steel chequerplate roof over service bridge
3 ramps up from service bridge
4 fire escape to Network SouthEast platform 19
5 up-only escalators
6 reversible escalators
7 passenger lifts
8 platform controllers' kiosks
9 reversible conveyors
10 down-only escalators
11 fire escape stairs

West elevation

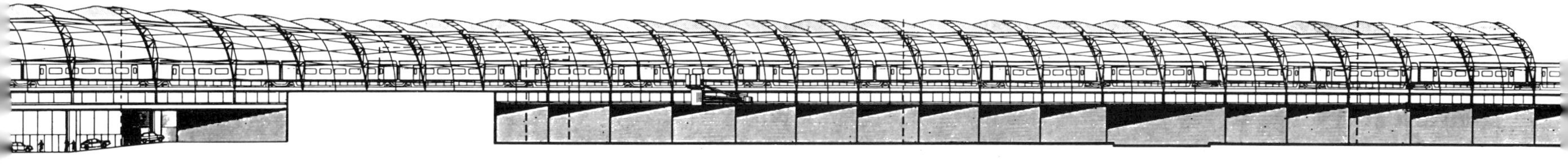

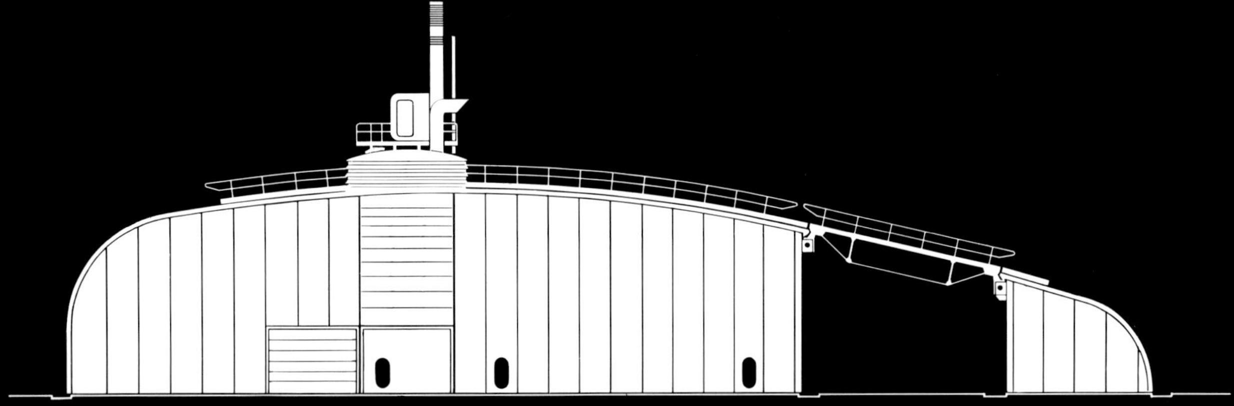

North Woolwich Pumping Station, London, 1988

'The site was a wasteland and the loneliness of the building was a strong influence on the design. The structure had to be both economic and virtually indestructible. The brief called for minimum maintenance and the longest possible life for all the materials. We tried to think of this quite large object as a soft shape with no distinction between roof and walls. This was partly to simplify maintenance – to apply a coat of North Sea oil-rig paint every 10 years or so would be a very easy task. However there was also the feeling of trying to reduce the bulk and impact on the skyline. As well as this, the toughness and ruggedness of the building seemed to match the process inside.' **NG**

Previous page
Model viewed from the south-east.

The pumping station at North Woolwich is part of a government-financed programme to improve London Docklands' drainage systems. Perhaps in response to criticism of under-investment in infrastructure, the London Docklands Development Corporation (LDDC) has chosen to commemorate this programme by appointing imaginative architects to design its visible structures. Grimshaw's pumping station joins others by John Outram and the Richard Rogers Partnership. In so doing, the LDDC has revived the Victorian tradition of taking pride in utilitarian structures.

The design, therefore, had to produce a satisfying object but also, in so far as it responds to a highly specific and technical brief, a very functional building. The wells and pumps it contains, and the headroom and swings of the cranes needed to move machinery, were all specified in the brief and defined the dimensions of the enclosure to a high level of precision. The architect's role was largely to supply walls and roof, capable of lasting 100 years with regular maintenance, and be robust enough to withstand vandalism. The site, a wasteland, also indicated a tough building.

The design is accordingly embattled, not to say apocalyptic, in appearance with only a few rounded windows denoting occupation, or tempering its massive scale. It resembles another robust and self-reliant construction – the submarine – and is clad, like a ship, in a continuous shell of butt-welded steel plate, strengthened with integral stiffeners. The steel plate spans between tapering steel portal frames which, in turn, span more than 40m, to give unobstructed internal space.

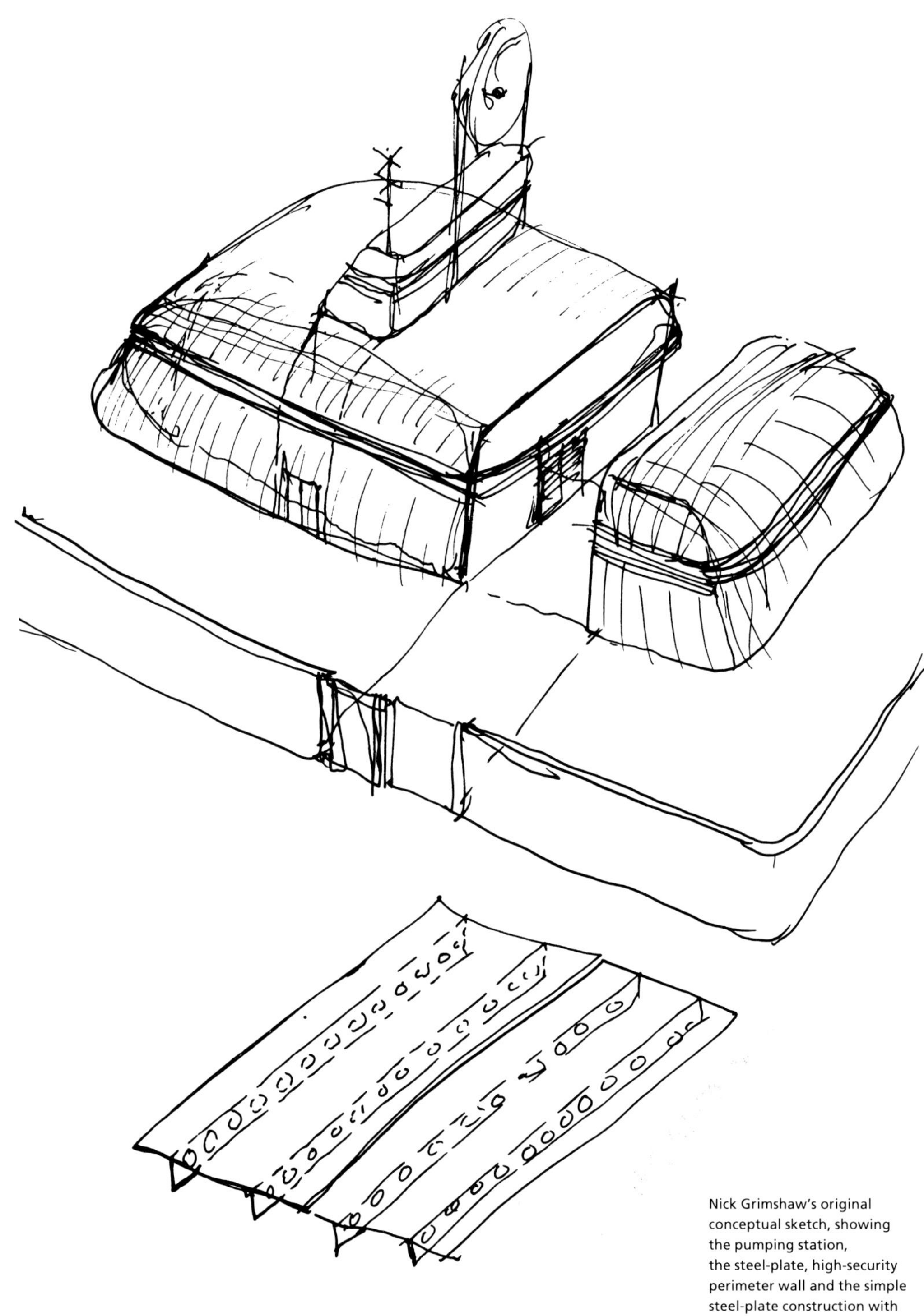

Nick Grimshaw's original conceptual sketch, showing the pumping station, the steel-plate, high-security perimeter wall and the simple steel-plate construction with perforated stiffeners.

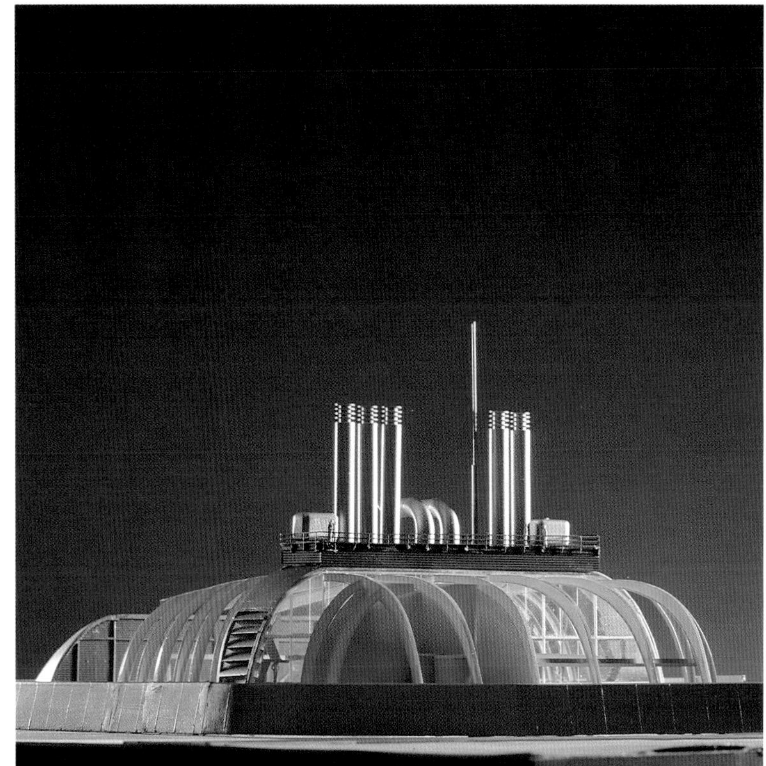

Model used for planning presentations. The external shell has been removed to reveal the central service and accommodation facilities with main pump halls either side.

A view of the model with the external shell in place, and perimeter, steel-plate wall.

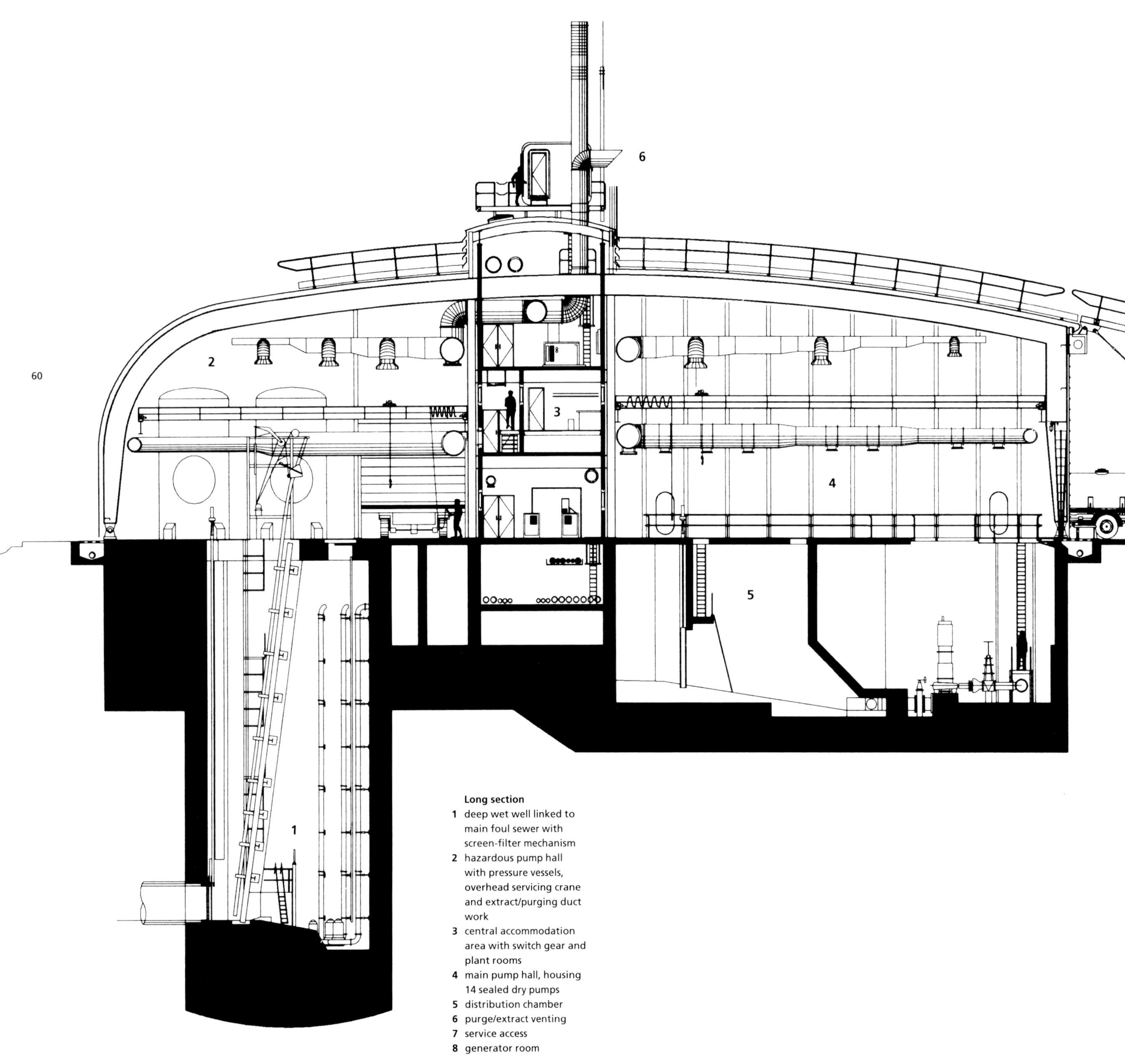

Long section

1 deep wet well linked to main foul sewer with screen-filter mechanism
2 hazardous pump hall with pressure vessels, overhead servicing crane and extract/purging duct work
3 central accommodation area with switch gear and plant rooms
4 main pump hall, housing 14 sealed dry pumps
5 distribution chamber
6 purge/extract venting
7 service access
8 generator room

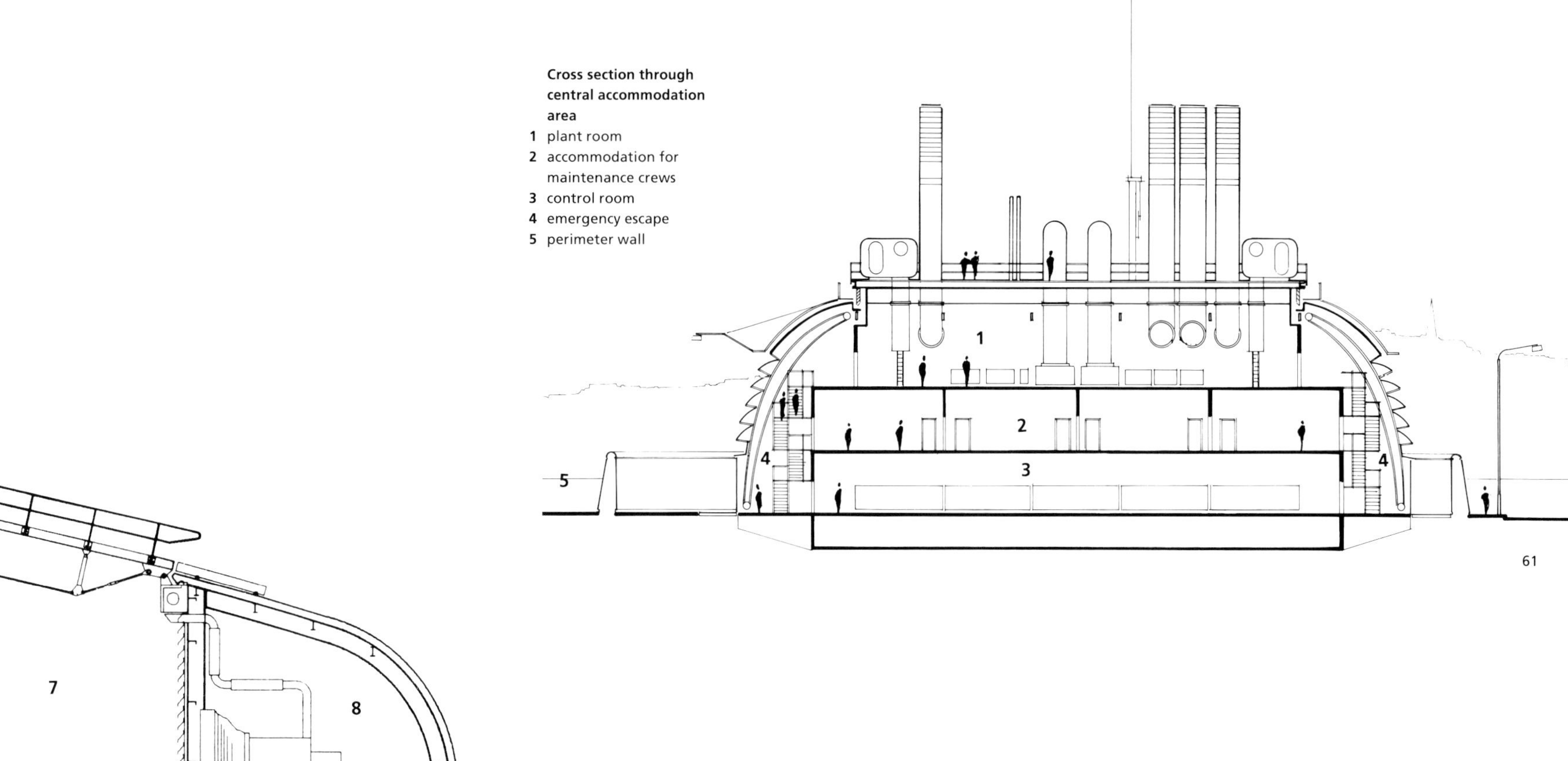

Cross section through central accommodation area

1 plant room
2 accommodation for maintenance crews
3 control room
4 emergency escape
5 perimeter wall

Thermal insulation is sprayed onto the inside to inhibit condensation in what is, apart from the intermittently used control room, an unheated building. The insulation and the long-lasting and resilient sprayed-metal coating are, like the structure, derived from marine and oil-rig technologies. A ship-building firm, consulted about the design of the plates, suggested that the structure might be prefabricated in four sections and floated up the River Thames to the site.

At one point the impermeable object becomes accessible. An access road decisively slices out a broad oblong slot through the building, separating the electrical plant from the rest of the pumping station. A parallel internal strip, narrower and less pronounced, houses the control rooms and separates the pump hall from the wet-well area which, in direct contact with the open sewers underneath, is subject to build-up of explosive and poisonous gases. The control room is marked on the outside by an array of extract flues, roof-mounted plant, and their associated access deck.

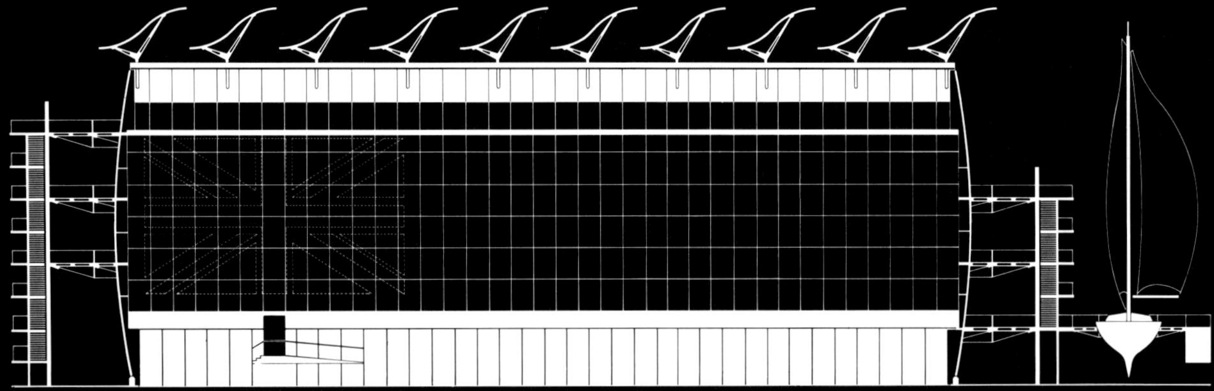

British Pavilion, Expo 92, Seville, 1992

'"Seville itself was dazzling – a thousand miniature patios set with inexhaustible fountains, which fell trickling upon ferns and leaves, each a nest of green repeated in endless variations around this theme of domestic oasis." I quoted this extract from Laurie Lee's book *As I Walked Out One Midsummer Morning* in our original presentations on Seville. Climate was always our theme and Seville is indeed dazzling. However, people have lived there happily for hundreds of years without air conditioning or indeed any form of technological aids to climate control. We therefore asked the question: why should an Expo building not respect these values and learn from them?

'We wanted to express a feeling about the age we lived in. We wanted to show our concern about energy and that we had the ability to reuse all the materials. But above all we wanted to get across something of the creative force that goes into architecture and the feeling of delight that can be gained by simply looking at something well made – like a finely crafted tool fit for its purpose.' **NG**

Previous page
Morning sunshine on the water-wall with sun louvres above.

Left: view of the British Pavilion from the north-east in International Avenue, as people queue to enter the building.

Since the 1851 Great Exhibition, world fairs have engendered some of the most inventive and influential structures of modern times: the Crystal Palace, the Eiffel Tower, Le Corbusier's Pavilion de l'Esprit Nouveau, Mies van der Rohe's Barcelona Pavilion. They have engendered, too, their share of kitsch, from the gondola-strewn World Columbian Exhibition in Chicago to the walk-through peacock that was the Indian pavilion at the 1992 Expo in Seville. In this divide Grimshaw, for whom the Crystal Palace has always been an inspiration, is, unsurprisingly, on the side of invention. When Grimshaw won the competition to design the British Pavilion, Grimshaw and his team were well aware of the tradition of previous exhibition buildings. However, at the end of the 20th century, technological invention is no longer seen as an unmitigated good. The British pavilion, therefore, is an affirmation of technology, but also a demonstration of its more environmentally benign applications.

Seville is the hottest city in Europe. In the field of construction, this primarily entails the creation of a cool space without consuming huge quantities of energy. Given Grimshaw's predilections for prefabrication, and the pavilion's function as an advertisement for British industries, the structure had to be constructed with components made in Britain and transported to the site. This in turn implied manufactured, lightweight materials, which are the opposite of the heavy masonry commonly used in hot countries to control heat. What Grimshaw actually built is a structure which, apart from its concrete foundations, was almost entirely prefabricated in Britain, but which harnessed the site's free resources of water, air and sun.

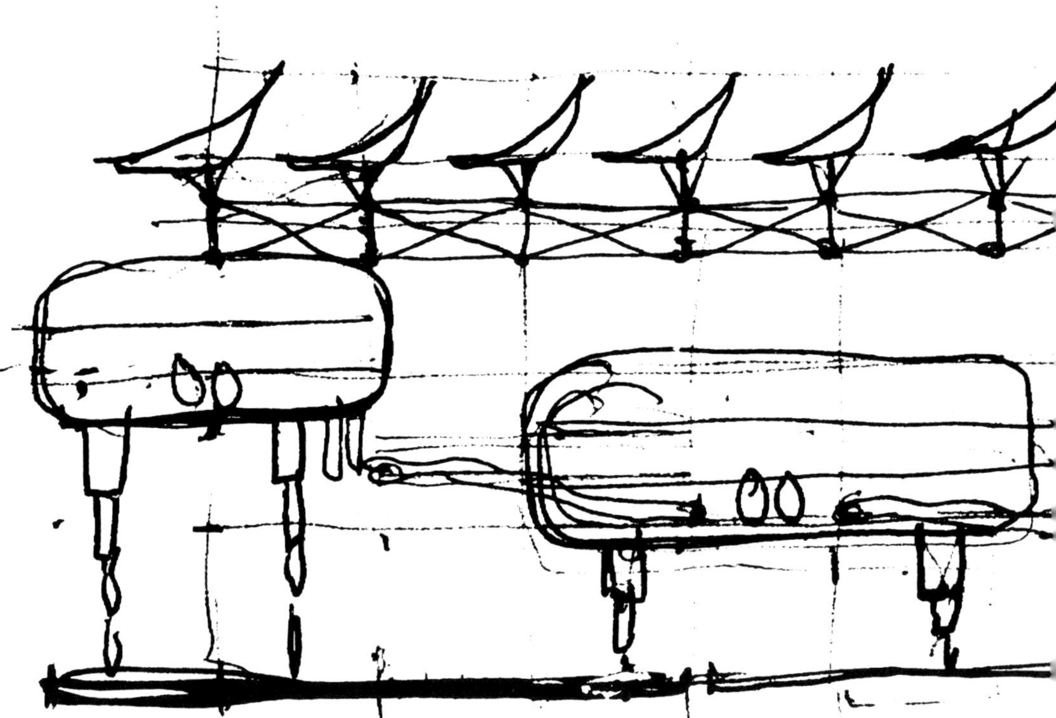

Early sketch by Nick Grimshaw illustrating the freestanding exhibition pods within the large single volume of the pavilion and the shading louvres on the roof.

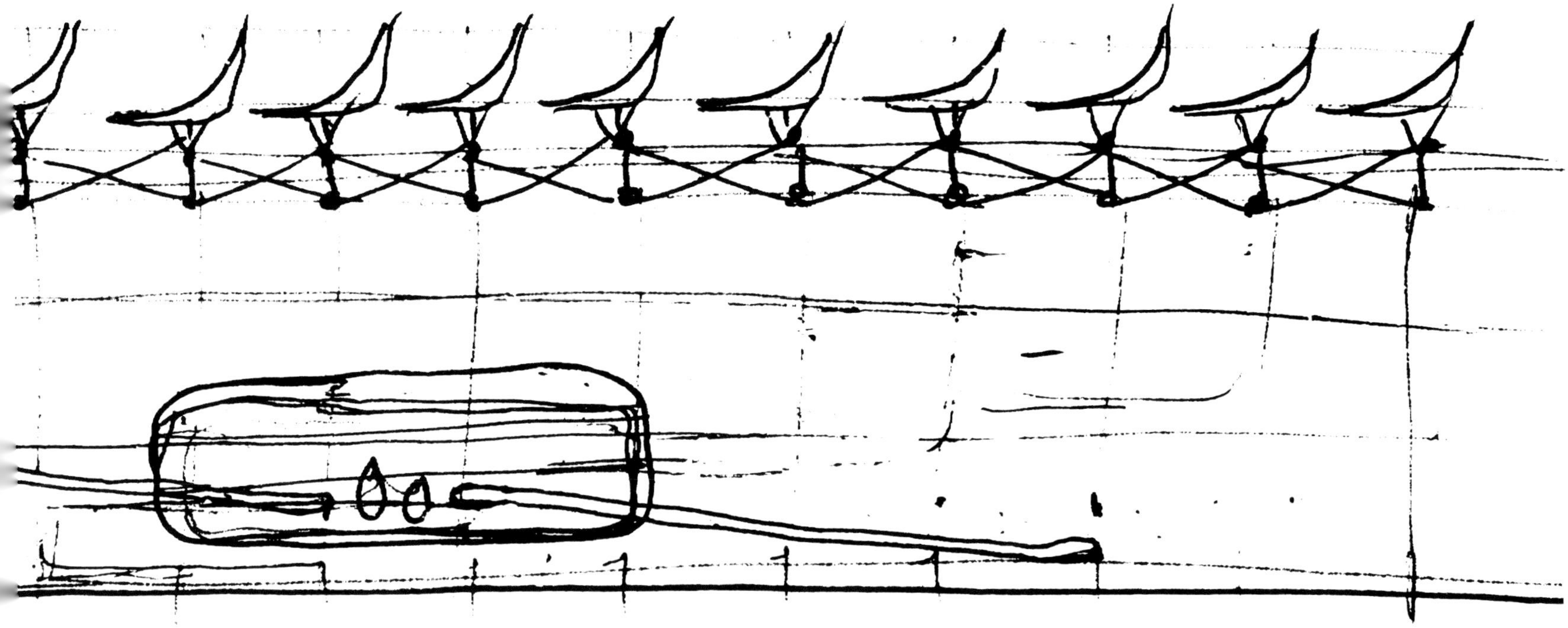

Model photomontage created for the competition submission.

Completed building viewed from the south-east corner, showing the water-wall by night.

Early sketch by Nick Grimshaw of the solar panels on the roof louvres, which contributed to the powering of the water-wall.

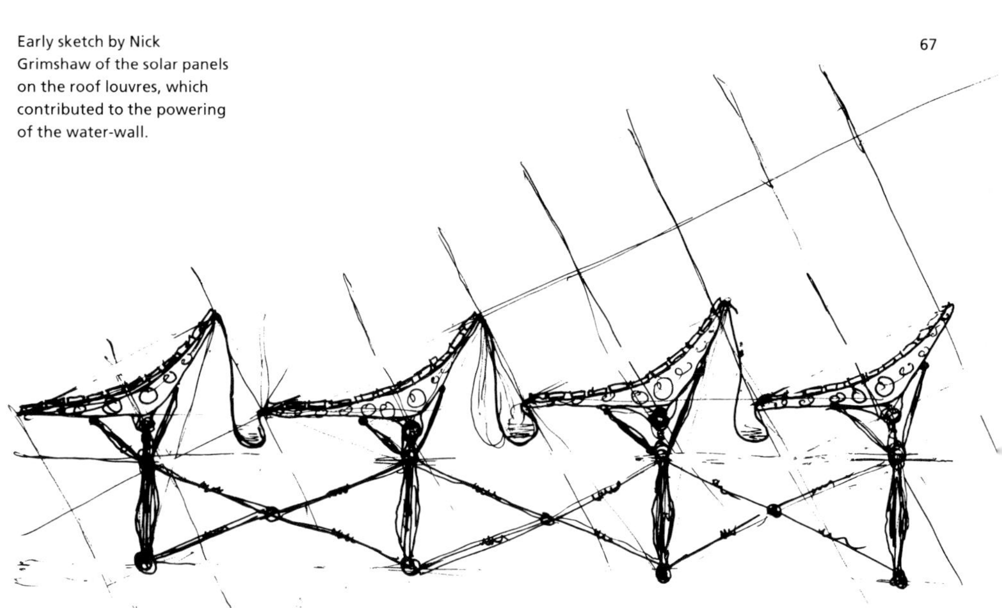

Diagrams showing the different surfaces of the building in response to the orientation of the sun.

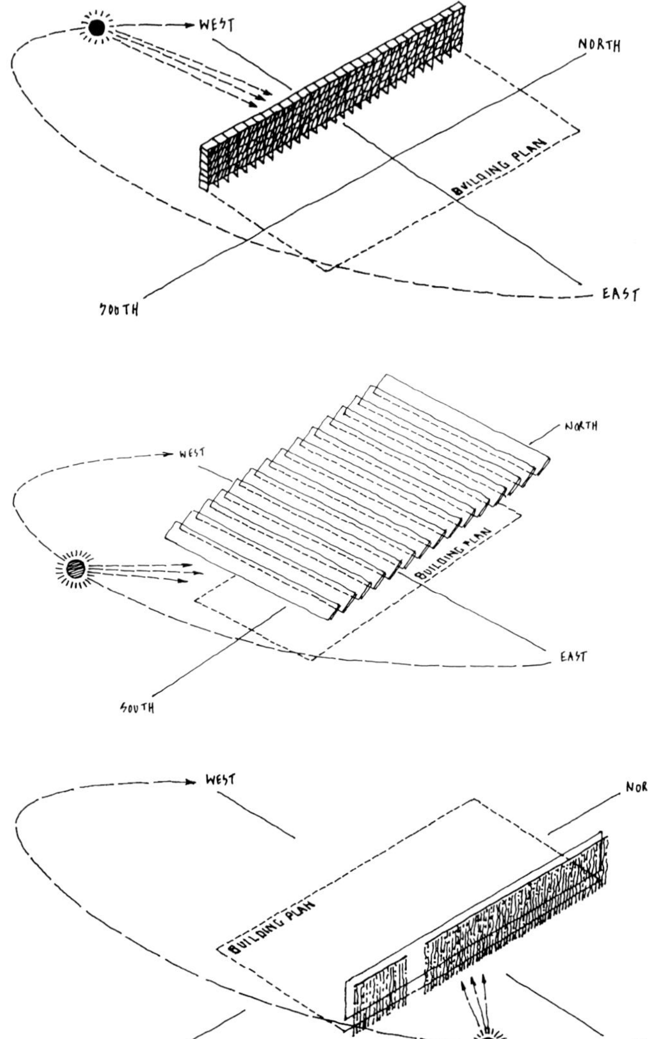

The most obvious example of this approach is the water-wall, which dominates the principal, eastern elevation of the pavilion. Water running down glass became a well-worked device of Expo 92, but the water-wall of the British Pavilion is the most convincing variation on the theme, by virtue of its sheer size, and of the attention paid to the flow patterns of water by Grimshaw and the water sculptor William Pye. The wall is a development of Grimshaw's love of very large glazed areas, but one (unlike, for example, the *Western Morning News* building) where the structure is on the inside of the planar glazing. On the outside, water adhering to the glass runs down in rhythmic patterns. Then, just above head-height at the entrance, a trough gathers it and redistributes it as a curtain of free falling 'rain', which falls into a pool that runs the length of the entrance elevation. This creates a play of two aqueous sounds, a swish and a hum, and two levels of transparency: a hazy upper level and a sharper-focused, lower one.

The environmental purpose of the water-wall is to create two zones of coolness: outside, for visitors awaiting admission and another inside. It is powered by solar panels in the roof, so the problem that governs most of the design, the Andalusian sun, becomes part of the solution.

Several other devices augment the water-wall. On the roof, S-shaped shades (with an obvious and acknowledged debt to Renzo Piano's and the late Peter Rice's Menil Museum in Houston) carry the solar panels and keep the sun from the sheet-metal roof. On the western wall, which receives sun during the hottest part of the day, stacks of shipping containers filled with

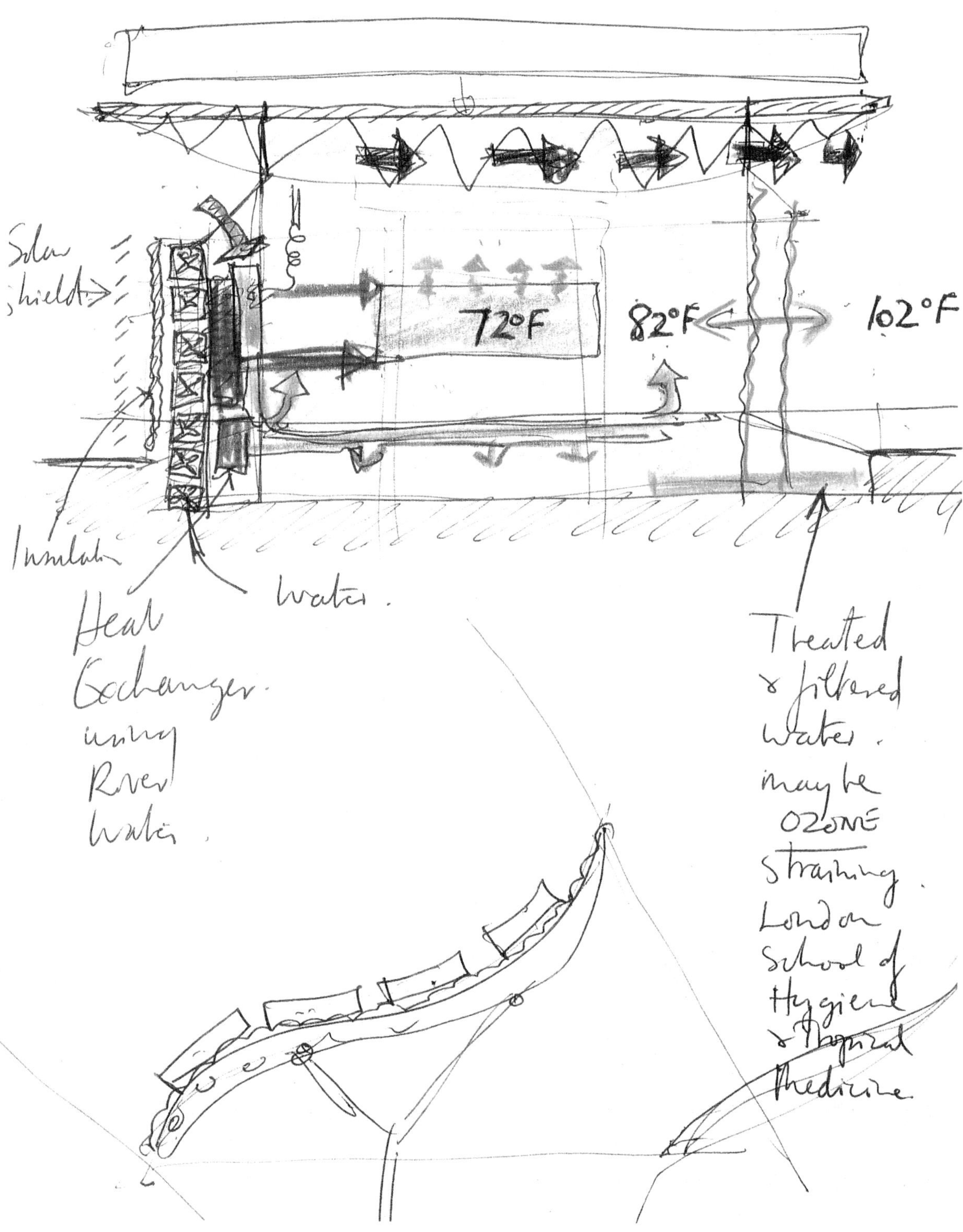

Nick Grimshaw's sketch demonstrating the idea of a passively moderated space between the extreme temperatures of Seville outside and the air-conditioned pods within.

Overleaf
Morning view looking up to the top of the water-wall and the shading roof louvres.

The structure of the water-wall is reflected in the internal pool.

water provide the thermal capacity – the ability to absorb heat – traditionally achieved with masonry. On the north and south walls another technology imported from outside traditional building construction is used: PVC-coated polyester fabric, made in the manner of yacht sails, is fixed to bowed-steel tubes by luff grooves, as sails are to masts. On the southern side a second layer of sailcloth in angled, louvre-like strips provides additional protection from the sun.

With the exception of the solar-powered pumps, all of these techniques are passive and require no external input of energy to function. Their combined effect is to reduce the internal temperature by 10°C which, in Seville, can mean the difference between unbearable and pleasant conditions. It is not, however, sufficient to handle the body heat generated by spectators of the audio-visual displays that were a requirement of the brief. These displays are contained in self-contained pods with localised air conditioning.

Given the building's role as a temporary pavilion, and as a built manifesto, it was not enough for its devices to work. They had to be seen to work. After all, the energy saved by them during the six-month life of the Expo is trifling compared to both the energy expended in the building's construction and the influence it could have on future building. Each component of the building's environmental thinking – the water, the roof-top shades, the fabric louvres, and the containers – is therefore emphatically expressed.

The expression of these elements is the dominant, but not the only, generator of the building's design. Almost as important to Grimshaw was a wish to articulate the building's structure, and its nature as an

Visitors move through the building from the concourse to the audio–visual performances in the pods via travelators. Bridges link the upper levels.

View of south elevation sail-wall. Fly sheets are attached, louvre fashion, to the pressed metal struts and tension cables that brace the masts.

The north and south walls of the building borrow technology from the boat-building industry. Membranes of PVC-coated polyethylene fabric are stretched between bow-shaped, circular section steel members and fixed by means of luff grooves in the same way that the sails of yachts are fixed to their masts.

Far left: external detail of sail-wall showing the use of yacht-sail technology.

Left: view of the sail-wall from within the pavilion demonstrating its translucency.

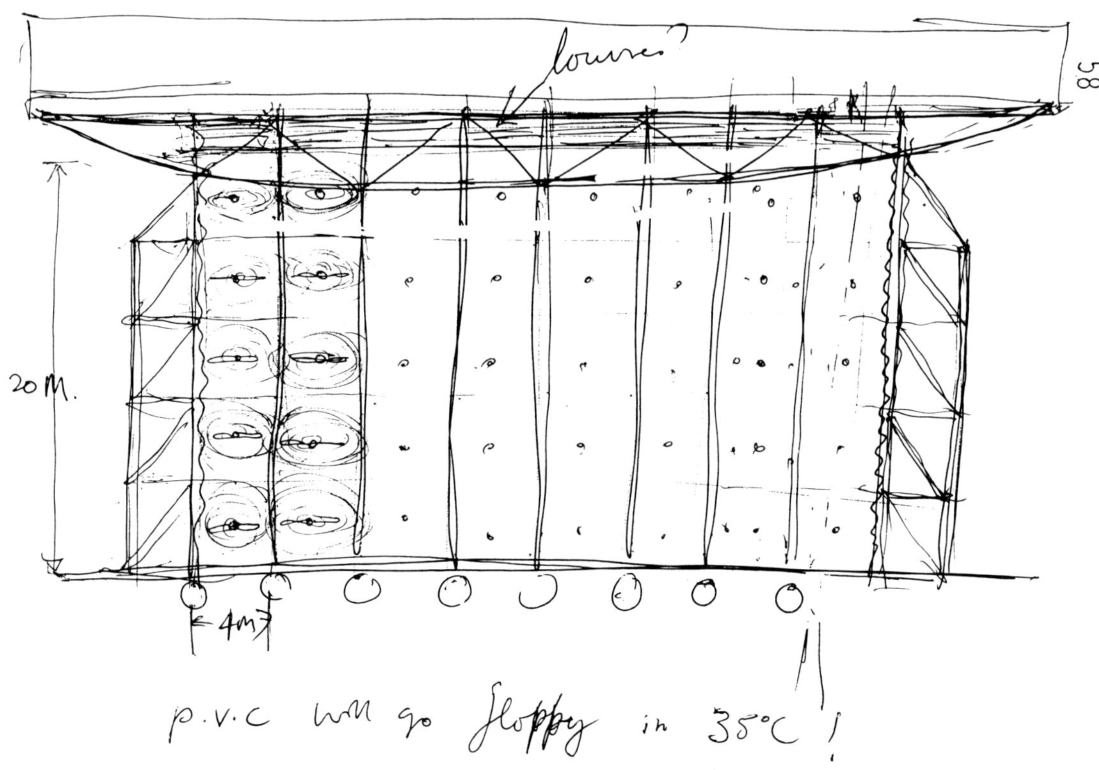

Detail of the water-wall showing how the water free-falls for the last 5m of the wall below the cowl section, allowing clear views into the building at ground level.

Nick Grimshaw's sketch exploring the use of fabric on the north and south elevations.

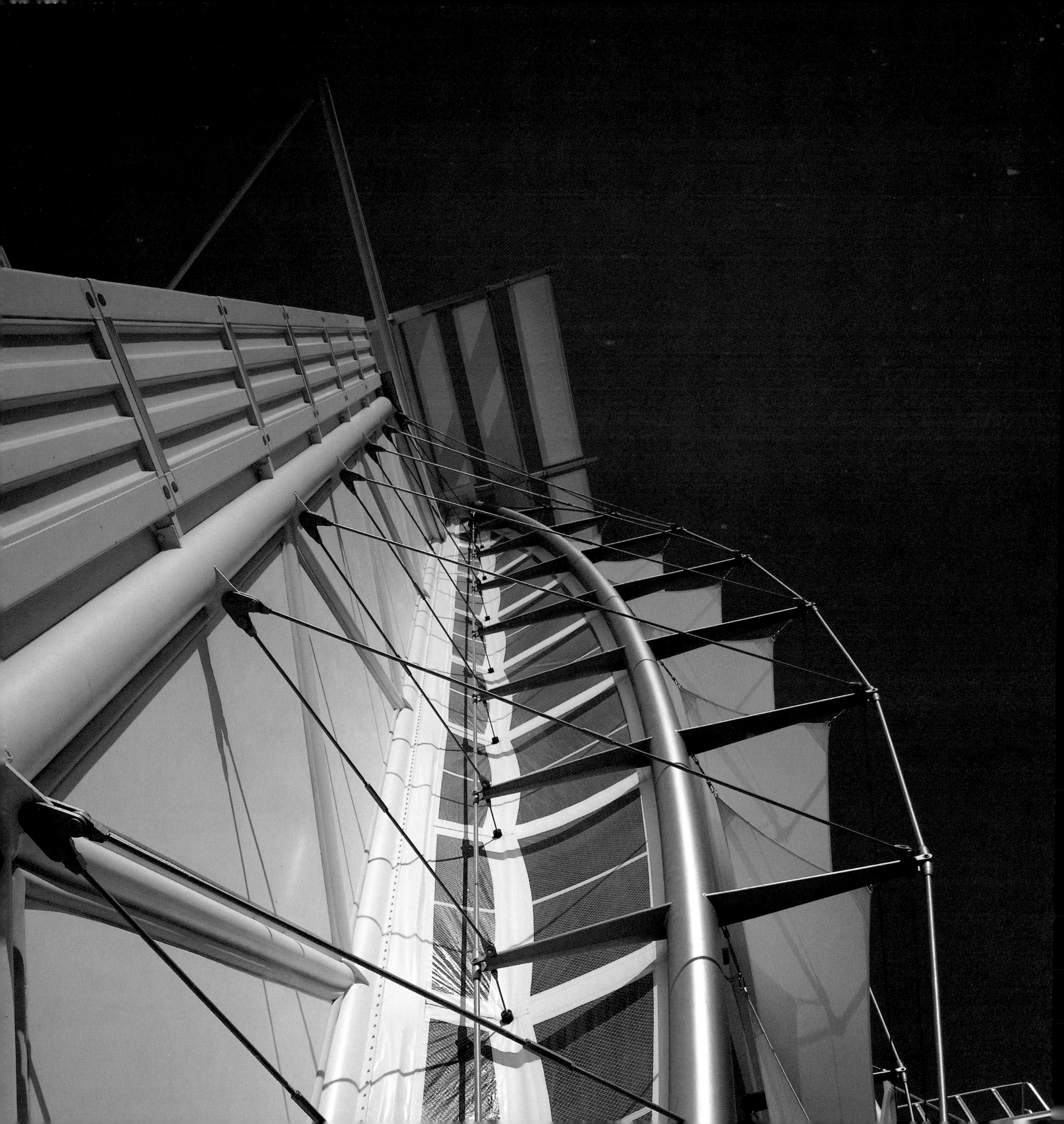

South-west corner of the building, showing stacked containers of the west elevation and junction with the sail-wall.

Pin joint at the foot of the sail-wall, bow-string truss.

assembly of parts. The building accordingly emphasises joints between components, all of which are pinned or bolted (there was no on-site welding), and distinctions between the structure and skin. The structure is constantly present as the visitor travels up, across and down the building. The ascent up the two travelators at the front is dominated by the spectacle of the building's vertical structure and the roof trusses. The trusses also project through the wall onto the main elevation. At night, illumination from inside articulates the cladding as light and the structure as silhouette. The building also records its making more surreptitiously: the flatness of the trusses and the bowed 'masts', for example, enabled them to be stacked efficiently on the back of low-loader trucks.

The structure of the external envelope is itself distinguished from that of the internal platforms, with the two meeting only where escape balconies penetrate the north and south walls. Even here the encounter is mediated with polyester sheet. The structural steelwork of the internal platforms is again exposed, together with the services ducts, as are the V-shaped trusses that support a tertiary structure, that of the walkways and travelators.

In all this, the spaces served by the structure are the least articulated parts of the design, not least because Grimshaw had only limited influence over the displays they contained. What he provides are open decks, large volumes and a circulation system that awaited transformation by an exhibition designer sufficiently strong-minded to exploit them. They also act as special viewing platforms for what, in the event, is the pavilion's principal exhibit, itself.

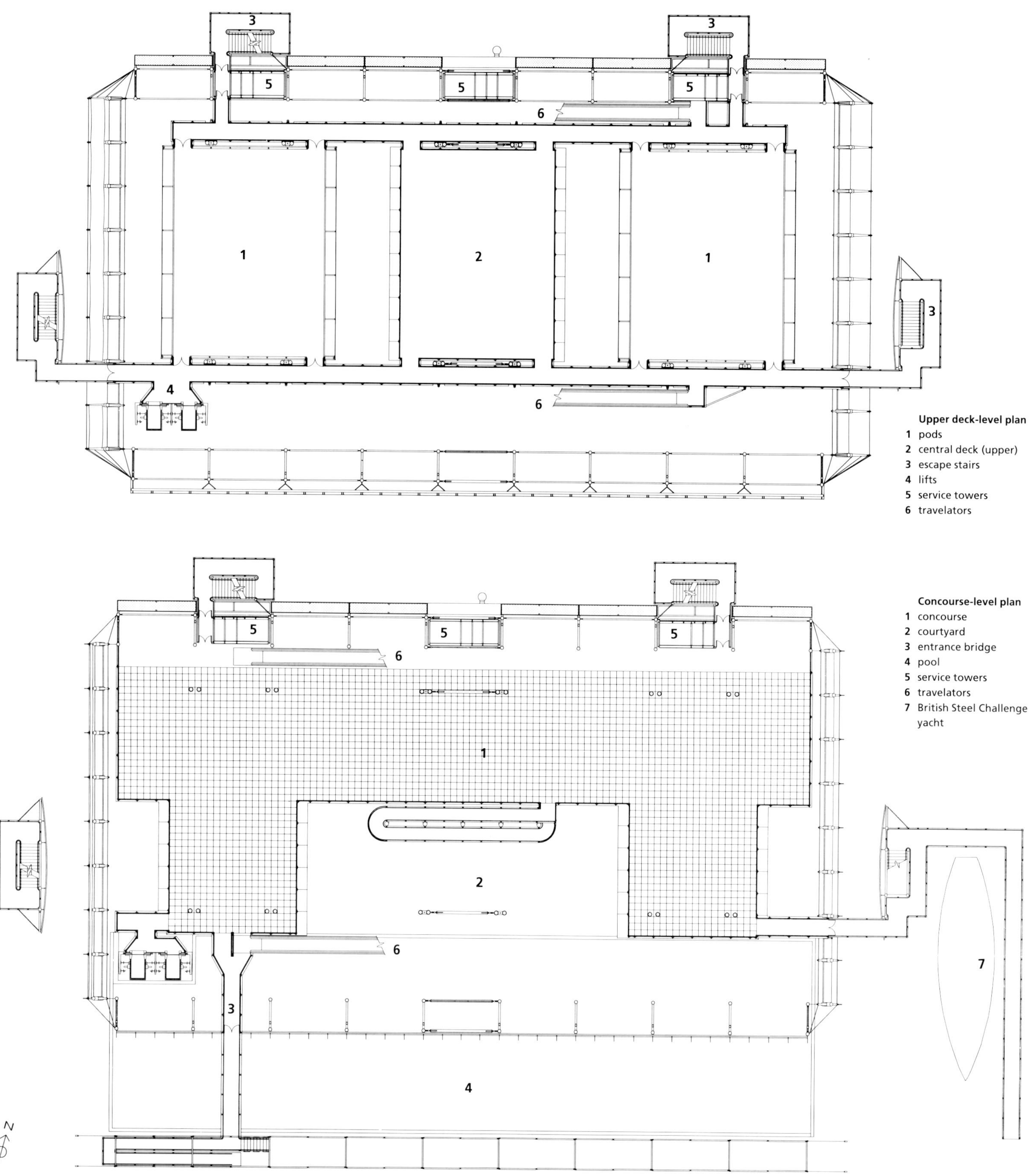

Upper deck-level plan

1 pods
2 central deck (upper)
3 escape stairs
4 lifts
5 service towers
6 travelators

Concourse-level plan

1 concourse
2 courtyard
3 entrance bridge
4 pool
5 service towers
6 travelators
7 British Steel Challenge yacht

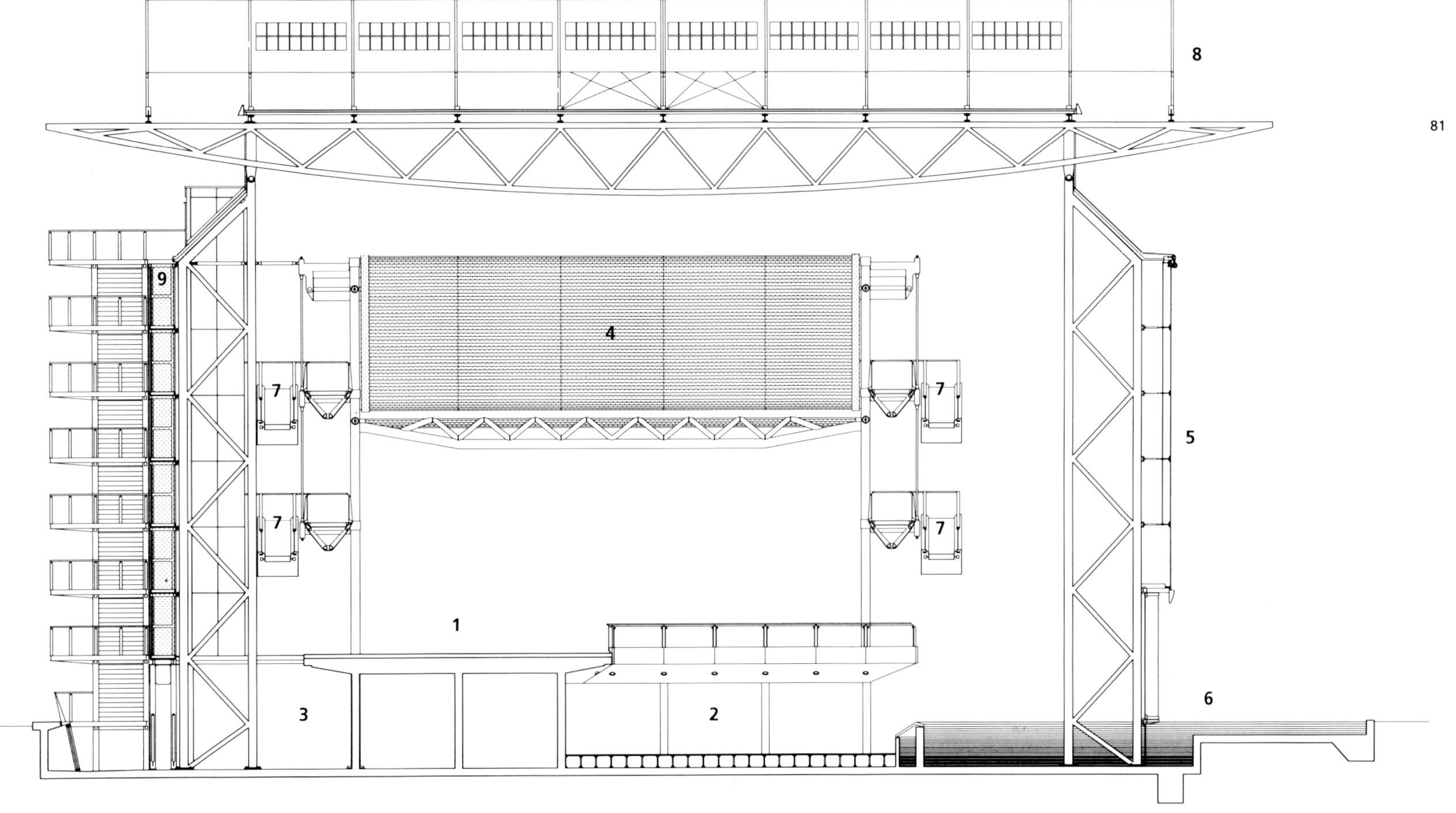

East–west section through courtyard

1 concourse
2 courtyard
3 plant
4 pod (in elevation)
5 water-wall
6 pool
7 travelator
8 sun louvres
9 water tanks

North–south section through pool

1 entrance bridge
2 pods (in elevation)
3 travelators
4 VIP lounge
5 sail-wall
6 sun louvres
7 fire-escape stairs
8 British Steel Challenge yacht

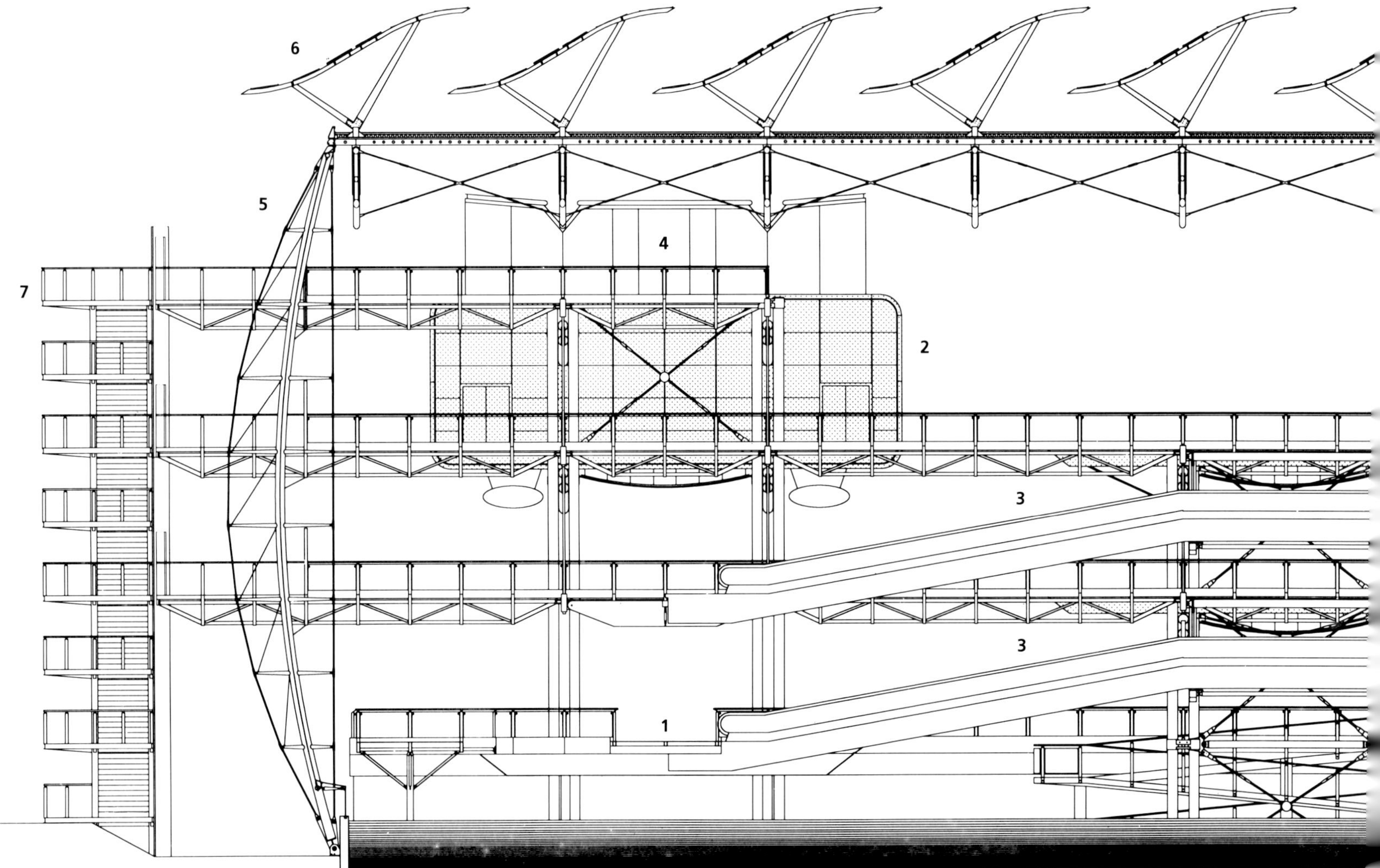

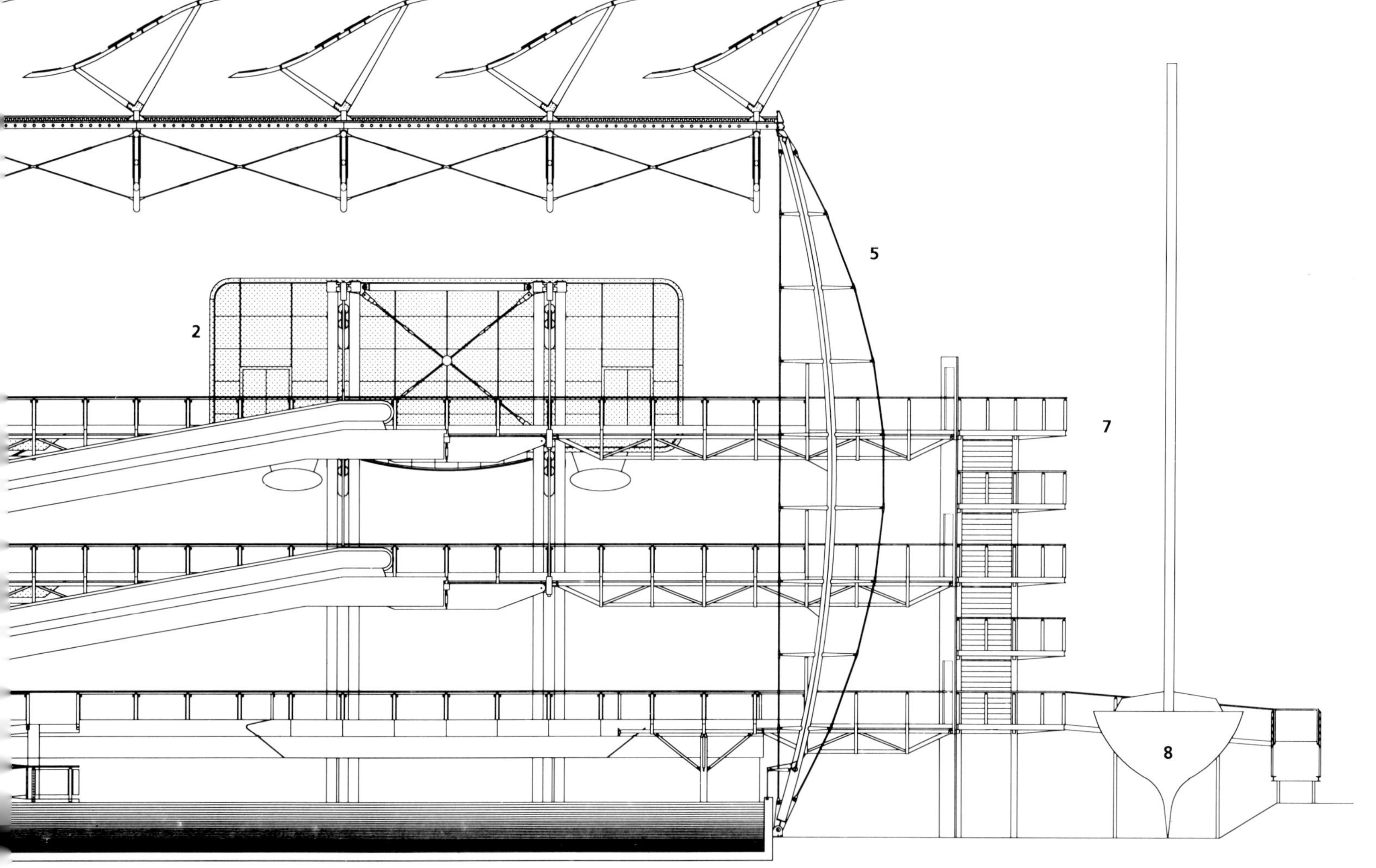

2
5
7
8

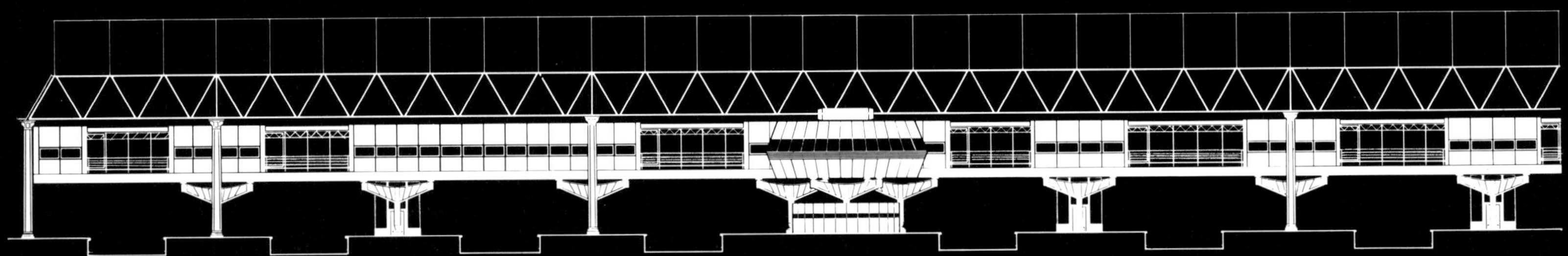

Operations Centre for British Rail at Waterloo, London, 1990

'Waterloo is the busiest railway station in the world. To construct new amenities for the train drivers and accommodation for 100 operations staff without disruption to the passenger-flow was a real challenge. The "tree concept" came early as the only place we could bring columns down was in the centre of the platforms. The trees were therefore planted there and reached out their arms to support beams of variable lengths, which spanned to the next tree. It was then a simple matter to place a metal deck over the beams, and to introduce a concrete slab to form a working platform on which to build the accommodation. The complexity of planning for this project was incredible – different lines had to be closed each night. Everyone in the design team was very pleased when we completed the project on time and even more pleased when they heard that the train drivers were happy.'

NG

Previous page
Columns during fabrication in workshops.

When Grimshaw suggested to representatives of British Rail that they might build their Operations Centre at Waterloo without people noticing, they reacted with resigned amusement. Since users of other London rail terminals – Liverpool Street, Victoria, Cannon Street – had been subjected to severe and long-term disruption by building works, it seemed improbable that anyone could unobtrusively insert an office and retail building into the air above the platforms of Europe's busiest railway station. This, however, is what happened. Eighty million passengers pass through Waterloo each year, none of whom complained, and most of whom, videoed during construction for their reactions by Grimshaw's team, did not notice anything.

The Operations Centre was prompted by the need to relocate the train-drivers' accommodation, which had been demolished to make way for the Channel Tunnel Railway Terminal, but it also provided the opportunity to provide a completely new Operations Centre for Waterloo. Office space was consolidated into the new building and drivers' walking time, from accommodation to trains, was reduced. The development enabled a new, unobstructed circulation route above platform and concourse level. All these ends were achieved with the completion of phase one in 1991; phase two will provide a control room, further staff facilities and shops.

The development as a whole will extend the full 175m width of the domestic platforms and is above the line of greatest passenger congestion, at the ticket barriers. The scope for disruption, therefore, was enormous. Other constraints were a tight budget and programme (six months for design, one year for

South facade of the Operations Centre bridging the tracks.

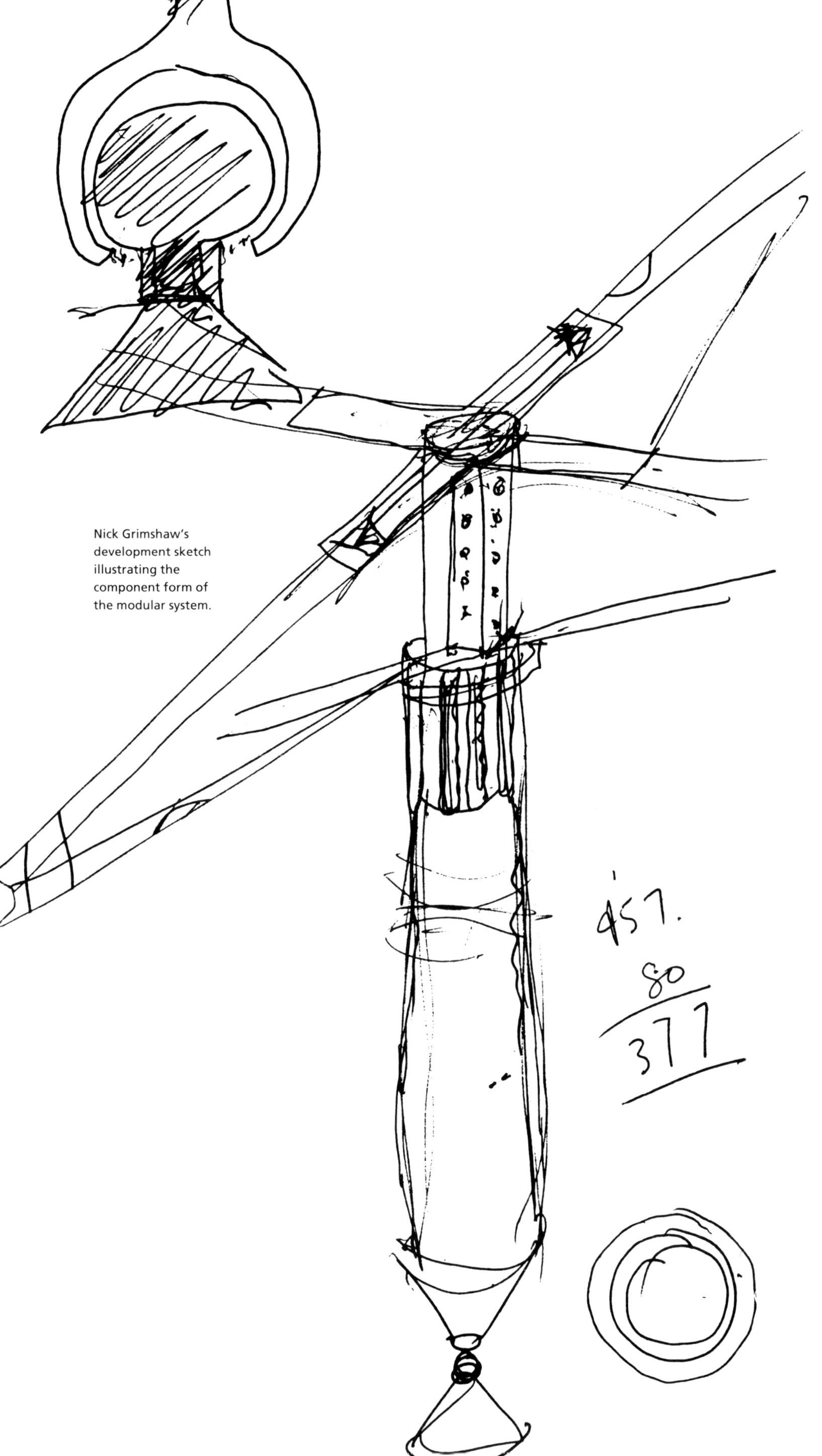

Nick Grimshaw's development sketch illustrating the component form of the modular system.

Construction shot showing the raising of the 'raft' structure. In order to minimise disruption at the station, the structure was raised in three, round-the-clock weekends.

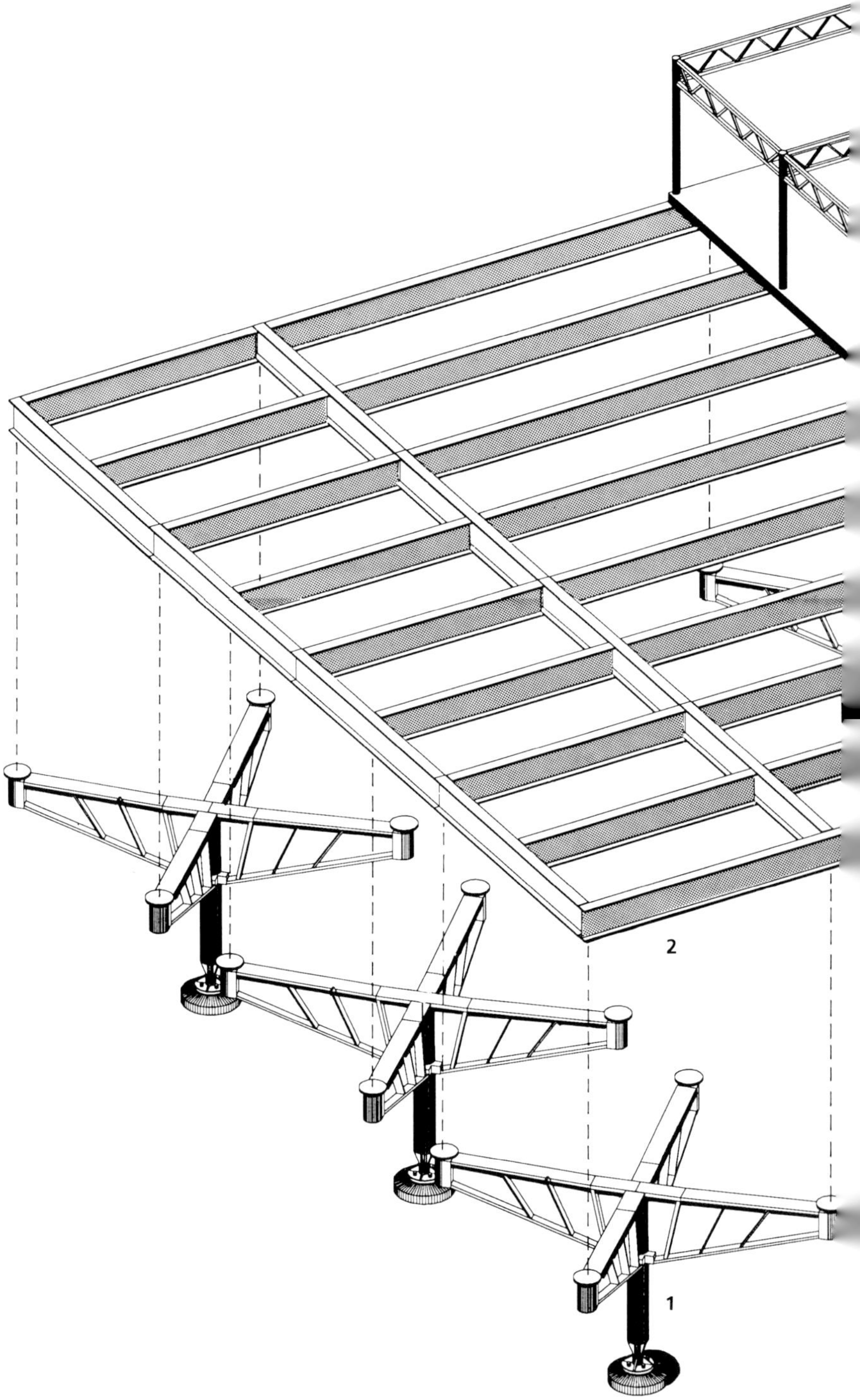

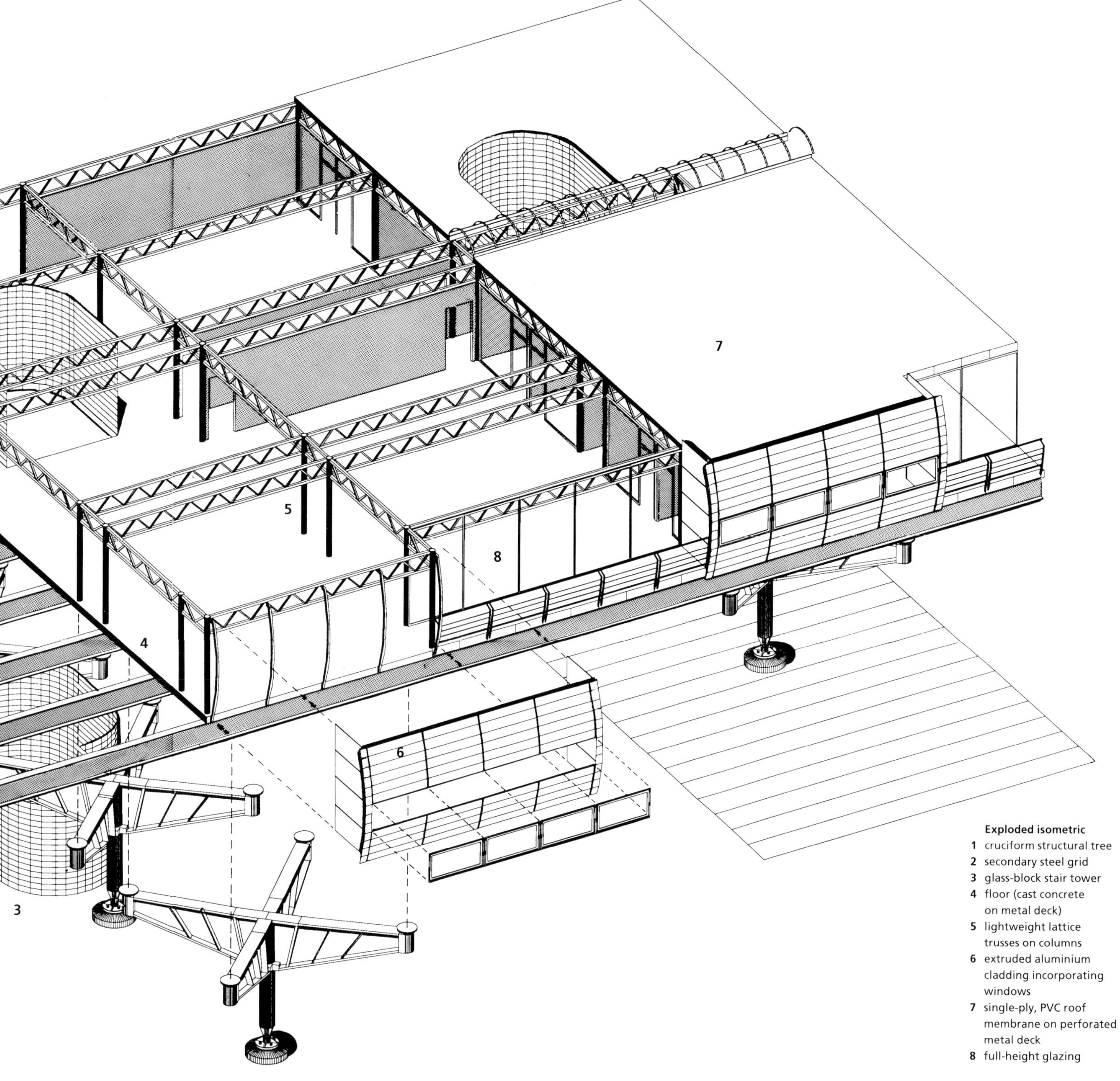

Exploded isometric

1 cruciform structural tree
2 secondary steel grid
3 glass-block stair tower
4 floor (cast concrete on metal deck)
5 lightweight lattice trusses on columns
6 extruded aluminium cladding incorporating windows
7 single-ply, PVC roof membrane on perforated metal deck
8 full-height glazing

Sectional elevation detail of 'tree' structure.

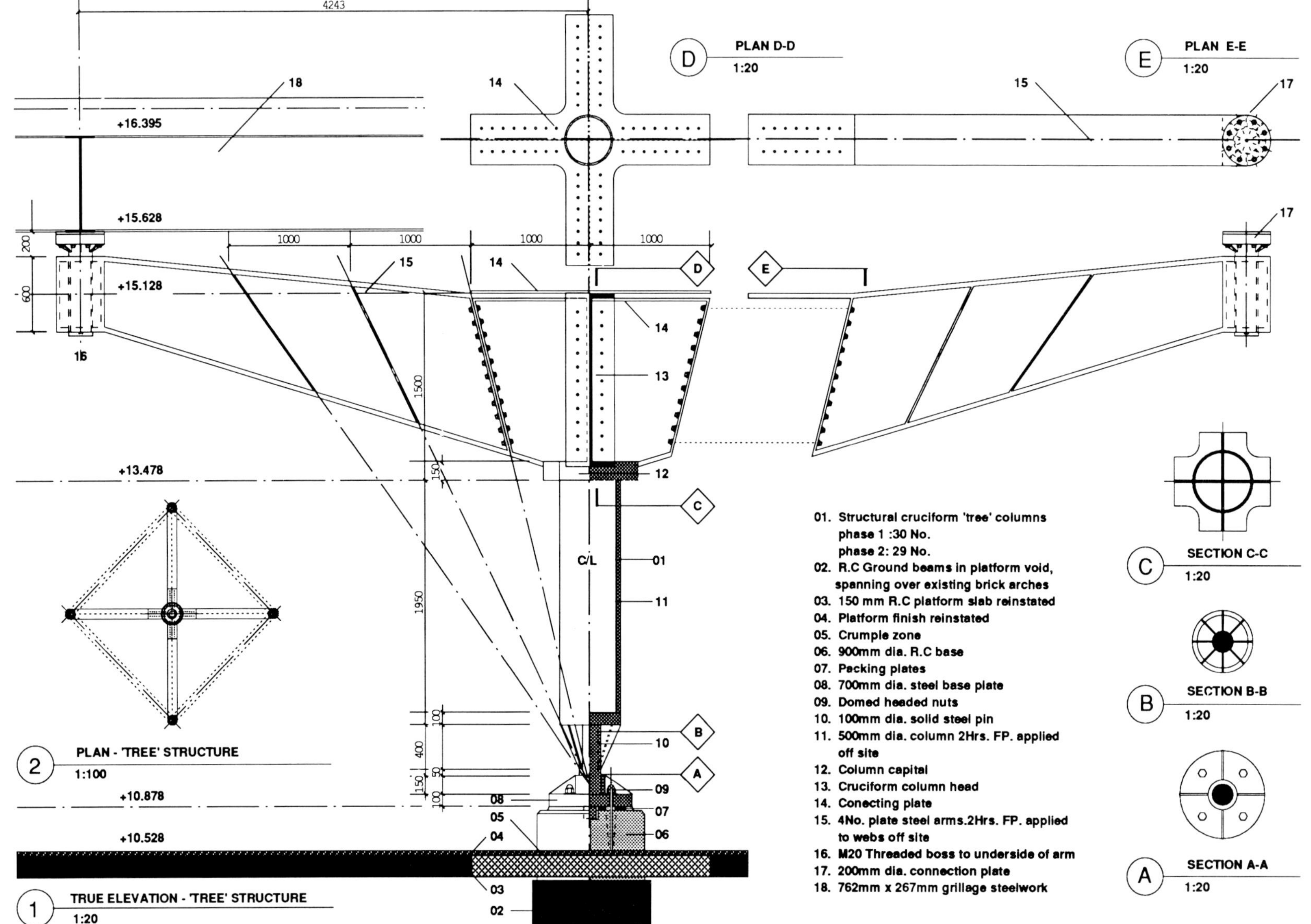

4243
PLAN D-D
1:20
PLAN E-E
1:20
+16.395
+15.628
+15.128
+13.478
+10.878
+10.528
1000
1000
1000
1000
200
600
1500
150
1950
100
400
50
150
100
C/L
SECTION C-C
1:20
SECTION B-B
1:20
SECTION A-A
1:20
2 PLAN - 'TREE' STRUCTURE
1:100
1 TRUE ELEVATION - 'TREE' STRUCTURE
1:20
01. Structural cruciform 'tree' columns phase 1 :30 No. phase 2: 29 No.
02. R.C Ground beams in platform void, spanning over existing brick arches
03. 150 mm R.C platform slab reinstated
04. Platform finish reinstated
05. Crumple zone
06. 900mm dia. R.C base
07. Packing plates
08. 700mm dia. steel base plate
09. Domed headed nuts
10. 100mm dia. solid steel pin
11. 500mm dia. column 2Hrs. FP. applied off site
12. Column capital
13. Cruciform column head
14. Conecting plate
15. 4No. plate steel arms.2Hrs. FP. applied to webs off site
16. M20 Threaded boss to underside of arm
17. 200mm dia. connection plate
18. 762mm x 267mm grillage steelwork

Nicholas Grimshaw & Partners

Computer models used to develop the detailed design of the tree structures.

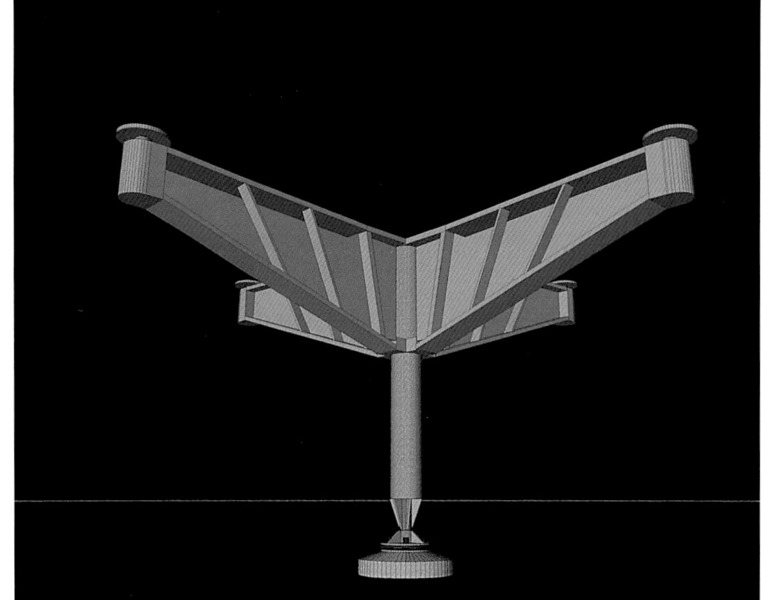

construction) and headroom limitations: the station's existing roof formed an upper limit while the new structure's underside had to be kept well above the tracks to avoid damage in a crash. Although the site conditions encouraged prefabrication, a further difficulty was the irregular spacing of the platforms, which made a simple modular design difficult.

Grimshaw's design concentrates vertical loads in a series of steel columns with cruciform heads fabricated, and part fireproofed off site. The columns, pin-jointed at their bases, are placed along the central axis of each platform to avoid risk to the structure in a crash and minimise obstruction to the passengers. A grid of simple steel beams spans the tracks from column to column, their length adjusted to fit the varying platform widths. With the arms of the columns placed diagonally to the beams, the structure achieves horizontal rigidity.

This arrangement enabled the primary structure to be erected over three weekends, leaving the platforms unobstructed during the working week. Once columns, girders and deck were complete, a clear, flat working area was created at the raised level, where the building could be completed out of the way of passengers and trains. The design also concentrates structural depth over the platforms, in the arms of the columns, leaving the greatest possible headroom over the tracks, where it is required.

The superstructure is an extremely light steel frame, to minimise the bulk of the primary structure. It is enclosed by a series of alternating bays. Above the platforms, walls of standardised width, curved in section, are clad in a development of the extruded

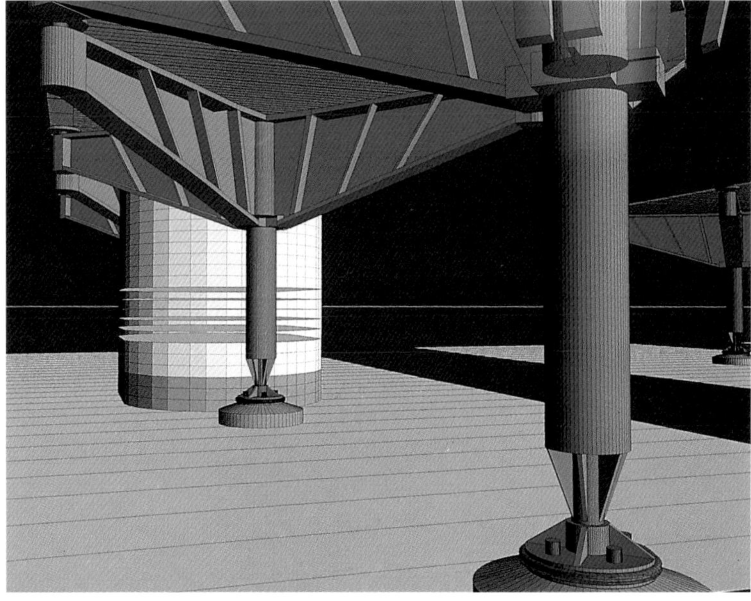

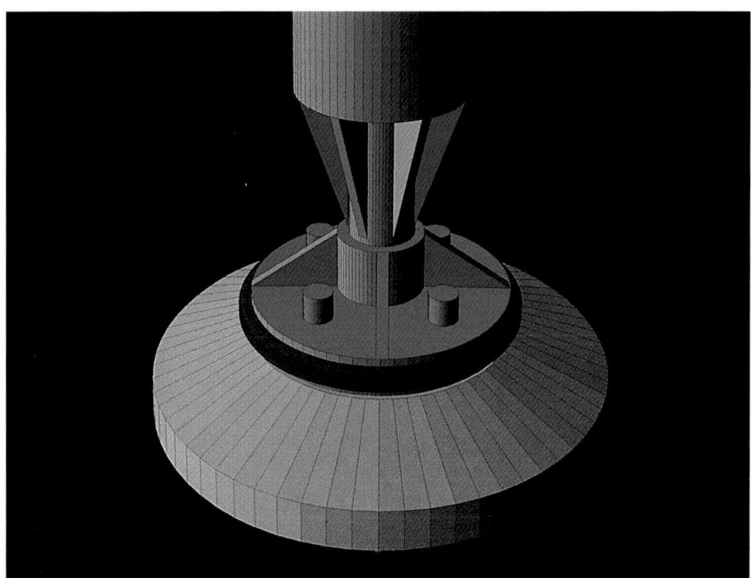

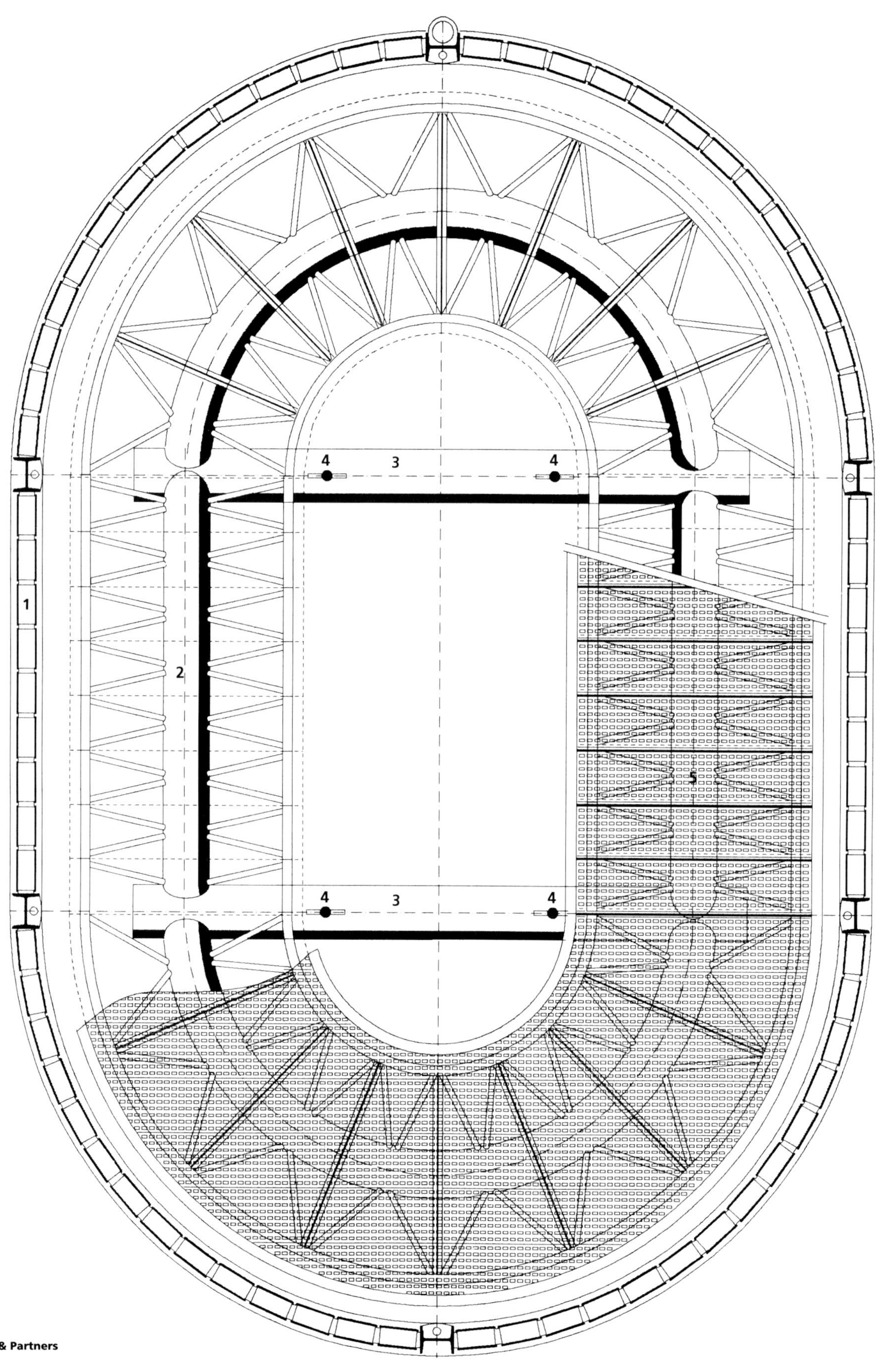

Glazed staircase plan
1 glass-block wall
2 circular, hollow-section support for stairs
3 suspended circular hollow section
4 steel suspension rods
5 aluminium, extruded decking

Interior view of the suspended access stair within a glass-block tower.

aluminium plank system used at Sainsbury's in Camden Town, north London. These correspond with cellular offices behind while, above the tracks, recessed glass walls of varying widths adjust to the irregular platform spacing. These bays simultaneously bring light into the open plan offices behind, create balconies with imposing views over the station, and conform to the fire officer's requirement that glazing should be 1.5m away from the edge of the structure.

If the design averted the organisational chaos associated with building work at railway stations, it also sought to improve the interior environment in which railway employees have to work. The site dictated that the plan should be deep, and with only one aspect, but borrowed light from the glazed open-plan offices filters into the centre of the plan. Lightwells, lined with glass block, penetrate the structure on the centre line of each platform to bring light to the driver's accommodation to the rear of the plan. They create an alternating pattern of light and dark in the central corridor. Alternate lightwells contain lightweight steel stairs suspended from the structure, with perforated aluminium treads of the type used in Grimshaw's own office. These bring down drivers at points near their trains. Additional stairs can be inserted, if required, in the remaining lightwells.

At the eastern end the Operations Centre aligns with the station's existing windows, to give light and views out of the station. By exposing services and dispensing with suspended ceilings, the office interiors achieve a generosity of height, which the site's constraints would otherwise have denied.

Along with the Satellite and Pier at Heathrow

Interior view showing suspended stair. A single continuous circular hollow section supports both the cantilevered treads and the radial landings.

Exploded sketch by Stefan Camenzind illustrating stair components.

Airport, and the neighbouring Channel Tunnel Railway Terminal, the Operations Centre embodies a developing Grimshaw theme. All three are transport buildings with fearsome constraints of programme, budget and, most of all, of site, in which the architecture derives from considered responses to the conditions. All three, however, seek to be elegant as well as practical, and to be civilising influences in abrasive environments.

External view of glass-block stair tower from within the train drivers' accommodation.

View of completed tree and stair tower from the station platform.

Far left: supporting trees hanging from the raised, raft structure prior to being lowered and fixed at platform level.

Left: erection completed before the morning rush hour.

Network

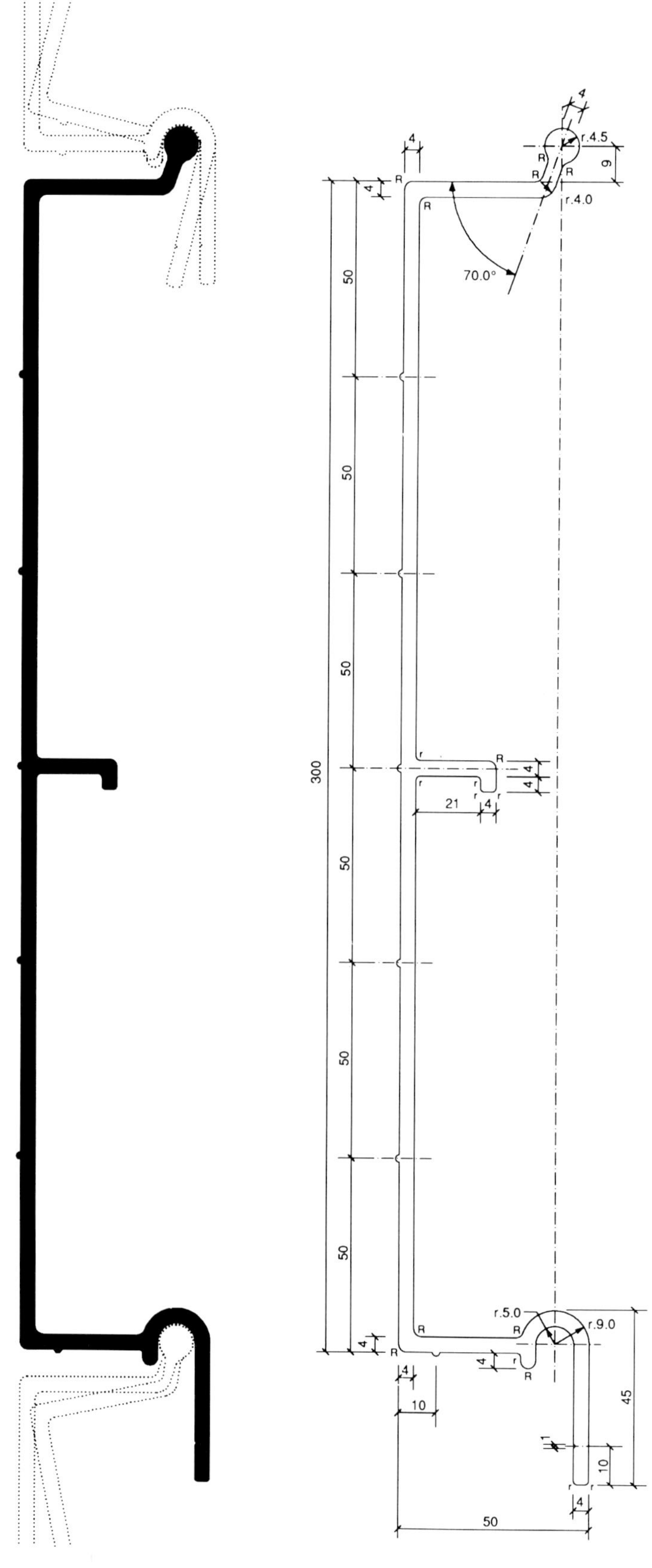

98 Section through a single extruded plank of the cladding to the office development. The aluminium extrusion was specifically designed to cope with both curved and flat walls.

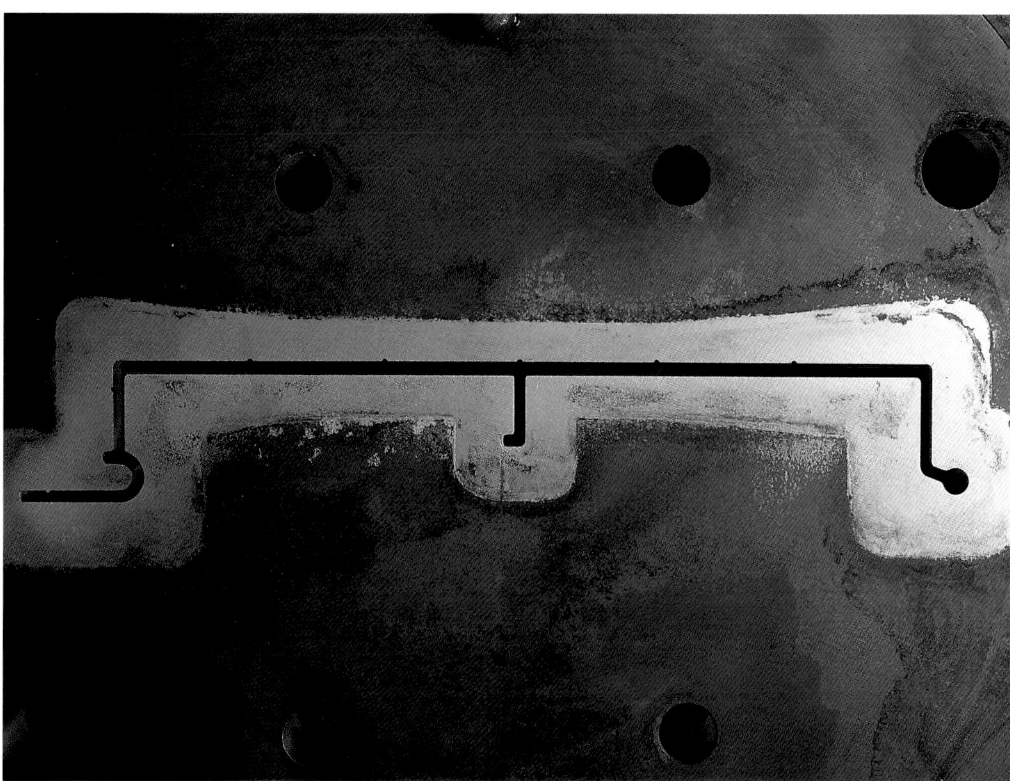

The stainless-steel dyes, used to extrude the aluminium plank sections.

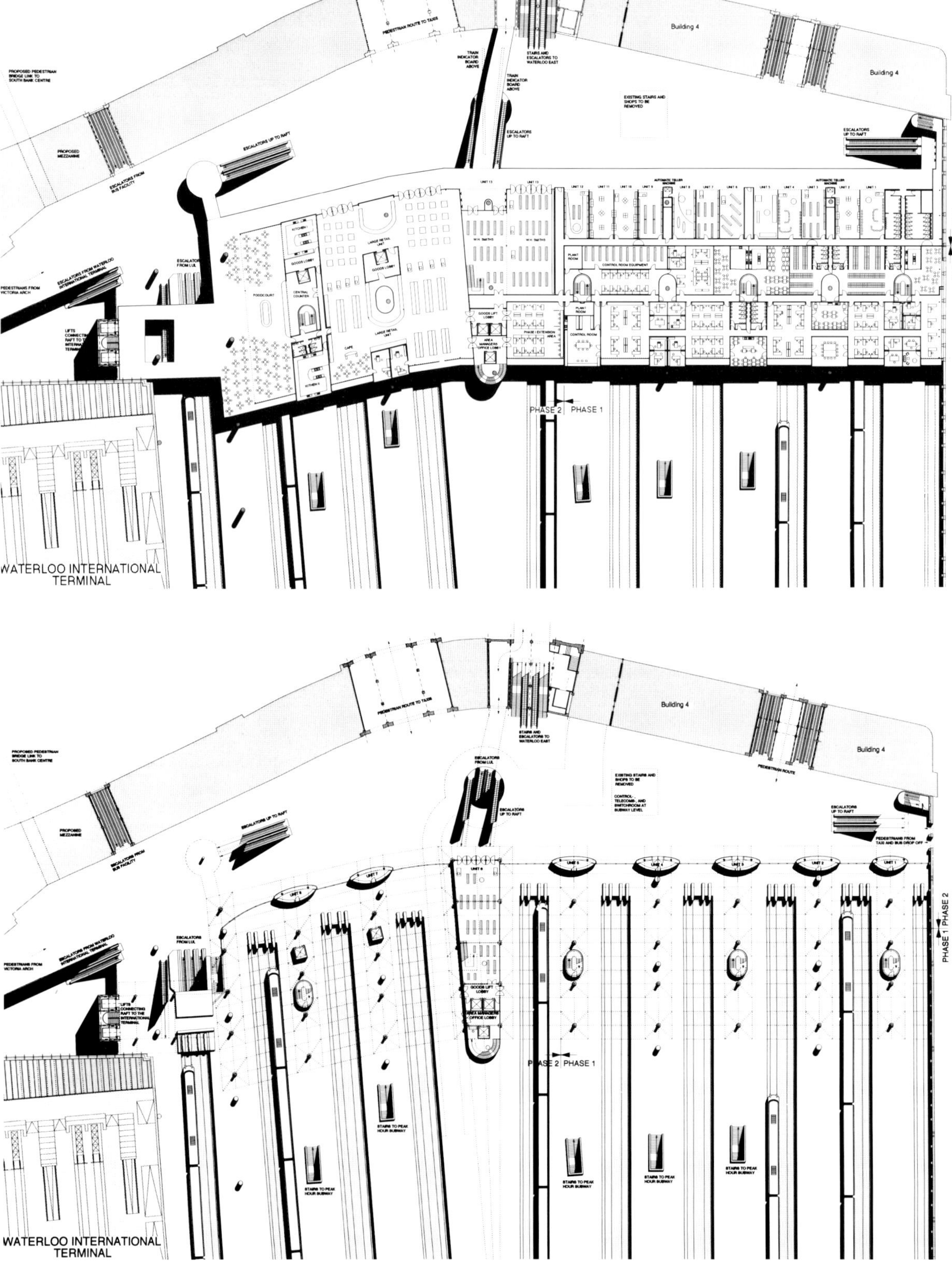

Overall development (phase one and proposed phase two) at Operations Centre-level, in relation to the Channel Tunnel Railway Terminal.

Platform-level plan showing structural grid, stair towers and retail units.

Computer model showing raised retail units, which will be accessible from the existing concourse. They will be constructed in phase two of the development.

Long elevation of the complete 175m-long raft spanning the width of 18 tracks to connect with the Channel Tunnel Railway Terminal.

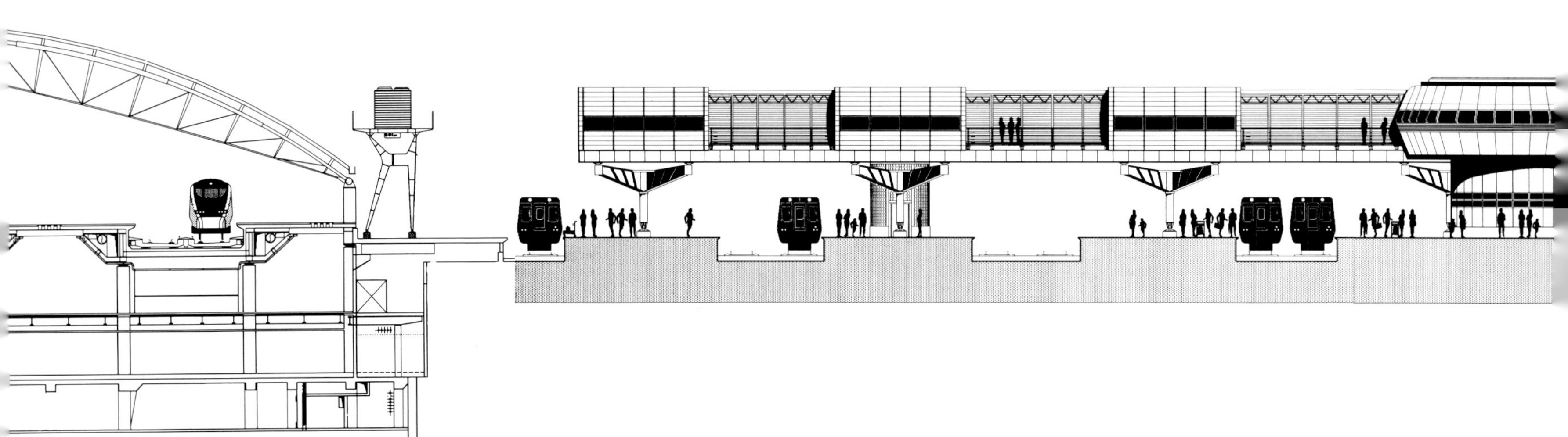

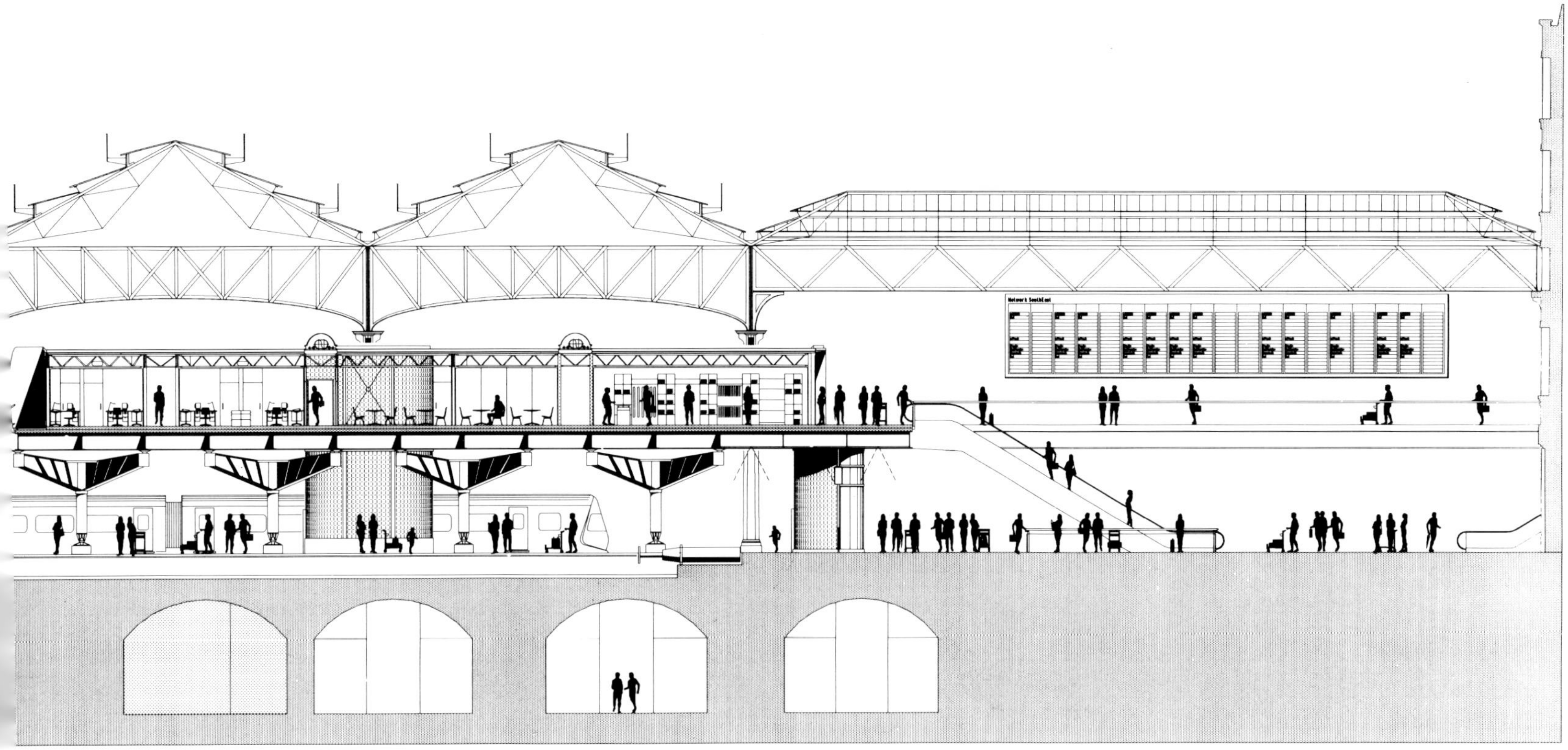

Cross section through the Operations Centre showing its relationship with the existing station structure.

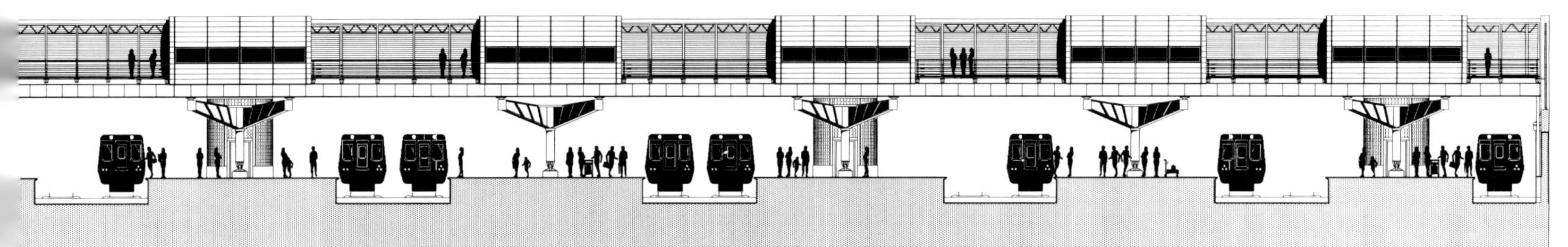

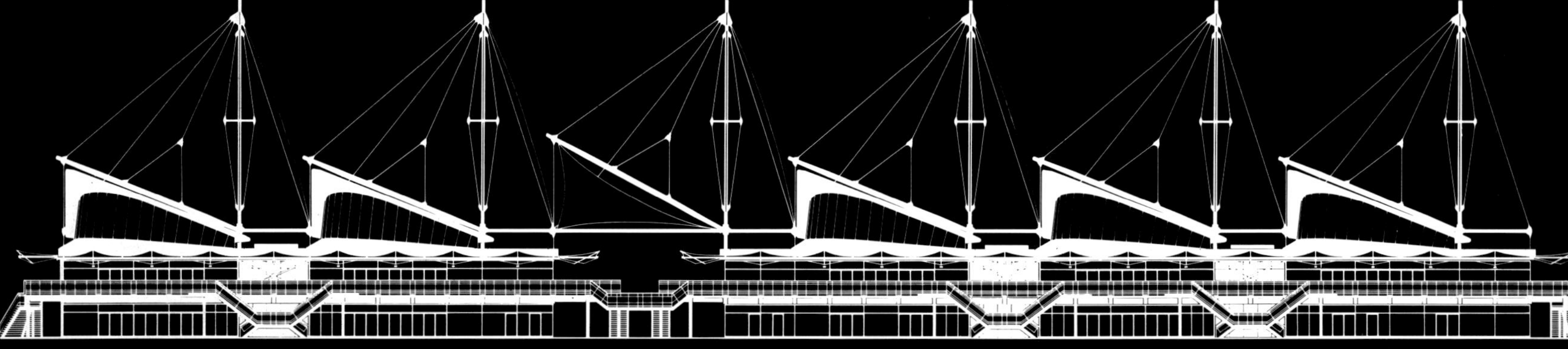

Shopping and Leisure Project,
Port East, London Docklands, 1989

'The brick warehouses behind our site were some of the best buildings in London Docklands; they really evoked the bustle of the dockside activity of the past. One could imagine the great sailing ships unloading there with ropes and spars creaking in the vicious easterly winds. We wanted our building to have a quality of lightness so that it literally seemed to perch on the edge of the dock in complete contrast to the heavy brick warehouses behind. The masted structure greatly helped to break down the bulk of the scheme and gave a strong structural discipline. The requirement for decks and walkways of course implied ship-like qualities. But why not? The activities of leaning on the rail, looking at the water and promenading on the deck were exactly the same as those on board a ship.' **NG**

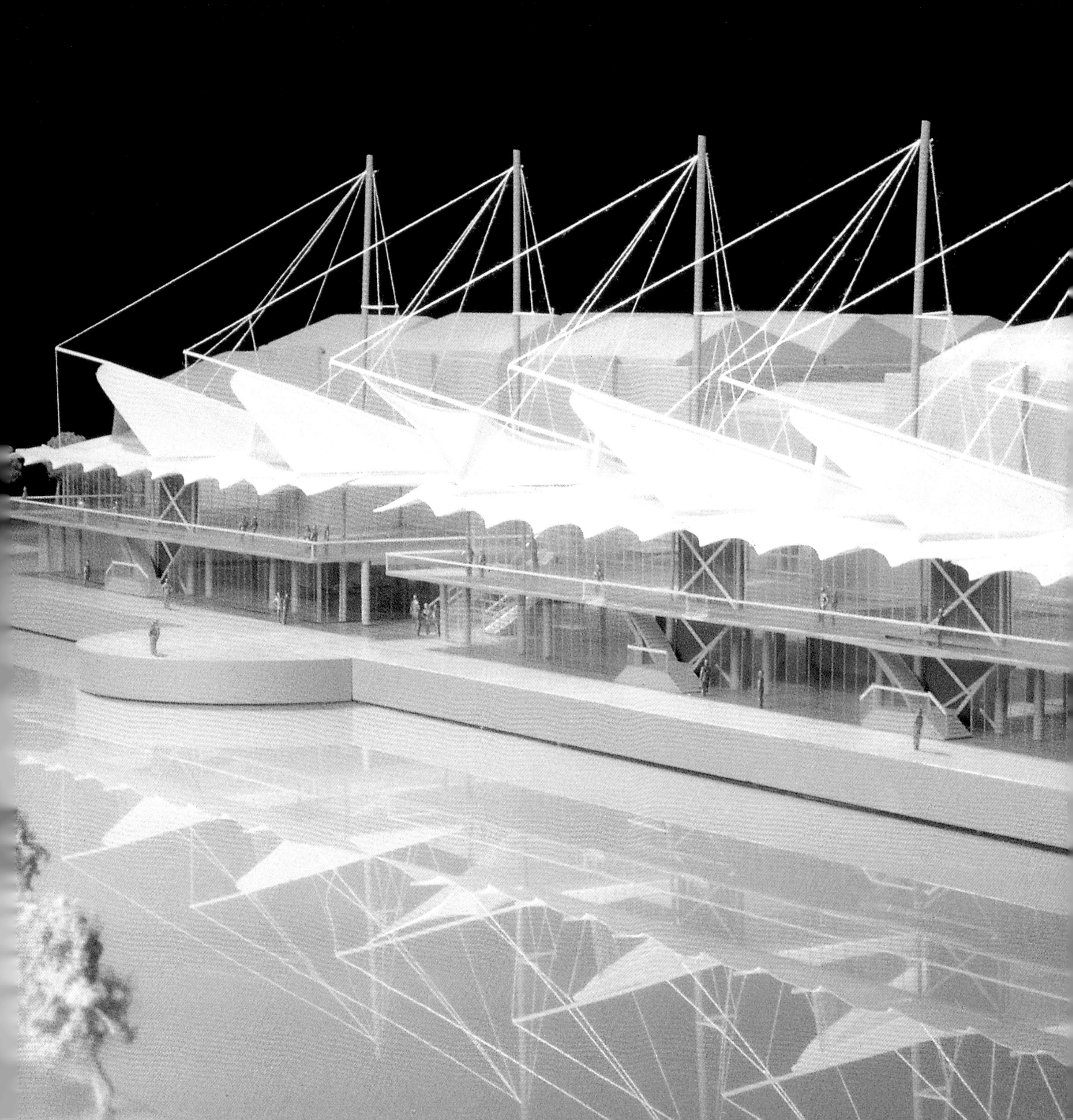

Previous page
Model of the waterside building, seen from the south-east corner, revealing a series of masts and sail-like roofs in front of the grade one-listed brick warehouses.

A 19th-century print of the site illustrating the warehouses and sailing ships. The picture was found by the client after the scheme had been designed, and has an uncanny similarity to Grimshaw's concept.

Nick Grimshaw's original sketch showing an early concept for the opening roof. The roof is based on the mechanism of Thames Barge hatches that hinge upwards from the centre. This sketch also shows the existing grade one-listed brick Banana Dock wall and the later false-quay structure, which was necessitated by the squarer-hulled ships of the early part of this century.

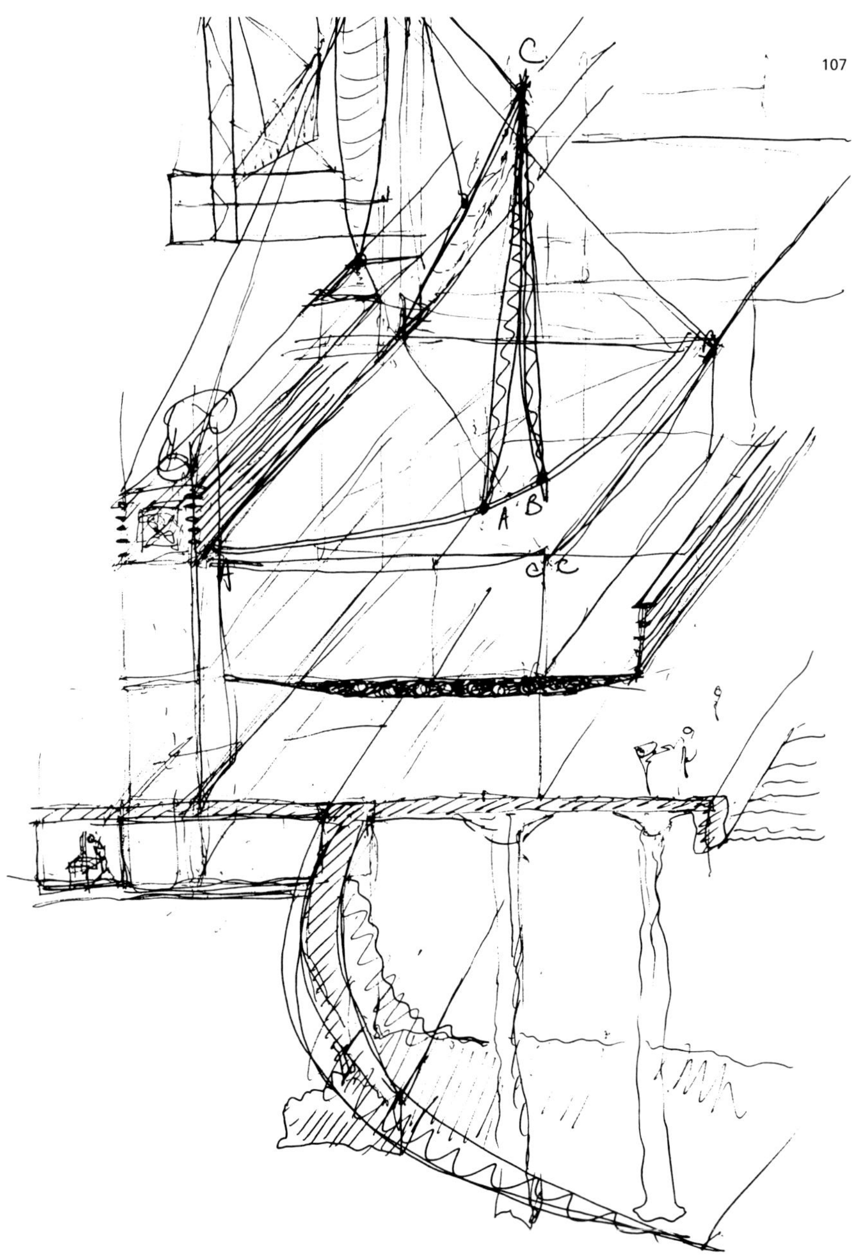

Grimshaw's building for Port East Developments in London Docklands is part of a larger project, which was designed to provide the Isle of Dogs with the variety of uses it notoriously lacks. Facing the office blocks of Canary Wharf across the northernmost part of the old West India Docks, the development as a whole was to house shops, restaurants, cinemas, a hotel and offices in four new buildings and in a linked pair of listed warehouses built by Napoleonic prisoners of war. Grimshaw's quayside building was to run parallel with the warehouses and contain shops and restaurants.

The design responds to, and reacts against, its setting. The dignified solidity of the brick warehouses is visible through, and complemented by, a comparatively delicate two-storey structure that echoes the rhythm of their facades. It is a striking shape, designed to be seen from the upper floors of office blocks as much as at ground level. At the same time Grimshaw's building – light, open, accessible, lively at street level – is everything that the impermeable blocks of Canary Wharf are not.

The form that grew from these concerns is unashamedly boat-like. A row of six masts, anchored by steel rods, support sail-like, hyperbolic paraboloid roofs which, before the client opted for a construction of more proven durability, were to have been of PVC-coated polyester. The boat theme is reinforced by the nautical detailing of the handrails and the light fittings, and the repetition of the roofs. Each of these is oriented south-west recalling, to use the architect's image, the way that moored boats collectively align themselves with winds and currents. The discovery,

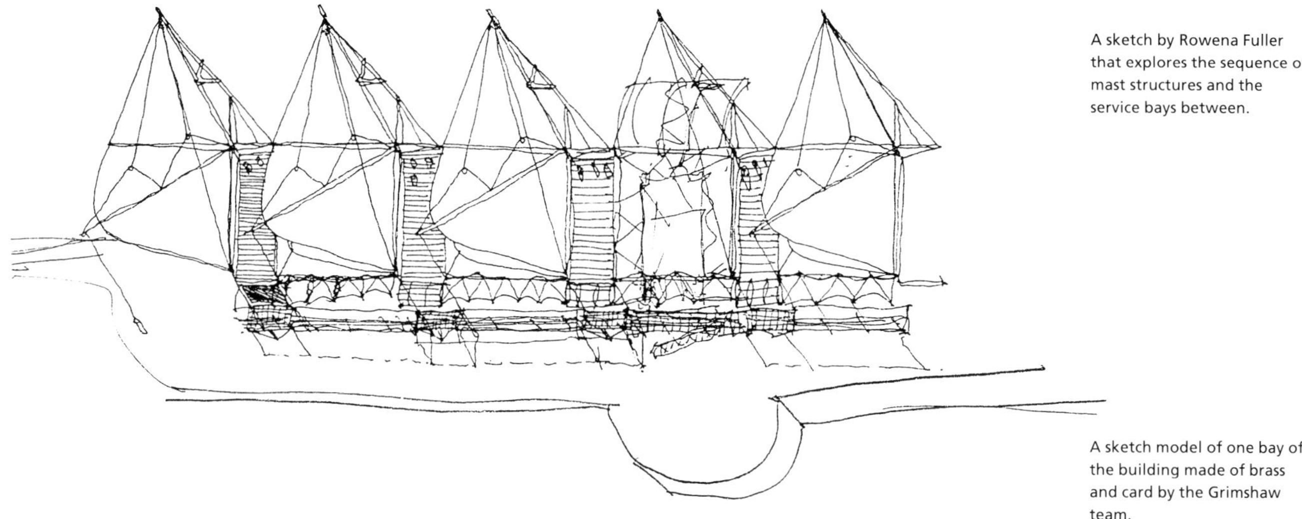

A sketch by Rowena Fuller that explores the sequence of mast structures and the service bays between.

A sketch model of one bay of the building made of brass and card by the Grimshaw team.

after the design was complete, of a 19th-century view of masted ships moored outside the warehouses gave it retrospective authority.

In addition to the pursuit of elegance, the masts serve a practical purpose. The building straddles the original quay, which was designed for smaller, round-hulled boats, and a pier added later for larger, square hulls. Between the two, and running down the long axis of Grimshaw's building is the 'banana wall', a curved retaining wall which is listed grade one and – although concealed – is, therefore, untouchable. By concentrating much of the load in the masts, the design transfers it to the more solid ground of the original pier and keeps major piling away from the banana wall. By introducing wide spans, the mast structure allows the number of columns, and hence of piles, to be kept to a minimum.

At first-floor level, five of the masts and roofs create airy, well-lit spaces, completely unobstructed by columns. In a variation of a favourite Grimshaw theme, a tent-like outer structure provides shelter for a more

Sketch model of the scheme at a stage when the roofs were of rigid construction. The roofs tilt up towards the south-west above the inclined glazing, which is supported above the prow structure. The glazing continues under the two low sides of the roof so that, particularly when lit at night, the roofs appear to float above the building. Small canopies provide shelter for the first-floor walkway.

solid fireproof concrete table which, using where possible the existing piles of the false quay, bears the first floor. Conceptually, each structure is separate, but they interact to give mutual support. The sixth mast supports the only fabric roof to survive the client's caution, and shelters a semi-external space. This space opens up a route from the warehouse to the water's edge, houses a formal staircase connecting the two levels and acts as an *ad hoc* auditorium for a semicircular performance space that projects into the dock.

Port East was an opportunity for Canary Wharf to mature after its first, embattled phase, to connect with its surroundings, and to be more readily and pleasantly inhabited. In the event, the planning authority for the area, the London Docklands Development Corporation, would not accept the density proposed for the Port East development as a whole, and the project was abandoned after piling had been completed, in 1990.

A model commissioned by the client to market the scheme. It shows the hyperbolic paraboloid roofs, a development of the rigid roofs in the earlier sketch model. The fabric roof over the open, event area has also been simplified.

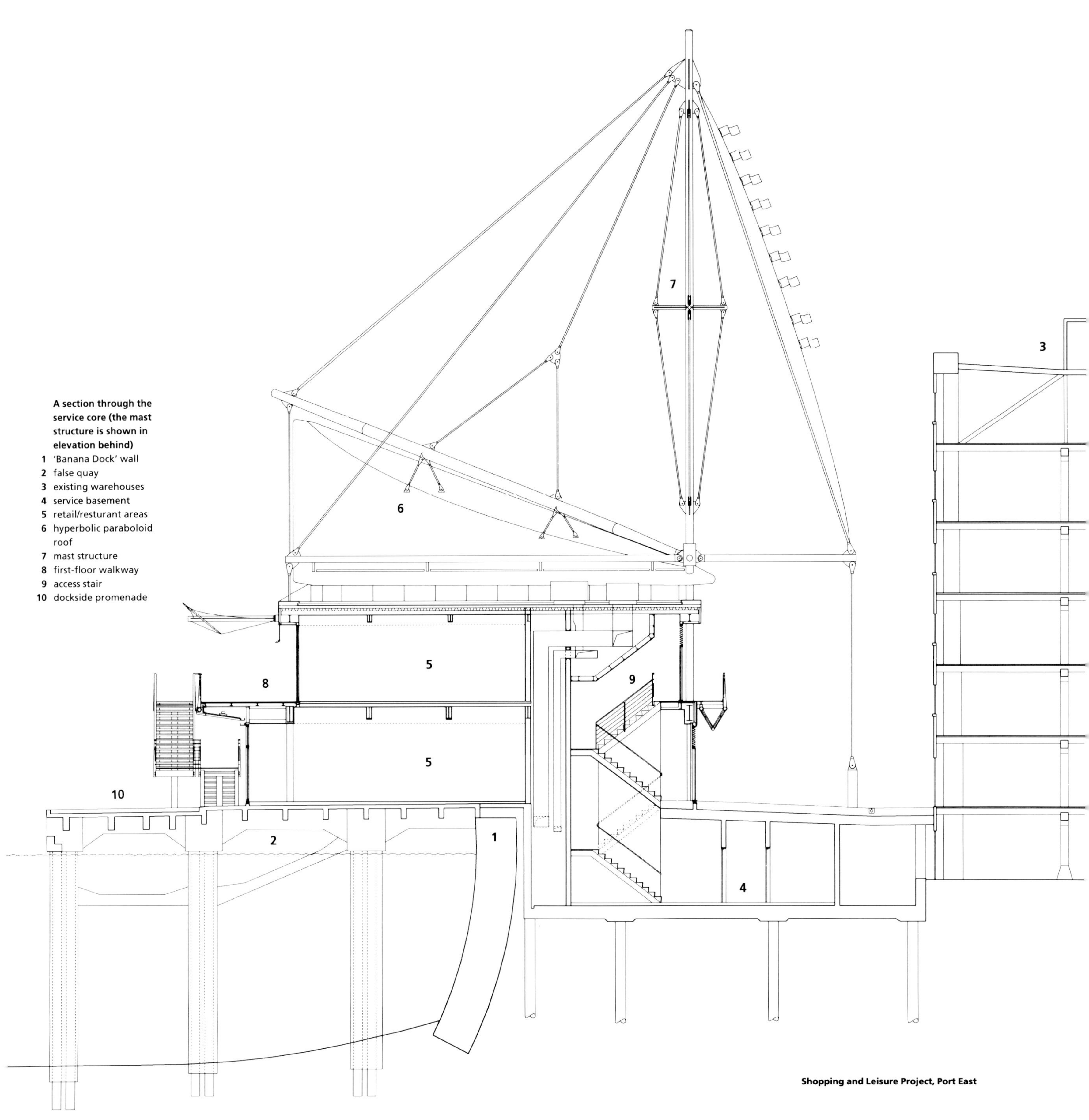

A section through the service core (the mast structure is shown in elevation behind)

1 'Banana Dock' wall
2 false quay
3 existing warehouses
4 service basement
5 retail/resturant areas
6 hyperbolic paraboloid roof
7 mast structure
8 first-floor walkway
9 access stair
10 dockside promenade

Shopping and Leisure Project, Port East

View of the south elevation
rendered by Chloë Grimshaw.

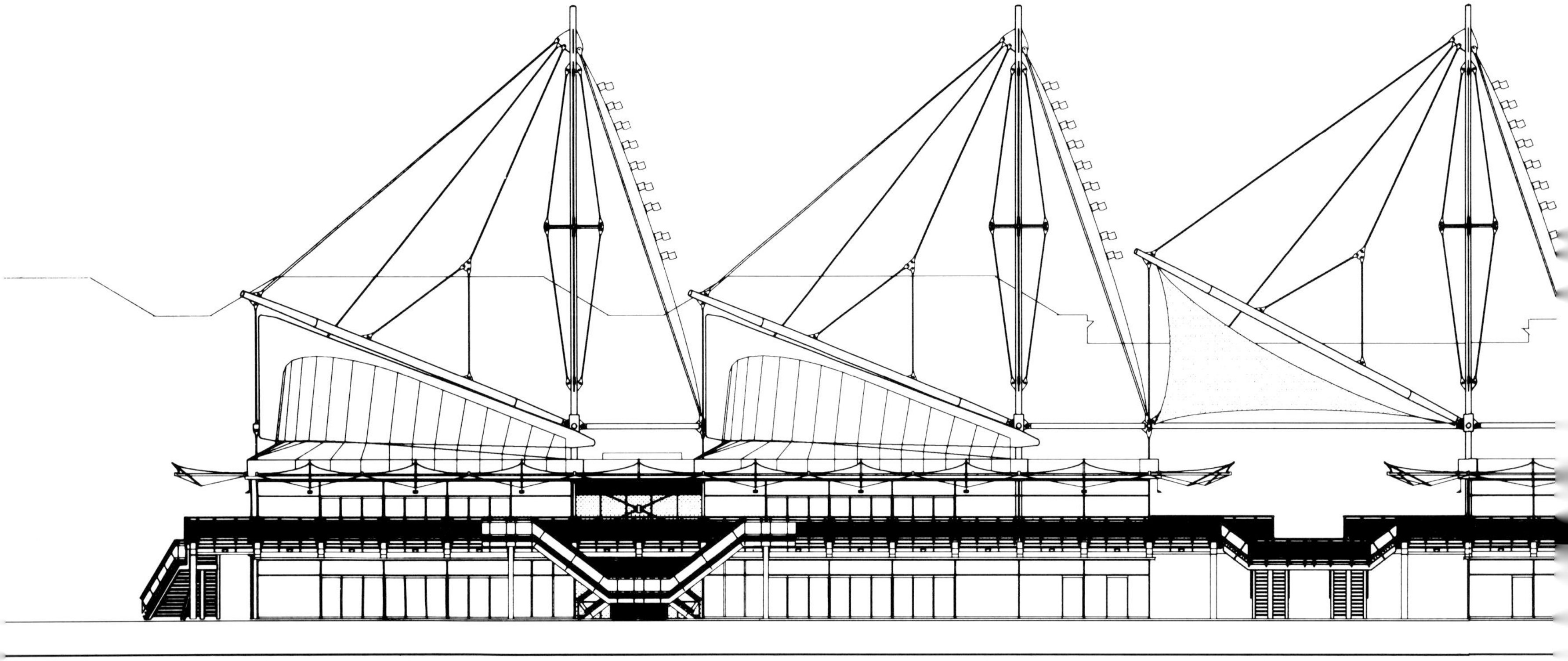

South elevation as viewed from the Canary Wharf development across West India Dock.

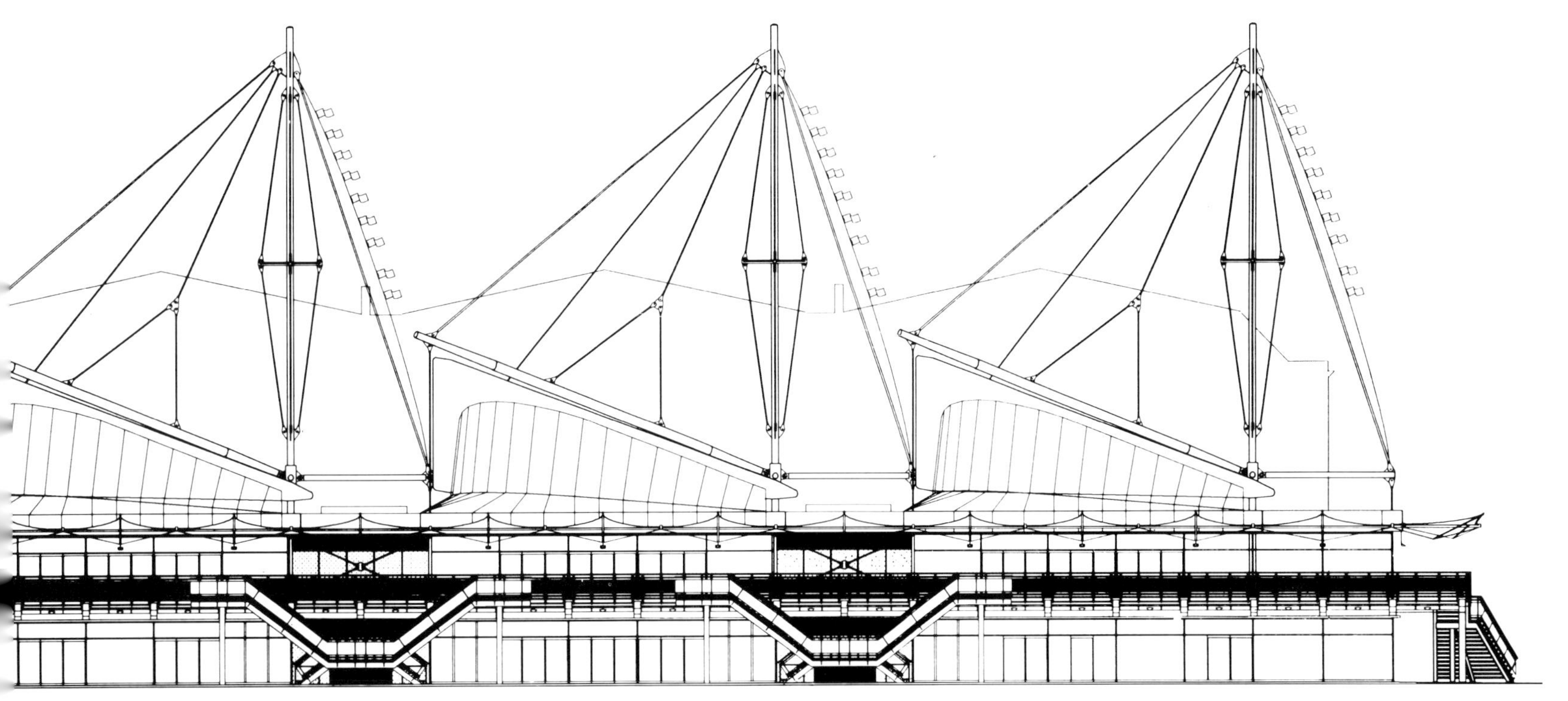

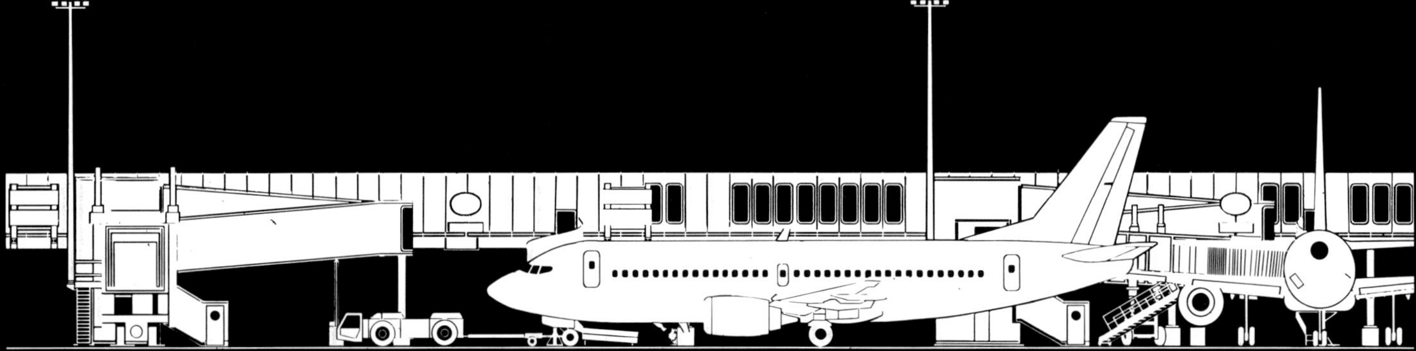

Satellite and Piers, Heathrow Airport, London, 1993

'The challenge here was to create a new "environment for movement"; to lift the spirit when moving along those endless corridors that dominate life at any airport anywhere in the world. We tried to strip the spaces of visual clutter – no structure, no rubber plants, no freestanding ash trays, no signs on posts. We were looking for a sleek, streamlined tube, with up-lighting that was subtle and that emphasised the sculptural shape of the elliptical walkways. I think we achieved our aim. It is not possible to cut down the distance the passengers had to walk but we did achieve a considerable improvement in the environment.' **NG**

Previous page
Suspended lighting unit containing uplighting, public address system, emergency lighting, feature lights, wireways and downlighting.

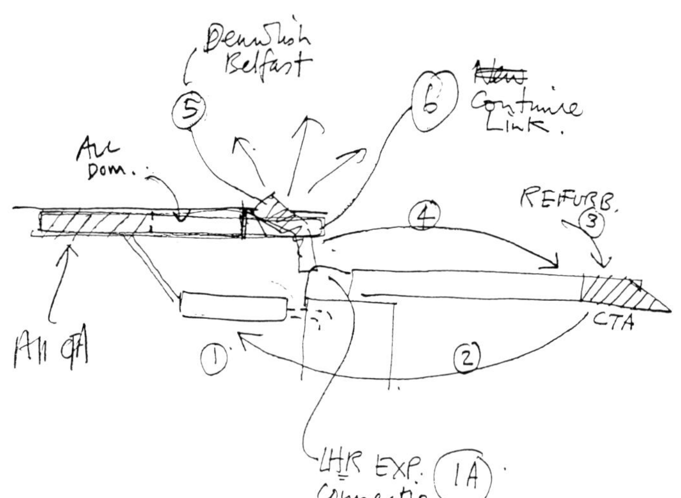

Development sketch by Hin Tan showing the elements of the project and the phased construction sequence.

The demand for a new satellite and piers for domestic passengers at London's Heathrow Airport presented gruelling demands of site and brief. Meeting these was in itself a complex task, but Grimshaw had a further ambition, to demonstrate that airport corridors need not be characterless and cluttered, and to show that the quality of the architecture need not decline on the journey from terminal to aeroplane.

The new piers are attached to Terminal One and serve domestic flights, flights to Belfast, and flights within the Common Travel Area (CTA), which includes the Republic of Ireland and the Channel Islands. Before they were built, inadequate facilities meant that many passengers on these flights had to travel by coach to or from their aeroplanes. Belfast passengers had to walk to the aircraft, in all weathers. The purpose of the project was to raise present standards and anticipate future demand.

Passengers to each of the three types of destination have different security and customs arrangements. Belfast flights have exceptionally thorough security checks and CTA passengers are subject to customs' controls; this means that, although they share the piers, their circulation has to be rigorously segregated.

The site is used intensively, like most of Heathrow: some of the piers are built over a service road, which means their supports could only occupy narrow strips on either side of the road, and their underside has to be sufficiently high to provide headroom underneath. At the same time an upper limit was imposed on the height of the structure to maintain sightlines and radar visibility from the control tower, leaving a narrow zone between these lower and upper limits in which the

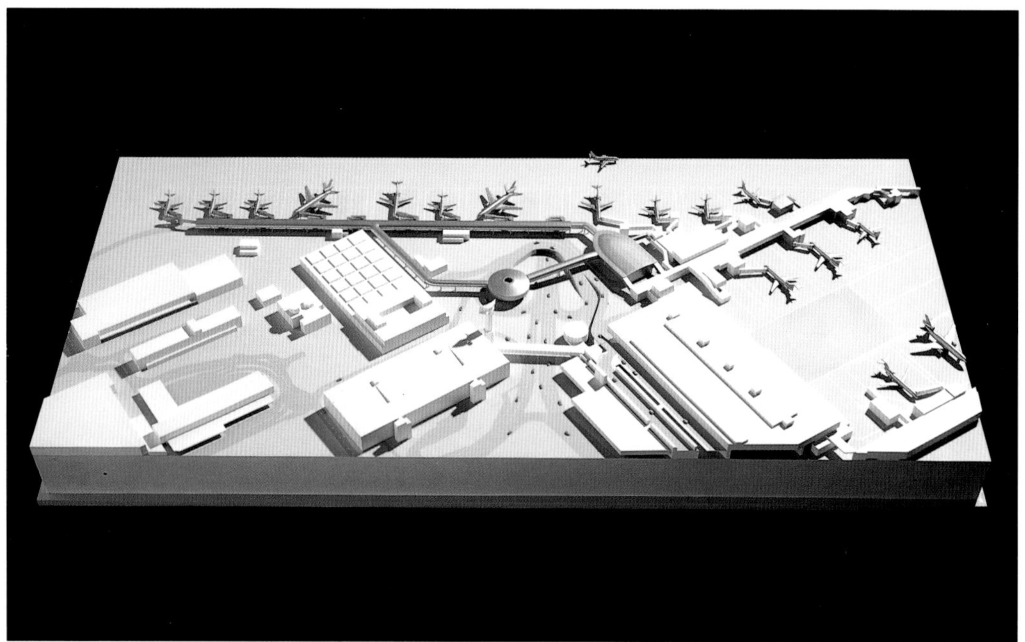

Site model showing the relationship of the new piers with Terminal One, the aircraft stands and taxiway.

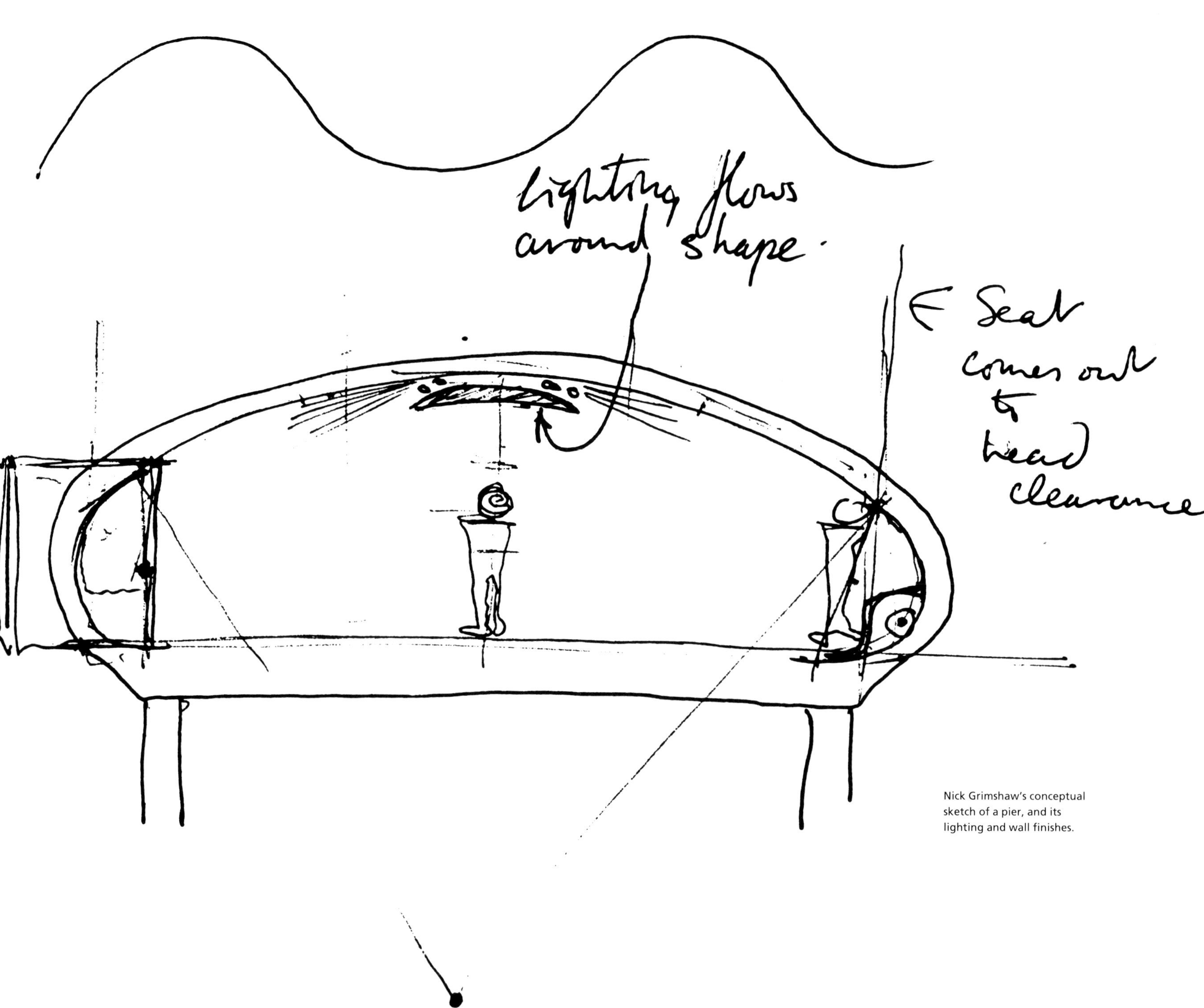

Nick Grimshaw's conceptual sketch of a pier, and its lighting and wall finishes.

piers could be built. The airside/landside boundary, the secure line that defines the controlled territory of the airport, had also to be respected.

Further complications arose from the demands of a tight programme and of an intricate structure of client bodies, airlines and other interested parties, such as the customs and security services. Most significantly, the airport's capacity had to be maintained during construction: only three aircraft stands could be closed at any one time.

Grimshaw's first contribution was to question the sketch layout that accompanied the brief, which the clients thought the only one possible. It involved separating the different passenger groups by subdividing the piers into parallel and, inevitably, narrow strips. Grimshaw pointed out that land and airspace outside the designated boundaries of the site

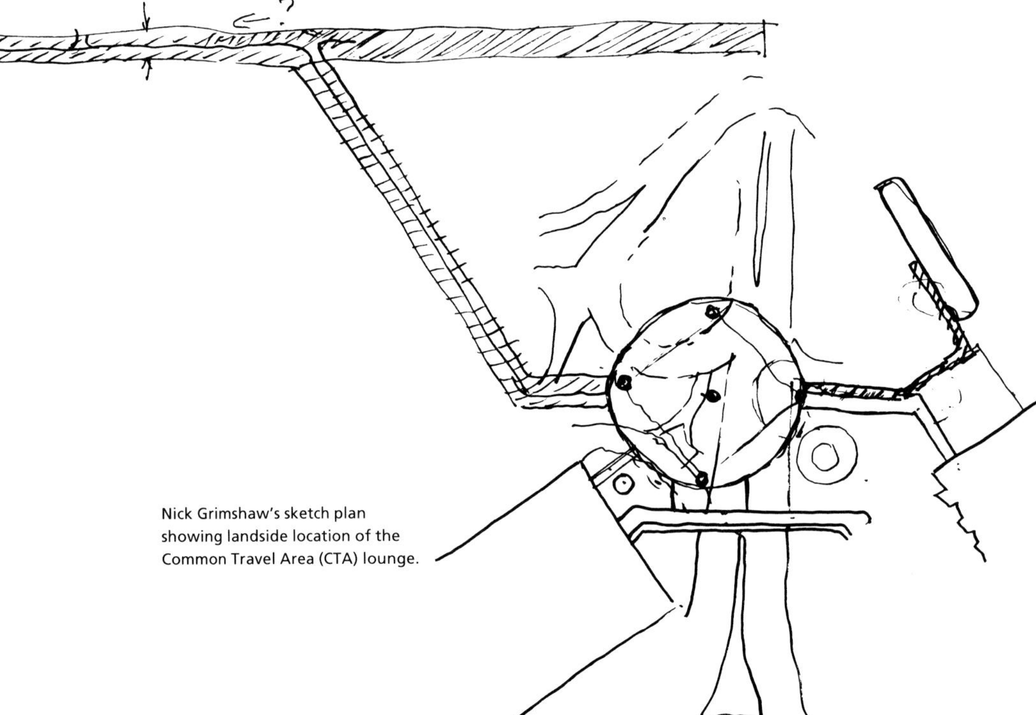

Nick Grimshaw's sketch plan showing landside location of the Common Travel Area (CTA) lounge.

External view of CTA lounge and link showing the two principal cladding elements: sinusoidal-aluminium, pre-curved sheet (internal and external); extruded aluminium mullions, which are elliptical in section towards the interior and which are expressed as perforated fins externally. The glazing is held in place by a structural gasket.

View of the CTA lounge during construction, showing the steelwork that surrounds the central rooflight.

Construction shot showing the erection of the structural steel hoops, which form this pier's envelope, at 2.4m centres spanning 9m.

View of the cantilevered supports to one of the links.

could be enlisted to construct a second route from the baggage area to the piers. With this, the main pier building can be split across its short dimension into two sections, with five of the nine gates dedicated to CTA passengers and four to domestic flights. Each section can be reached without passing through the other. The lounge for Belfast passengers was relocated at the end of the existing pier and exposure to the weather was eliminated.

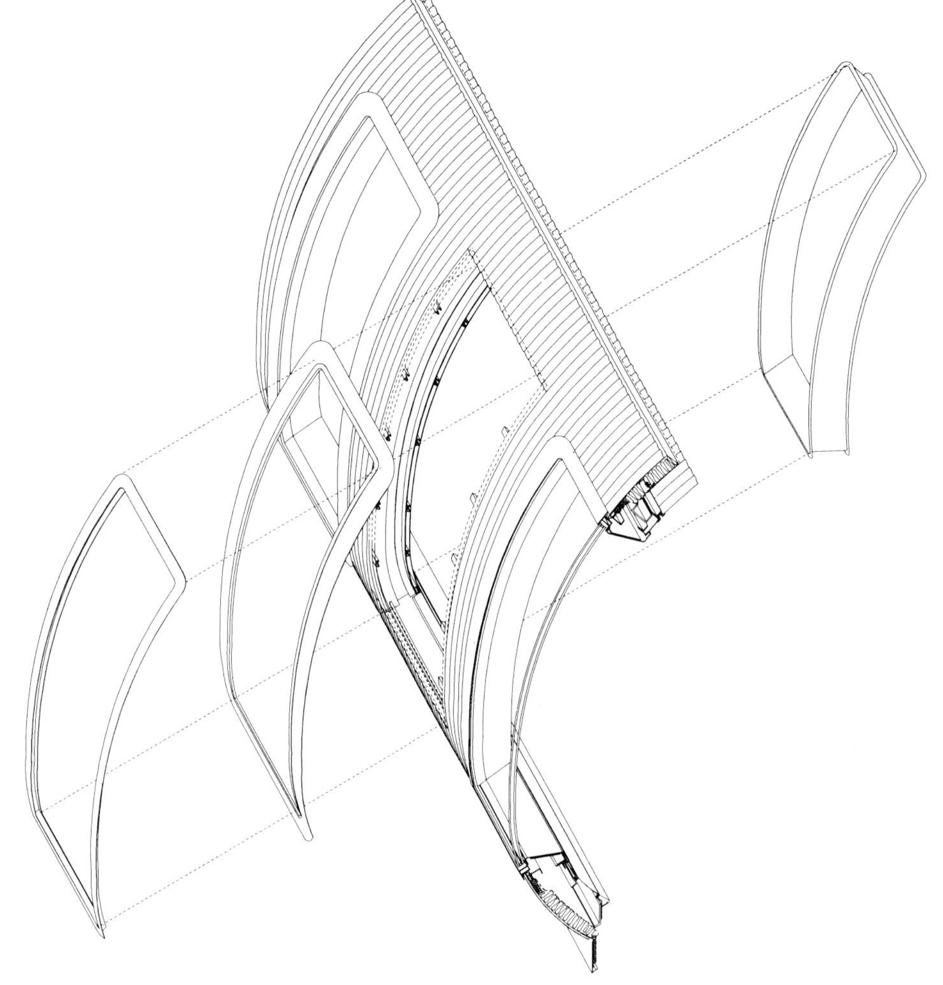

Exploded isometric showing the assembly of the curved window and inner linings of one of the piers.

View of aircraft stand and runway from within a pier.

The route for CTA passengers passes through two elevated corridors linked by a circular duty-free and waiting area, which is built on the previously unused centre of a traffic roundabout. This arrangement breaches the airside/landside boundary, but security is maintained by keeping the corridors at a raised level and by making the roundabout secure. As well as segregating passengers more gracefully, this layout simplified the phased construction, so that the CTA pier opened while other phases were still being constructed.

Both CTA and domestic flights are connected to a building which, shaped like an aeroplane nose, houses the baggage reclaim and customs for CTA passengers, and leads domestic passengers to and from the main Terminal One building. The shape of the 'nose building' derives from the need for efficient separation of the

View of Link 3 from within the CTA arrivals' corridor.

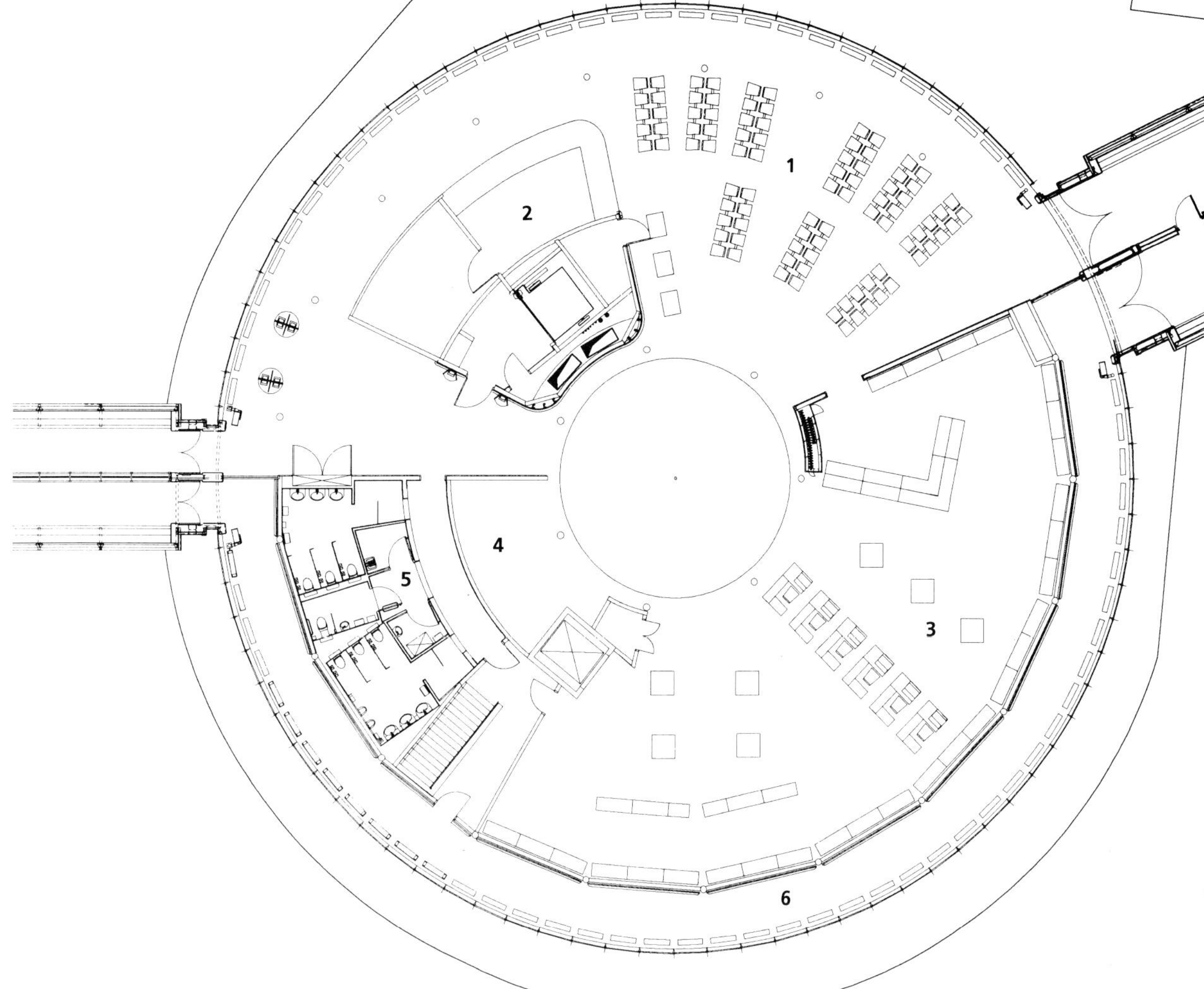

CTA lounge plan

1 departures' lounge
2 cafeteria
3 duty-free shop
4 retail unit
5 passenger toilets
6 CTA arrivals' corridor

two passenger flows, while exploiting views of the runway through an arc of 180 degrees. The wall that segregates the baggage area is of glass, like the external wall, so that, in contrast with the cavernous interiors of most airports, passengers can see out from the heart of the space.

The main pier's structure is a creative response to its constraints. Given that it is confined by minimum and maximum height restrictions, and by a fixed width, a structure that used depth effectively was essential. The solution was to employ steel portal frames spanning the road beneath the pier, with steel beams running between the frames supporting a concrete floor. This creates a platform which in turn carries a very light steel frame, its lightness achieved by the structural efficiency of its elliptical cross section. Close spacing of the frame

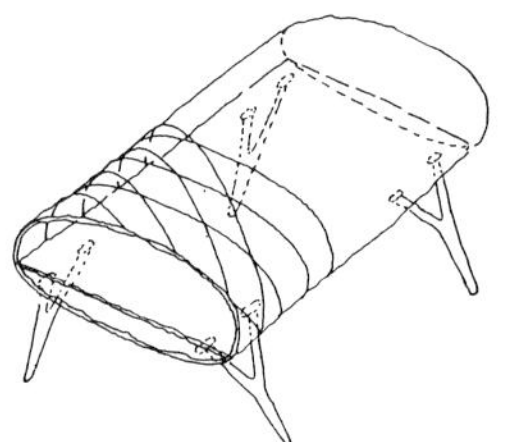
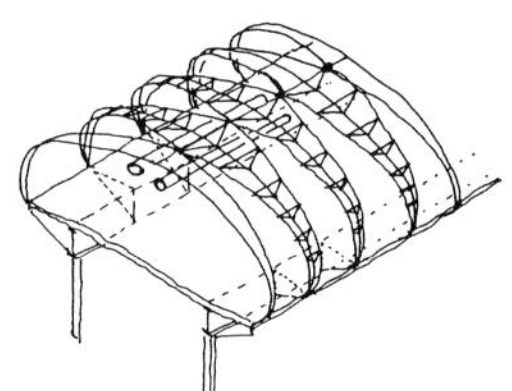

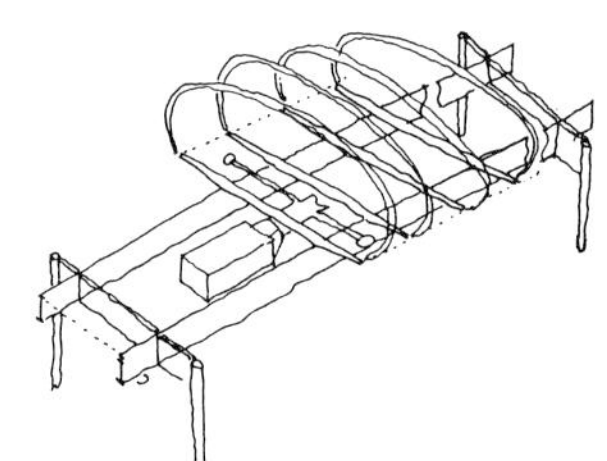
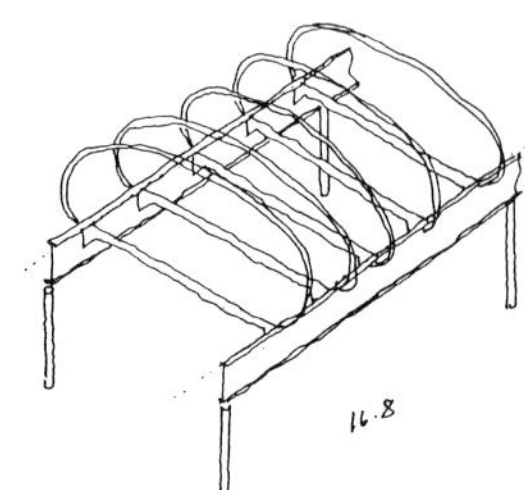

Diagrams by Hin Tan investigating structural alternatives for one of the piers.

members keeps their structural depth to a minimum and enables lightweight cladding rails to span between the frames.

To provide visual cohesion for the disparate and dispersed elements of the scheme, only two enclosing materials are employed. On the piers and the links sinusoidal aluminium cladding sheaths the structure both inside and out, while the circular CTA lounge and the nose building are clad in glass. The effect, in marked contrast with most interiors at Heathrow, is of a sleek, uncluttered tube, which enhances rather than neutralises the effect of travelling along it.

The interior's aesthetic – industrial but civilised – is developed by its finishes and fittings. Chequerplate aluminium sheets enclose power cables and, together with a neoprene bumper rail, protect the walls against damage from luggage trolleys. Carpets and seating match the metallic tone of the walls. Two aerofoil-shaped lighting booms throw light upwards so that it washes down the curved walls, and project direct light down onto the seating areas to achieve the high lighting levels required by the BAA. The booms are of pop-rivetted steel sheet and, along with the other fittings inside the pier structure, have a silvery-grey finish that complements the rougher, matt surface of the walls.

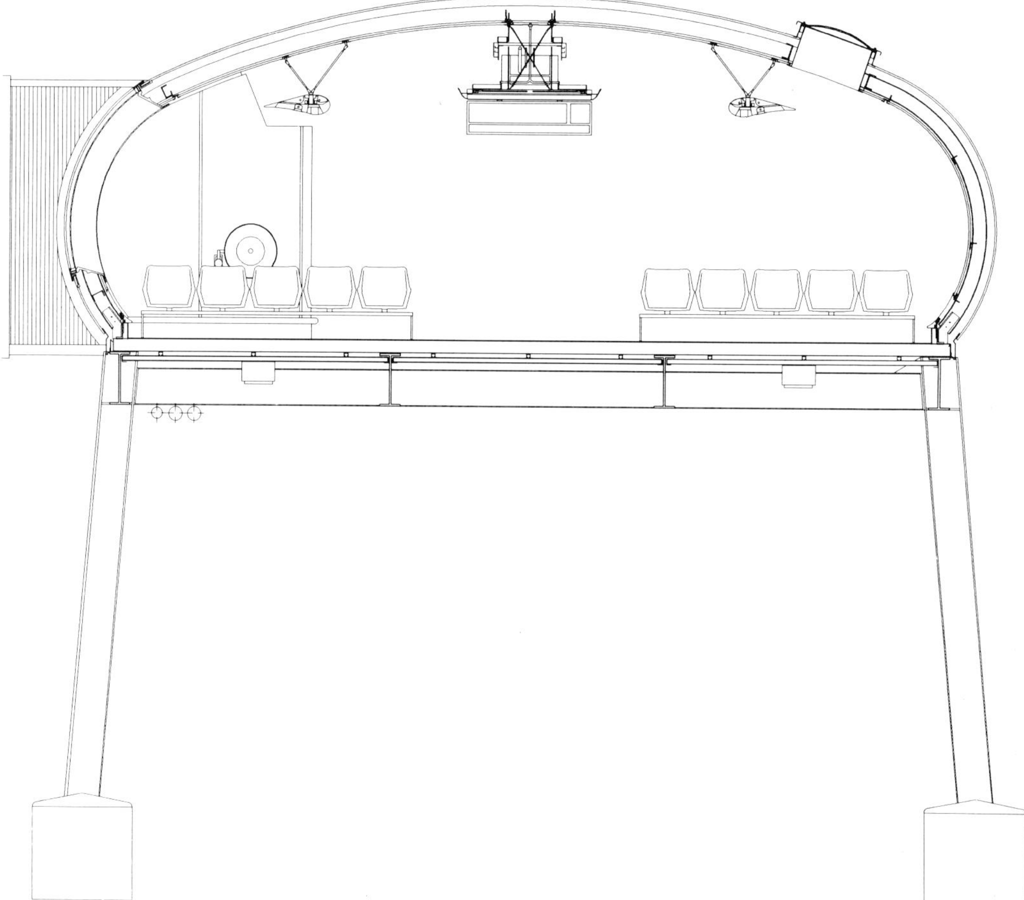

Cross section through the main pier.

Interior view of main pier showing seating, uplighting and departure gate.

90

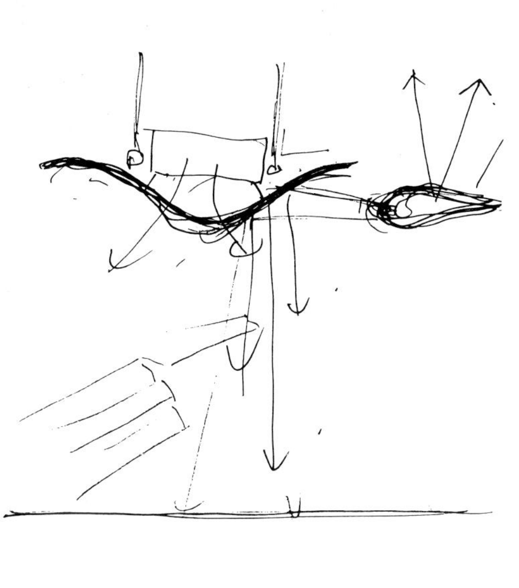

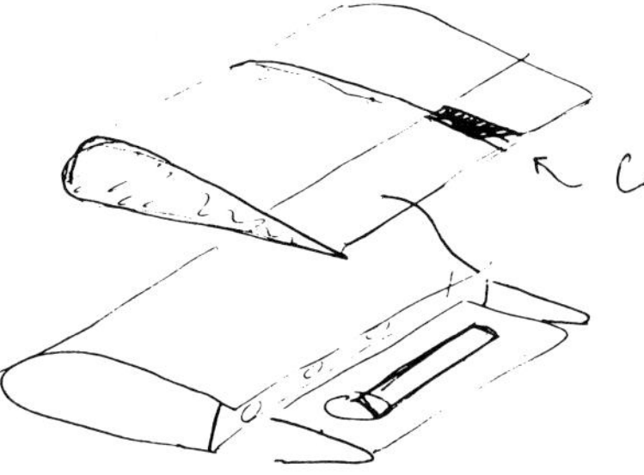

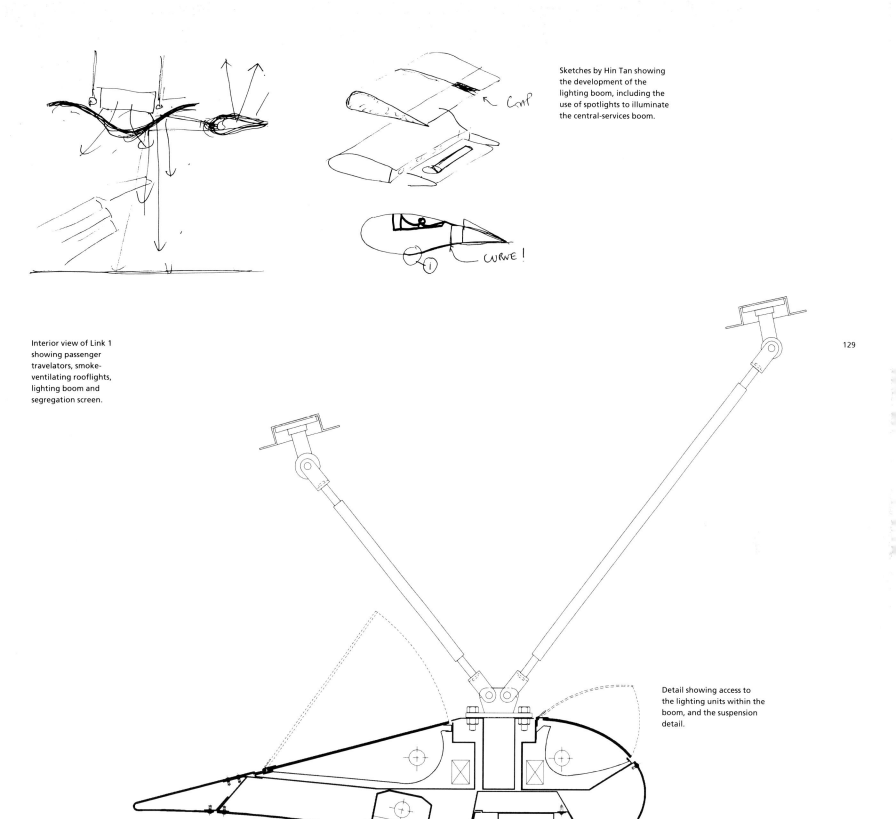

Sketches by Hin Tan showing the development of the lighting boom, including the use of spotlights to illuminate the central-services boom.

Interior view of Link 1 showing passenger travelators, smoke-ventilating rooflights, lighting boom and segregation screen.

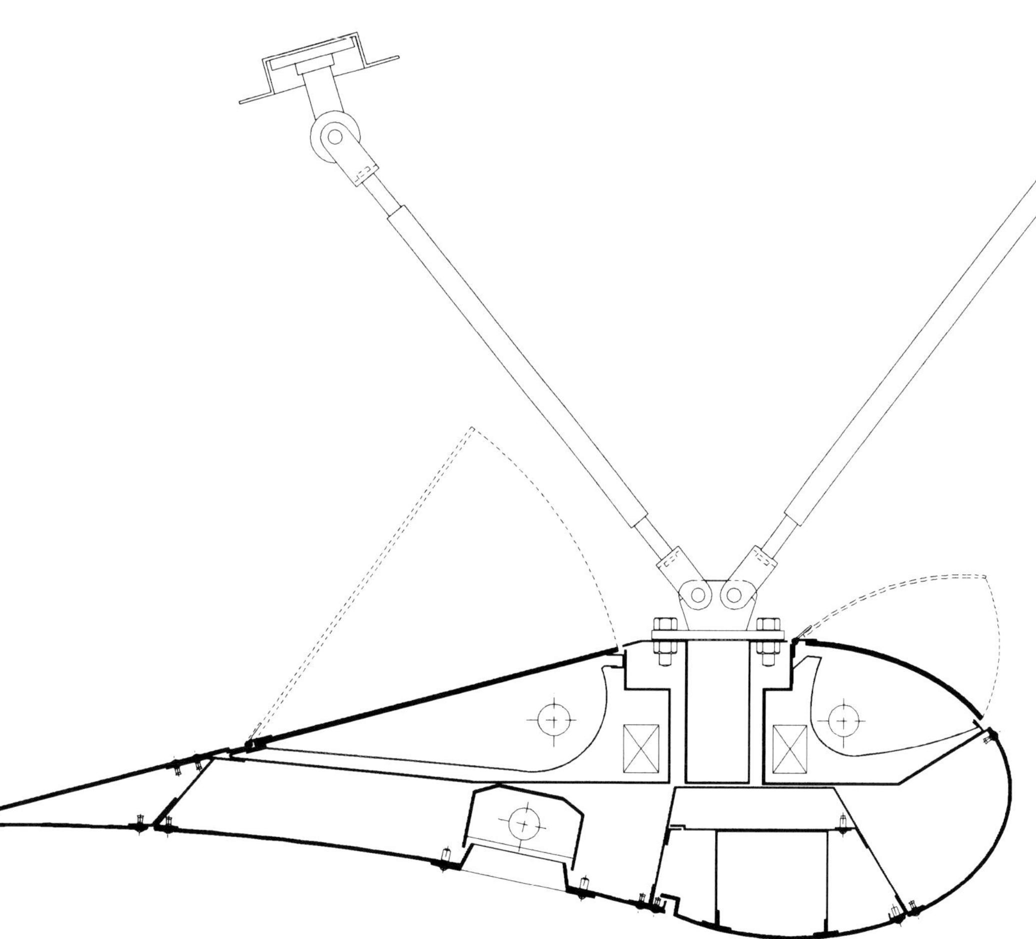

Detail showing access to the lighting units within the boom, and the suspension detail.

N88

View of a pier showing glazed gable end and the air-bridge node.

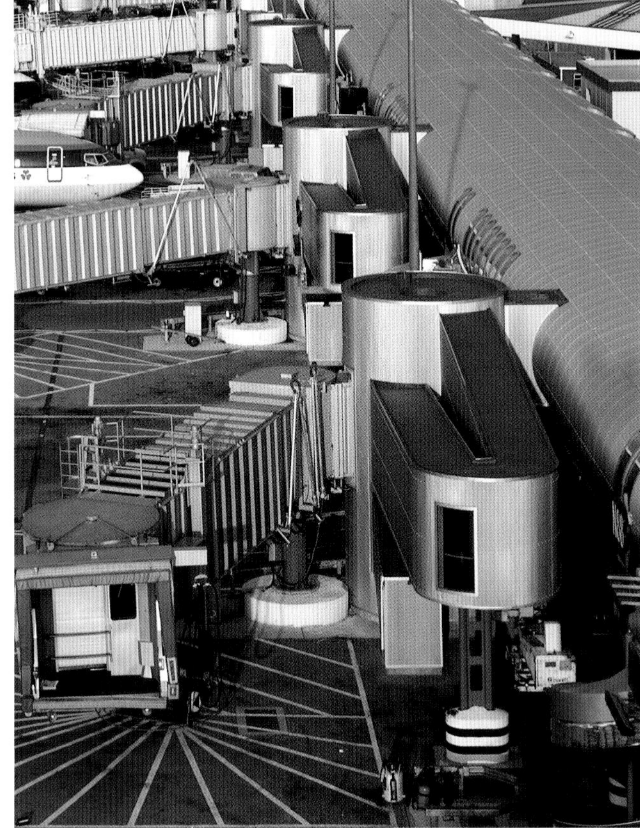

Air jetty connection with aircraft on stand.

View of the air-bridge links to the CTA pier.

Departure-level plan

1 CTA pier
2 link with travelators
3 CTA lounge
4 link between CTA and nose building
5 nose building with baggage reclaim hall and customs
6 domestic pier with connection to nose building and shuttle lounge
7 new Belfast lounge
8 Terminal One

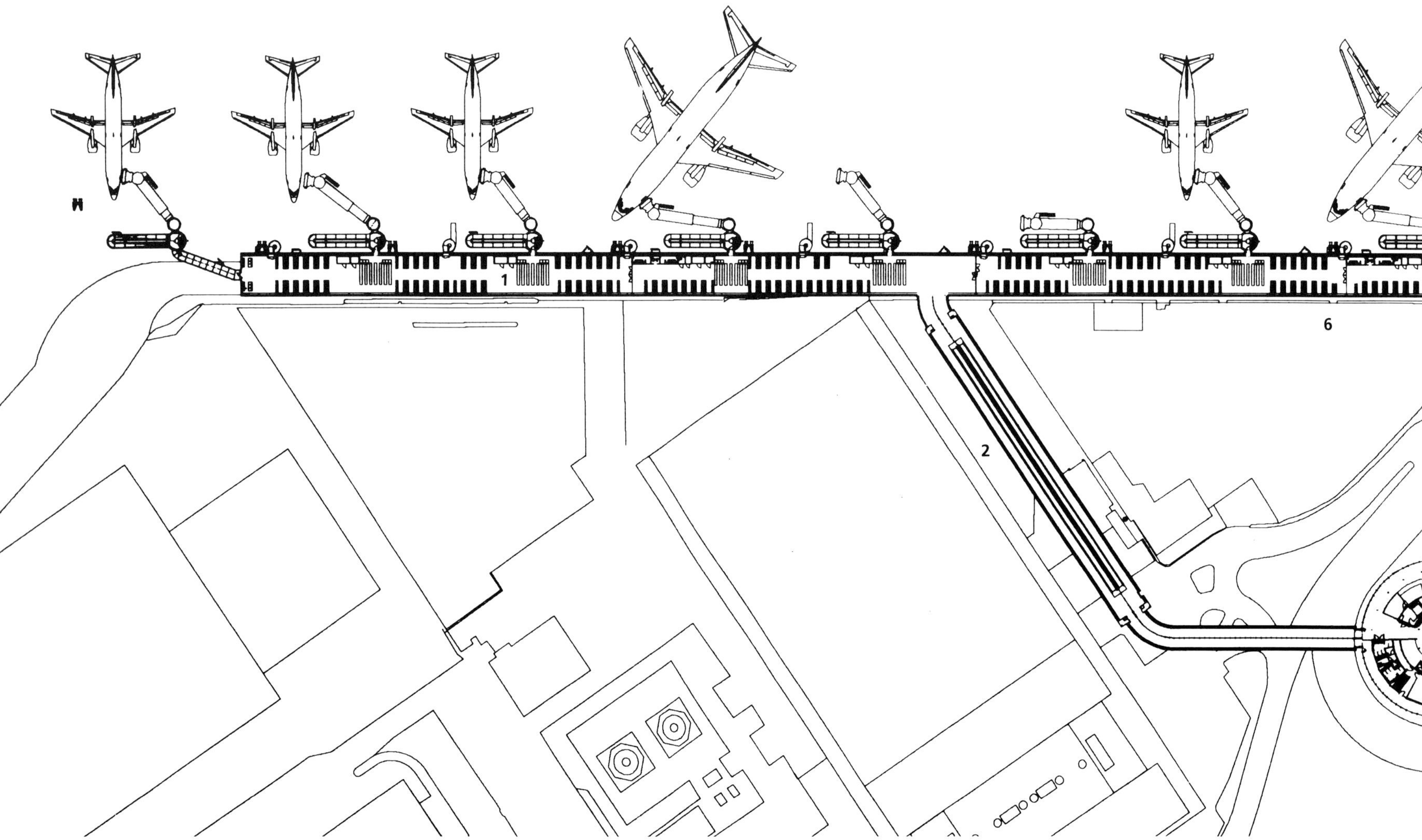

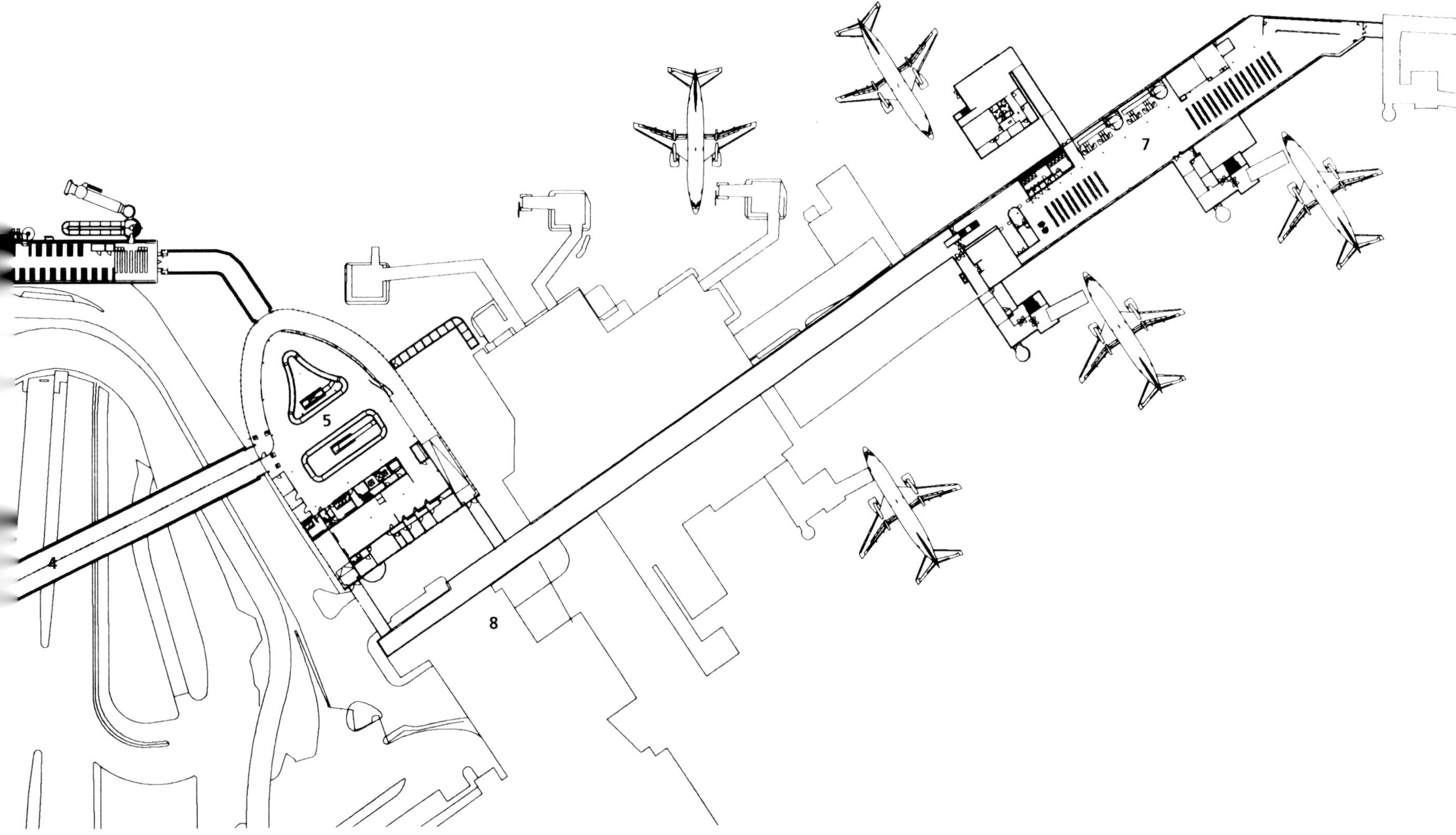

Satellite and Piers, Heathrow Airport

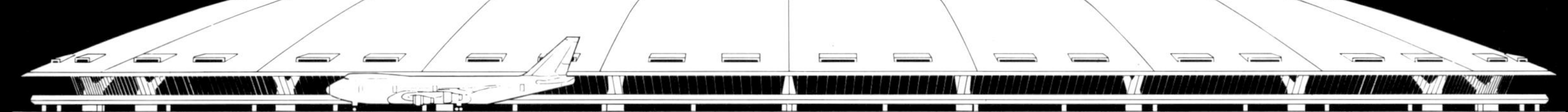

Venice Biennale, 1991

'First and foremost the idea was to construct a piece of sculpture, which would stand in the centre of our small room and be seen as a creative thing in its own right. We constructed the airport model on a glass plate and lit it from below. This gave it the most marvellous floating quality – as though it was airborne. The design of the up-lit sculptural shape of the roof with radiating steel pylons encased in smooth aluminium skins could be imagined easily when looking at the model. I believe we really did create the feel of the space and get across the simplicity of the idea – that everyone would stay in one vast enclosure until the plane was ready to take off.' **NG**

Previous page
The main model photographed in the British Pavilion at the Venice Biennale 1991.

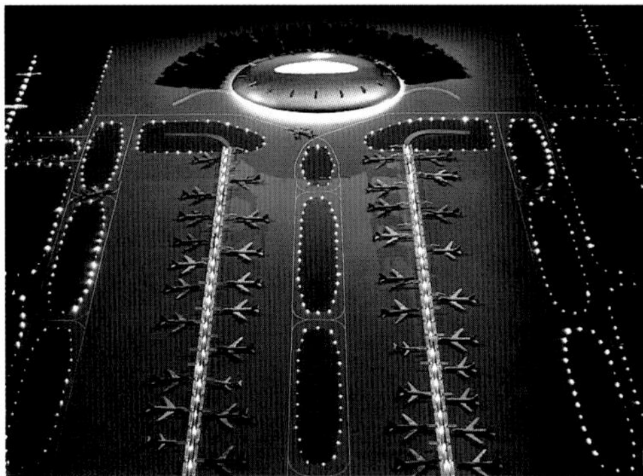

An early model, used for the competition, shows the terminal from the air.

The 1991 Venice Biennale was a multinational, multi-faceted, city-wide event that transcended conventional architectural exhibitions in its scale and imagination. In the same spirit, Grimshaw's exhibit for the British pavilion transcended the predictable arrangement of photographs and models with which architecture is commonly displayed. Instead of two-dimensional echoes of work elsewhere and in the past, it was architecture in its own right, both a thoroughly present conjuration of light, space and materials, and an image of the future.

The exhibition space was dominated by a model that, placed at eye-level, forcefully engaged the viewer, who could circulate round it rather than contemplate it from a fixed point. Its metallic substance and its scale gave an immediacy and a tangibility that penetrated

Nick Grimshaw's sketch developing the solution for the radiating ribs that formed the model.

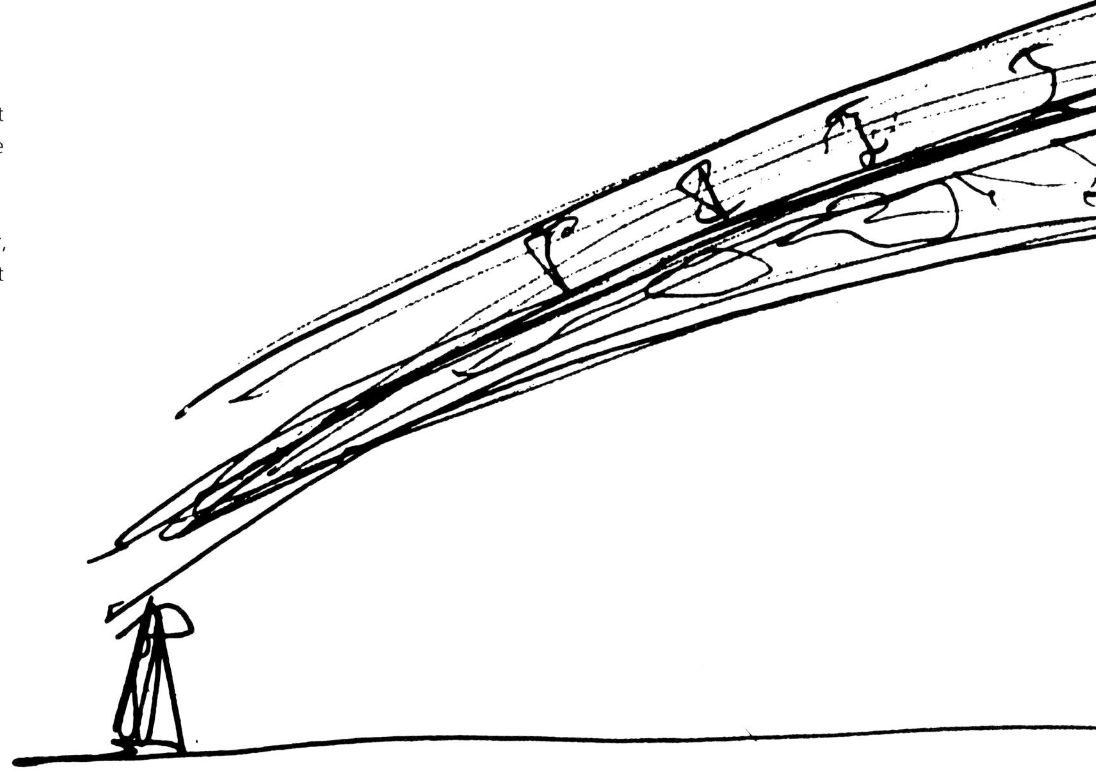

A mock-up of a structural bay of the model was built to explore the choice of materials and colour. A glass floor allowed experimentation with various lighting sources to emphasise the form of the roof.

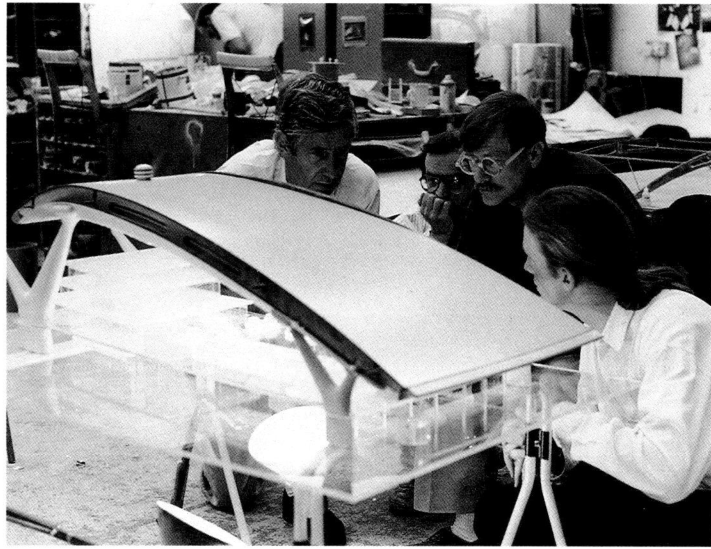

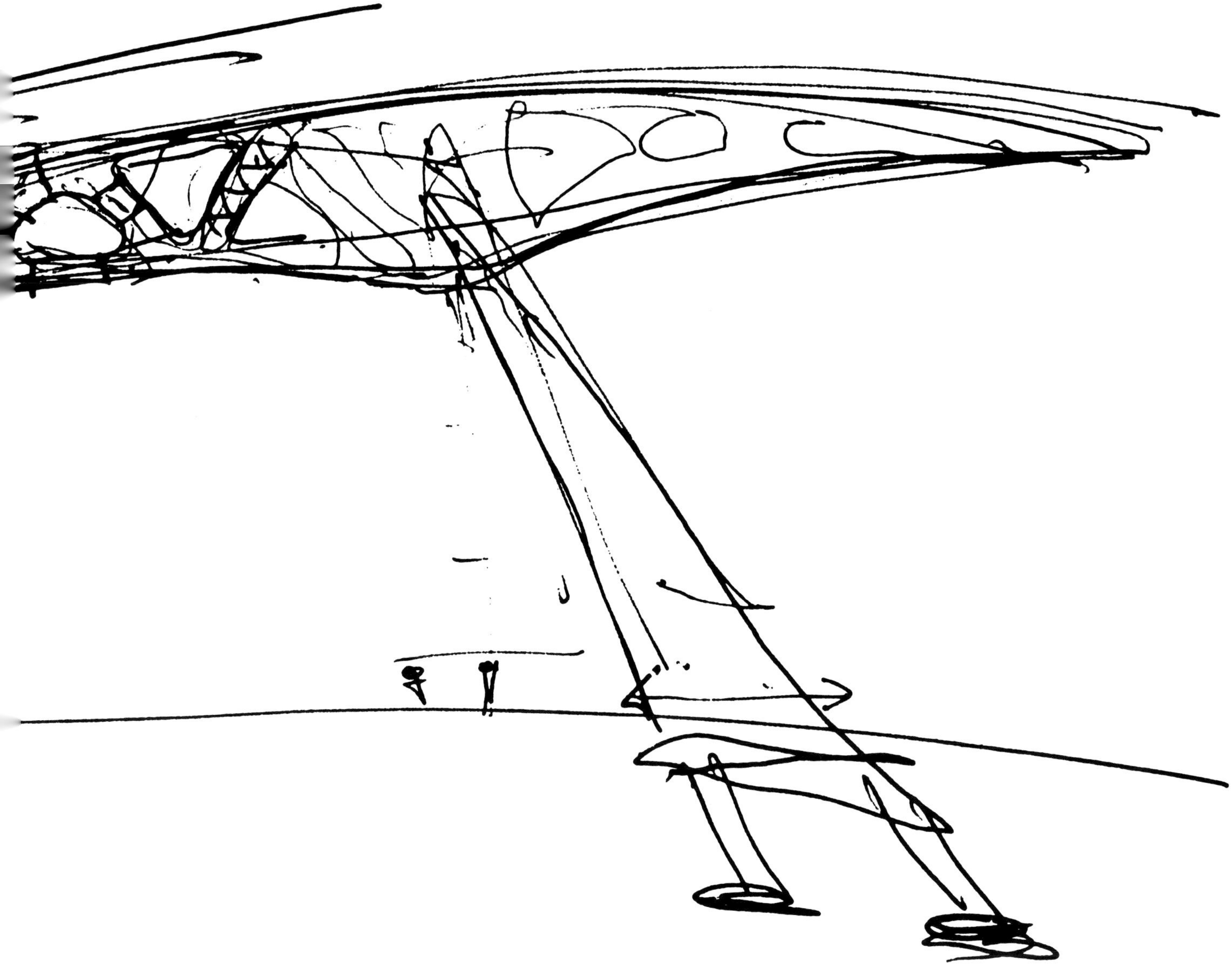

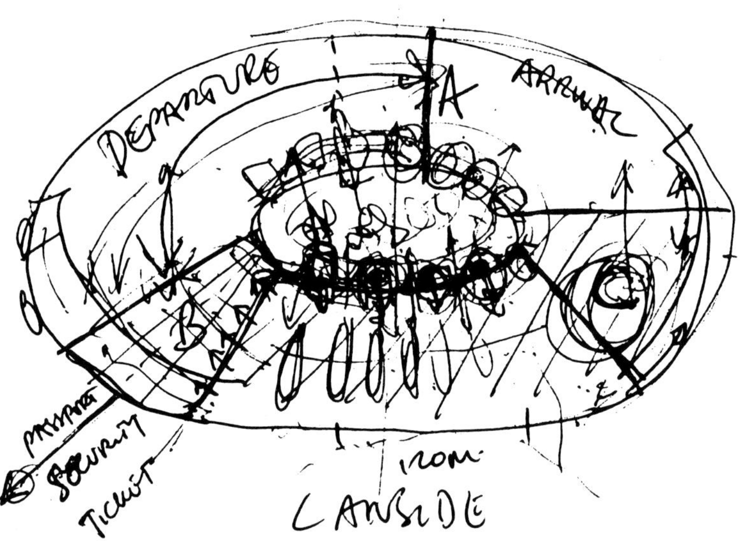

Nick Grimshaw's early conceptual sketch showing the plan of the terminal with the division between landside and airside, and landscaping in the centre.

the barrier between viewer and object, which is commonly erected in galleries. Light, rather than falling on the installation from outside, emanated from it into the dimmer light of the exhibition space from fluorescent tubes at the perimeter, halogen uplighters in the floor and incandescent lights within the model.

The structure that supported the model was continuous with the floor and the guardrails, and through them with the exhibition space, but it was a representation as well as an installation. It used the freedom allowed by the exhibition to portray a prototype airport which, through the application of fresh thinking, sought to restore dignity and grandeur to air travel.

A single idea dominated the design, that of replacing the conventional paraphernalia of piers and walkways that conventionally link terminal to aeroplanes with a system of trains. These would take passengers from a central terminal building directly to their aeroplanes only when the aeroplane was ready to take off. The confusion, wasted time and fatigue associated with modern airports would be eliminated, and its claustrophobic network of corridors would be replaced by the huge, airy volume of the terminal building.

A similar wish for simplicity informed the project's structural and environmental design. The 80m roofspans would be achieved with steel trusses sheathed in aluminium, in a structure similar to that of an aeroplane. As with an aeroplane, the visible surfaces would be smooth and uncluttered, and the spaces created within the structure would allow ample room for services.

Cutaway axonometric showing the internal layout of the terminal, where all passenger facilities are included in one space.

Nick Grimshaw's sketch illustrating the concept for the circulation of the transport system bringing passengers to and from the aircraft and the terminal. Direct, dedicated train connections with the aircraft banish the need for departure gates.

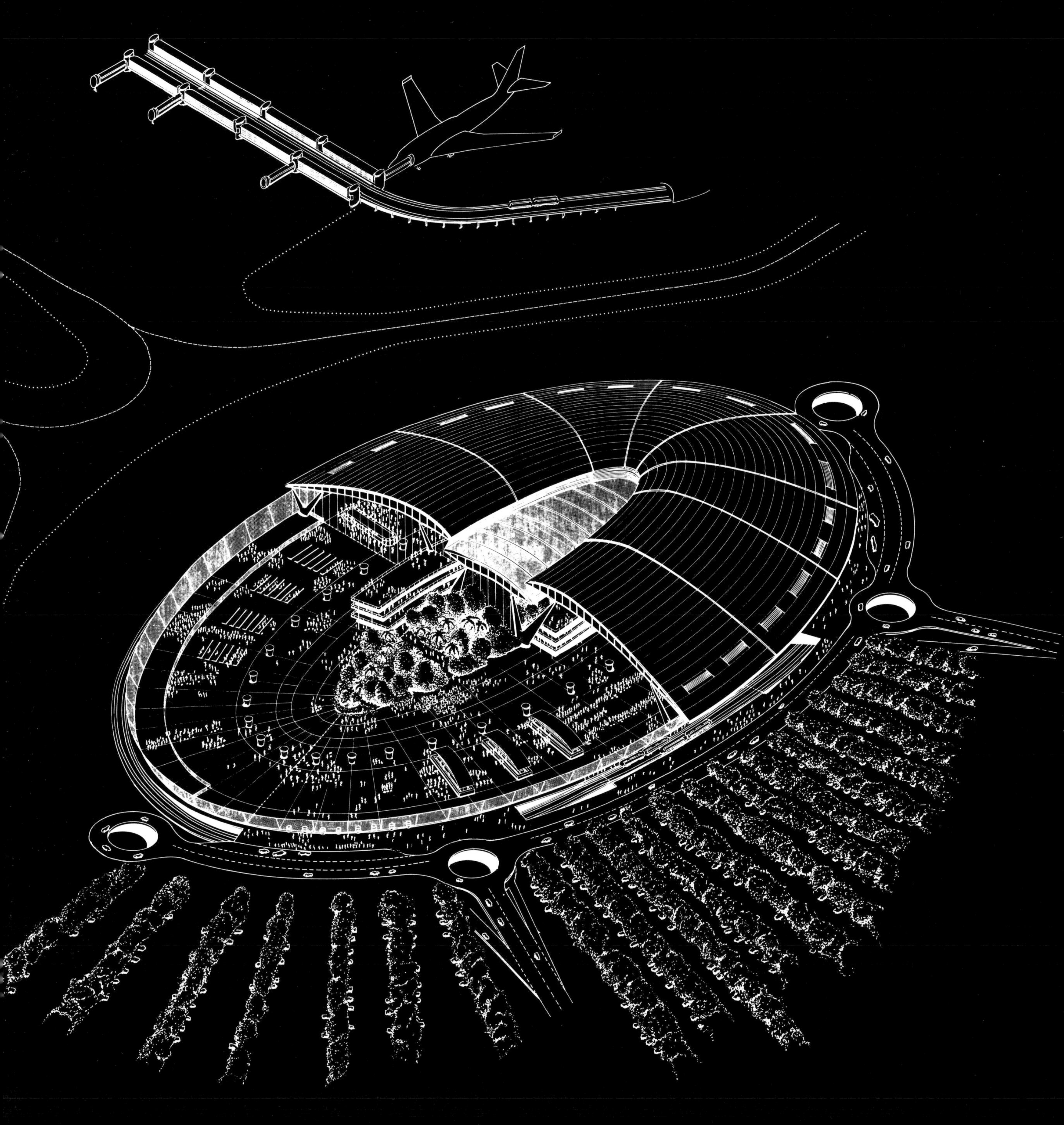

4mm-thick, laser-cut, steel ribs formed the structural skeleton of the model.

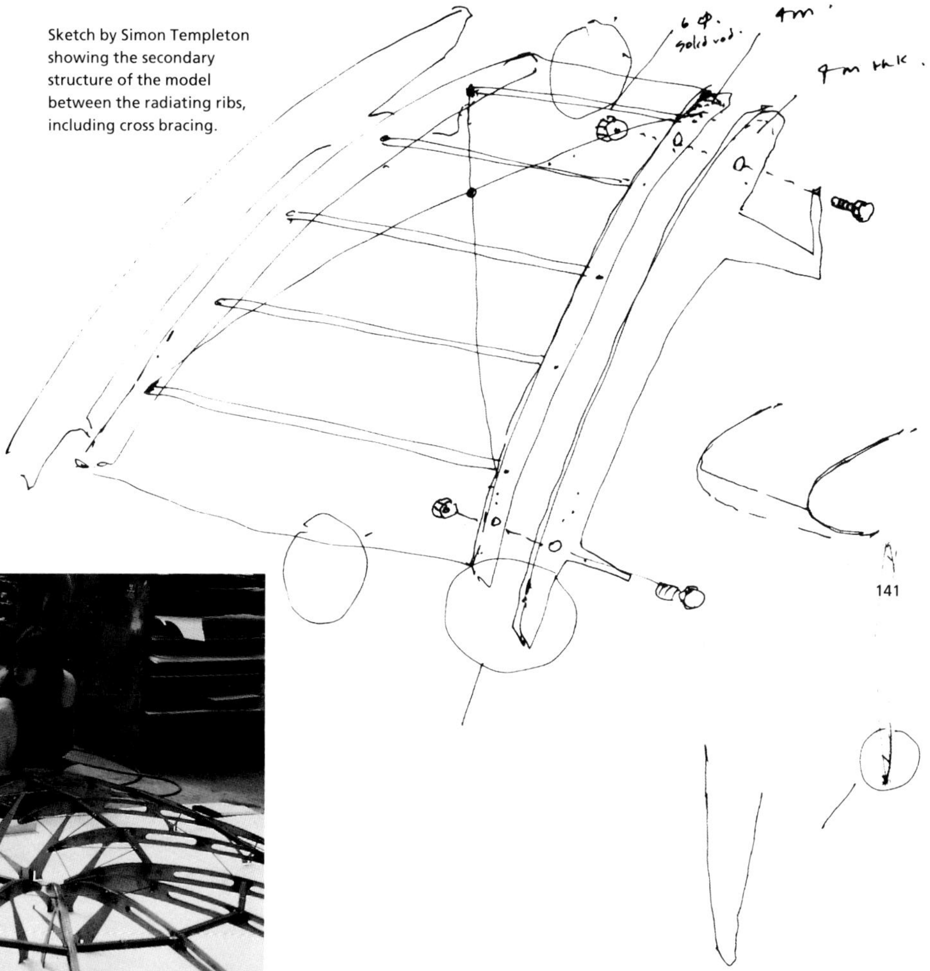

Sketch by Simon Templeton showing the secondary structure of the model between the radiating ribs, including cross bracing.

Initial assembly of structure.

Competition cross section showing the vertical organisation of the building.

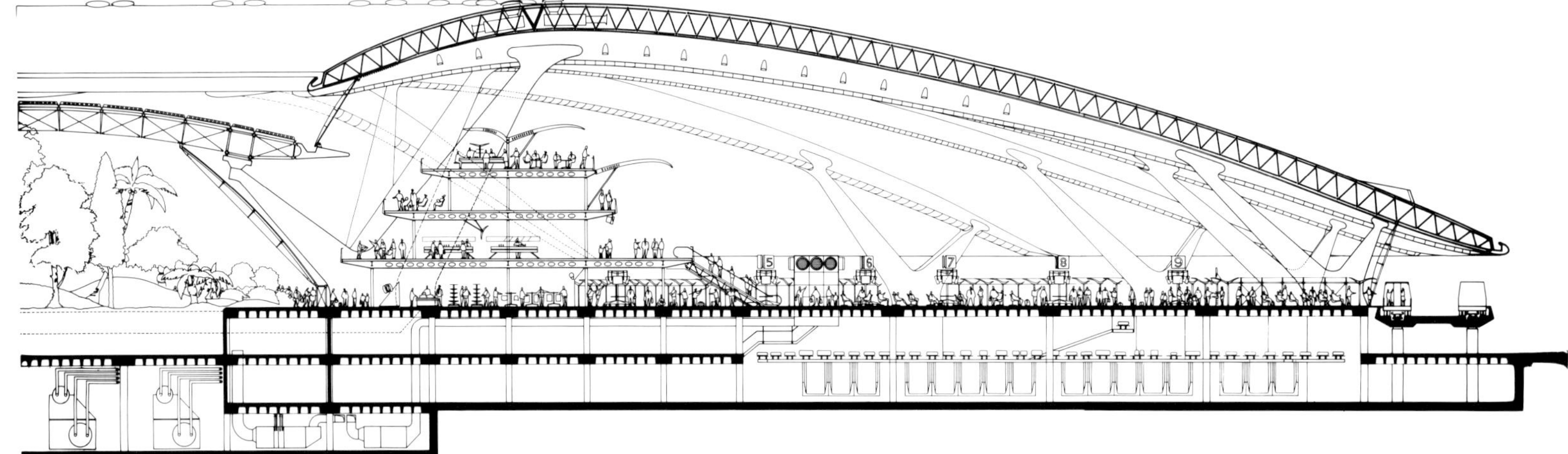

The airport's ventilation techniques continued Grimshaw's investigation of ways other than air conditioning to cool large buildings. The design acted on the principle that, in a temperate climate, external air is seldom hotter than the desired internal temperature, and that the main problem, therefore, is not cooling the air intake but extracting heat generated inside the building by bodies and machines. Fresh air, admitted at low level, would be drawn through the space by the tendency of hot air to rise, and would leave through the top of the building, taking excess heat with it. The floor would be used further to cool or to heat the building, as necessary. The main air intakes also would be the fire exits, in keeping with the economy of means applied to much of the project.

Interior views of the model showing the main concourse area and the internal, landscaped area.

Overleaf
View of the model, uplit with recessed, tungsten halogen lights.

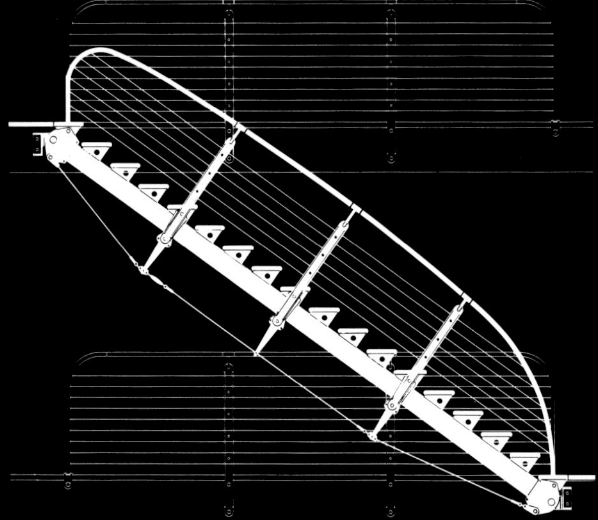

Nicholas Grimshaw & Partners' offices, London, 1992

'I have always seen the office as part workshop and part studio. My ideal is for each team to have a working model beside them so that they can be continuously aware of the scale and size of the spaces on which they are working. Pieces are added and removed so that in the end the model has the feeling of a battered tapestry. One can also see pieces of buildings, castings and fixings lying around people's desks. This illustrates our constant dialogue with all the various manufacturers and suppliers. I enjoy showing the staircase to potential clients. I think they can appreciate the care that has gone into it. I hope they feel that if they appoint us as their architects they, too, will get the same degree of care and attention.' **NG**

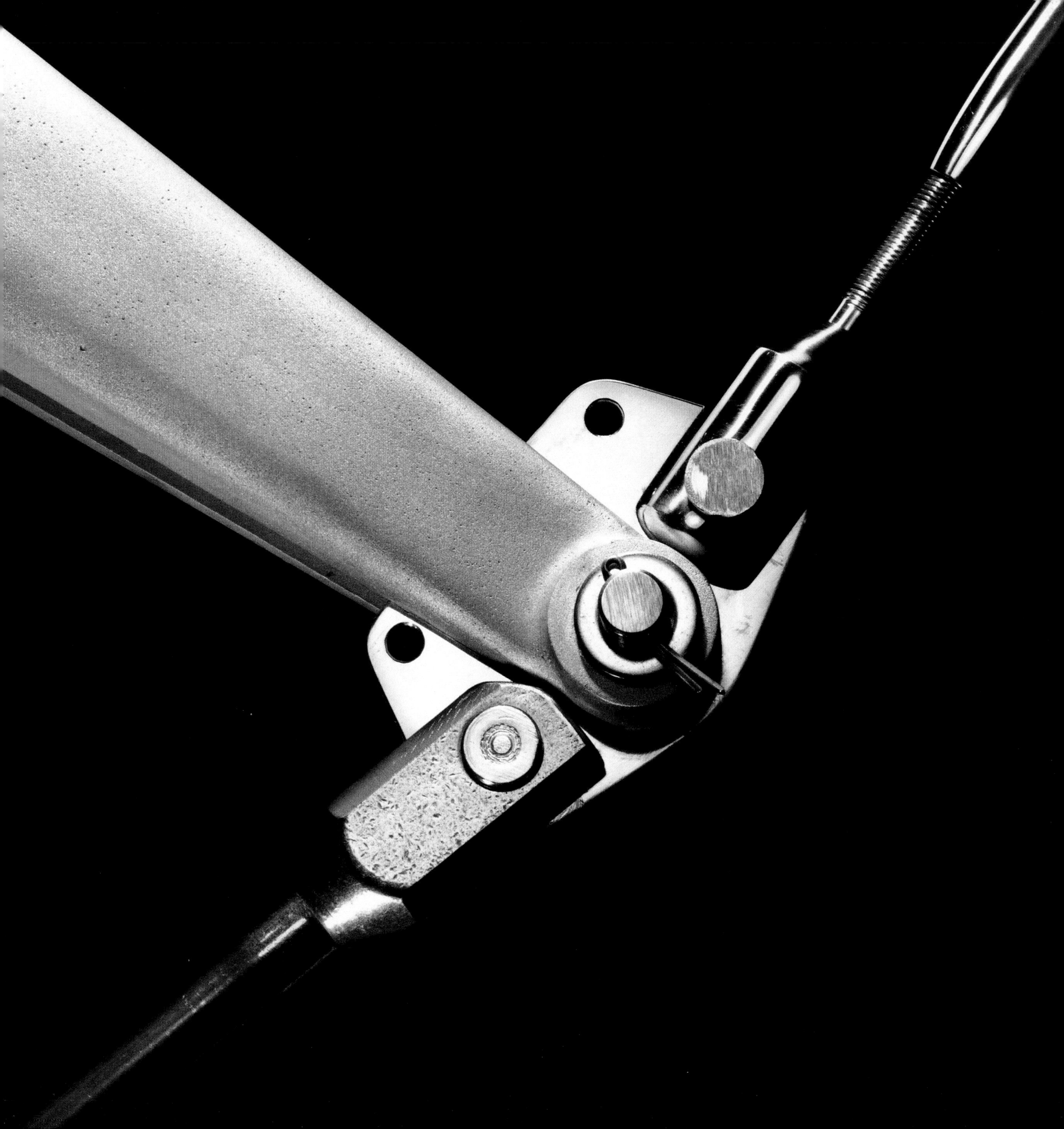

Previous page
The stainless-steel pin plate at the lower end of the aluminium leg casting. Stainless-steel tie rods strengthen the aluminium stair.

In moving offices, Grimshaw's decision to remain in central London keeps his team near to the engineers and other consultants with whom they work closely, and accessible to clients, but it made other desirable ends harder to achieve. Light, airy, open spaces, allowing good communications within the practice, are difficult to find in London's West End, and there are limited opportunities to create public demonstrations of the practice's work. Achieving these ends in an existing building just off Fitzroy Square was the main objective in the conversion of No 1 Conway Street.

The existing building, built in the 1920s, was a six-storey former belt factory in an area largely comprising Georgian houses. Both industrial and urbane, the combination of building and setting suited the ambiguous nature of an architects' office which is, according to Grimshaw, 'a cross between a workshop, a studio, an office and a manufacturing plant'. Its disadvantage was its subdivision into small rooms with little or no daylight, a problem compounded by a three-storey 1970s' addition, which extended to the rear boundaries of the site.

The conversion opens up the building sideways and upwards. A steel frame has replaced the internal loadbearing walls and partitions have been removed to make each floor into a single open space, capable of housing design teams for even the largest projects. Vertically, the top-lit stairwell on the boundary between the original building and the extension brings light into the centre of the building. To the front the section of basement that extended under the pavement has been removed, together with its pavement lights and the ground floor elevation. This creates an external

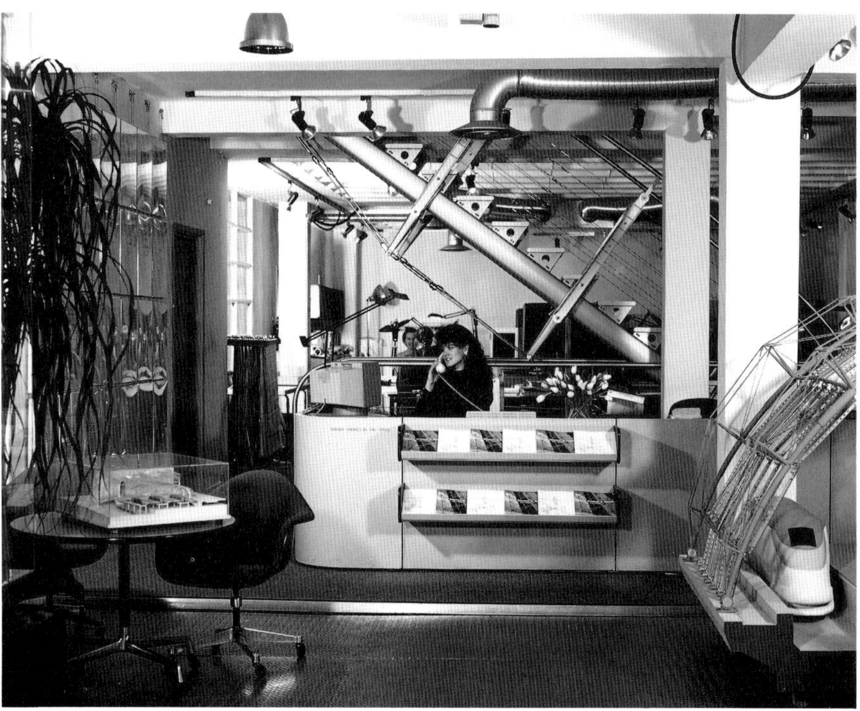

Interior view of the reception area from the model exhibition space at the entrance. The staircase behind leads to studio floors on three levels and is positioned below a central lightwell.

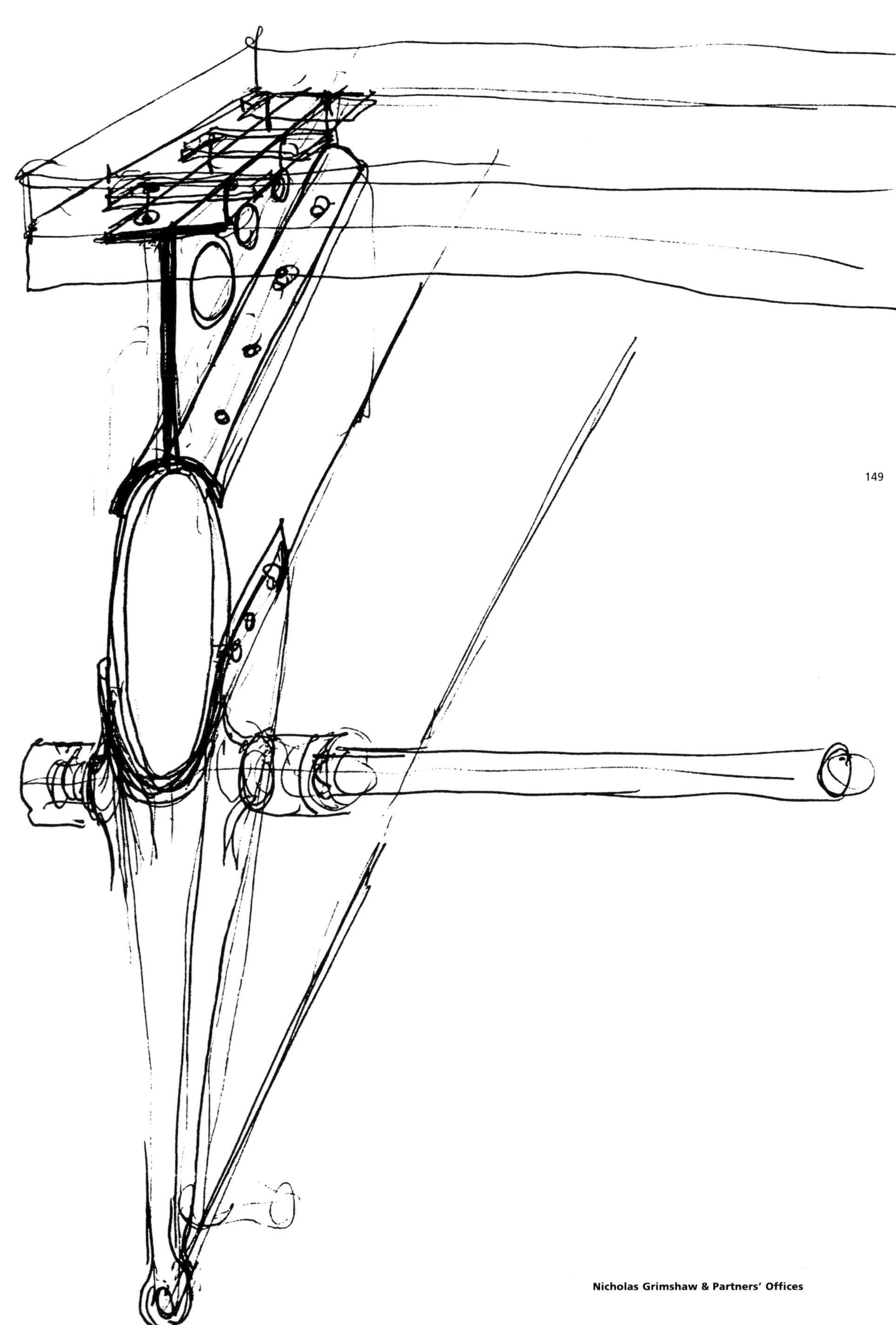

Nick Grimshaw's sketch developing the idea of using a yacht mast as the stringer of the stair.

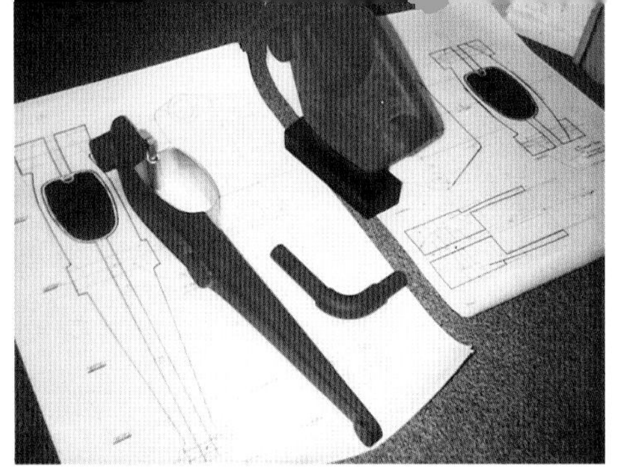

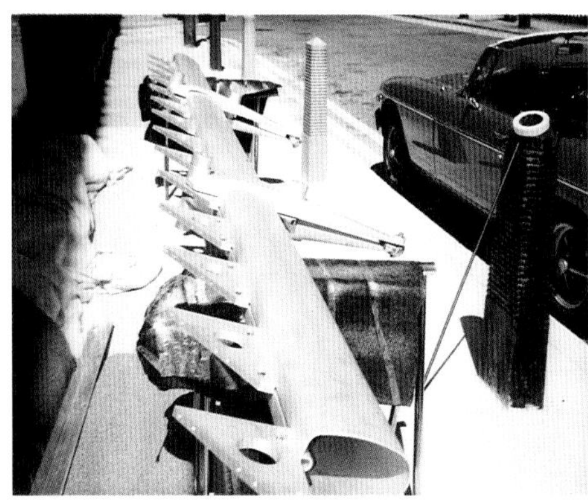

Top to bottom: wooden patterns used in the aluminium sand-casting process; the entire stair in component form before erection; a single stringer of the staircase being assembled on the pavement; the stair was fabricated and installed in one day.

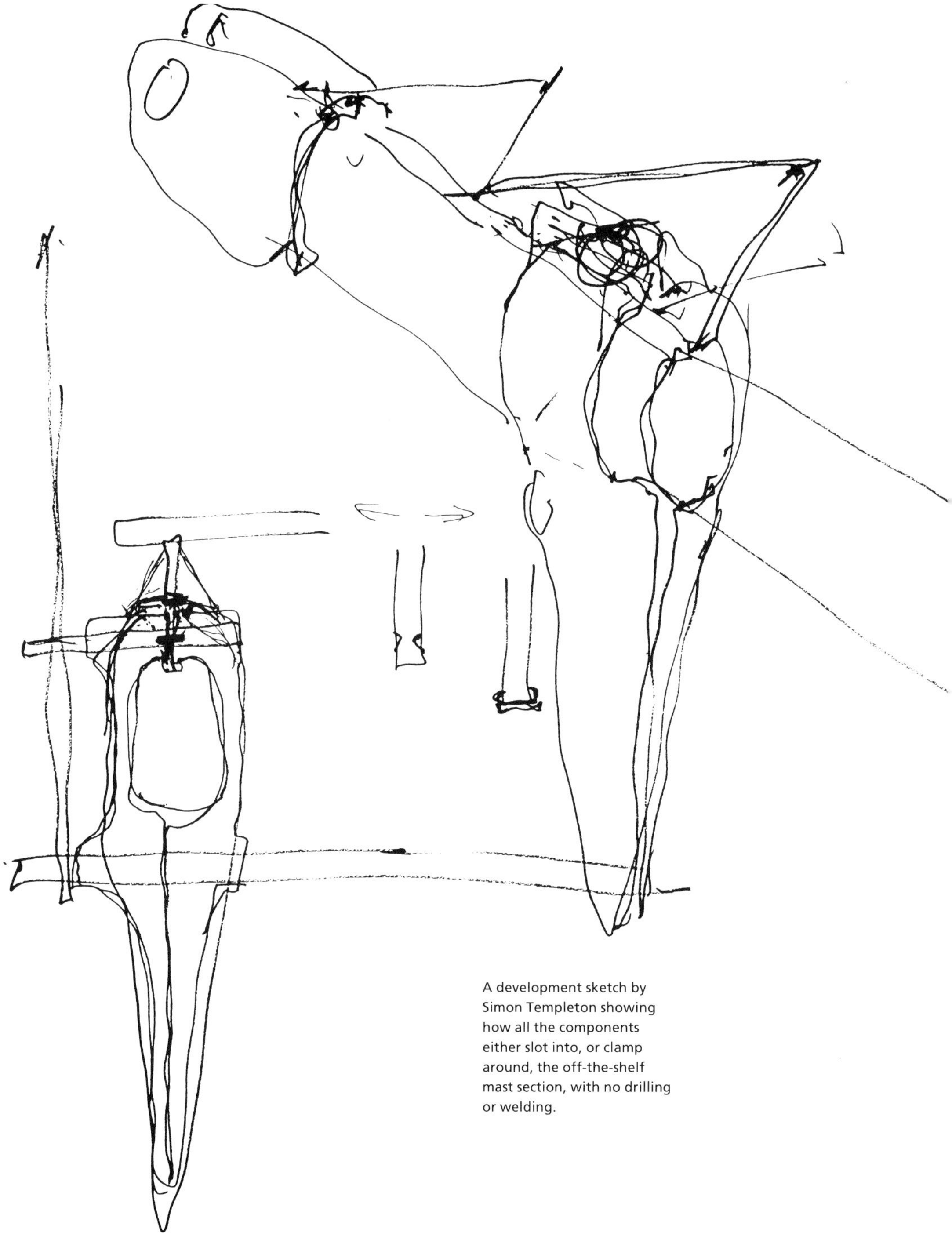

A development sketch by Simon Templeton showing how all the components either slot into, or clamp around, the off-the-shelf mast section, with no drilling or welding.

basement area and two-storey glazed opening that bring light into the basement.

The alterations that now make the building 'open', make it work, too, as a showpiece. The glass wall gives a view into a reception space, reached by a bridge across the area, where the practice's output of models and building components is displayed. As one moves through the offices all theworking areas are on show. Most importantly, both visitors and staff circulate on the central stair which, visible from the street and most of the interior, is a self-conscious display of Grimshaw's approach to detailing.

The stair, predominantly of aluminium, is light and open allowing for penetration of light and crane-free construction. It was assembled by hand in the reception space when the offices were already in use and carried into place by Grimshaw and his staff. It demonstrates Grimshaw's fondness both for prefabrication – the parts were made to exacting tolerances so as to preclude on-site drilling and welding – and for creatively combining available materials with the selective use of purpose-designed elements.

The stair's strings are mast sections more usually found on yachts, with the supports for the treads inserted into the sail grooves. The treads and their supports are cut from standard aluminium sections while purpose-designed castings provide bearings for the masts at either end. At the mid-span, cast 'legs' provide fixing points for stainless-steel tie rods (supplied by a yacht-rigging manufacturer), which work with the strings and the legs to form trusses, and so give strength to the lightweight structure.

A detail of the staircase showing how the two stringers are clamped together at each aluminium leg casting.

A sketch by Simon Templeton that shows how the aluminium mast section slots into the head casting. Three stainless-steel pins act as dowels to secure the two halves of the casting.

The stair being lifted, while the foot castings are secured to the floor, before being dropped into position.

The finished assembly. The treads are 250mm aluminium-extruded plank, which is commonly used in North Sea oil-rig decking.

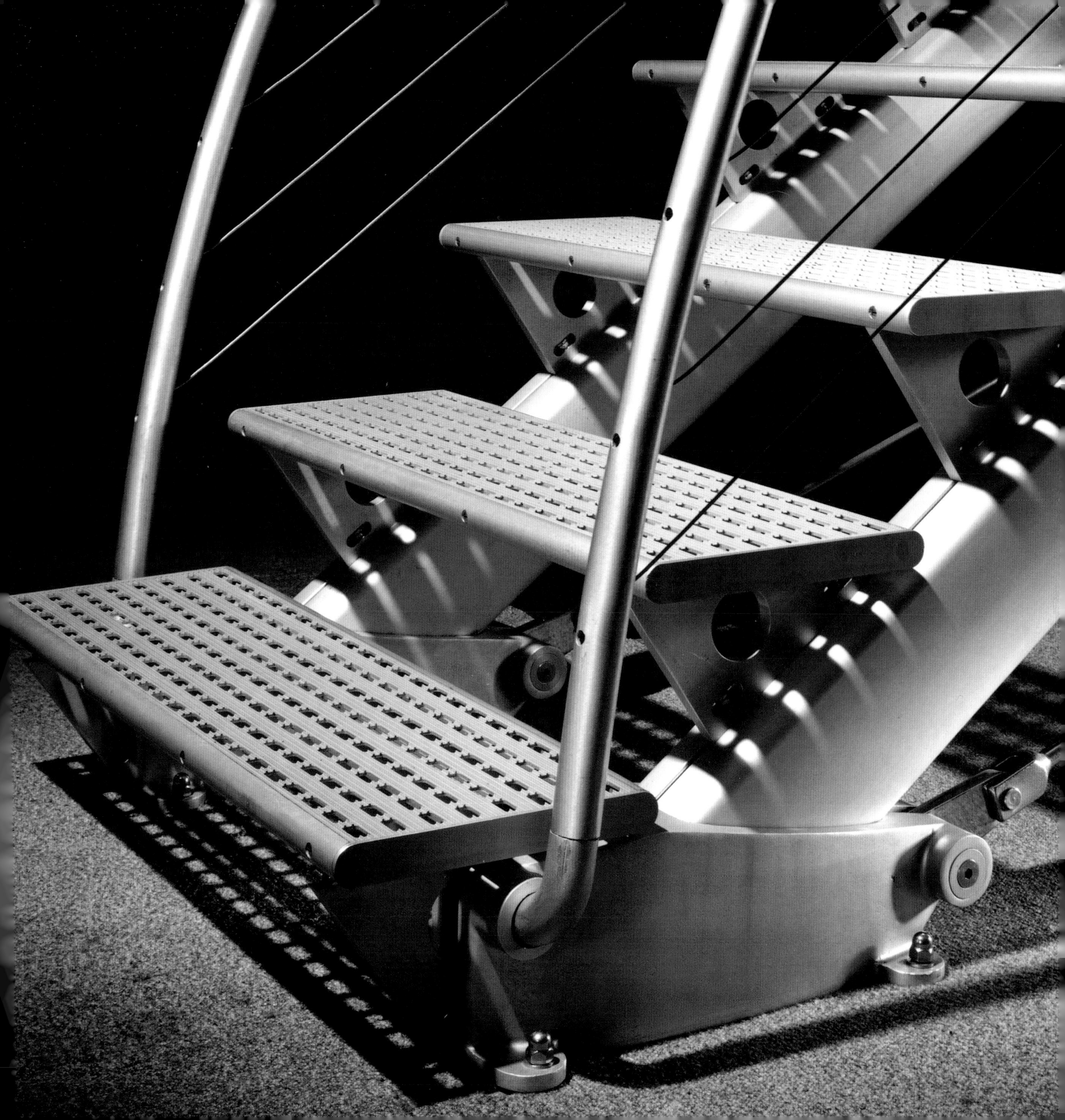

A view of the stair and balustrade between the ground and first floors.

An elevation of the complete stair and balustrading. The handrails are continuously radiused aluminium tube sections. A third staircase is planned to the floor above.

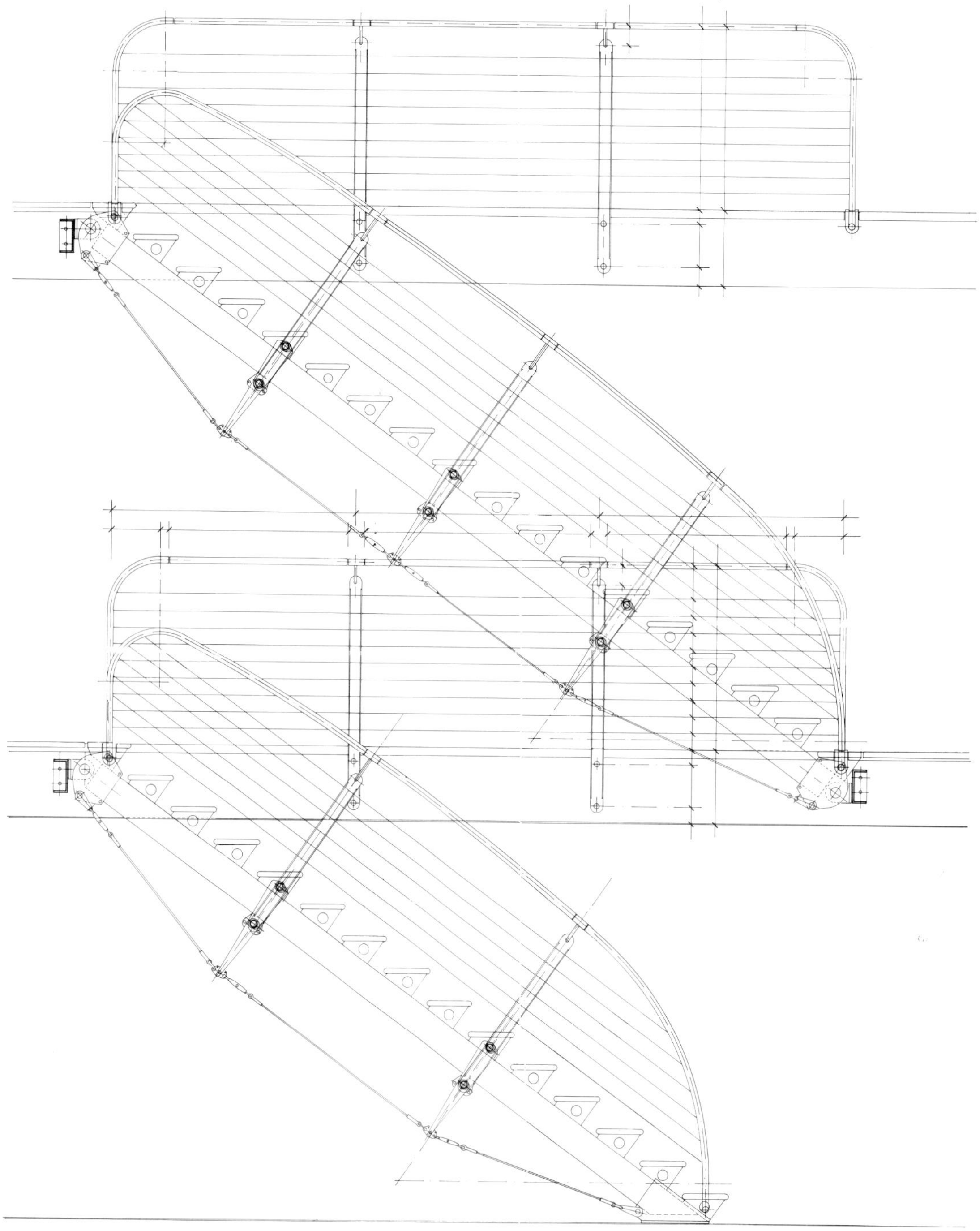

Overleaf
View of the lower-ground floor of the offices.

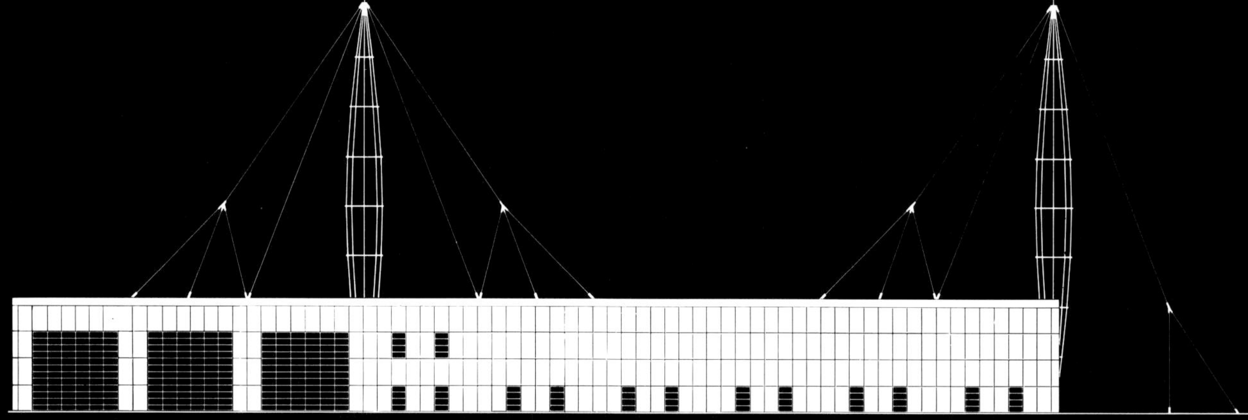

Igus Headquarters and Factory, Cologne, 1992

'If a client places a lot of confidence in you, then this tends to be returned with interest. You will do almost anything for him and it is hard to stop the creative team from working all night and every night.

'The brief was challenging: a landmark but also an up-to-the-minute totally flexible manufacturing plant where 'anything could happen anywhere'. Furthermore the building had to be capable of extension.

'I make no apology for the powerful impact of the structural masts. I believe they give the project a great image and excitement. They also allow much greater flexibility internally as they make it possible to remove so many columns. We used our past experience of prefabricated panels for the cladding but added refinements that made it much easier to erect. The roof domes with their north-facing roof lights give grandeur to the space and a marvellous studio-quality of light to the workplace. The client calls the building "his cathedral" – not bad for a low-cost factory.' **NG**

Previous page
Detail of the east elevation, with the entrance pod reflected in a window.

Grimshaw likes to tell the story of his first meeting with Günter Blase, Chief Executive of Igus, a firm that makes injection-moulded plastic products: 'He turned up at the front door and said, "Mr. Grimshaw, I've chosen you to be my architect"'. It turned out that Blase had already visited several of Grimshaw's buildings and was familiar with his approach: 'when I was going on about flexibility he would say, "You don't have to tell me. I know"'.

Blase knew what he wanted: an innovative building and a striking one, that would raise the profile of the successful, but insufficiently known, company he and his wife had built from nothing. It should demonstrate the principles of clear-headed design on which he had based his own work. It would also embody Igus' non-hierarchical management structure, described as a 'solar system', whereby the company is composed of different groups of equivalent status. Clients deal directly with individual groups and can move readily from one to another according to their needs.

The building is not, however, a public relations folly or a monument to Blase, as its first task is to provide the flexibility and the ability to grow that his company requires. The nature of the company's work involves an unpredictable future, and the capacity to change internal factory layouts rapidly and often.

The result is a building that is as much an approach, or a process, as it is a finished object. Its plan of four blocks, each six bays by six, can be built in up to seven phases: first one complete block, followed by the others in halves. Each block has an open-lattice steel mast at its centre from which steel rods reach out to carry the roof, creating huge, unimpeded internal

A view of the finished building showing the structural pylons.

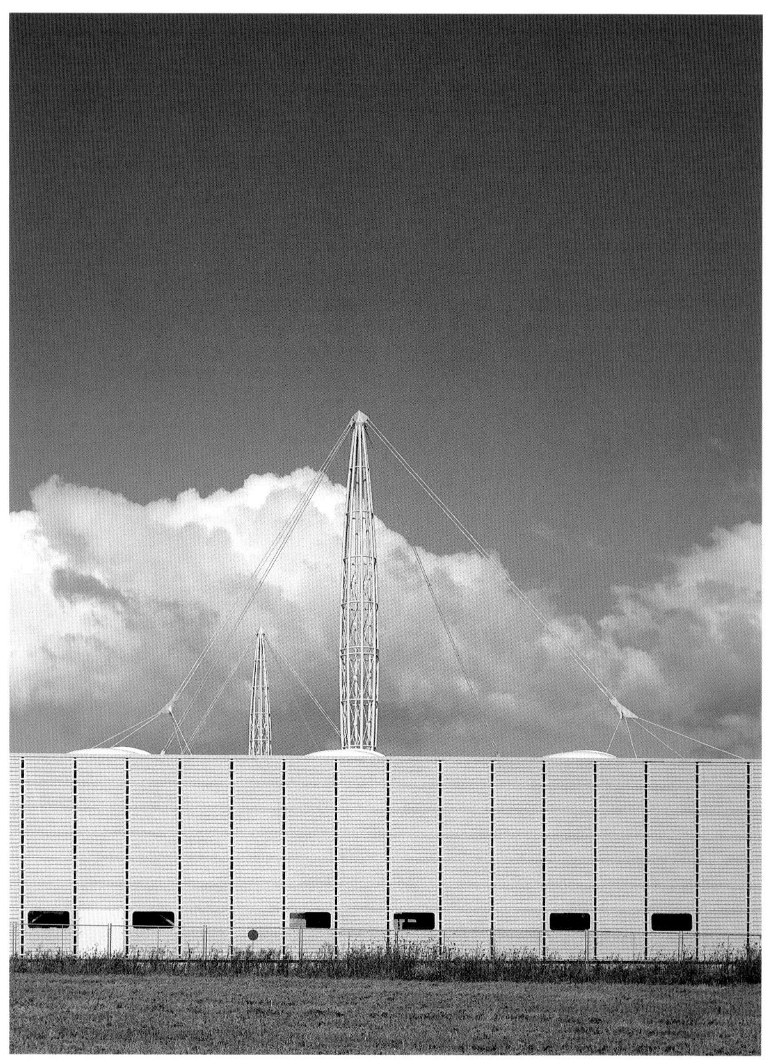

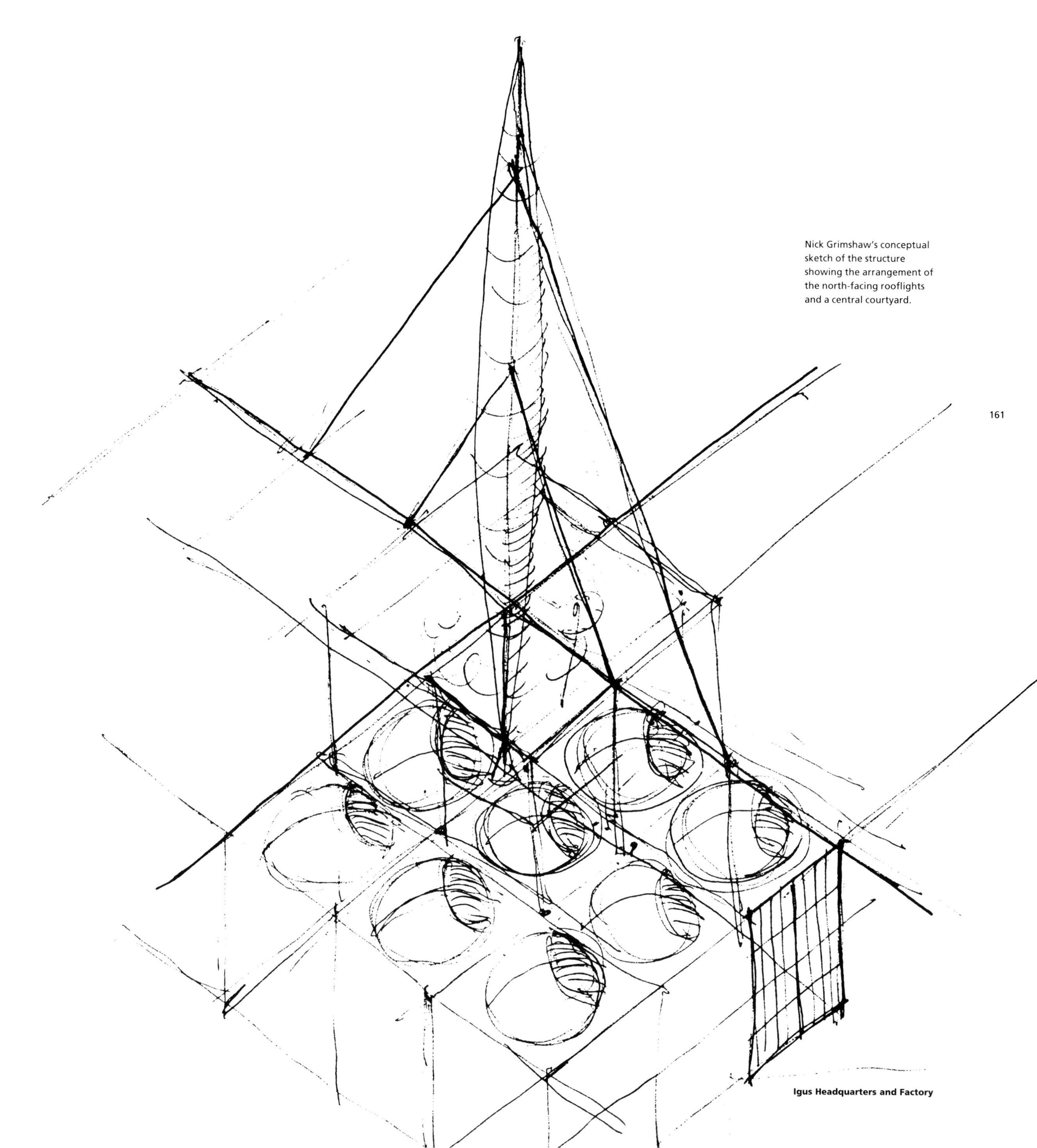

Nick Grimshaw's conceptual sketch of the structure showing the arrangement of the north-facing rooflights and a central courtyard.

Detail of the factory roof showing roof domes and high-level service distribution. The arrangement of roof domes, windows and interior courtyards ensures that natural light and ventilation are available in all areas of the factory.

spaces. Working with internal beams, the mast structure enables spans of up to 33m.

The only insertions into these spaces, other than the factory machinery, are the elevated walkways and the movable pods for offices, WCs and recreational rooms. The walkways enable visitors to tour the factory and clients to move about the different groups with which they deal, while providing 'expressways' for employees to move rapidly about the building. Placed on the cross axes of each block, they distribute the services, all of which – including pumped drainage – are located overhead. This liberates the factory layout from the need to match fixed connections in the floor. A siphonic rainwater disposal system, of the type pioneered by Sir Norman Foster & Partners at Stansted, drains the roof. By using suction as well as gravity, this enables the use of horizontal pipe runs and smaller pipe diameters.

The office pods can be dismantled and assembled in two weeks, and Grimshaw's team is working on a variation for the later phases that will rest on air cushions, so the pods may be moved over a weekend. The pods' splayed feet spread their load, which avoids the need for localised foundations. Each pod has its own services box, which can be plugged into the building's overall system through flexible ducts. The upper levels of the pods are reached by stairs assembled in two parts, each of which can be carried by a forklift truck. Inside the basic structure there is virtually nothing that cannot be moved or altered.

The external walls are composed of panels fixed to standard Unistrut shelving uprights, reinforced to span the full height of the wall. These allow shelves and

The interior of the factory space looking towards one of the courtyards.

Wooden pattern of roof domes from which the moulds were taken.

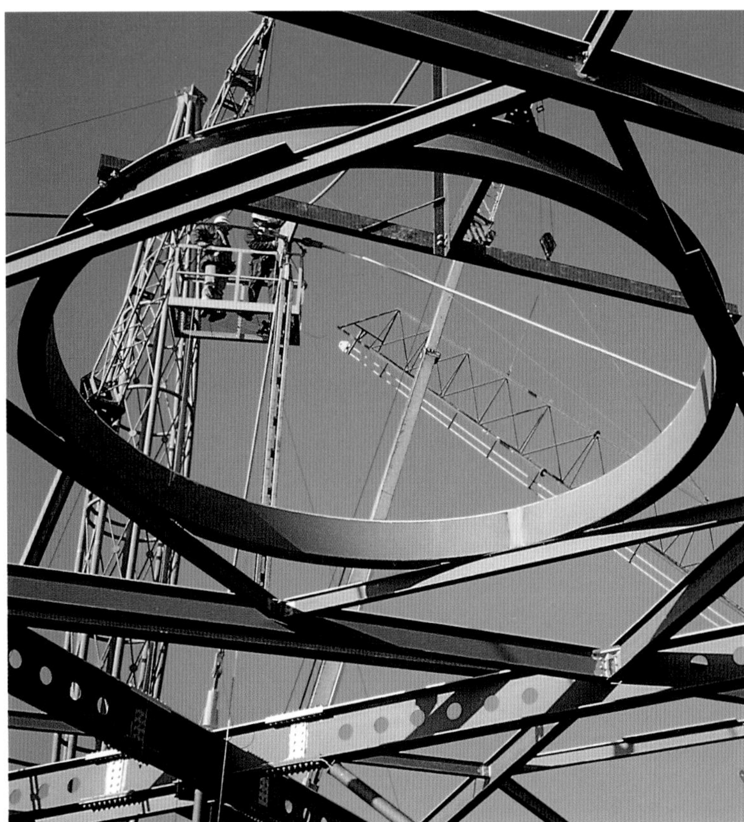

Construction shot showing the main steel structure that supports the roof and roof domes.

internal paraphernalia, such as fire hydrants and light switches, to be fixed directly to the uprights; externally, solid or glazed panels, doors and loading bay openings can be removed and interchanged at will simply by loosening a clamp and turning it through 90 degrees. On the roof, grp domes fitted with opening glass windows provide daylight and natural ventilation through north-facing elliptical glass lights. The domes are of a size designed to fit container lorries. They are designed to collapse during a fire at the point at which the internal temperature begins to threaten the steel structure, thus reducing heat build-up.

The abundance of moving, portable and repeatable parts has a clear value in giving flexibility; these parts also play a less obvious role. As Igus grows, and successive phases are built, the systems can be refined and improved in response to the company's experience of using the building; the design is interactive, one that can be adapted in the light of experience. It also means that short-term solutions can be employed without the fear that they will become permanent by default. The courtyard of the first phase, for example, is walled in the standard cladding used elsewhere, rather than a specialised glazing system that would allow more light to enter the factory. As the building grows, economies of scale will mean that the additional cost of the specialised glazing will diminish in proportion, and it will be possible to reuse the present elements of standard cladding elsewhere.

Igus is a highly considered piece of machinery, in which components have been thought through from first principles, but it is not purely mechanistic. Attention has been paid to the quality of the internal

Computer-generated images showing the geometry of the roof domes. The 6m-diameter and 1.5m-high roof domes are manufactured in three pieces so they fit into a pantechnicon lorry for ease of transport. Each roof dome has an 'eyebrow' to prevent glare from the low-angled sun and the glazed area of the dome acts as a smoke vent. In the event of a major fire the entire roof dome softens and collapses to allow heat to escape, thus reducing the risk of the steel structure supporting the roof reaching the critical temperature at which it would fail.

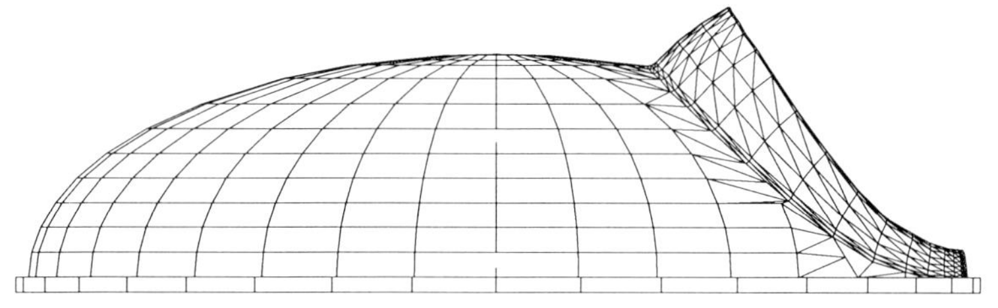

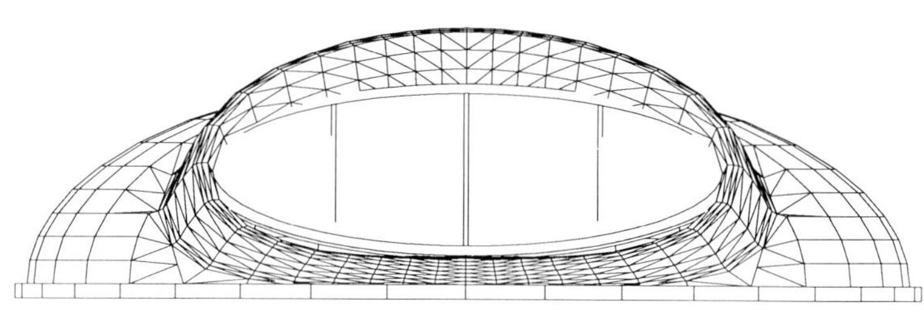

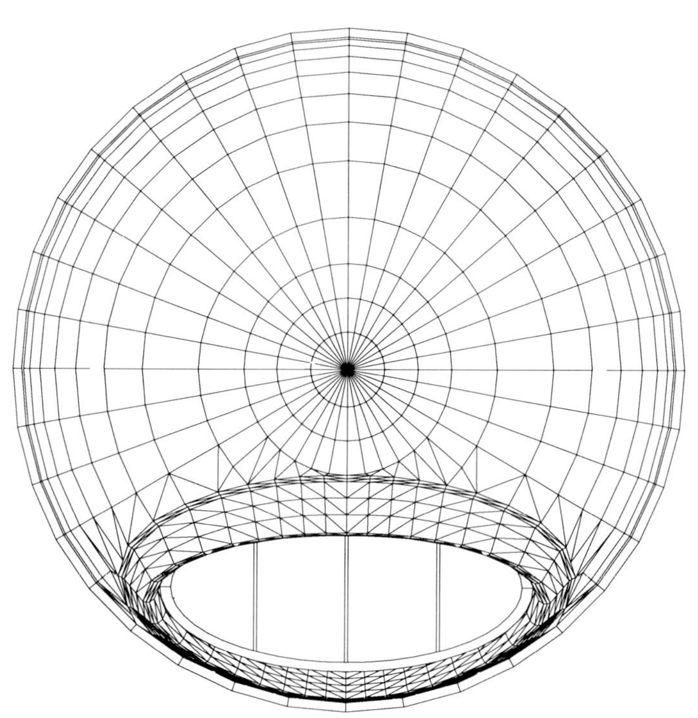

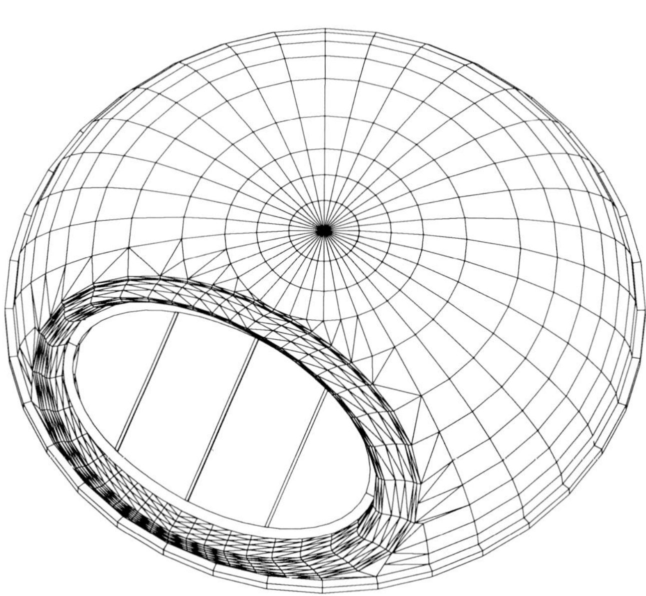

Interior view of the cladding system looking out into the courtyard.

View looking along the vertical junction between cladding panels.

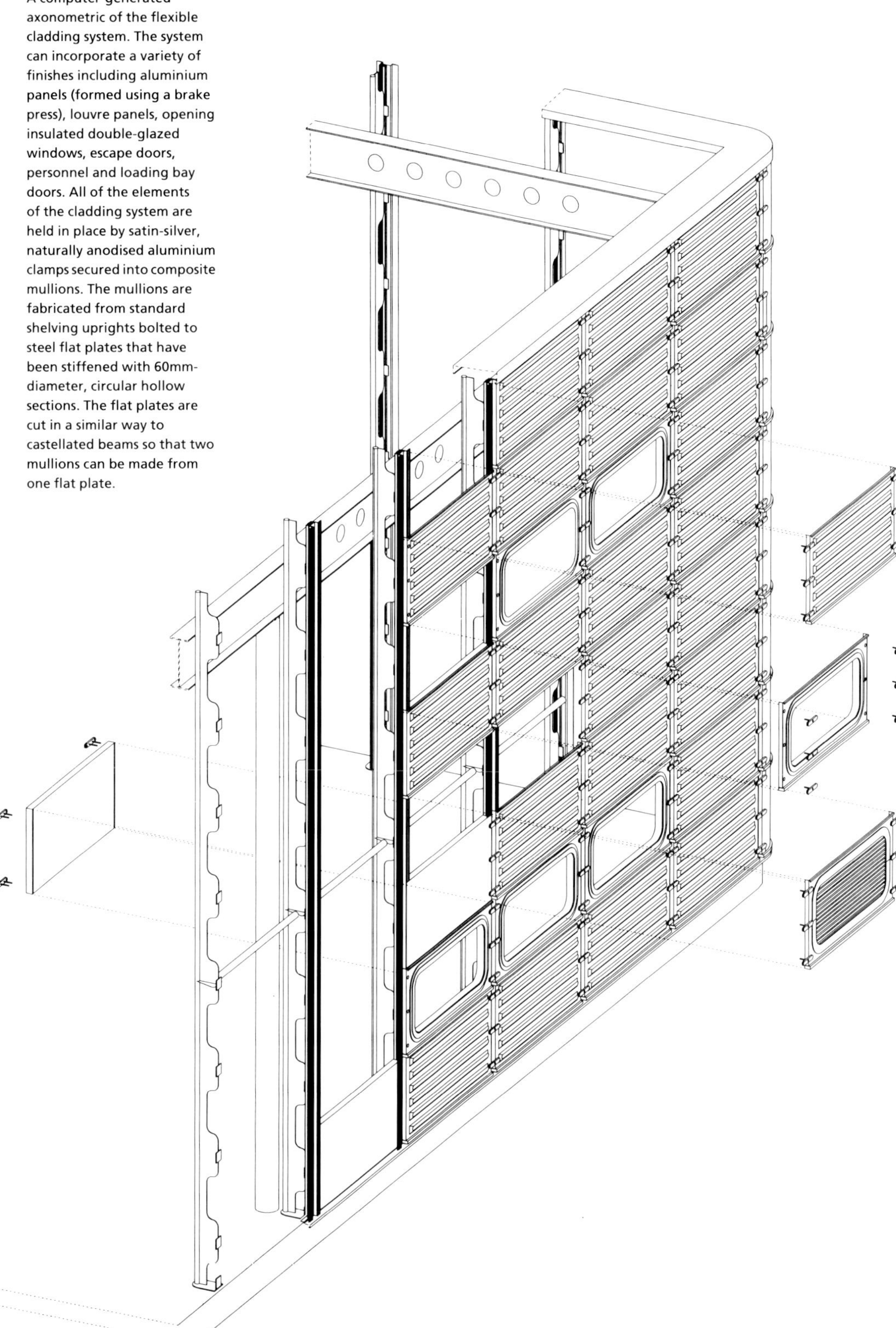

A computer-generated axonometric of the flexible cladding system. The system can incorporate a variety of finishes including aluminium panels (formed using a brake press), louvre panels, opening insulated double-glazed windows, escape doors, personnel and loading bay doors. All of the elements of the cladding system are held in place by satin-silver, naturally anodised aluminium clamps secured into composite mullions. The mullions are fabricated from standard shelving uprights bolted to steel flat plates that have been stiffened with 60mm-diameter, circular hollow sections. The flat plates are cut in a similar way to castellated beams so that two mullions can be made from one flat plate.

environment. In each of the four blocks the structural pylon rises from a central landscaped courtyard (each one is planted to flourish in a different season), which bring daylight into the workplaces and a degree of enclosure and intimacy otherwise lacking in Igus' somewhat barren site. Abundant natural light comes from the roof, and mechanical ventilation has been minimised. With air entering through the walls at low level, the opening rooflights create a stack effect that draws air through the entire building.

The building also seeks to give visual expression to its technical thinking. The construction is highly legible, offering the same satisfaction as comprehending the workings of any machine. The purpose of each element is made clear, and the building is visibly an assembly of components. In the pods and the cladding the boundaries between the fixed and the moving parts are delineated. At the point where so much transience begins to disquiet, the building finds coherence through its four-square geometry and the masts' decisive assertion of stability and fixity.

Igus is the latest in a line of flexible, panelled, wide-span buildings that goes back to the Herman Miller factories and Grimshaw's other industrial projects of the Seventies. This is the work on the strength of which Blase chose Grimshaw. What he has got is the most sophisticated building of the genre, and one which also serves its purpose as a landmark. In a largely featureless landscape, the masted structure is conspicuous from the nearby *autobahn*, the railway line and even the flight paths to the airport. It announces, as Blase intended, a company and building wedded to inventiveness.

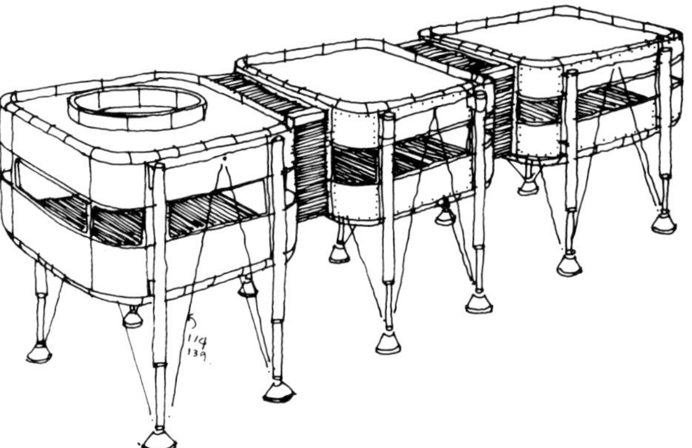

A sketch by Mark Bryden of the internal office pods. The pods contain general administration offices, while the space directly beneath forms 'factory offices' where quality control, research and development or testing can be carried out. These spaces serve as a buffer zone between the noise of the factory and the quiet of the administration areas above. It is envisaged that future pods will be able to be dismantled and moved at short notice.

An interior view of the factory looking towards the internal pod that houses shower rooms and toilets. The staircase leads up to the first-floor walkway, which forms a direct route through the building.

The distinctive pod legs frame the service route and the main circulation route across the factory floor.

A view along the roof, showing the pylon structure and its cables, and the north-facing domes.

The 'hand' detail of the pylon structure; two rods are fixed to the top of the pylon and this assembly allows individual rods to be connected to the main steel structure in the correct locations. Strain guages can be seen in the top right corner of the photograph.

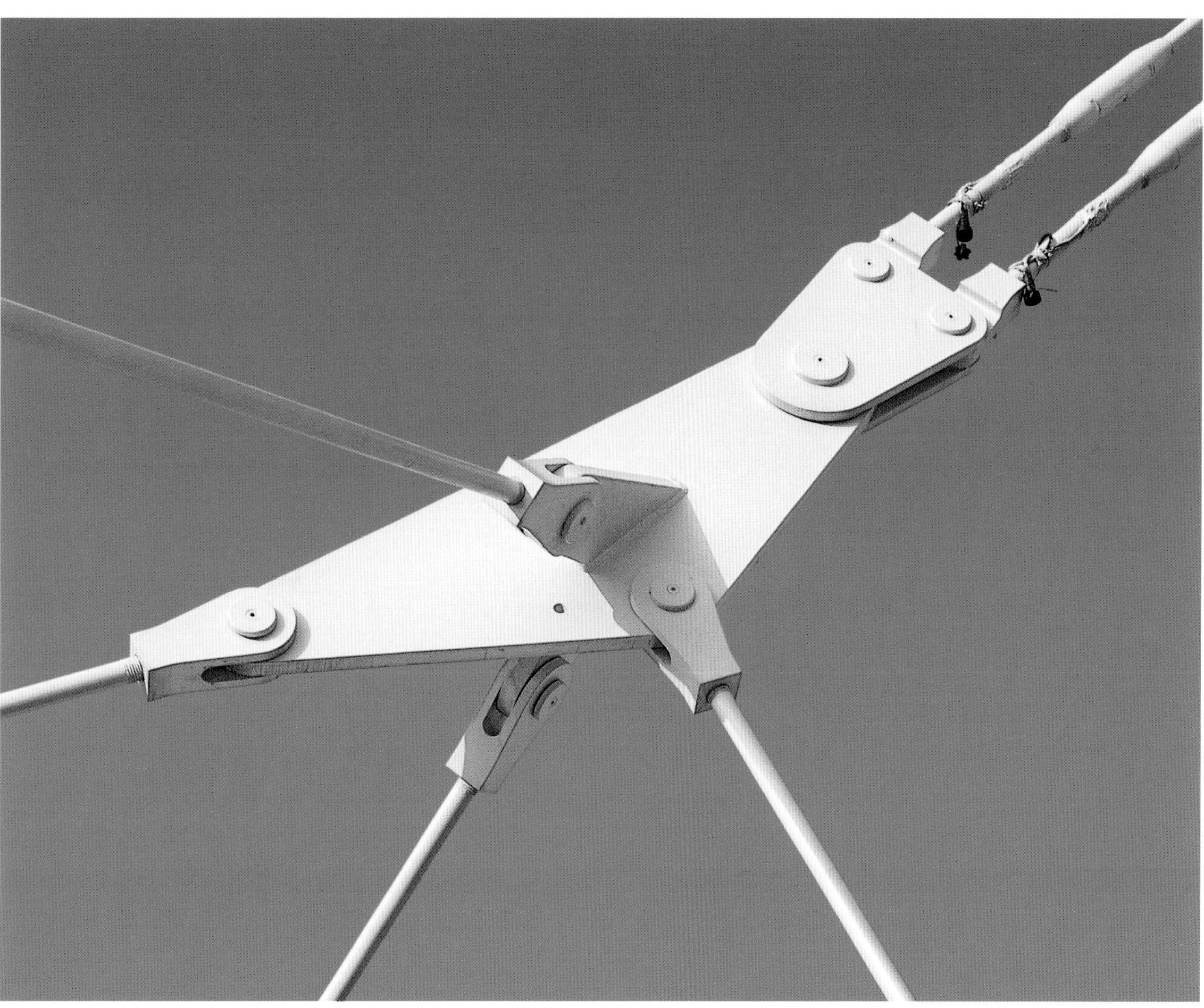

View of the finished building.

Main external escape stair.

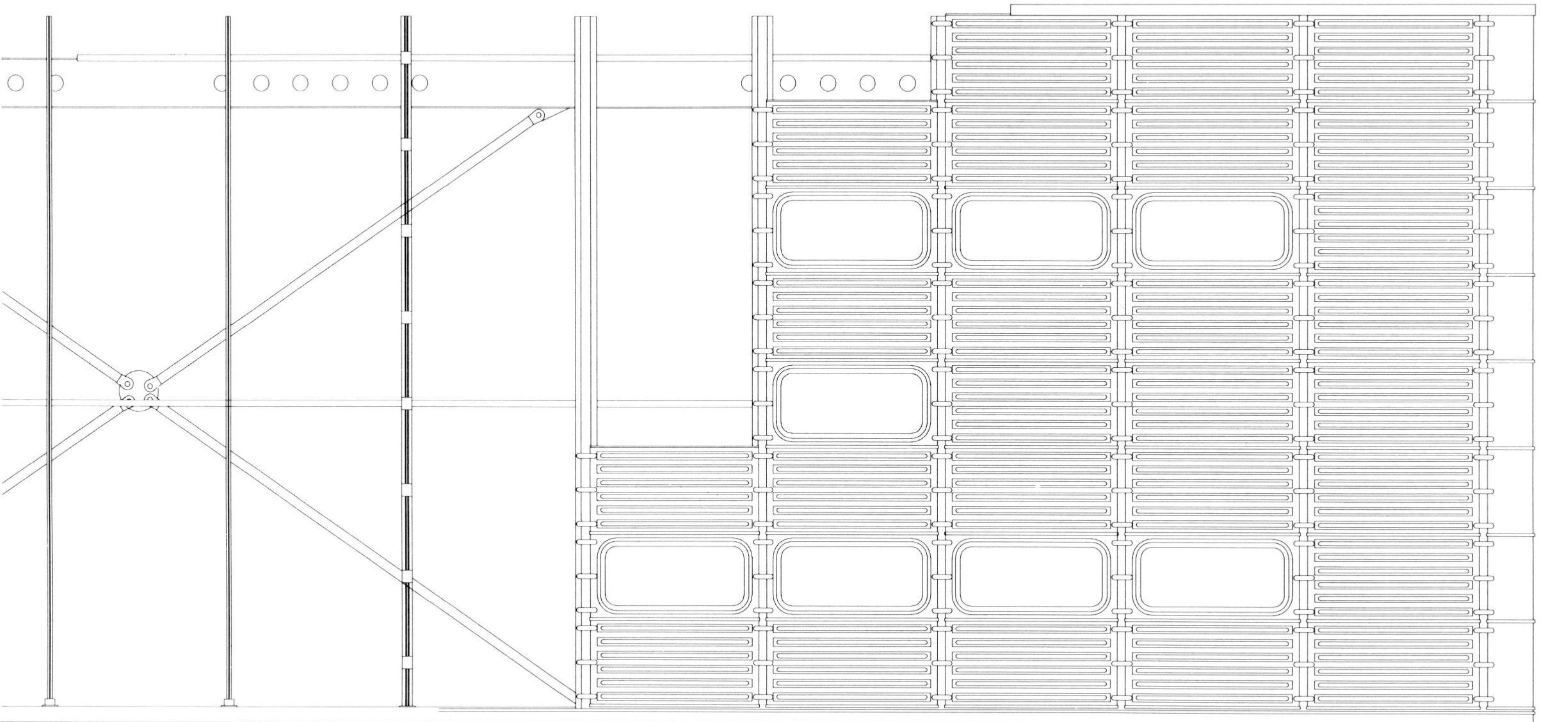

Drawing of the cladding system in various stages of assembly, showing the main structure, secondary structure, cladding metalwork, panels and windows.

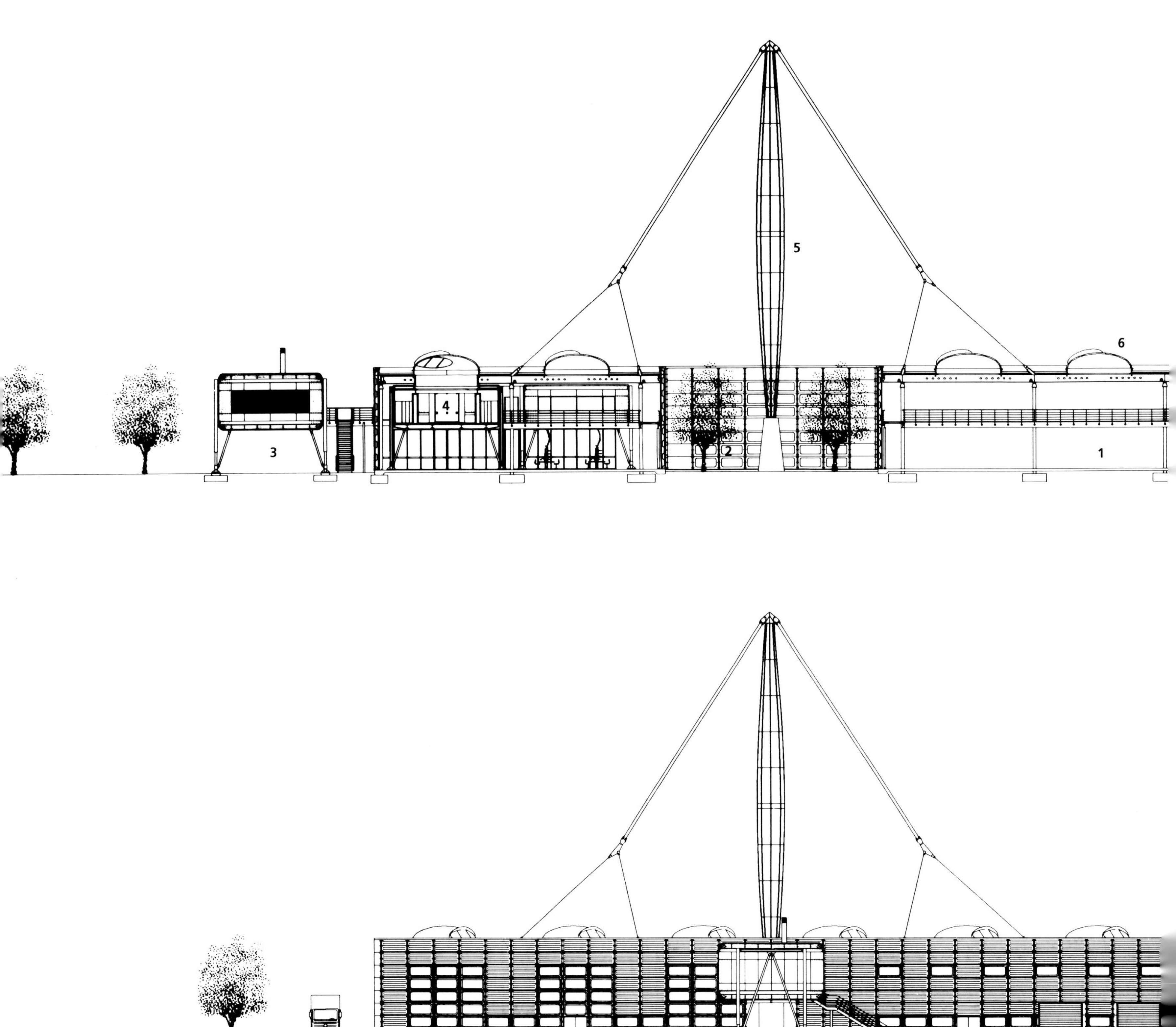

Nicholas Grimshaw & Partners

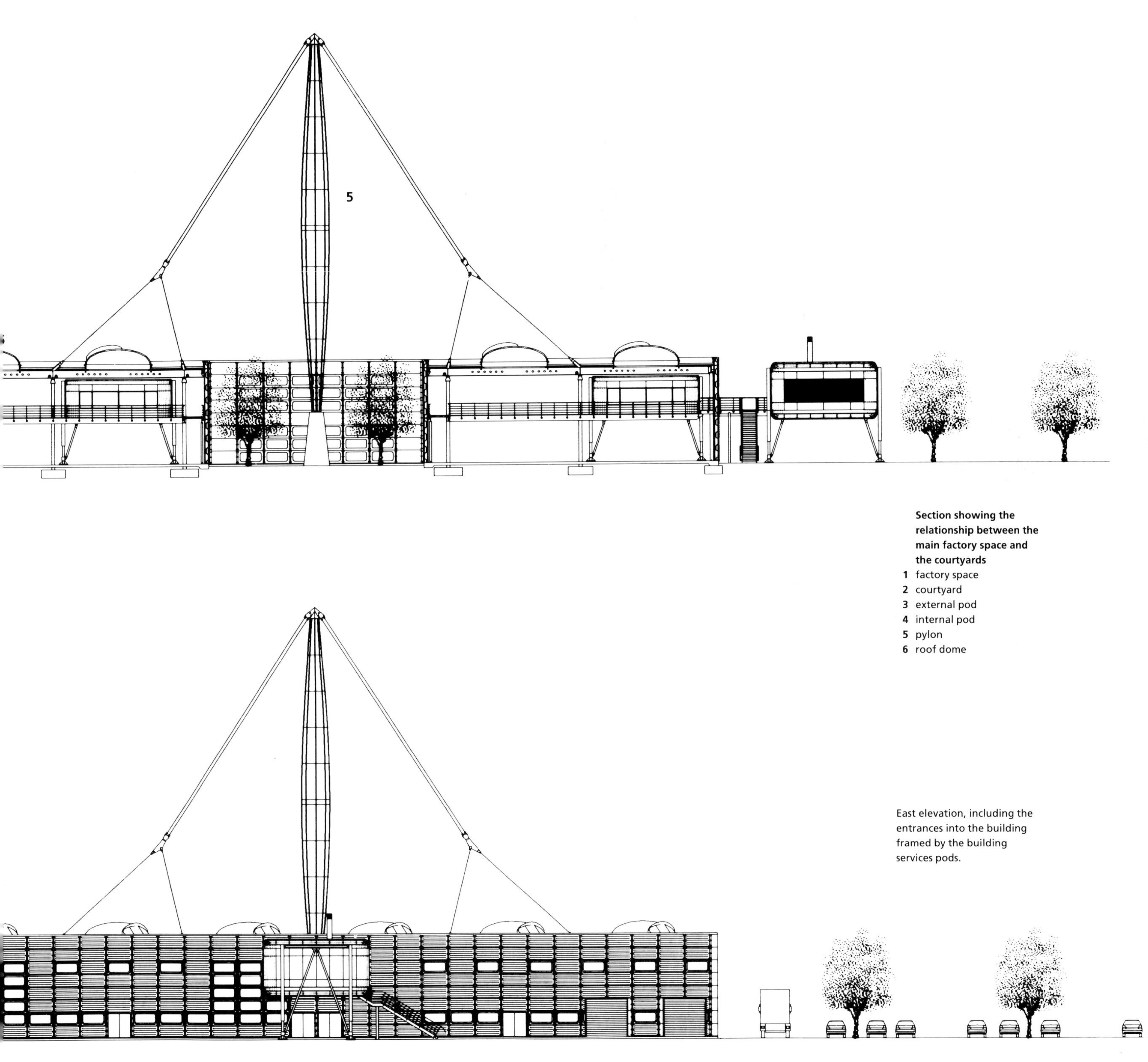

Section showing the relationship between the main factory space and the courtyards

1 factory space
2 courtyard
3 external pod
4 internal pod
5 pylon
6 roof dome

East elevation, including the entrances into the building framed by the building services pods.

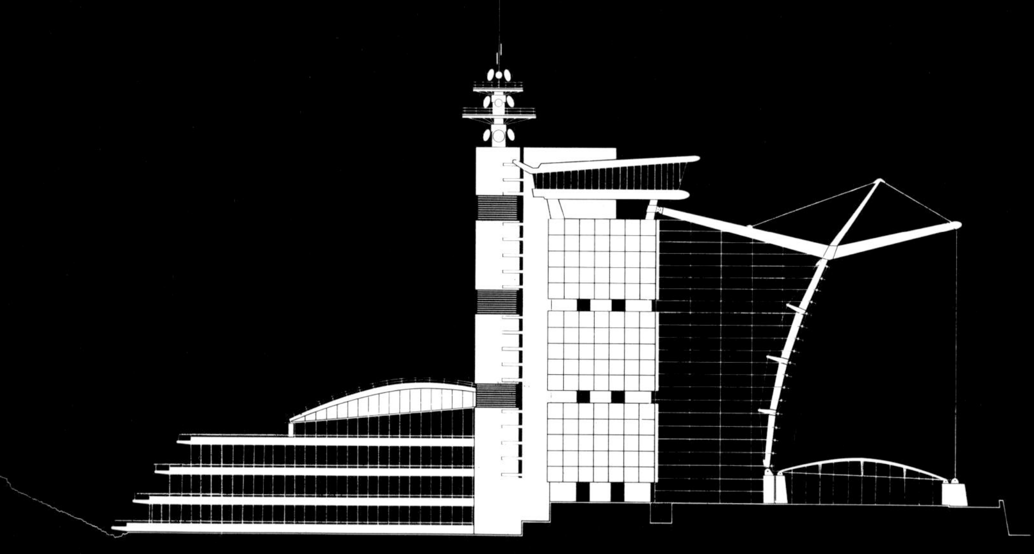

Bibliothèque Nationale de France, Competition, 1989

'The Bibliothèque Nationale had to be not simply a vast and historic store of books but also a living organism of evolving collections. It seemed to us essential to offer the most up-to-date, information-retrieval system for every form of communication, from the written word to film and television. We felt this process should be displayed to the world. We sought to create a public street or spine from which people could reach all the libraries and also see the automated book-retrieval process happening before their eyes. The site on the River Seine was spectacular and we felt that maximum use should be made of it. A brilliantly lit wall of books could be seen even from the other side of the river. At night there was a plan to project images onto the face of the building, which would have added greatly to the riverside scene.' **NG**

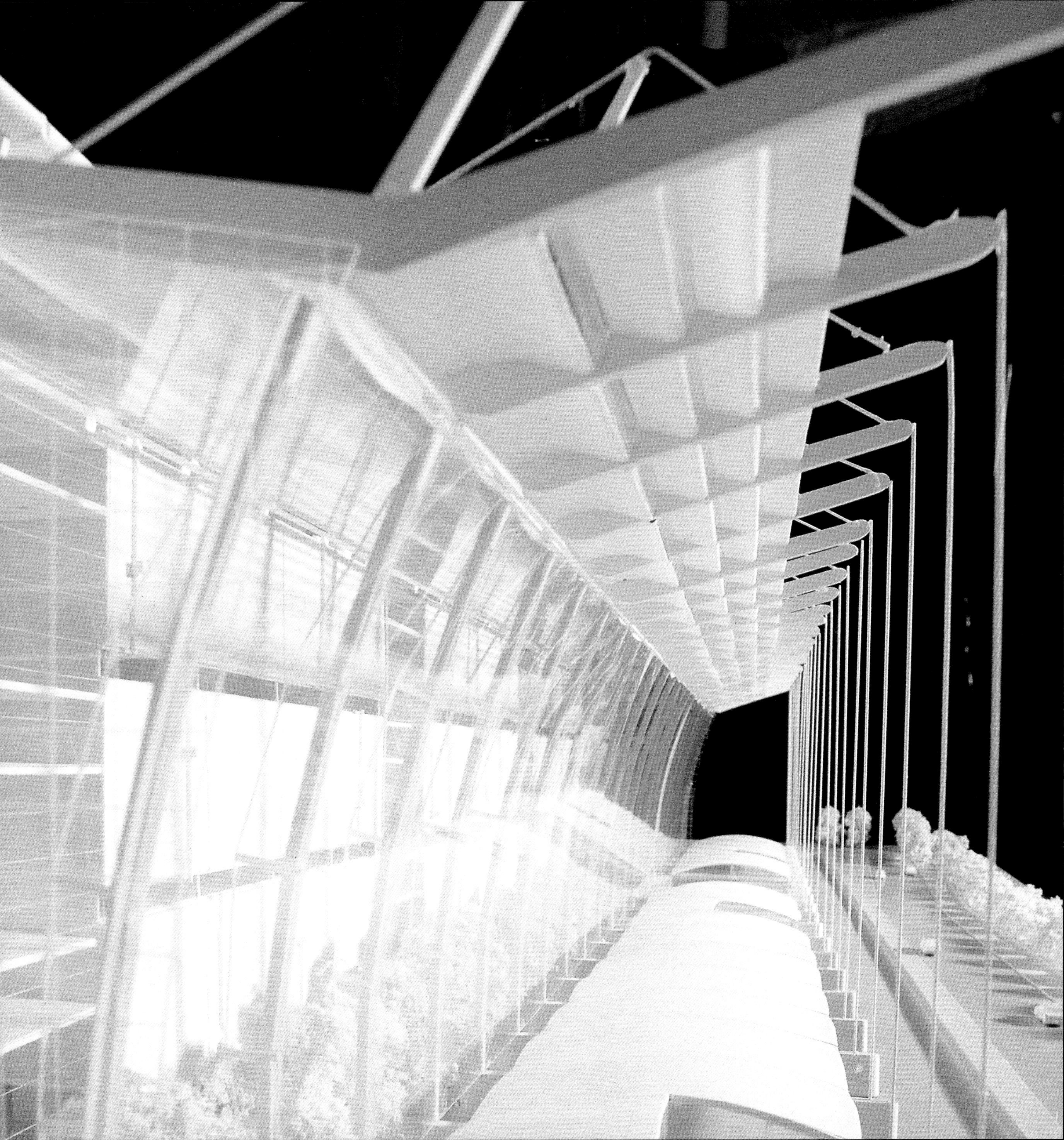

Previous page
Detail of the model with robotised book-retrieval system on the left.

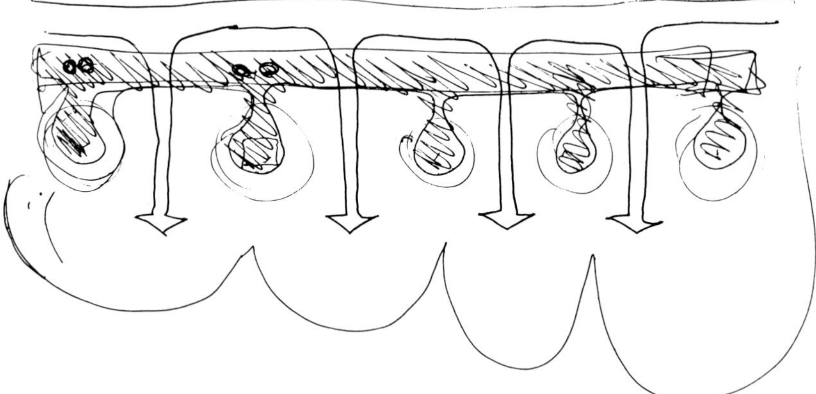

Nick Grimshaw's conceptual sketch showing how the central wall of books separates quiet contemplative spaces of the four individual libraries from the bustling internal street.

Grimshaw's competition design for the Bibliothèque Nationale in Paris replaces the enclosed, torpid quality associated with libraries with transparency and animation. In this, his principal tool is an extendible 14-storey storage wall containing 7 million books that presents itself to Paris through an immense, reflection-free, concave glass wall. For conservation reasons, the books are not visible, but are represented by a series of containers and a robotic retrieval system, so that the activity of the library is expressed as a continually shifting spectacle of travelling carriers. This machine-in-a-window recalls other Grimshaw designs such as the *Western Morning News* building and is this project's big idea, but the Bibliothèque is many times larger than Western Morning News and rather more complex. The design, therefore, operates at several different scales and levels.

At the largest scale (Grimshaw calls it a 'European' scale), it is a monument –an image powerful enough, like the other Parisian *grands projets*, to project itself across the Continent. In its more immediate setting it is a memorable piece of structure that forms a set piece with the Parc de Bercy across the River Seine. Huge screens are intended to project images of events to an audience on the opposite bank. Closer to the building's edge, the design generates a public esplanade and connections with the quay. A pedestrian route, open at all hours, penetrates the library, continues across the Seine over a bridge and connects with the Parc de Bercy. A raised terrace, overlooking the river, runs round the building's front perimeter.

The public space continues into the library's interior, as controlled but still accessible spaces. A grand, tree-

Nick Grimshaw's sketch showing the principle of a concave, glass wall cutting out sky reflections, and thereby allowing views of the kinetic wall behind.

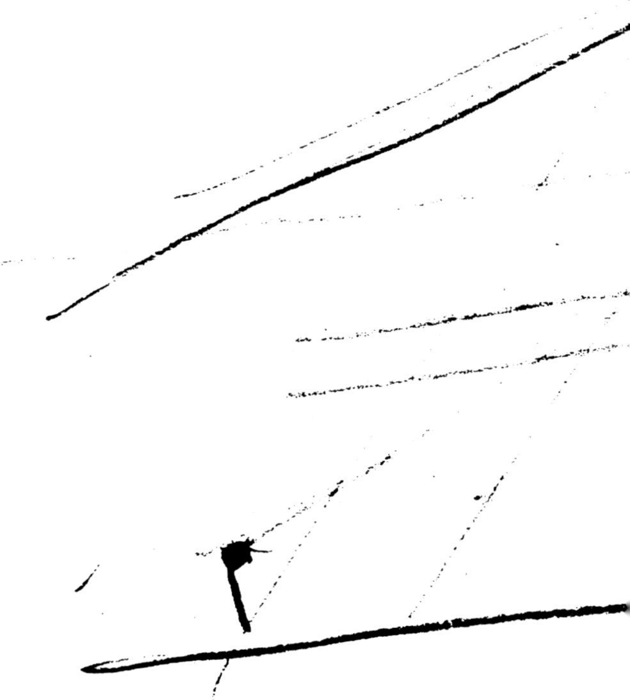

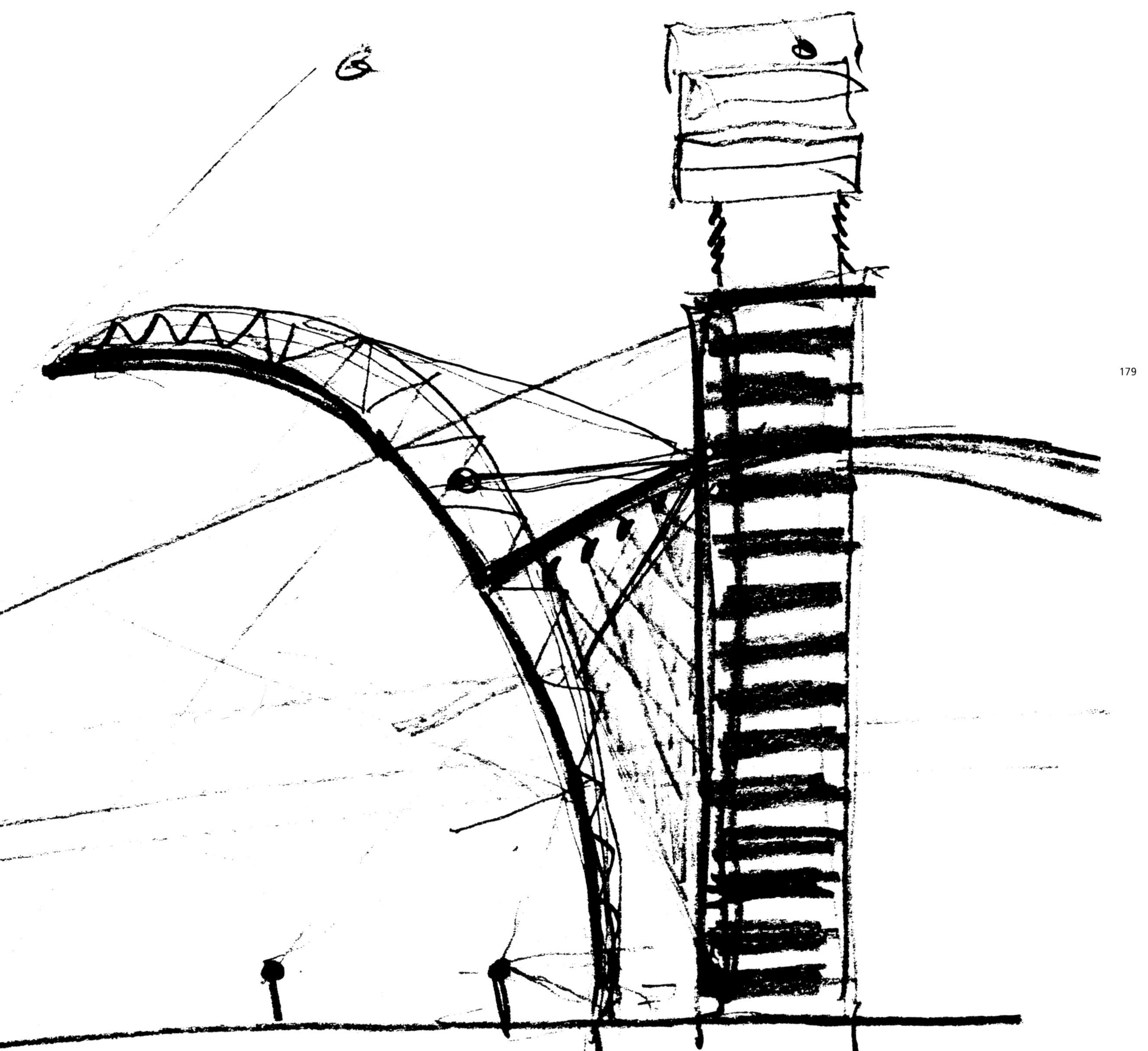

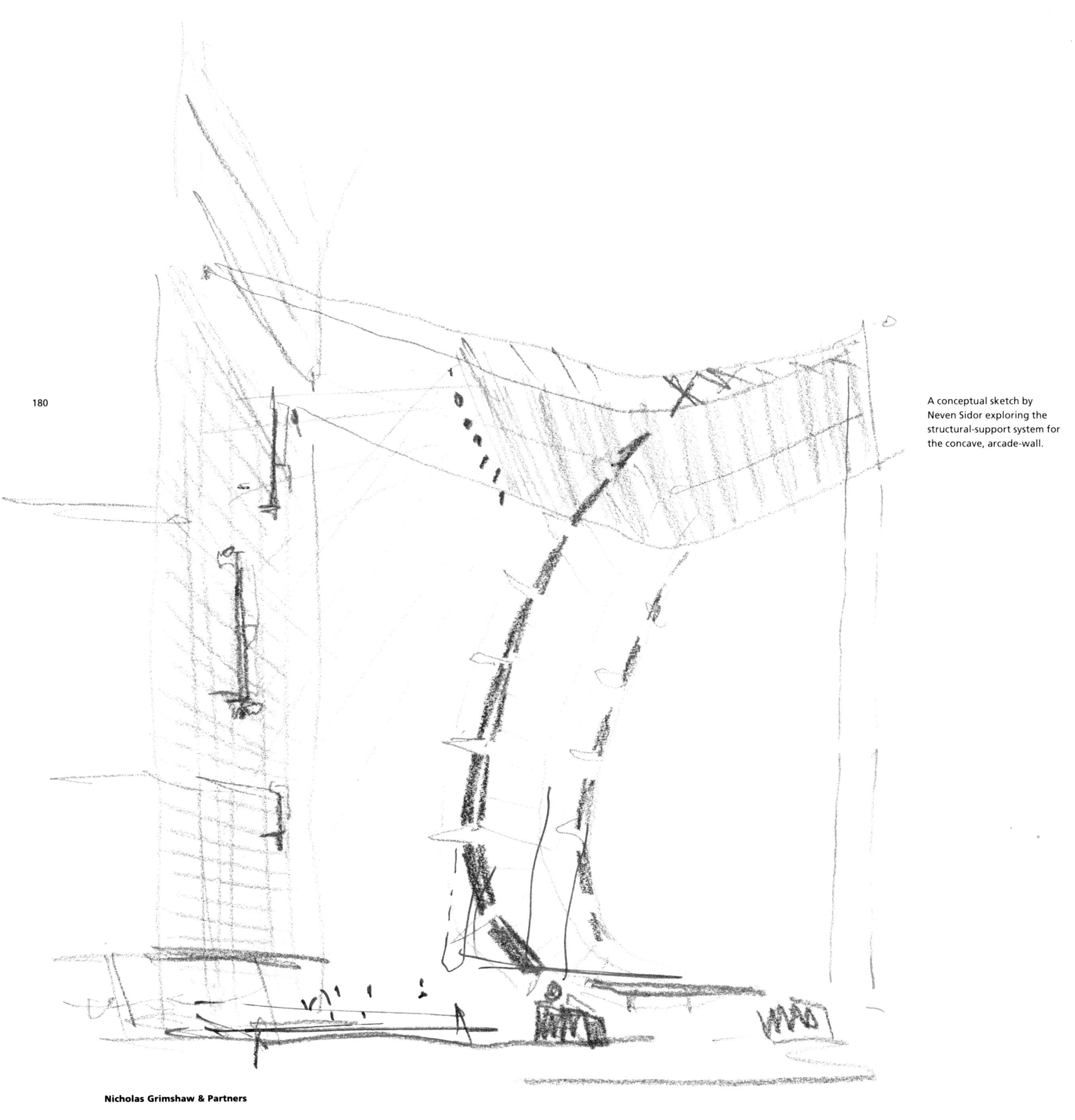

A conceptual sketch by Neven Sidor exploring the structural-support system for the concave, arcade-wall.

Two views of the project model. The site steps down to the River Seine opposite the Parc de Bercy and the scheme tries to exploit this relationship. The robotised wall of books would offer a grand spectacle. The structural outriggers along the building edge create a means of erecting huge cinema screens, for the benefit of people sitting in the park.

lined internal street, which is open all the time, runs the length of the vast space between the stacks and the concave glass wall. Along one side a low, curved roof shelters a loose arrangement of the more public, less strictly controlled rooms of the library: a children's library, a lending library, exhibition space, cafés and restaurants. These look out to the park, the river, and to the quays and terraces.

On the other side of the internal street, openings in the book storage wall lead into the more specialist areas, the reference and research reading rooms and the audio, media and film and video libraries. These quieter spaces occupy a stepped, three-storey structure, penetrated by clerestory-lit internal courts, which is sunk into an enclosed garden. The garden is sheltered from the streets outside by a colonnade supporting a three-storey office building. The storage wall itself is inhabited by administrative offices, served by five lift towers. At the top, a floor of offices looks out onto spectacular views of Paris.

From the scale of the city to that of individual working areas, the design articulates a progression from public to individual, and from active to reflective. The storage wall and its glass portico serve not only as a spectacular object, but as the means by which the site is divided into two parts: the more public spaces that relate to the city outside and a more introverted area for contemplative work.

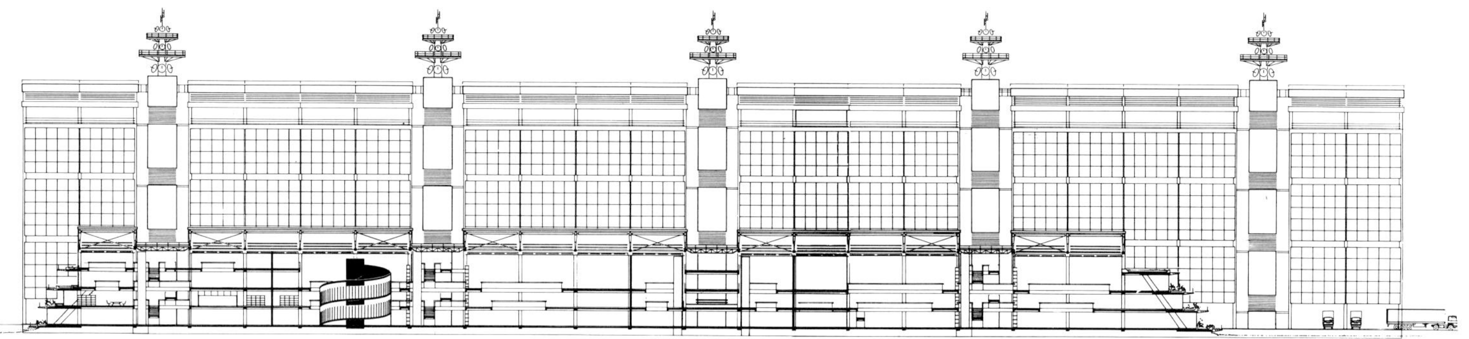

Cross section through terraced, three-storey libraries.

Ground-floor plan

1 ancillary open and covered public spaces (shops, restaurants, etc)
2 grand internal boulevard
3 zone of vertical, robotised storage
4 wall of books
5 terraced, three-storey libraries

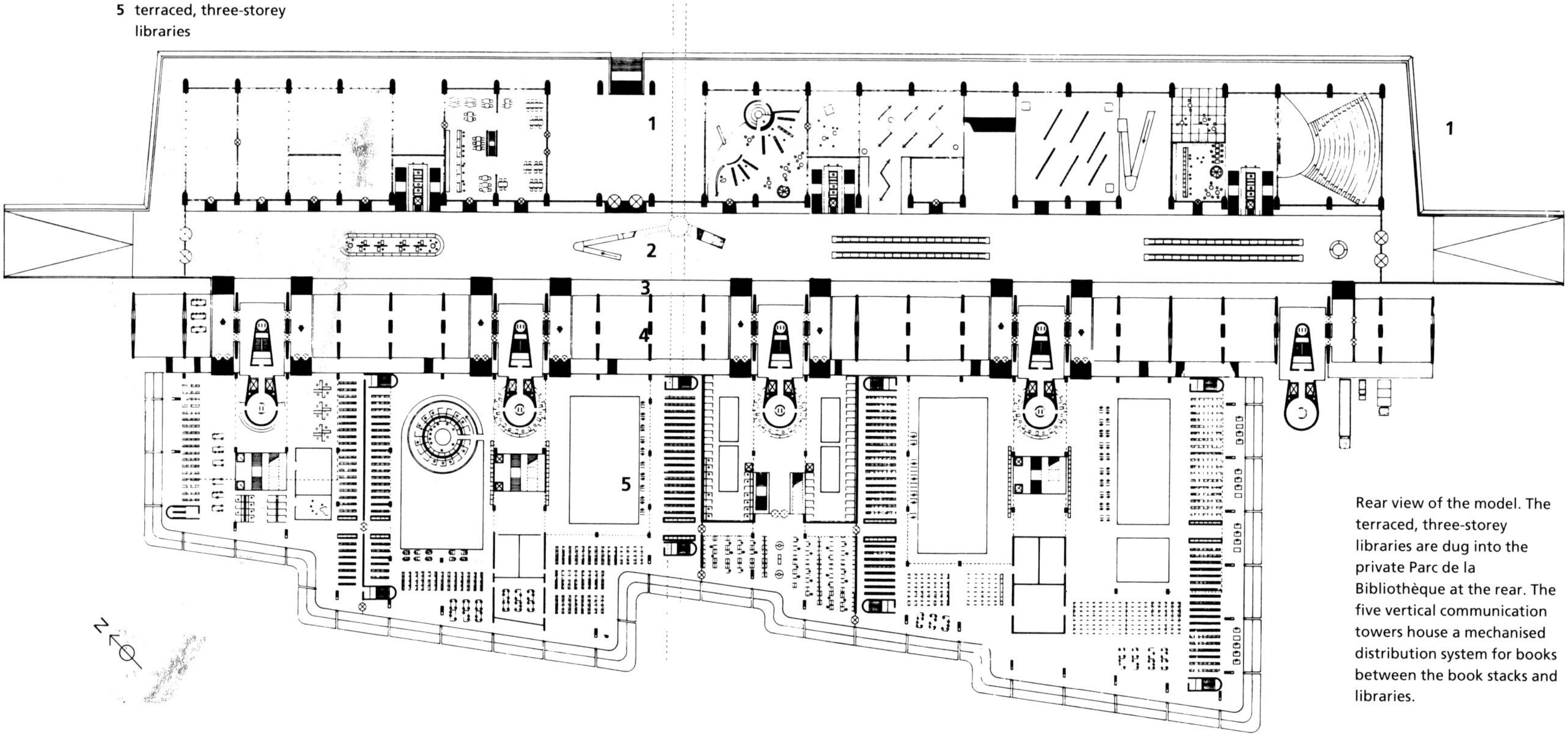

Rear view of the model. The terraced, three-storey libraries are dug into the private Parc de la Bibliothèque at the rear. The five vertical communication towers house a mechanised distribution system for books between the book stacks and libraries.

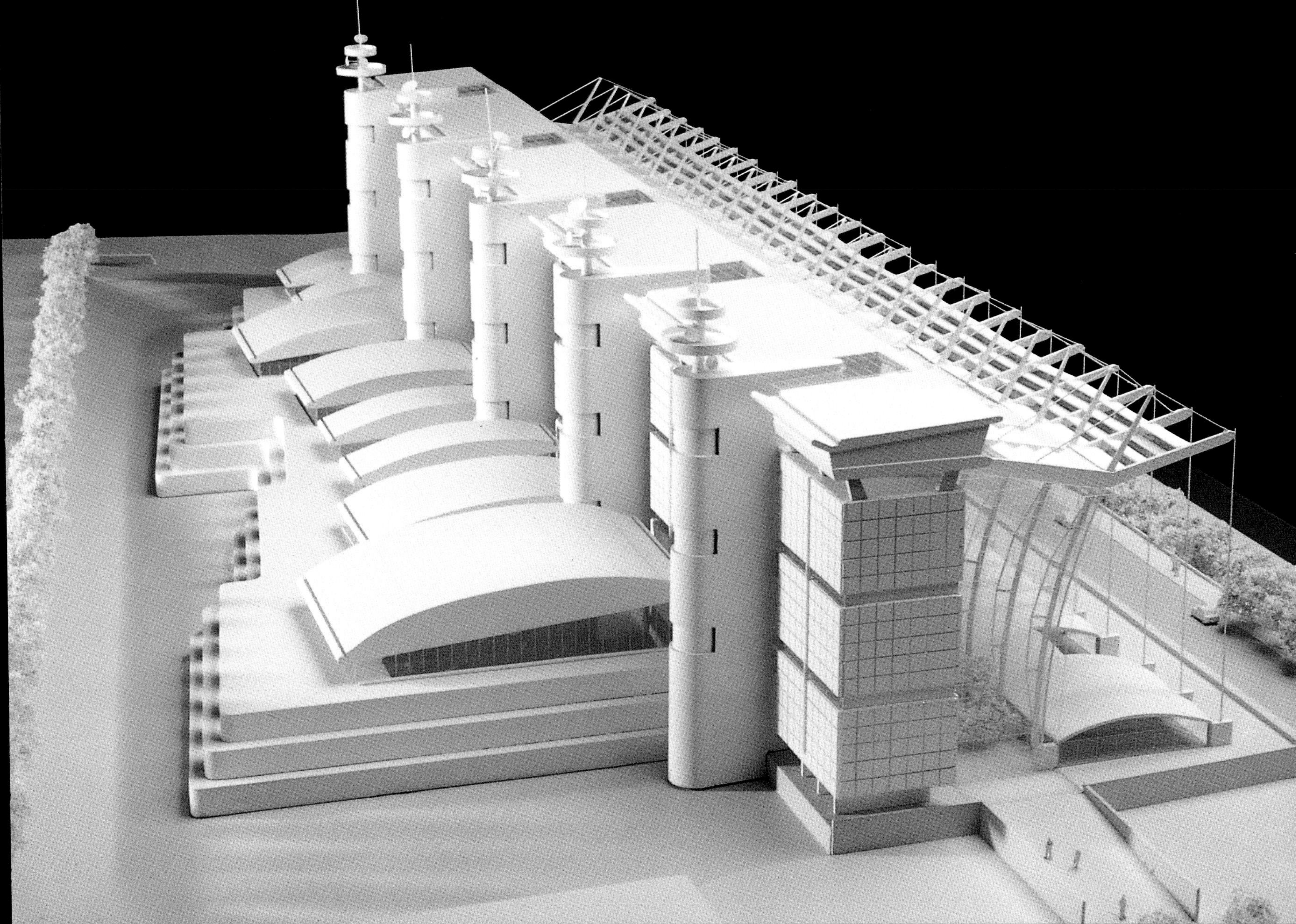

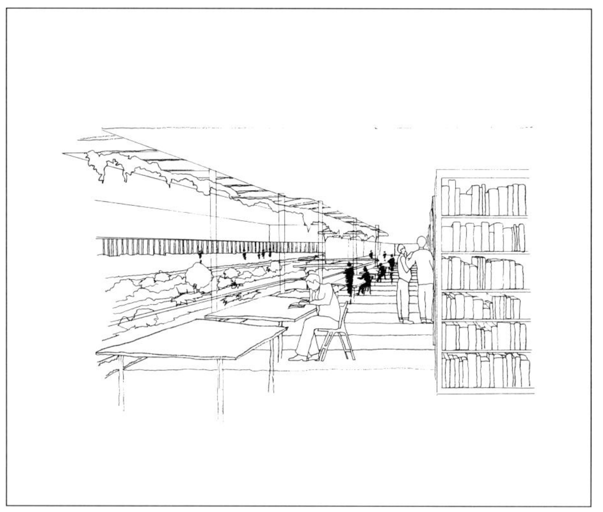

Neven Sidor's freehand sectional perspective through the principal building elements. Reading right to left: projection zone; terraced bars/restaurants etc; concave, glass wall; Boulevard de la Bibliothèque; zone for robotised book-retrieval system (these books are in insulated, metal containers and would be the more popular titles), static, archive-book storage with librarians' offices on every fifth floor, three-storey reading libraries grouped around top-lit wells and the Parc de la Bibliothèque.

Two sketch views by Sarah Hare of the reading libraries and restaurant space.

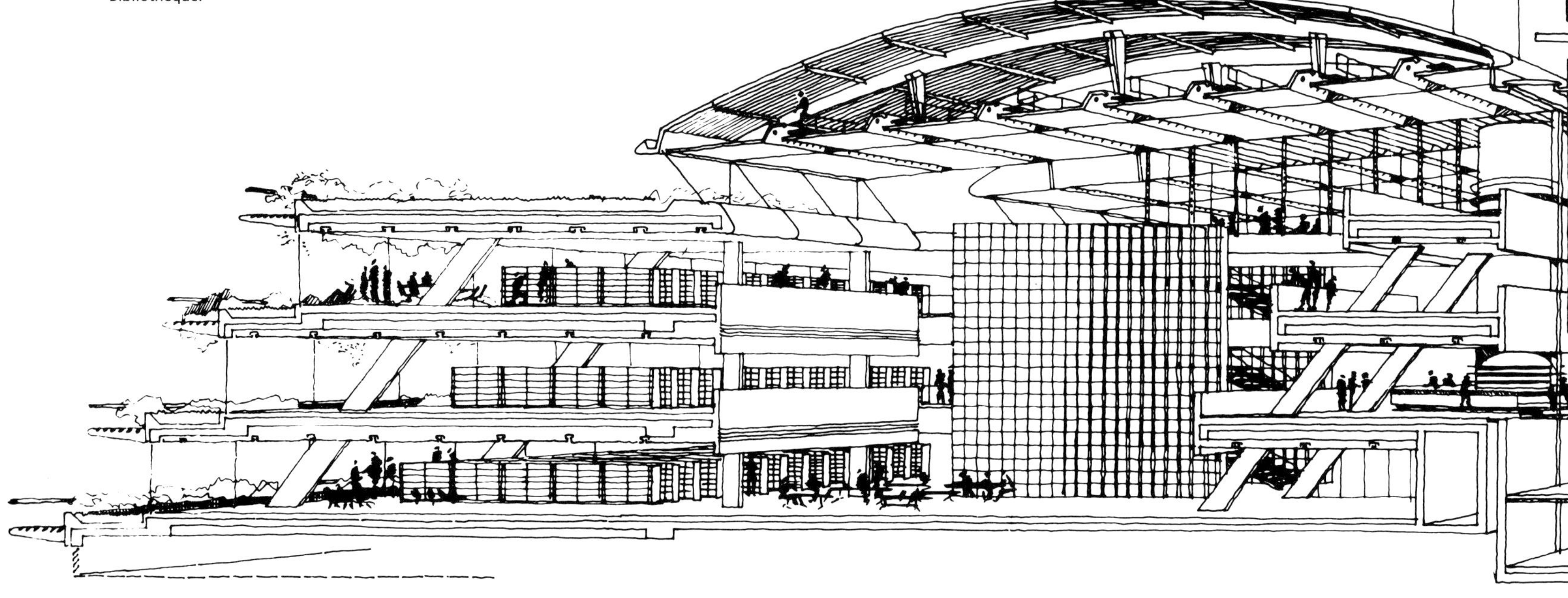

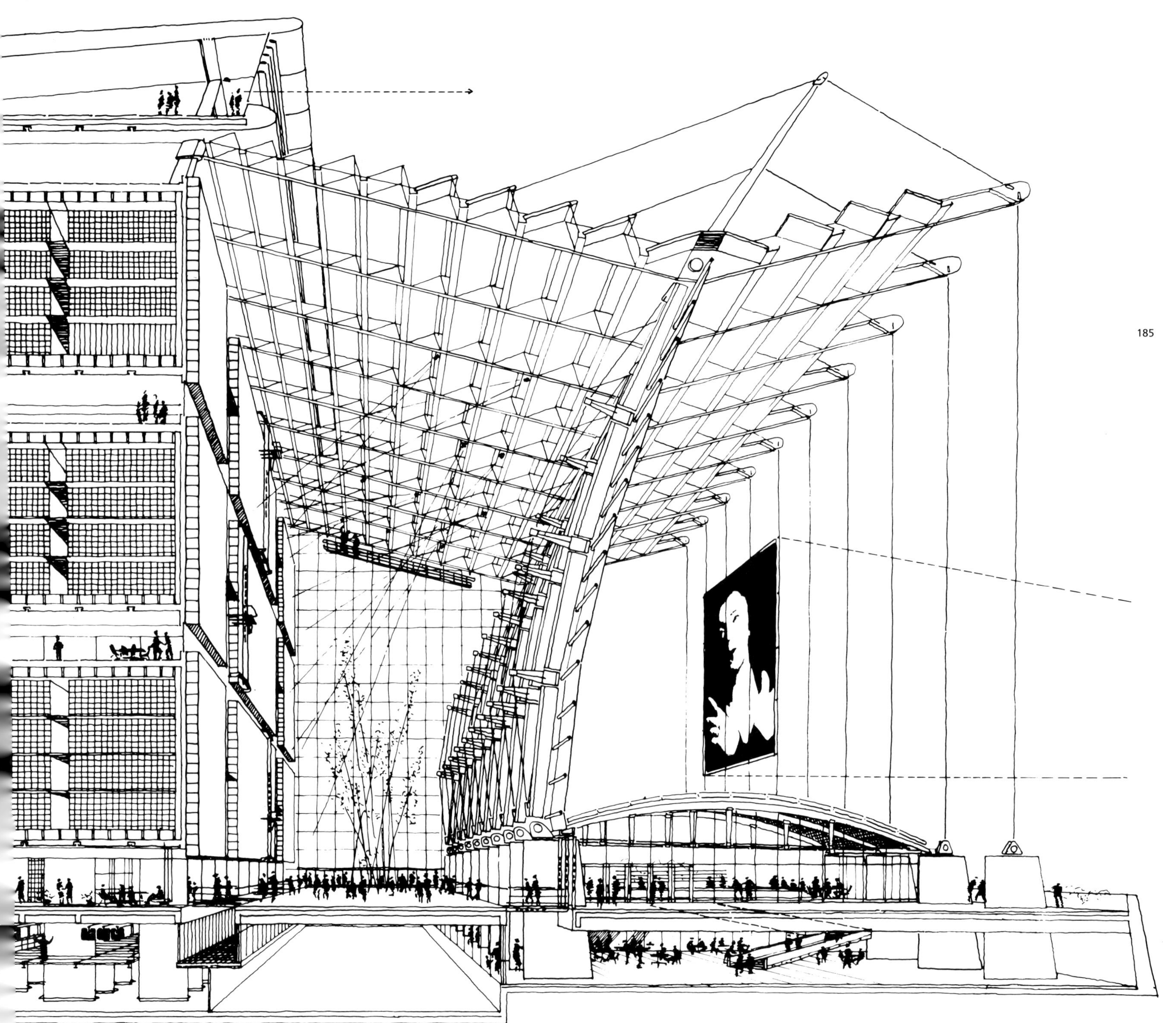

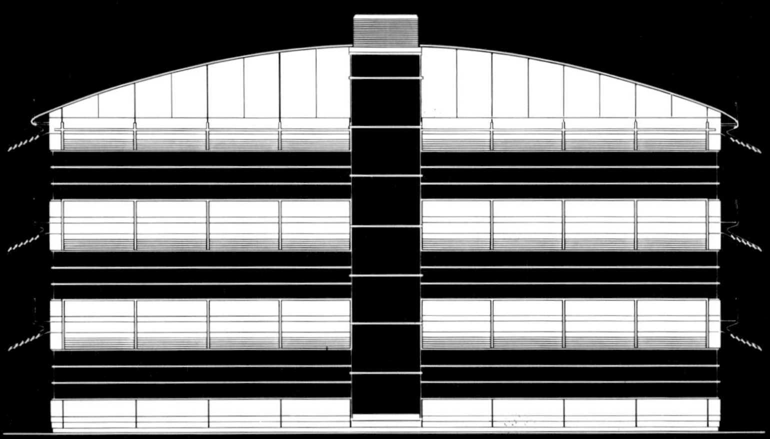

**Hartspsring Business Park,
Watford, 1986–**

'Because office rents were much lower than those in central London, the cost constraints were fierce. We had to ask ourselves what would make someone want to work here? First of all, the location was good: between the M1 and the M25. Secondly, this was real countryside with many amenities nearby and a huge tennis centre over the road. Thirdly, we felt we could genuinely lift people's spirits with the architecture. The buildings were conceived as sleek, low, silver forms with curved roofs helping them to nestle into the countryside. The immediate landscaping, however, was formal and this gradually blended into the fields and hedges surrounding the site. For a car-borne society this is an ideal place to work.' **NG**

Previous page
Study model showing an early version of the glazed stair tower with faceted, glazed end.

A model of a typical, two-storey building at night. It was used to present the scheme to a planning committee, to obtain detailed planning approval.

Site plan showing the arrangement of buildings around central landscaping, with perimeter parking.

The site for Hartspring Business Park, a scheme for 23,225m^2 of speculative offices, derives its value more from its connections with nearby motorways, the M1 and M25, than from the intrinsic quality of its surroundings. The first consideration, therefore, was to devise a plan that would create a pleasant local environment out of what had once been a quarry.

A new entrance route from the more important of the two roads that bound the site leads through the site's untouched eastern section. This part of the site lies just inside the London Green Belt, and so was left undeveloped. From here the entry route faces axially onto a symmetrical group of five buildings that look inwards into a green, pedestrian court with a central pool. The buildings increase in area towards the far end of the court, rising from two storeys to three, and culminate in a large block intended as a headquarters building. This is composed of two wings joined by a transparent glass link. The overall effect of the site plan is an orderly enclave protected from its surroundings by a ring of tree-lined car parks.

The different sizes of the blocks allow for varying patterns of occupation; they can be further subdivided and let in units as small as a quarter of each floor. This variety is achieved within a modular construction system, which is consistent across the site. Although the indeterminate nature of speculative office space gave the design team little to work with, the team sought to create elegant structures out of the considered design of the buildings' essential elements, their walls, glazing and stairs.

The basic cladding for all the buildings is a simple aluminium and glass curtain wall, which is given depth

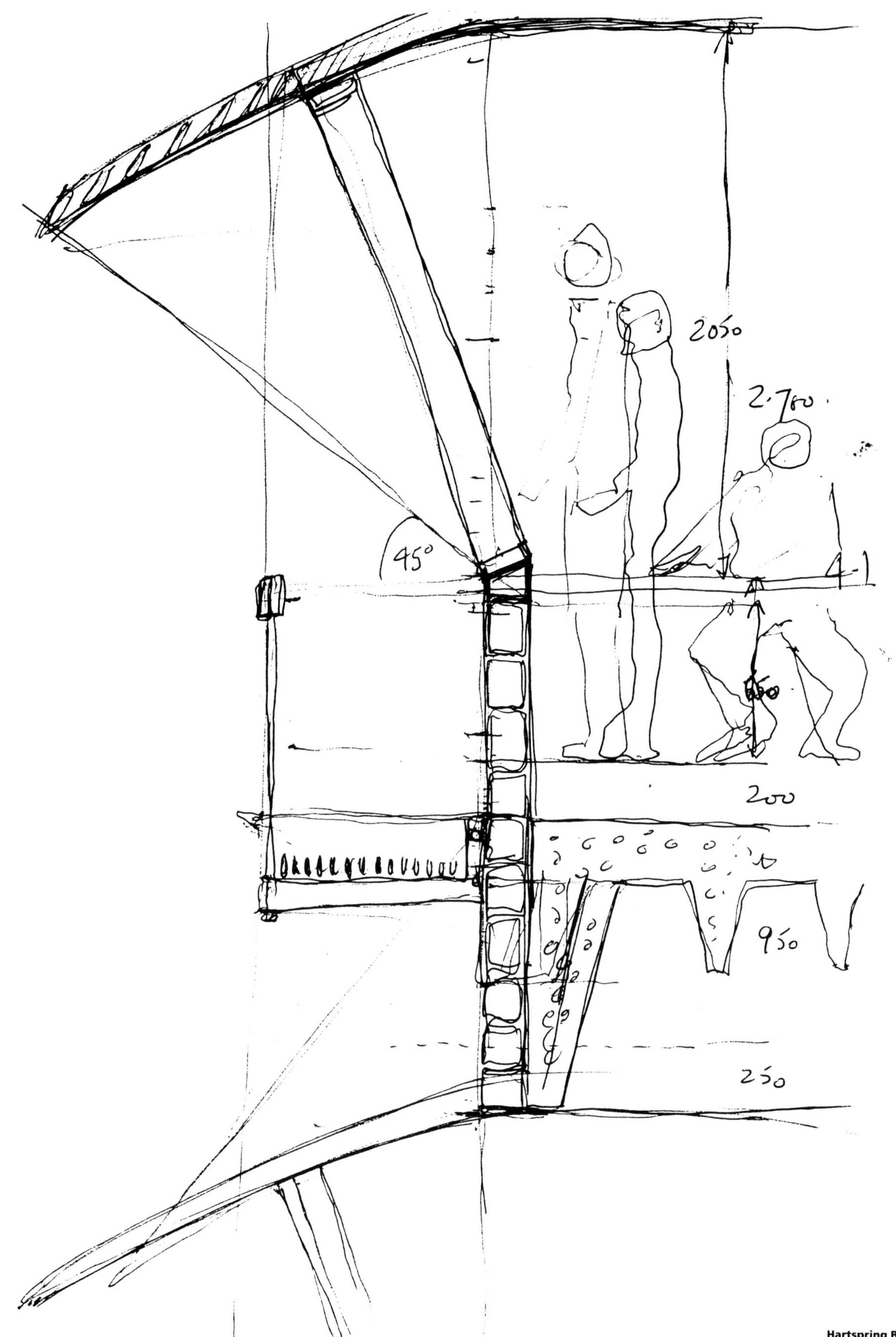

A sketch by Nick Grimshaw illustrating the early development of the envelope.

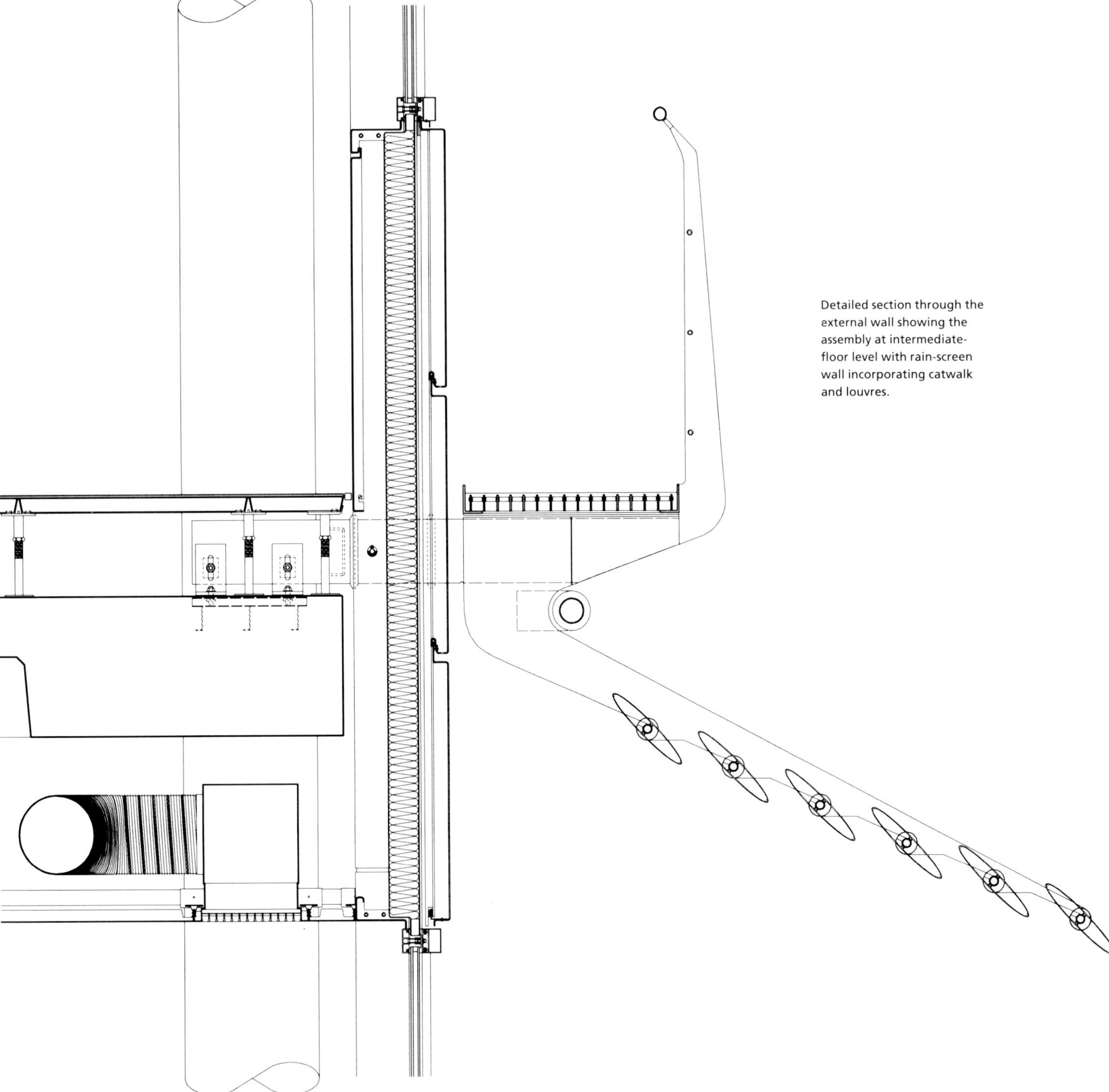

Detailed section through the external wall showing the assembly at intermediate-floor level with rain-screen wall incorporating catwalk and louvres.

by the addition of an external silver-anodised aluminium assembly that comprises louvred sunshades and catwalks. The catwalks continue round the end walls, connecting with the escape stairs, to form a self-sufficient and separate circulation system for maintenance.

Curved roofs of standing-seam aluminium sheets accommodate plant rooms, and the structure is concrete frame. This simple formula is then embellished by special elements. The glazed escape stairs project at either end of the buildings to form rounded, almost decorative objects which, illuminated at night, punctuate the composition with brightly lit towers.

The glazing of the stair towers is detailed to continue the horizontal emphasis of the buildings, with the transoms emphasised and the vertical joints butt-jointed and silicon-sealed, so as to be scarcely visible. This horizontality is then offset by the vertical, full-height entrance screens of suspended planar glazing restrained, in a variation of a favourite Grimshaw detail, by cast brackets connected to tapering masts by steel arms. In the smaller blocks an open, steel staircase spans between the masts and exposed-concrete landings, the soffits of which are lit from below.

In the link block of the headquarters building similar ingredients are used to more dramatic effect. Fair-faced concrete balconies, again lit from below, project from two steel-clad service towers, which are linked across a central void by an assembly of bridges, glass-clad lifts, and an open steel stair with granite treads. Stainless steel arms, with cast brackets at their ends, reach out from the balconies to restrain the suspended planar glazing that encloses both external faces of the link.

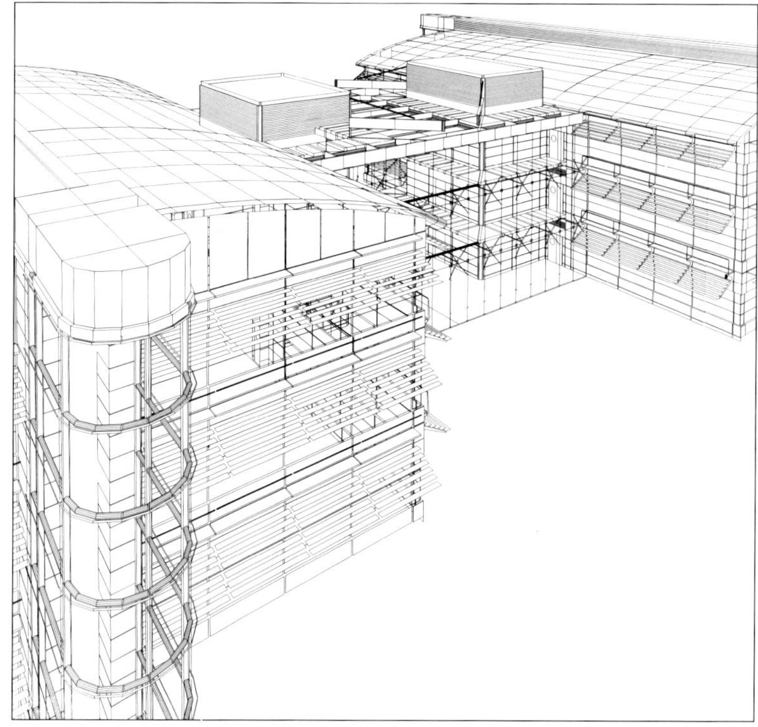

Computer-generated, three-dimensional model. It was used during the detailed design of building one and shows the office wings and glazed link block.

192

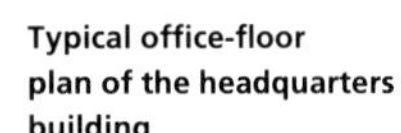

Typical office-floor plan of the headquarters building

1 office space
2 escape stair pod
3 atrium
4 toilet/service core
5 lifts
6 bridge link

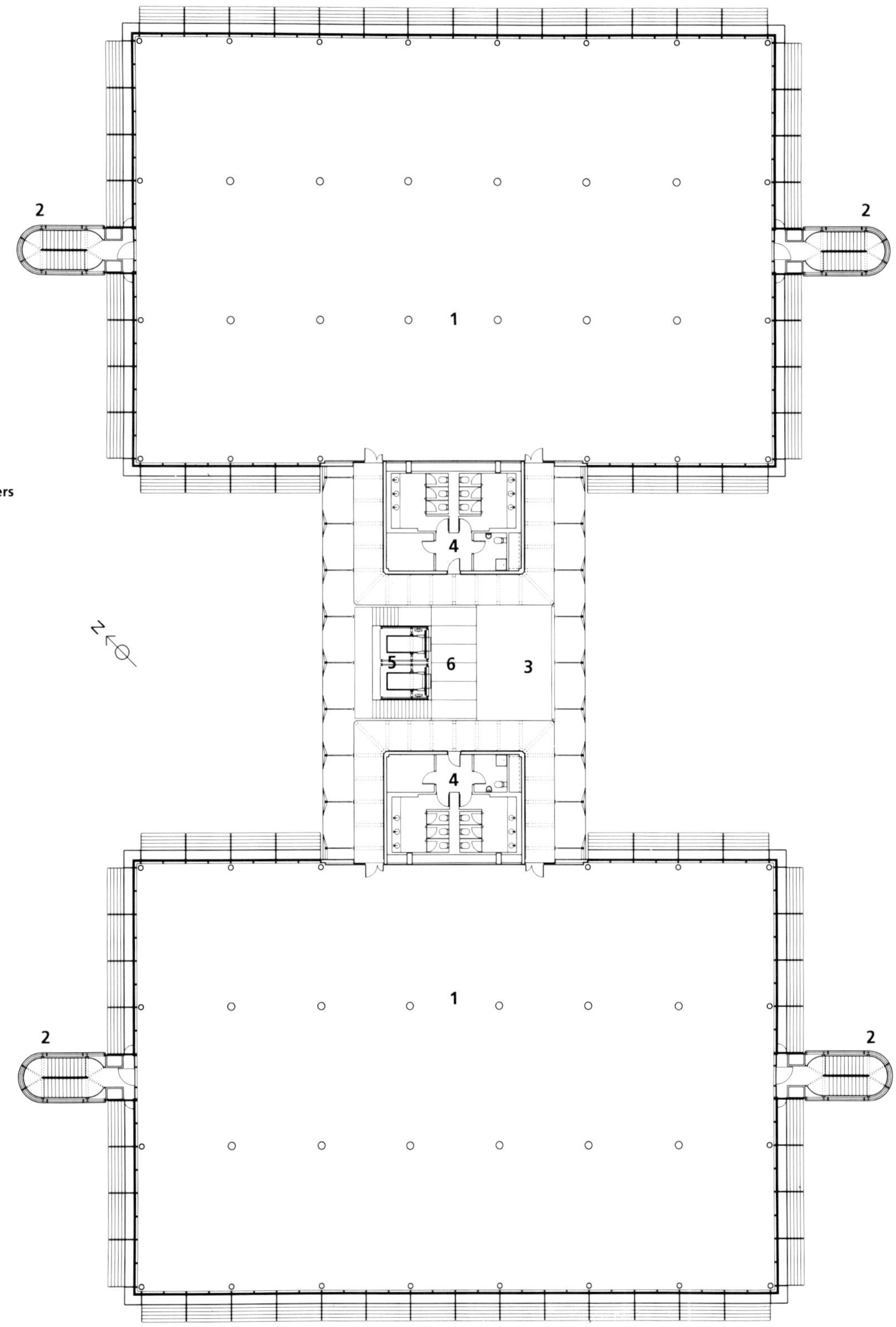

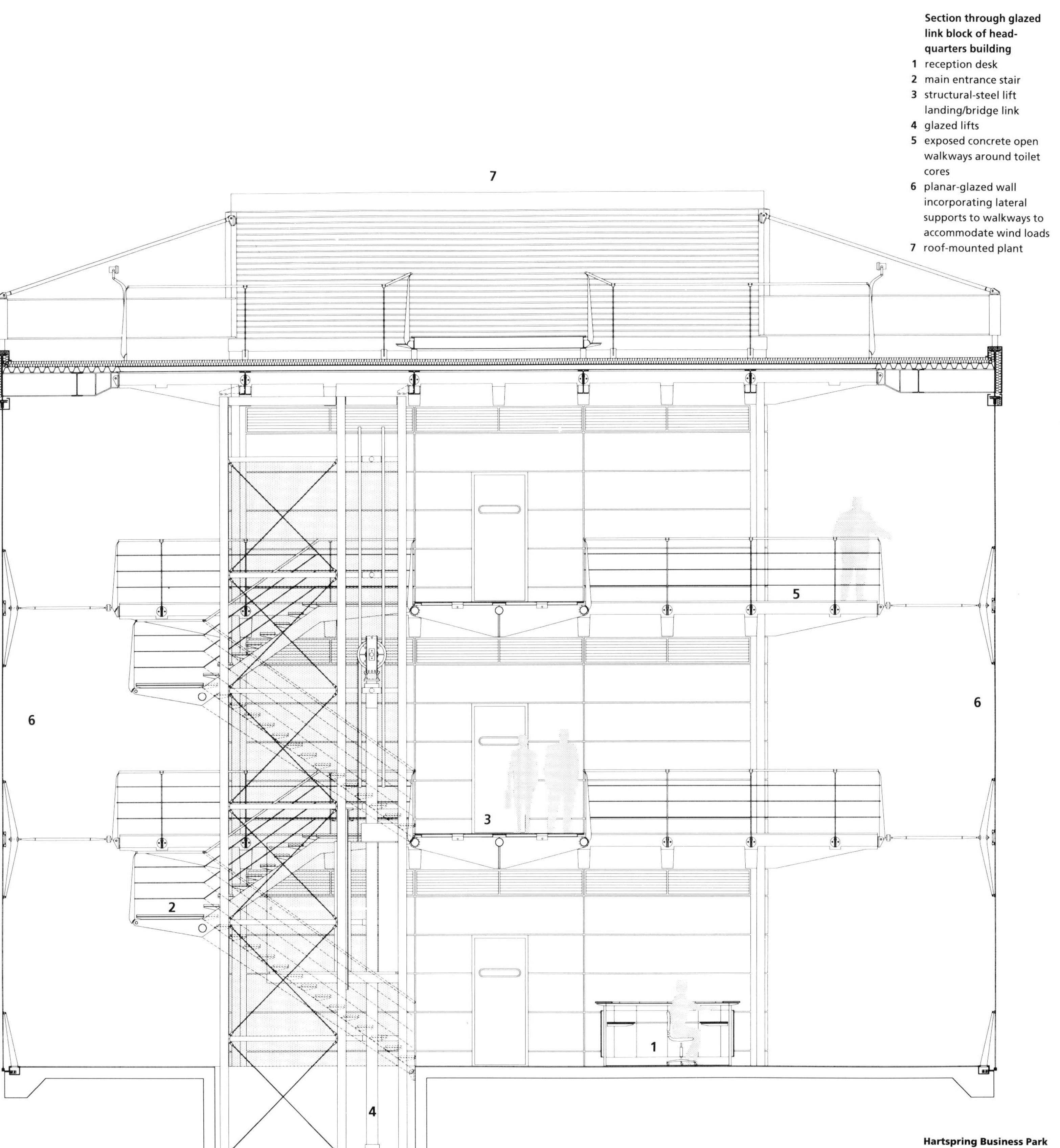

Section through glazed link block of headquarters building
1 reception desk
2 main entrance stair
3 structural-steel lift landing/bridge link
4 glazed lifts
5 exposed concrete open walkways around toilet cores
6 planar-glazed wall incorporating lateral supports to walkways to accommodate wind loads
7 roof-mounted plant

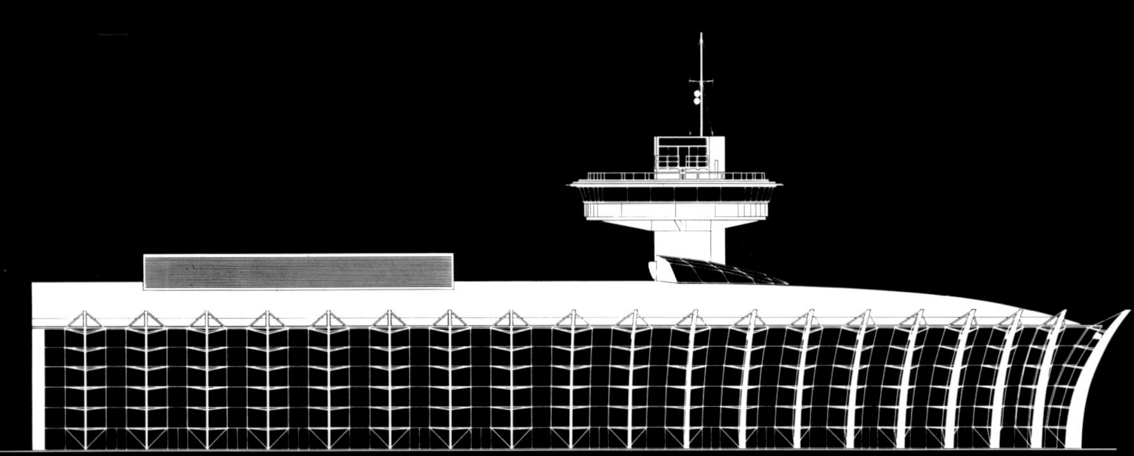

The Western Morning News, Plymouth, 1992

'The client was very good at getting his sense of excitement across to us. He wanted the best for his team and he wanted a landmark to show off to the world. But this was no mere football team, it was practically an Olympic village. Two hundred and fifty people all working together: printers, accountants, journalists, editors, cooks, cleaners, secretaries, advertising people, graphic designers and so on, all working in an intense atmosphere with a great belief in their own newspaper. We tried to express all this in the building. We gave the editorial side a real sense of community by arranging it around a great light well. We created sweeping spaces with fabulous views over the countryside. We displayed the press hall to the world like some great ship's engine room. We made obvious the structural skeleton, which excited everyone. And although this was a huge building I think it is in harmony with its surroundings – like a

Previous page
Detail of cast stainless-steel glazing boss assembly.

Sketches from Nick Grimshaw's notebook. They illustrate initial ideas for the shape of the building, and show how people working inside the building would have views of the surrounding countryside.

View of the completed building at night.

1) Executive in his office looking across editorial floor & through external wall to the landscape

2) "Johnson Wax" type view of overall office space.

The headquarters of Western Morning News Co Ltd is virtually a civic building, although its setting near Plymouth airport is on the edge of the city. The *Western Morning News* and the *Evening Herald*, two of the company's seven newspapers, have a much higher profile than most local newspapers: they are objects of local pride and forums for debate on local controversies. According to the *Western Morning News'* editor, the people of Plymouth 'think they own it'. The company's move from the city centre to a new building, therefore, is a matter of great public interest. The company's finances rely heavily on advertising (on average 250,000 small ads a year), which reinforced the case for a building that would make an impression on Plymouth's skyline.

The site is located on the edge of a nature conservation area. It slopes down steeply towards a wooded stream, giving views north-east towards Dartmoor and views back over the city towards Plymouth Sound. The brief was not, as at the Financial Times Print Works, only to house the printing works, but also to include editorial and advertising offices, an associated canteen, crèche, and fitness room. As in London, the demands of new technology and colour printing forced the move out of the city's centre, but the *Western Morning News* managed, as the Fleet Street newspapers did not, to keep all its operations under one roof.

All these factors combined to produce the design. The spectacle of the printing press in action is presented to the outside world, both by a visitor's route that winds through the building, and through glass walls. The concave glass wall reaches out as it rises,

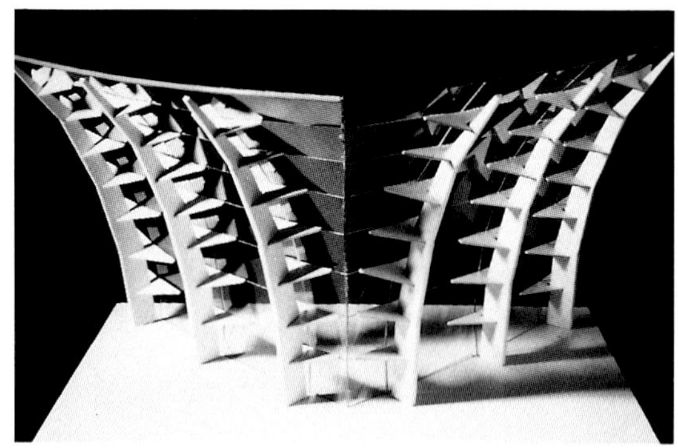

Early study model illustrating the curved-steel 'tusk' column.

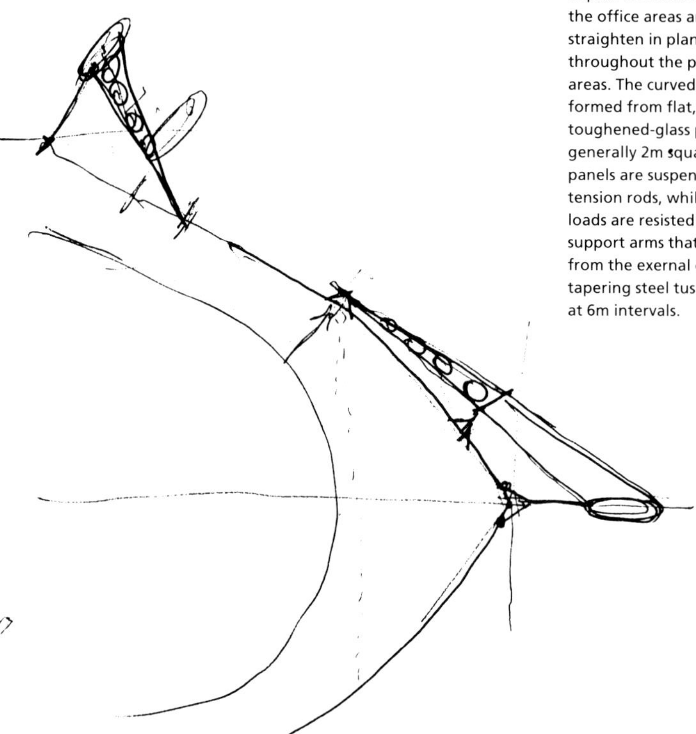

Glass walls on each side of the building meet at a single point in plan. The walls curve in plan and section to enclose the office areas and straighten in plan throughout the production areas. The curved walls are formed from flat, faceted, toughened-glass panels generally 2m square. The panels are suspended by tension rods, whilst lateral loads are resisted by glazing support arms that 'reach out' from the exernal curved and tapering steel tusk columns at 6m intervals.

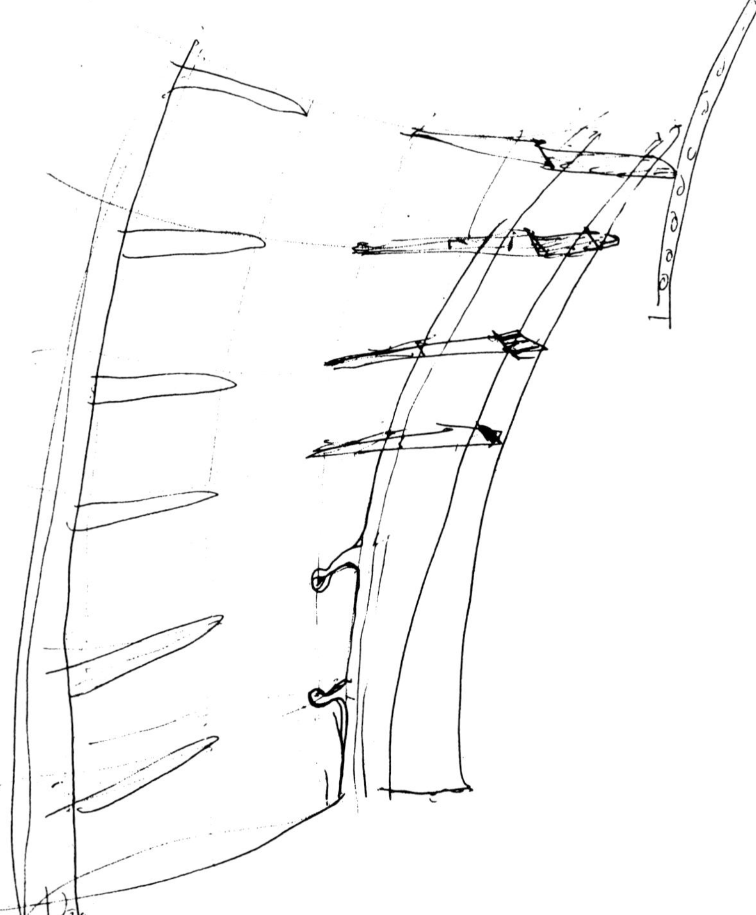

Nick Grimshaw's development sketches showing an elevation and plan of the columns.

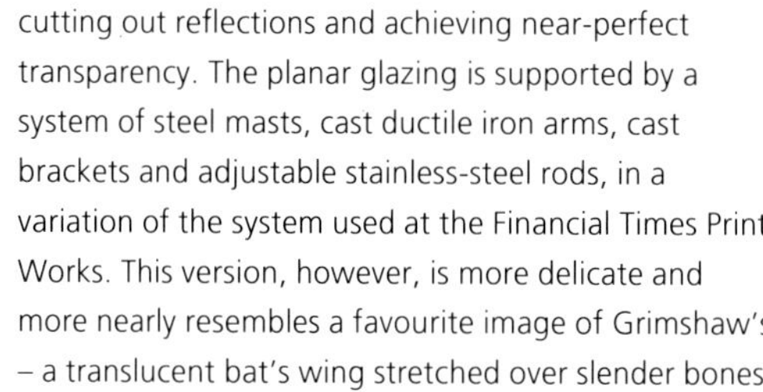

cutting out reflections and achieving near-perfect transparency. The planar glazing is supported by a system of steel masts, cast ductile iron arms, cast brackets and adjustable stainless-steel rods, in a variation of the system used at the Financial Times Print Works. This version, however, is more delicate and more nearly resembles a favourite image of Grimshaw's – a translucent bat's wing stretched over slender bones.

The walls curve in plan as well as in section following, on the northern side, the contour of the hill and turning the offices towards the the best view. The southern side echoes the curve, largely for the sake of symmetry, and gives the boat-shape that fortuitously alludes to Plymouth's naval connections. The imagery is reinforced by the 'masts' that hold up the glass, and the 22m-high 'bridge' which, from its boardroom and

observation gallery, gives views of the sea, the city, and the moor. Grimshaw insists that form followed function, the site and the Modern Movement's admiration for nautical design. But the adoption of such a memorable shape will certainly do the client's public image no harm.

The site gives other cues to the design. On the southern side the slope is dug out to receive (or harbour) the building, and the differential in height enables the main entrance to take printers, journalists and the general public inside on the middle of the building's three levels. This entrance can be reached directly from the road, through a car park lined with Devon hedges, but also by a scenic route through the greener, undeveloped part of the site and past the twin drama of the printing press and the building's

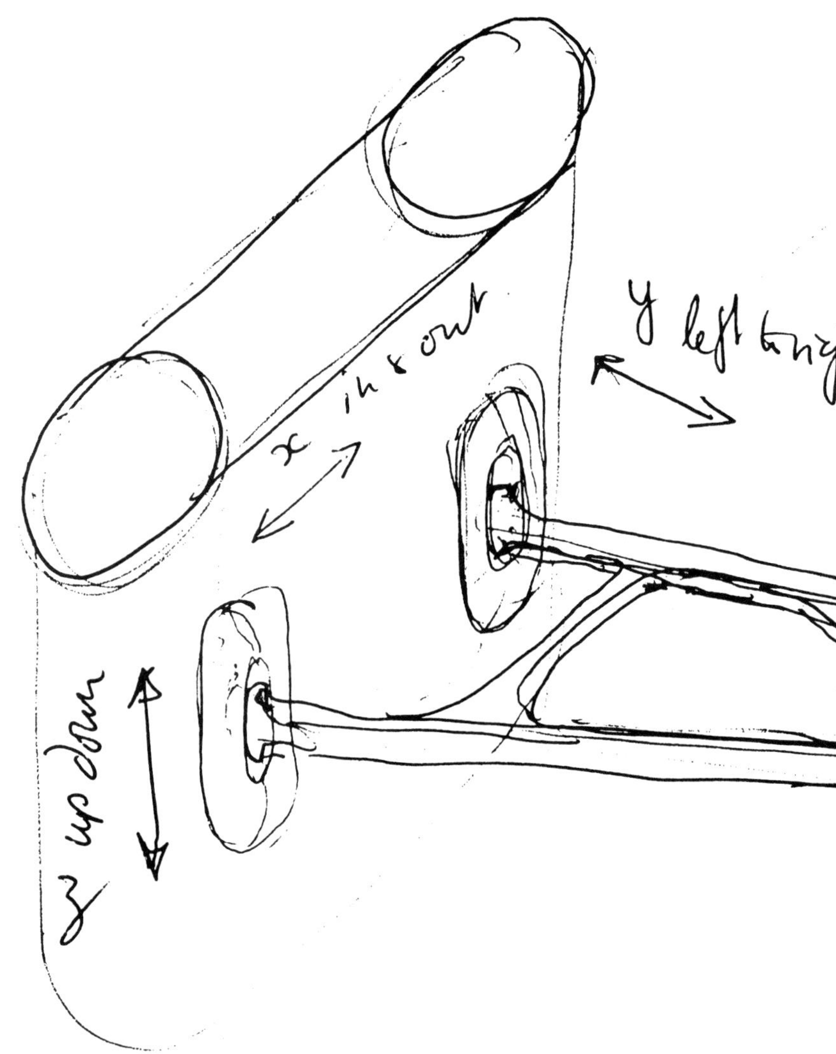

Early conceptual sketch by Nick Grimshaw exploring mechanisms by which building and movement tolerances could be accommodated by the glazing arm assembly.

Metal resin used to rigidify the connection between glazing arm and column.

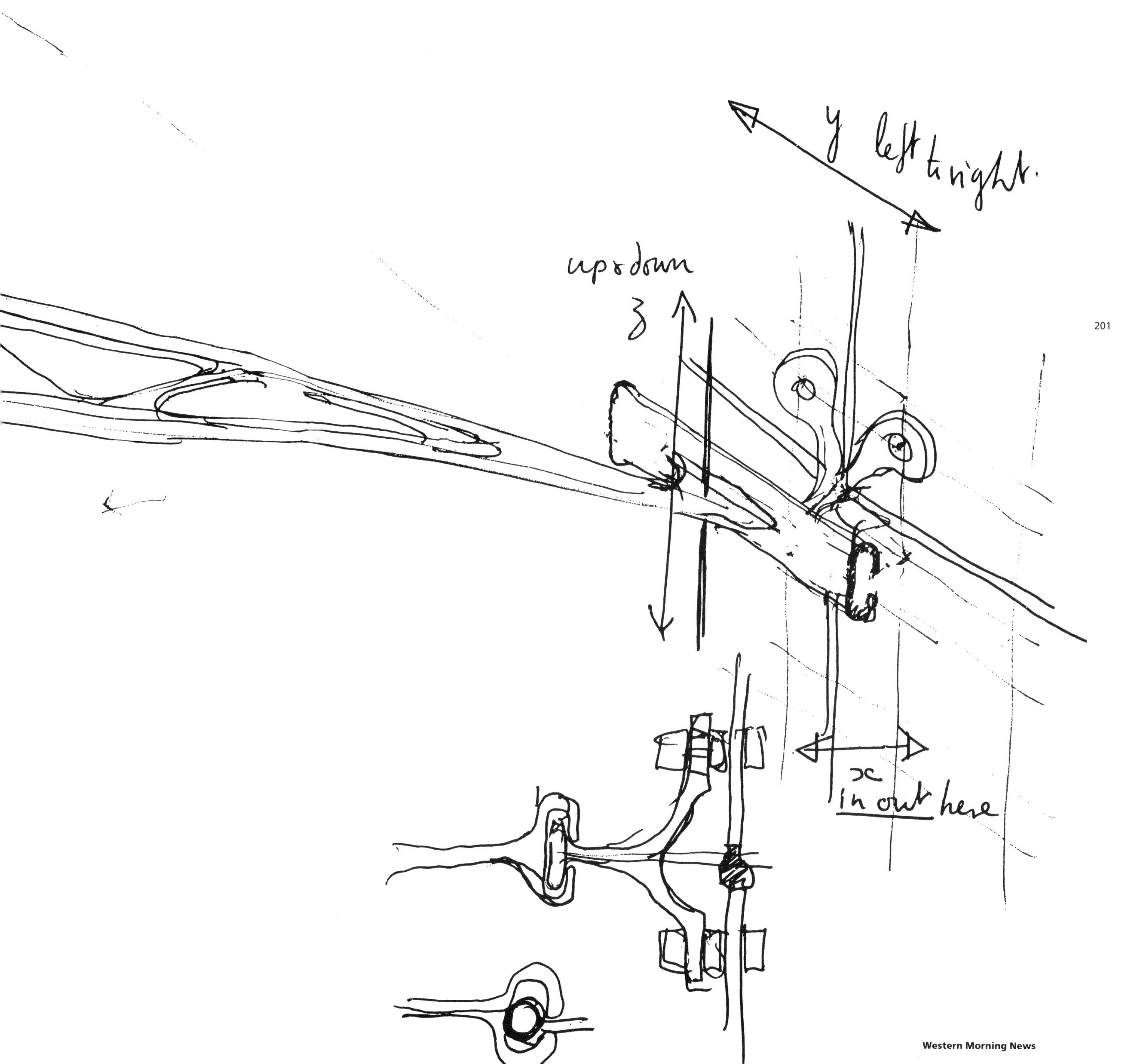
y left to right.
up & down
z
x
in out here

Detail of a spheroidal graphite, cast ductile iron glazing arm. Spheroidal graphite has a number of properties that make it particularly suitable for this project: in molten form it is less viscous than steel, enabling the use of narrower and more complex moulds; smelting occurs at lower temperatures than steel, reducing the degree of adhesion on the sand mould and improving the surface finish; it is more cost effective than steel for the casting of relatively small pieces.

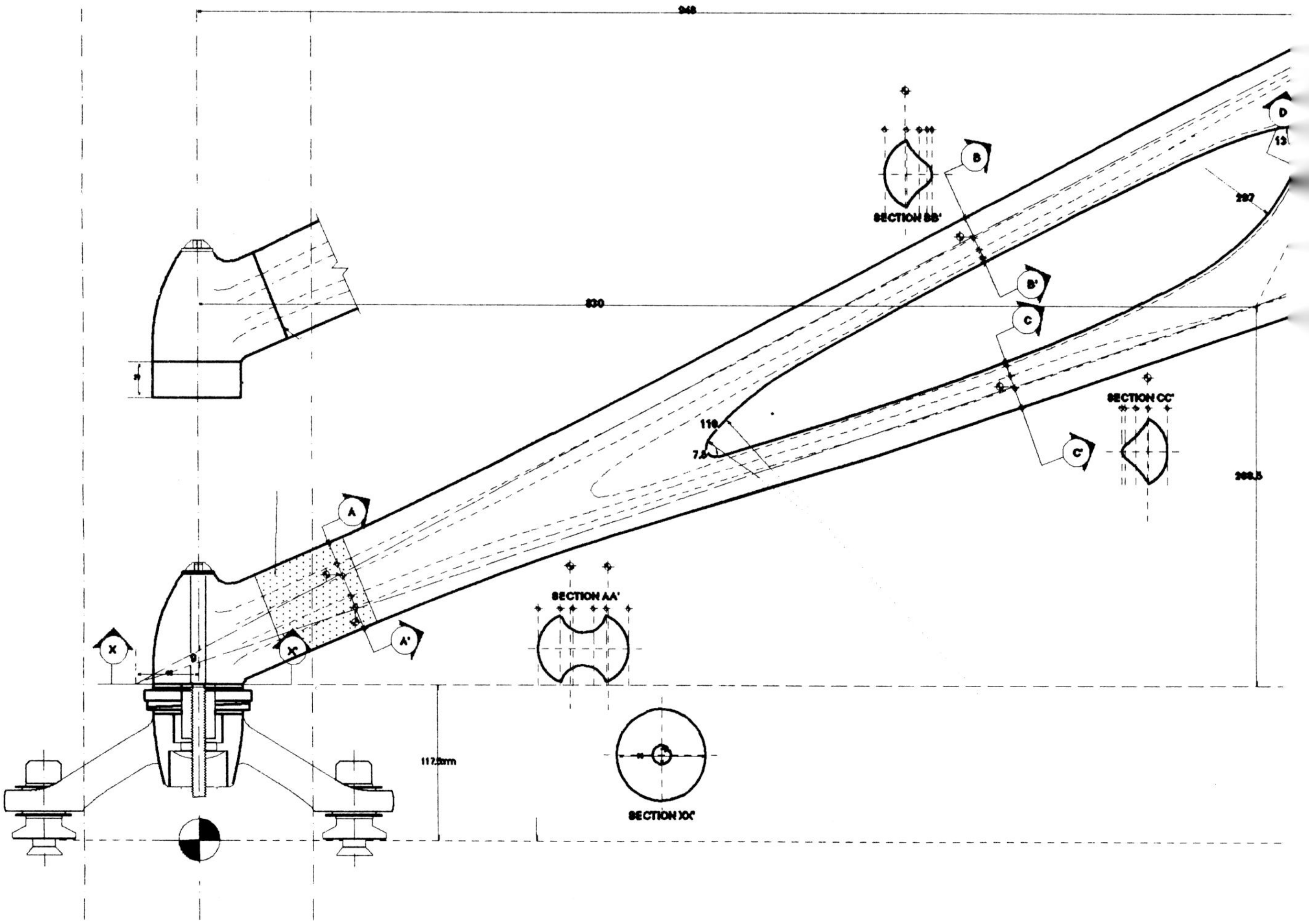

Detailed drawing of the relationship between glazing bosses, cast glazing arm, cast glazing strut and fabricated steel 'tusk' column. Sectional profiles of the cast components are indicated at critical intervals.

Nicholas Grimshaw & Partners

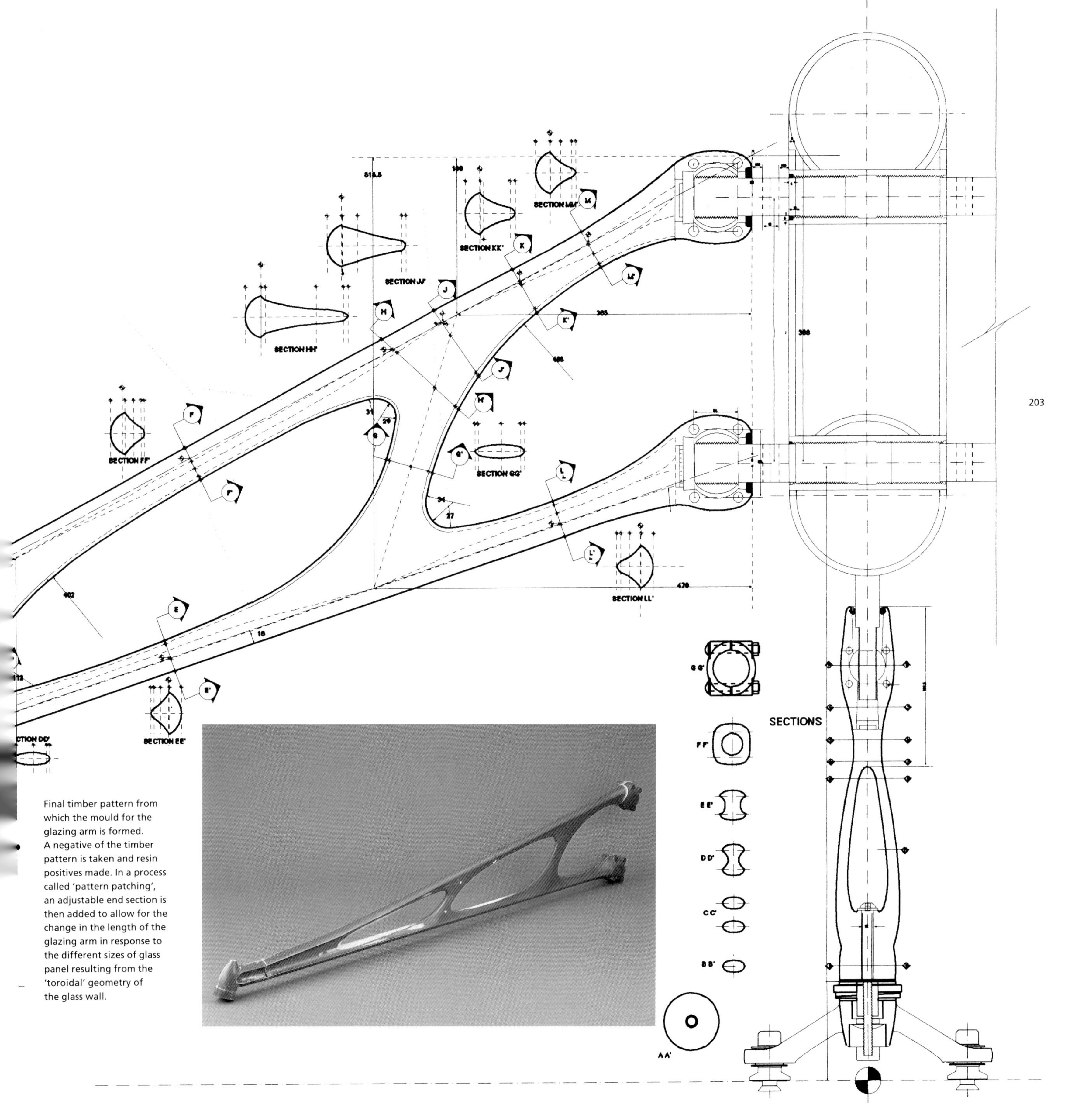

Final timber pattern from which the mould for the glazing arm is formed. A negative of the timber pattern is taken and resin positives made. In a process called 'pattern patching', an adjustable end section is then added to allow for the change in the length of the glazing arm in response to the different sizes of glass panel resulting from the 'toroidal' geometry of the glass wall.

A stainless-steel, glazing-boss casting. An assembly of more than 50 components including ball joints, sliding fixings and tapered washers allows the glazing boss to accommodate all variations in the geometry of the glass wall.

Completed glazing assembly.

Nick Grimshaw's sketch developing the form of the glazing boss

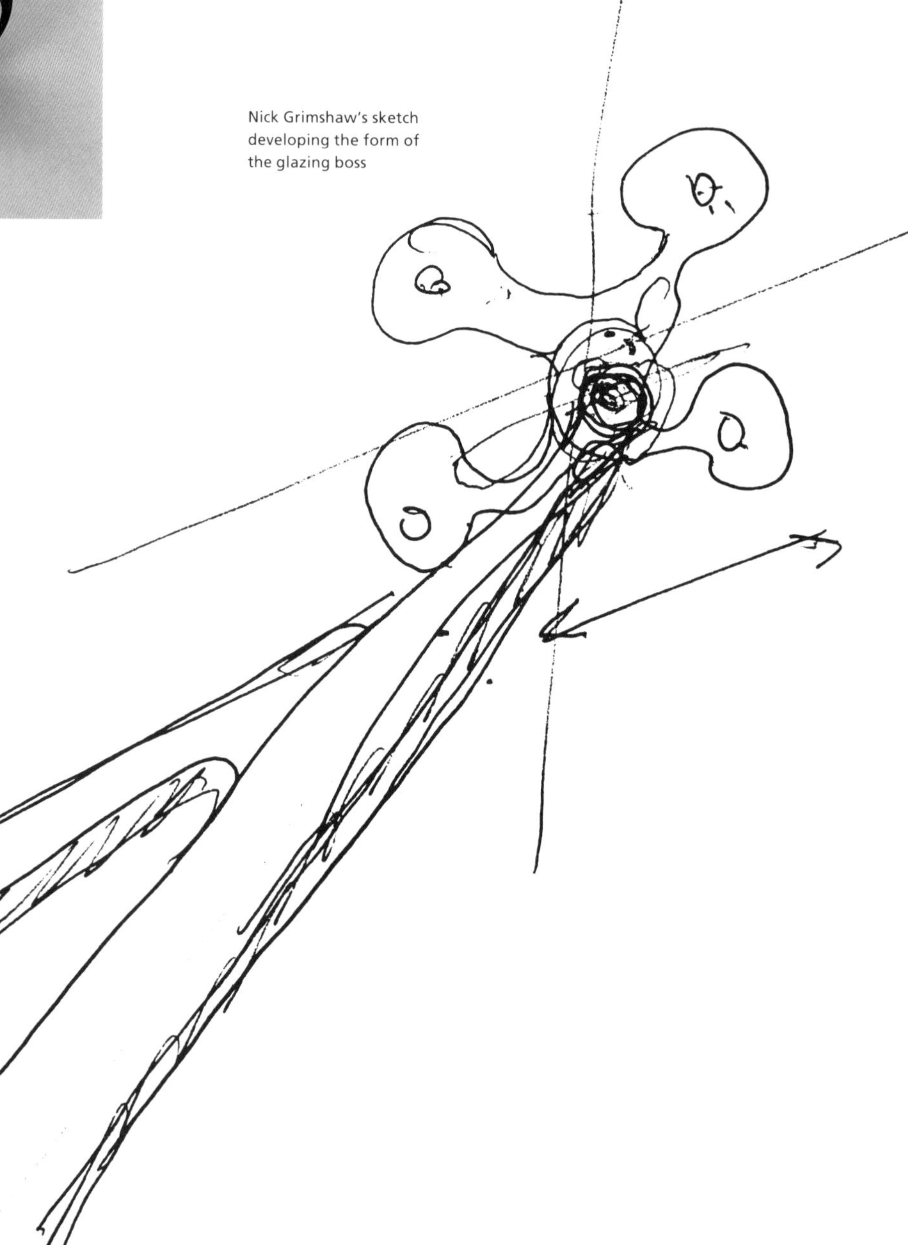

A ball and socket-clamp fixing to the column provides adjustability in construction to accommodate tolerances and geometry before being injected with metal resin to lock into the final position.

structure. The terrain is used for the environmental as well as the visual benefit of the building: trees and the cut into the hillside combine with the projecting eaves to shelter the southern face from the sun.

Internally the building's form divides in two: offices are located in the curved 'prow', while the rectangular section contains the printing and production areas. The plan and section of the latter are ordered by the demanding logistics of printing machinery: paper arrives at the lower level through the matter-of-fact, unglazed west elevation, is stored, and is taken up to the middle level as it is printed in the press hall. This hall rises through the full three storeys of the northern elevation. From there newspapers are packaged in the publishing hall, and they leave the building at the raised external level provided by the sloping site.

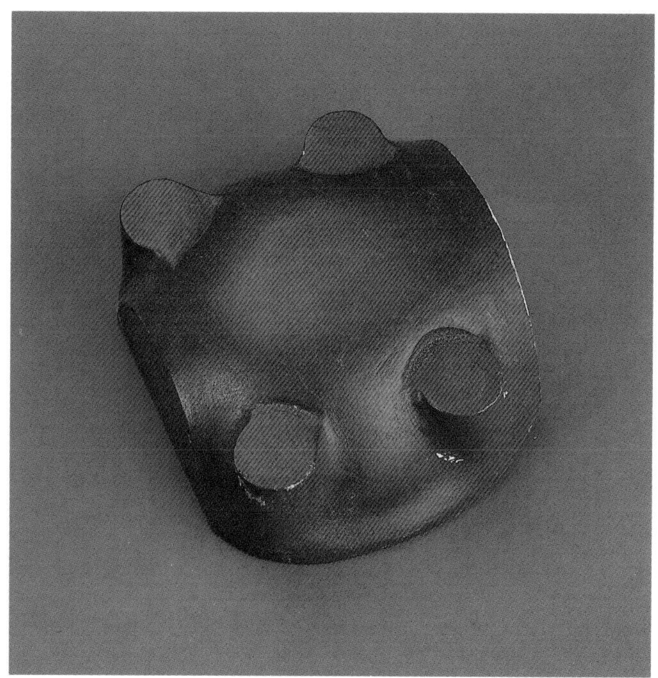

Detail of wooden pattern.

View of atrium.

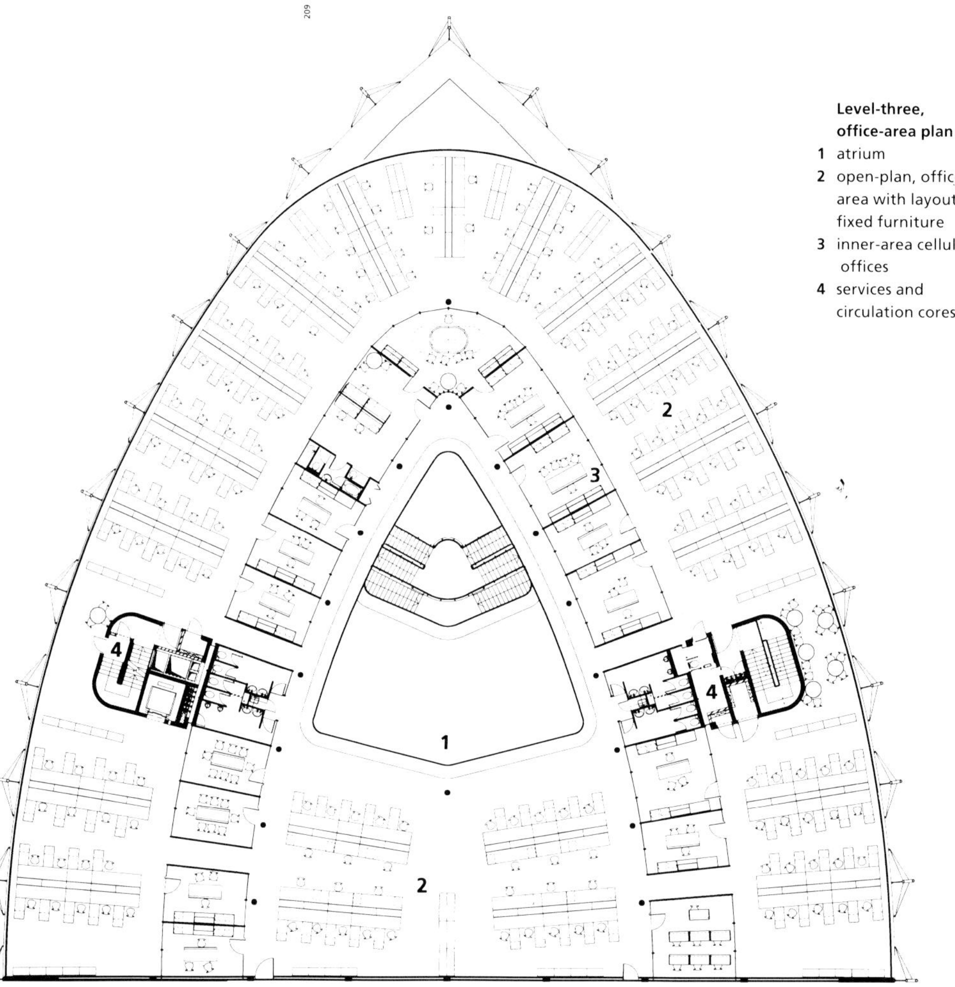

Level-three, office-area plan
1 atrium
2 open-plan, office area with layout of fixed furniture
3 inner-area cellular offices
4 services and circulation cores

Overhead are viewing galleries for the public, and the voluminous plant needed to handle the heat generated by the printing machines, which include heat exchangers to recycle waste energy. The machinery is supported on a substantial concrete structure kept separate from the external envelope of steel and glass. Towards the perimeter, more delicate steel walkways are attached to the concrete to form galleries. The offices are placed on the other side of a two-hour fire-resisting wall but, for directness of communication, the editorial, photographic and composing areas – the places where each issue is planned and put together – are placed on the same middle level where the main printing and publishing operations take place. Thus, on a single floor, news enters the building, is written up, edited and composed, printed and published. The

Detailed computer studies of atrium staircase.

A view of the completed building in its context.

The tusk columns, with glazing arms and tie rods pre-assembled at the manufacturer's works, are craned into position.

upper and lower floors support the middle one with subsidiary services, including the advertising, marketing and administrative areas.

On each floor the central atrium is ringed by cellular offices and then by open-plan space, reversing the conventional arrangement whereby the most prestigious but lightly occupied offices use up the best views and light. At Western Morning News the plan gives a more egalitarian distribution. Glass ends to the cellular offices allow views and natural light to permeate the building.

The furniture, designed in Grimshaw's office, also departs from conventional wisdom. In the open plan offices it is fixed along the structural lines of the building and perpendicular to the light which, in

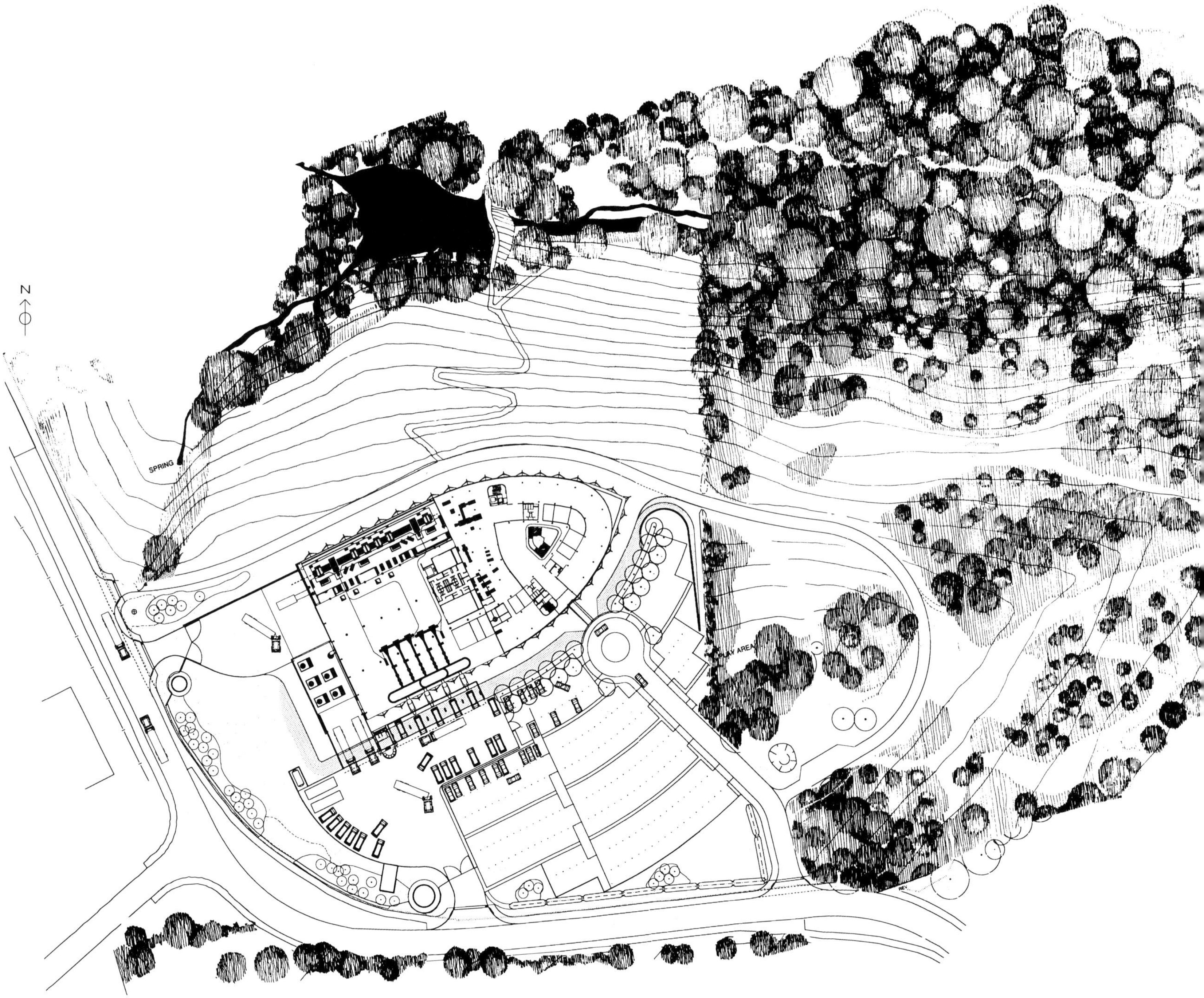

Site plan. The building footprint follows the contours of the site, taking advantage of the existing tree belt and nature-conservation area.

theory, reduces flexibility. In practice, Grimshaw's in-house industrial designer found that, by ruling out unlikely options, simplicity and cost savings could be achieved. Instead of a plethora of service risers, supports, and alternative floor sockets to cope with every conceivable eventuality, each of the long workbenches rests on either three or four central legs. Services rise through these to a structural and service spine from which detachable work services are cantilevered. Both above and below the working surface this system provides the minimum of obstruction. Additional sliding surfaces allow for all the variation the offices are likely to need.

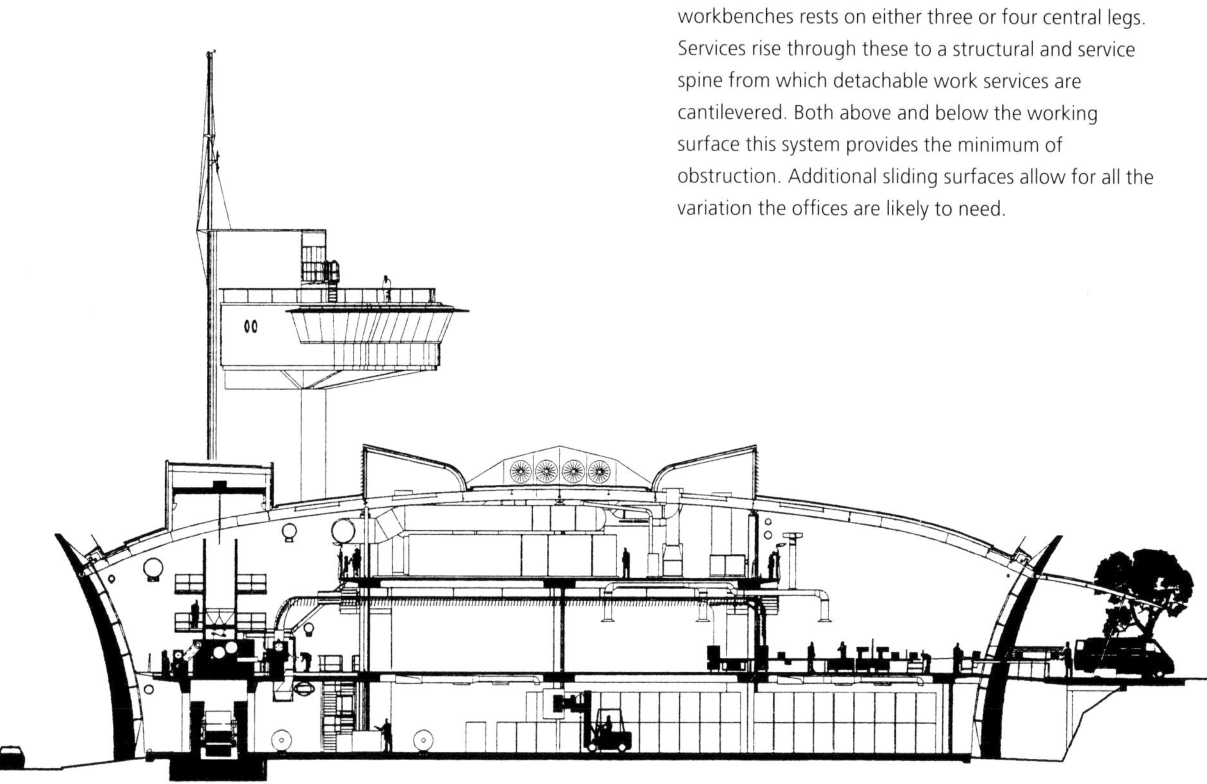

A cross section through the printing and production areas. The slope of the site has been exploited in the design of the building to facilitate the flow of the production process. Paper reels enter the building through the west wall at lower-ground level; paper is fed up to the printing press. The press hall, mechanised publishing hall and distribution areas are all situated on the middle or main entrance level.

Long section. A tower containing the boardroom provides views to Plymouth Sound and Dartmoor. The envelope or 'hull' contains three concrete decks, of relatively conventional, reinforced-concrete slab and column construction. The slabs are punctured by a central atrium with rooflight above to ensure natural light penetrates to all office areas. The atrium is the hub of the building where all the company's activities inter-relate.

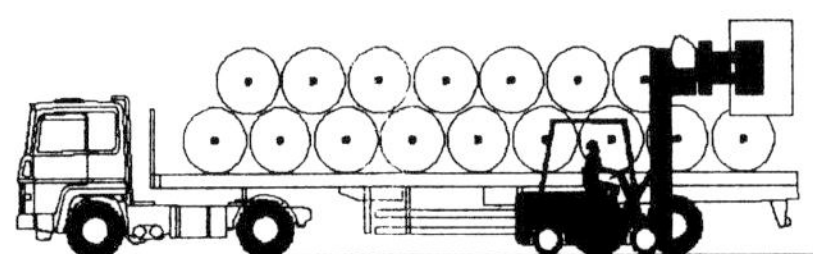

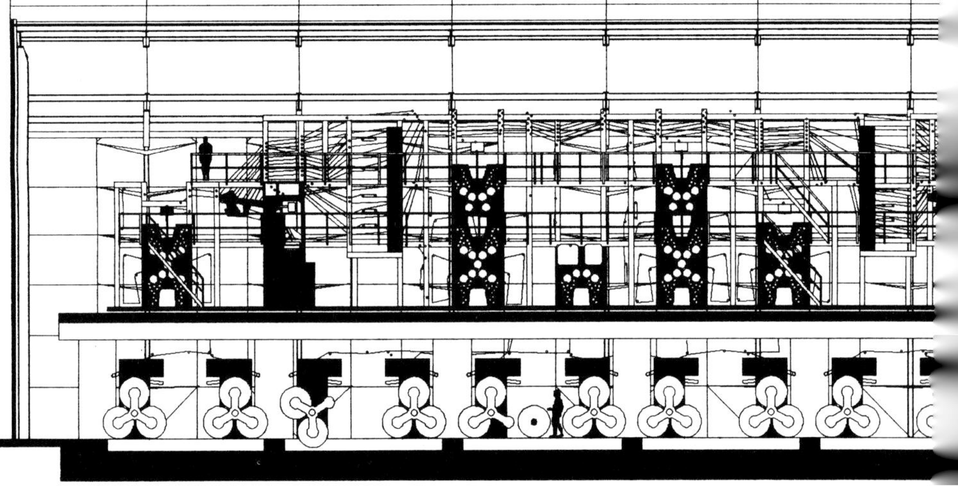

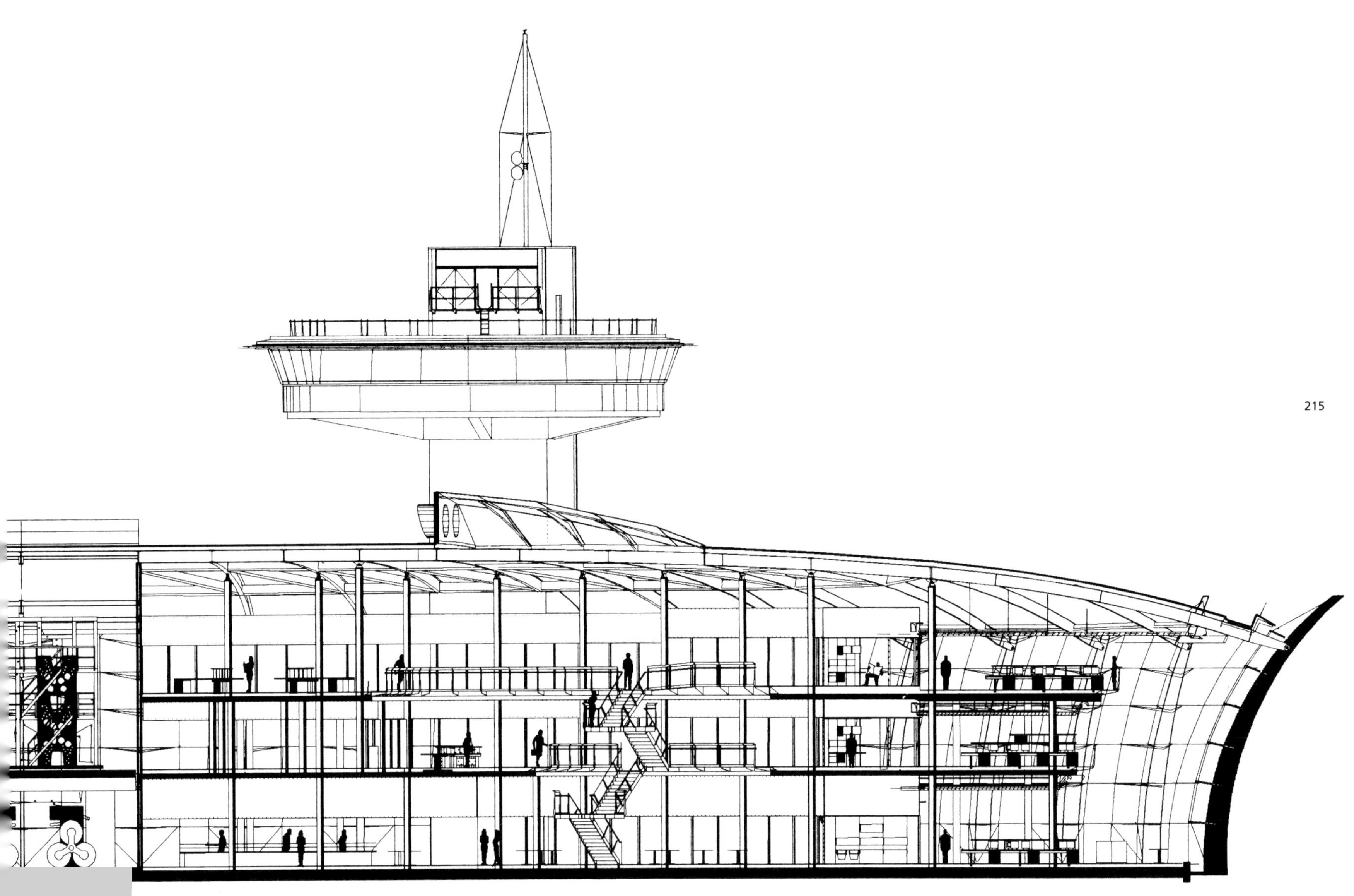

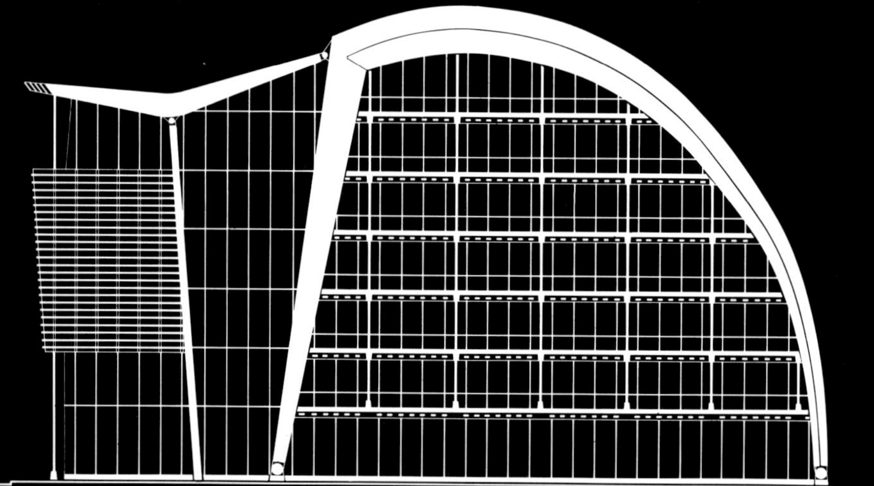

Berlin Stock Exchange and Communications Centre, 1991–1995

'I experienced a very strong reaction to the site. I felt that what was required was a building that not only responded organically to the constraints of the available space but which also displayed brilliantly its diverse activities to the world. Well over a thousand people would work in the building and their interaction with the public was vital. We created a pedestrian spine which linked all the main activities together. The conference hall, exhibition spaces, stock exchange, restaurants, the design centre, the energy advice centre could all be seen from the spine. This gave the building an open democratic feel, which seemed to us appropriate to the Berlin of today.' **NG**

Previous page
Structural model, made by the project team to show the concept of arches spanning from the central spine.

Since the fall of the Wall, projects in Berlin have had to reconcile opposing emotions. On one hand is the wish to recall the romantic, 1920s' city of Marlene Dietrich, on the other to make a fresh start on what again will be the capital of Germany. Grimshaw's design for a service and communications' centre for the Berlin business community responds to this ambiguity by firmly looking to the future.

Grimshaw won the commission in an invited competition, in which the brief called for a complex, dense development on an irregular site. To several of the entrants this suggested a freestanding tower, but Grimshaw felt that a tower would fit awkwardly into its immediate context and Berlin's flat skyline, and decided to work a comparatively low building into the crevices of the site. This decision also allowed Grimshaw to generate an energy-efficient form, with minimal surface area, as part of a larger interest in creating a 'healthy building'. To the same end the building is cooled by fresh-air ventilation rather than by recirculated air from an air-conditioning system.

The project mends a ragged part of Berlin's famous pattern of city blocks and harmonises with the prevailing parapet heights. But it does so without the brick and render deference of the Berlin housing blocks built by Aldo Rossi, Rob Krier and others for IBA, the international building exhibition of the 1980s. The materials – steel and glass – and the building's aspirations to democratic openness and transparency, represent the opposite of what Grimshaw calls the 'impenetrable' blocks of old Berlin.

The building is for two clients, the Berlin chamber of trade and commerce, IHK, and the local federation

Computer perspective of the scheme viewed from Fasanen Strasse, which was prepared for the competition.

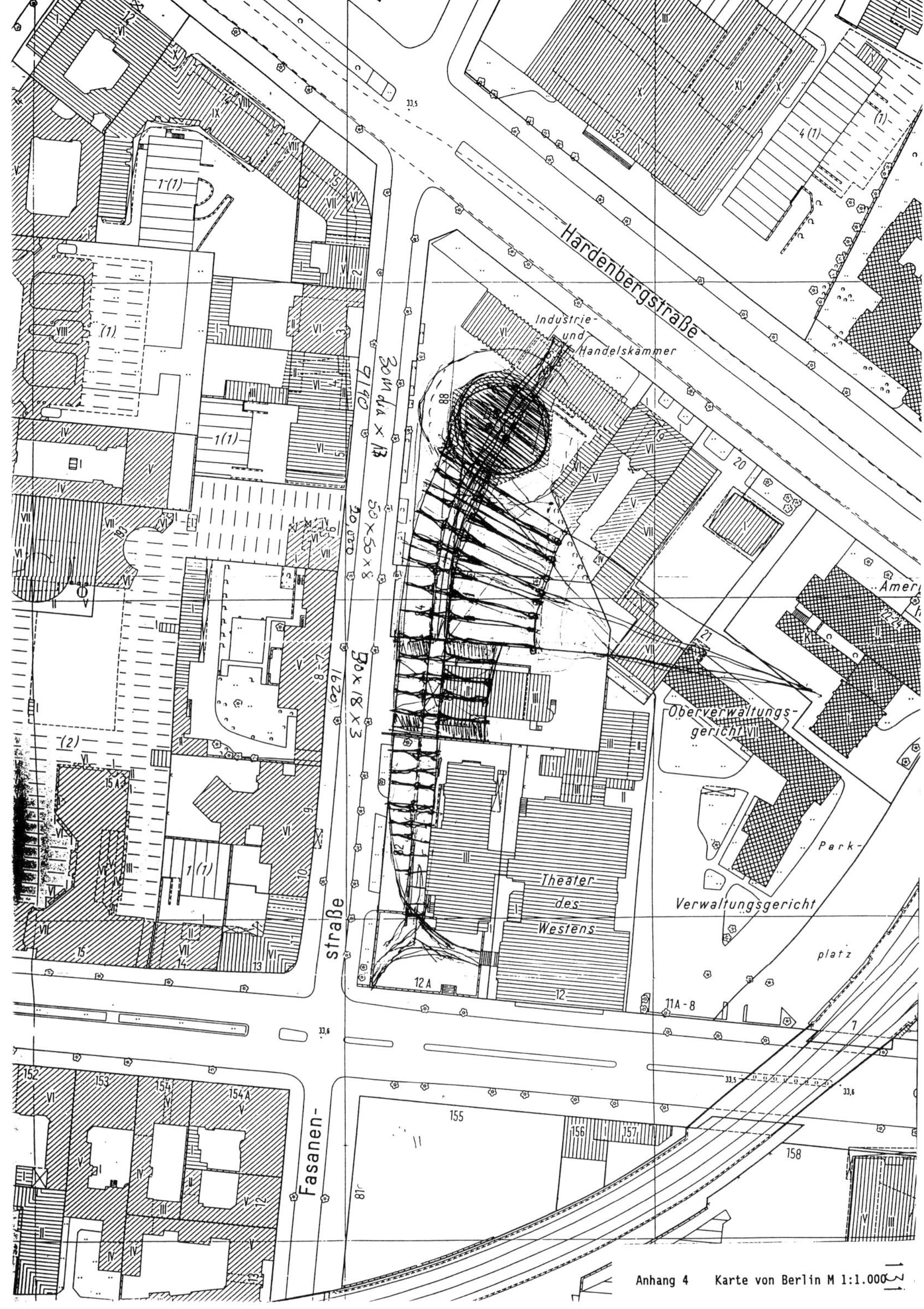

Nick Grimshaw's original concept sketch following the first site visit and briefing.

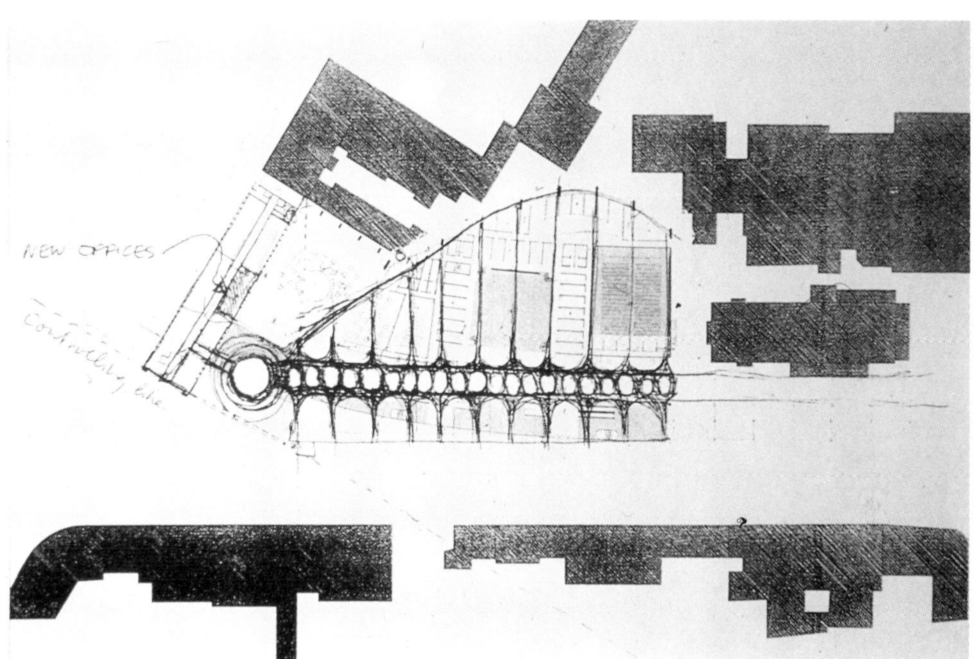

Nick Grimshaw's development sketch exploring the link between the old and new building; the rib-structure spans vary in response to the site limits.

of industrialists and businessmen, VBKI. It houses several functions: the Berlin Stock Exchange, a conference centre, an energy advice centre, exhibition space for the International Design Centre, a lecture theatre, offices, and four different restaurants and bars. Grimshaw's response to this complexity was to unify the community of spaces with a central spine, which runs down the middle of the site. Starting at the retained, listed, 1950s' building at the north end of the site, it is suggested that the central spine will extend off the southern boundary to form a new entrance for the Delphi cinema, site of the Berlin film festival and a place of historic significance for Berliners.

Running along the central spine is an internal street that is open to the public. On its inner side, it looks onto the trading floor of the stock exchange, and gives access to the offices, conference centres, restaurants and bars. On its outer side the double-height exhibition area, which includes the International Design Centre, rises from the basement to give an unobstructed, glass-walled void, traversed by two bridges. This allows views from the outside into the stock exchange and the exhibition spaces, and establishes a rapport between the internal life of the complex and that of the city.

Study model made by the design team to explore relationships between the client's existing building, the new building and townscape.

Competition model within the context of the surrounding city, viewed during the day, and at night.

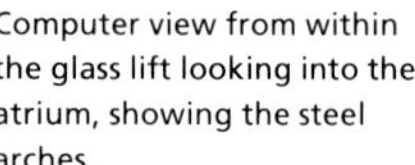

Computer view from within the glass lift looking into the atrium, showing the steel arches.

By its nature, a communications and services centre is a building type that demands a close relationship between the functions it houses. The brief called for large unobstructed spaces, such as the stock exchange and conference centre, to be accessible directly from ground level but also demanded a large amount of office space, which had to be on the upper levels because of the limited size of the site.

Grimshaw dealt with this difficult spatial relationship by suspending the offices above a large, column-free, flexible space on the ground floor.The office space comprises two elements. A small proportion of the space is designed as office suites, specifically for use by the Chamber of Commerce. The rest of the space is designed as 'combi' office layouts (groups of small offices with shared facilities), suitable for the Berlin businesses associated with the other services offered within the complex. These are suspended, in blocks seven and eight storeys high, from nine steel arches, which rise the full height of the building and span from the structural spine to the back of the site. Two large atria alternate with the office blocks to bring daylight into the depths of the building, and to take stale air out. To the front, a subsidiary, but still massive, structure leans off the central spine to carry a further block of offices over the space between the internal and external streets.

These nine arches give the design its most immediately striking quality, its resemblance to an unnamed vertebrate. The local press has called it, in a friendly spirit, a 'reptile', an 'armadillo' and a 'turtle', and Grimshaw's earliest sketches show a distinctly fish-like plan. It corresponds with a more organic imagery

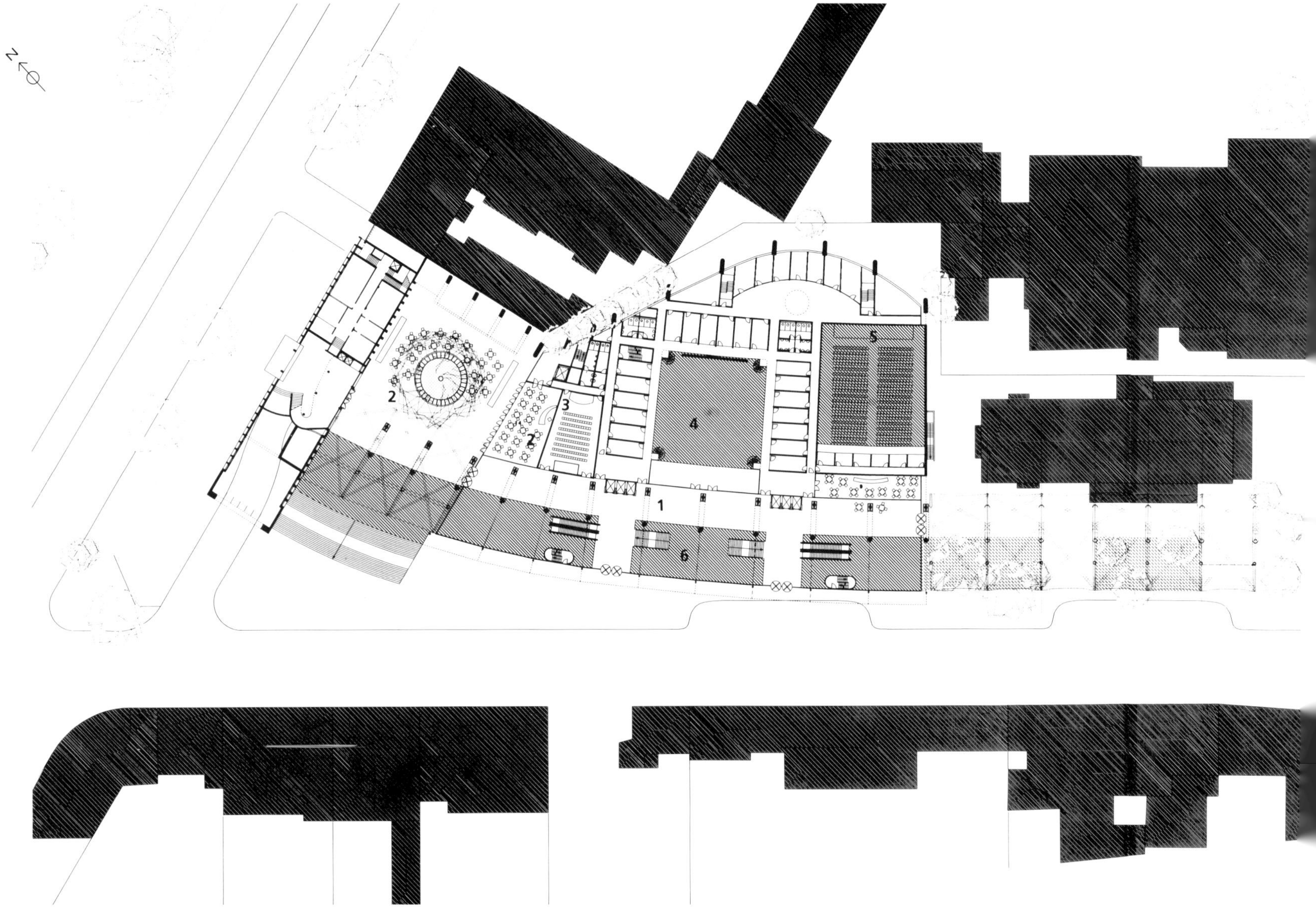

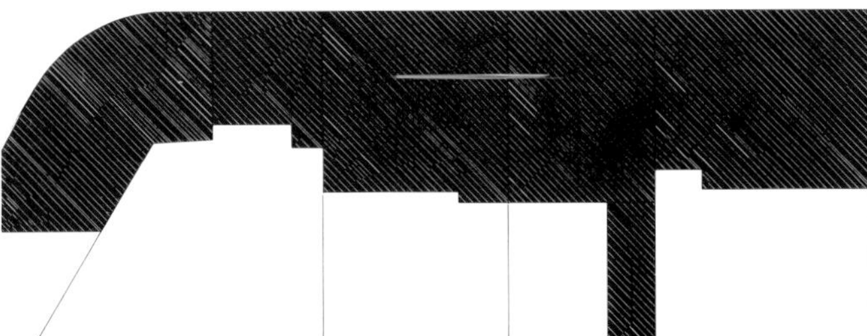

that can be seen in other contemporary Grimshaw projects, such as the Channel Tunnel Railway Terminal at Waterloo and Western Morning News. Grimshaw attributes this organic approach to circumstance, such as irregular sites, but it is too pronounced to be purely accidental. One factor is the practice's ever-increasing familiarity with ambitious technology, which gives it the confidence to take on complex forms. Another is that organic patterns give buildings, as they do at Berlin, a unity and a strength, without the inflexible finality of Classical hierarchies, or the clumsy imagery of Post-Modernism.

Ground-floor plan
1 internal street
2 restaurant
3 lecture theatre
4 stock exchange
5 conference hall
6 exhibition space

Section through atrium
1 atrium
2 internal street
3 stock exchange
4 exhibition space
5 offices
6 car park

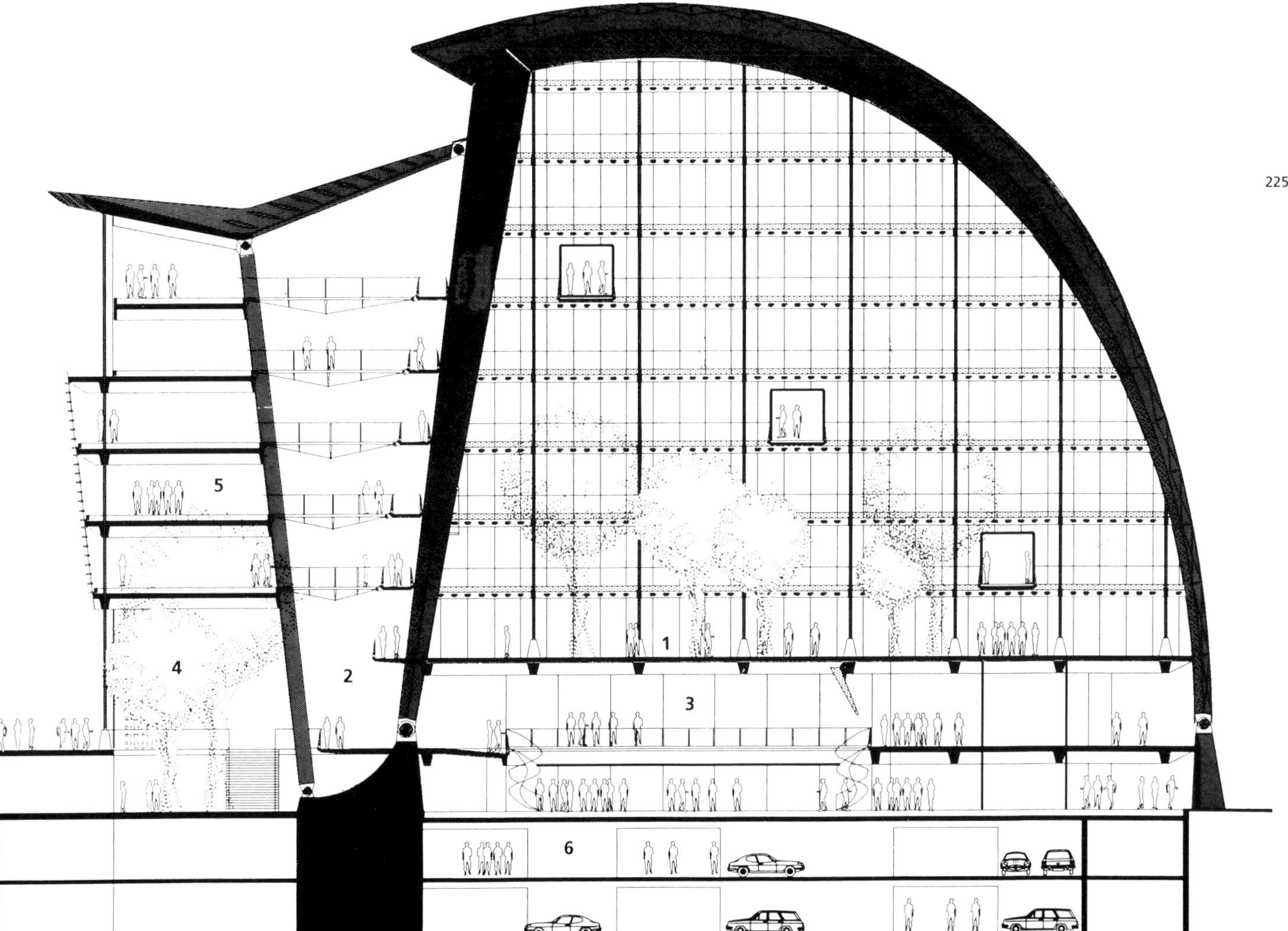

Long elevation

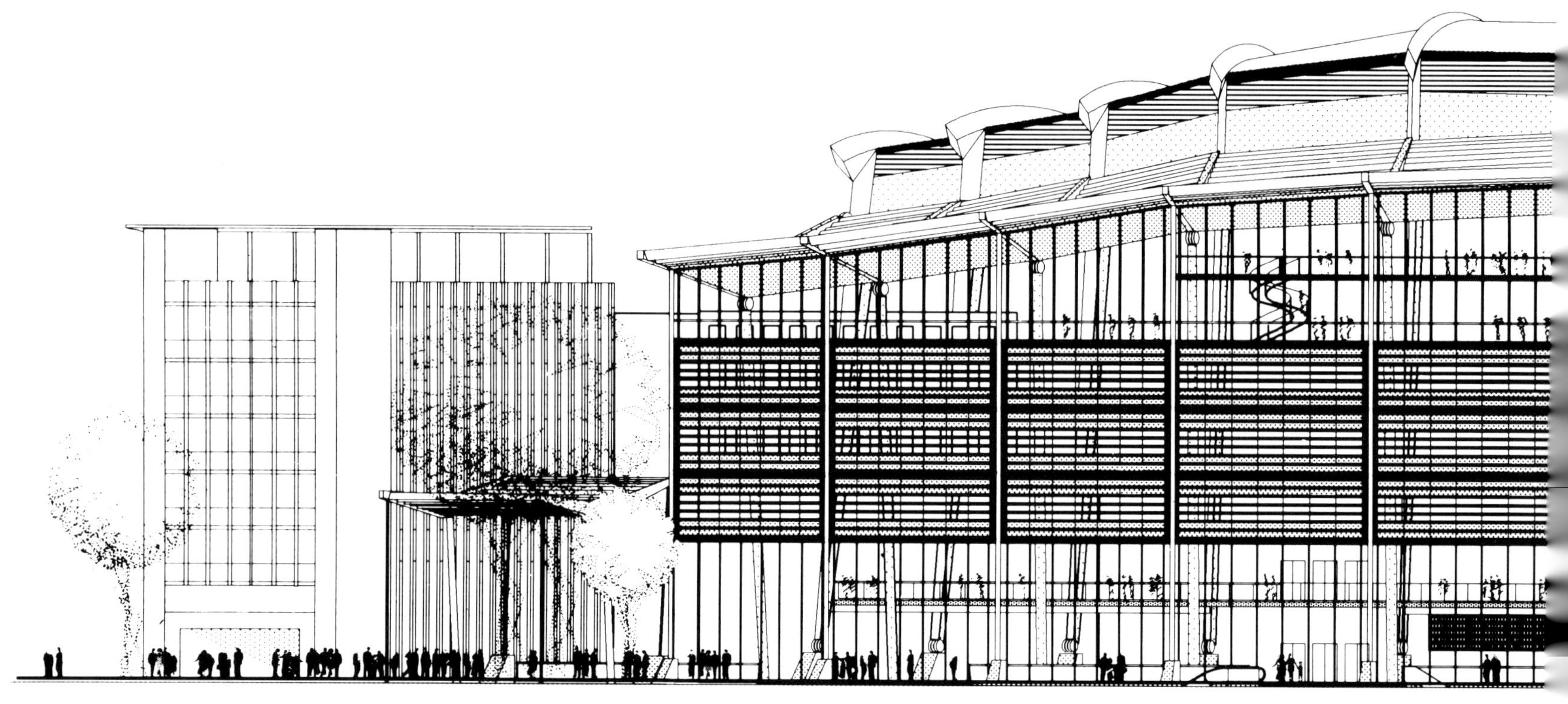

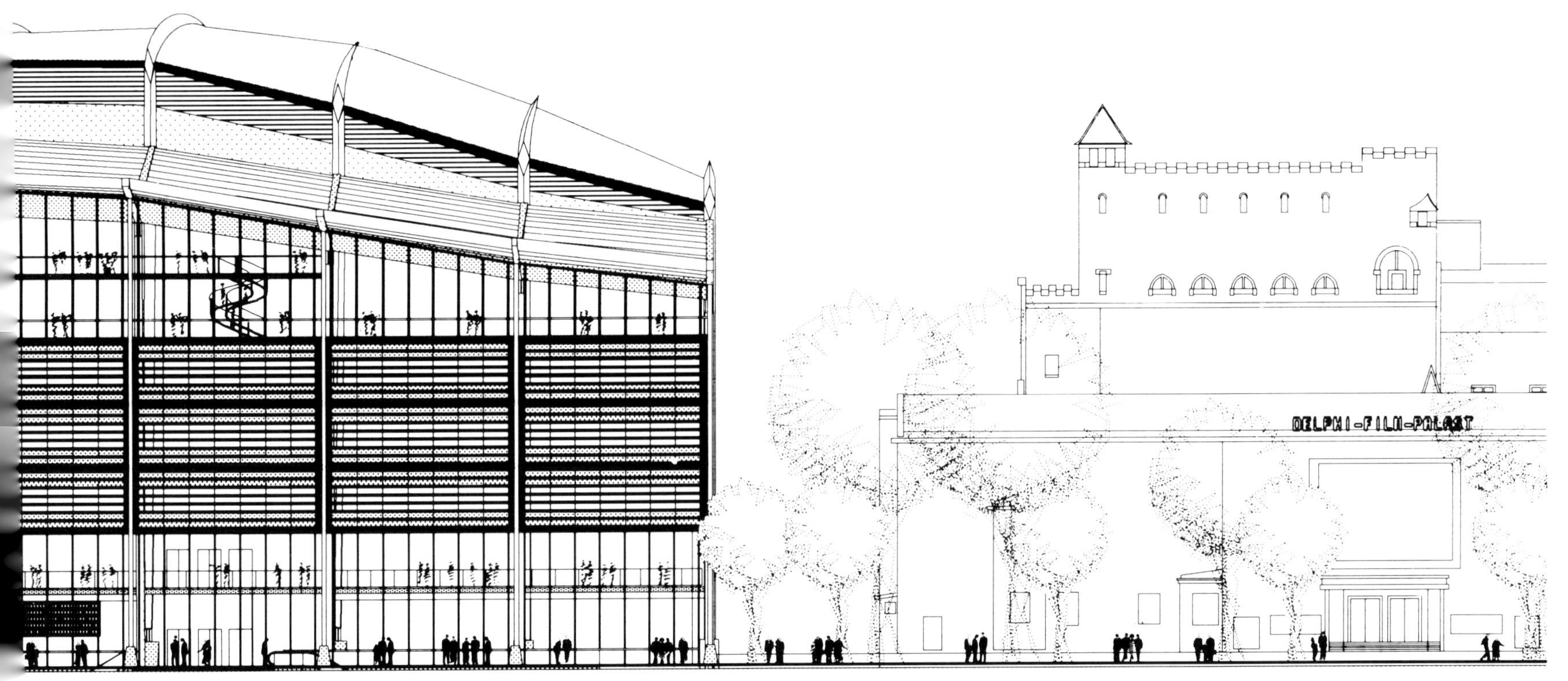
DELPHI-FILM-PALAST

Combined Operations Centre for British Airways, London, 1993

'The client was clear that, although he wanted the utmost rigour in terms of cost and spatial efficiency, he wanted a building of quality. The severe constraints of height, radar, orientation and materials had a very creative effect on the design. The building *had* to be all glass; six different kinds of glass and every kind of modern technique of toughening, fritting, coating and drilling have been exploited in its design.' **NG**

Previous page
View of south elevation and entrance canopy at night.

The Combined Operations Centre for British Airways is, in the words of Grimshaw's client, a 'symphony in glass'. Virtually all its visible surfaces use various forms of the material, from the clear glass of the windows to the blue-fritted louvred sunshades. The staircase towers at the end of each block have glass block walls, so they shine at night like beacons. They are flanked with service towers clad with convex, opaque-blue glass panels. The spandrel panels of the curtain walling combine a blue-fritted outer pane with a solid-blue inner pane to give a subtle sense of depth by day, and a deep blue glow at night.

This celebration of the material's many properties is a creative response to the conditions of the site. One requirement is that the building has to withstand severe environmental conditions ranging from

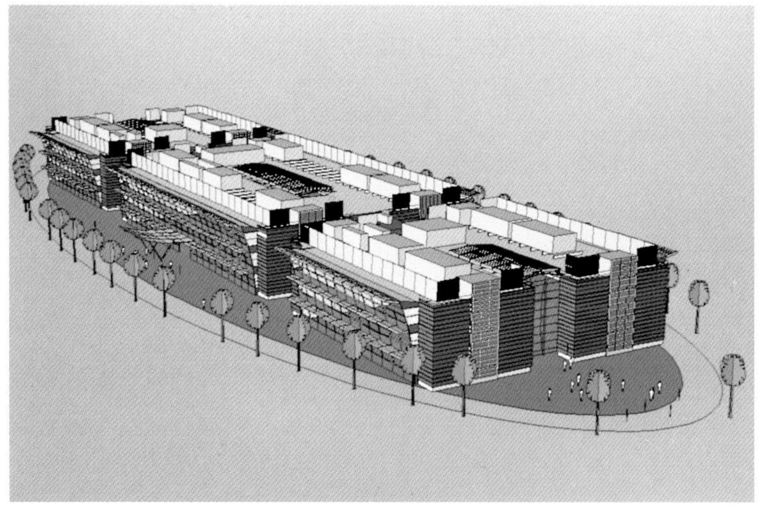

Aerial view of computer model showing the three linked blocks surrounded by the elliptical road.

Computer model view of the south-east corner of the building showing the main entrance to block C between the service cores, which are clad with deep-blue, curved, glass, rain-screen panels.

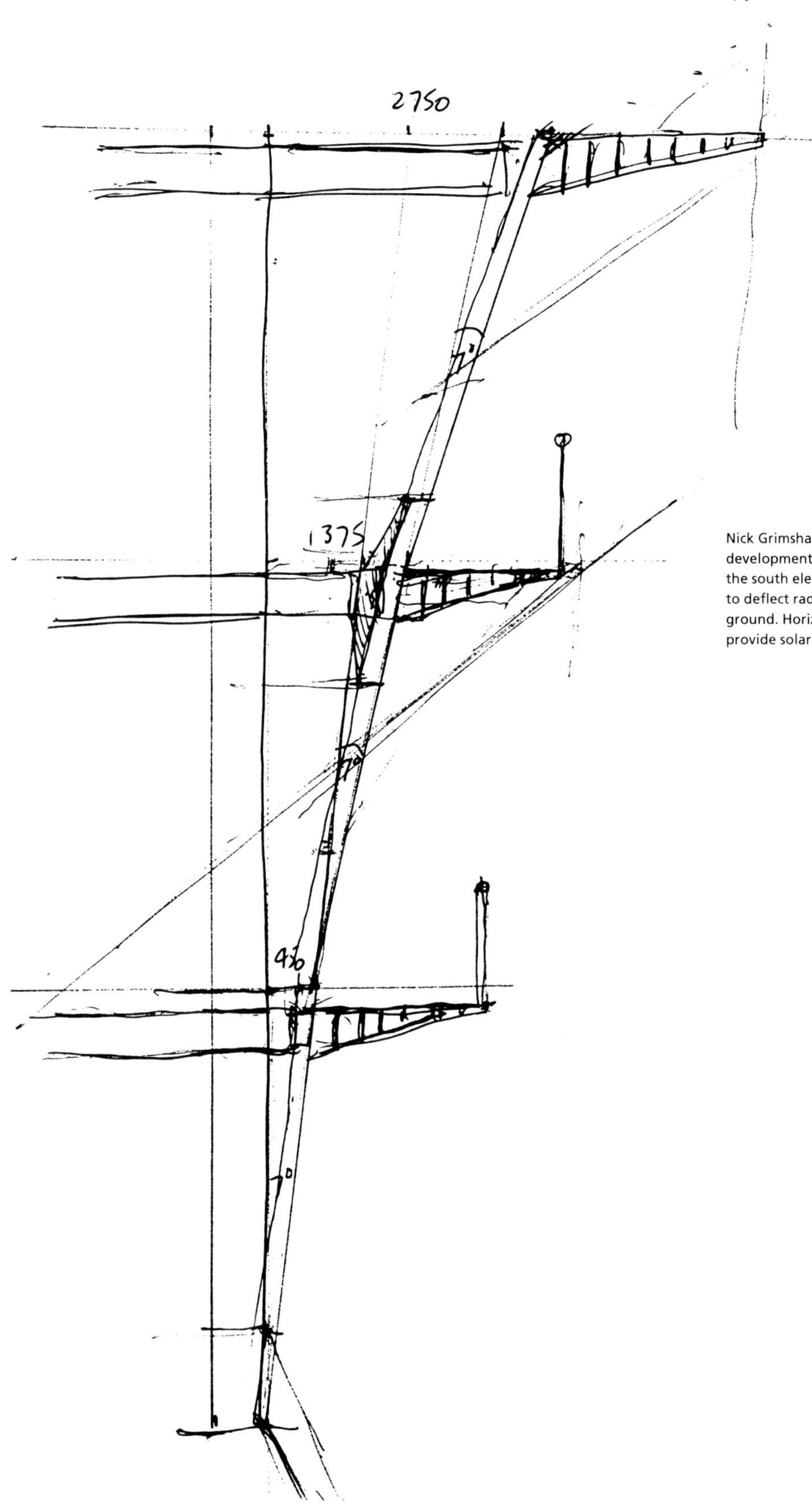

Nick Grimshaw's development sketch shows the south elevation faceted to deflect radar towards ground. Horizontal louvres provide solar shading.

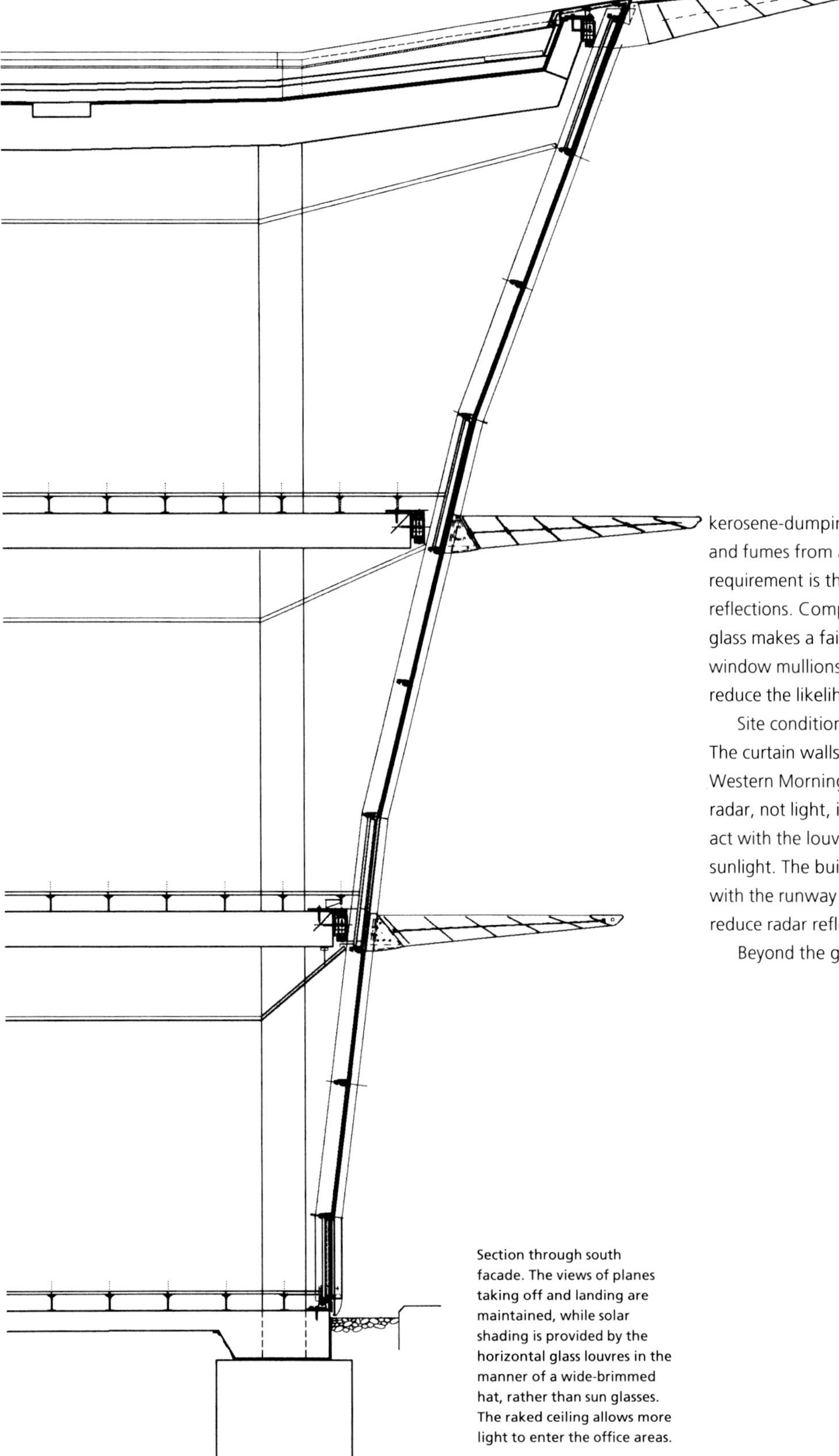

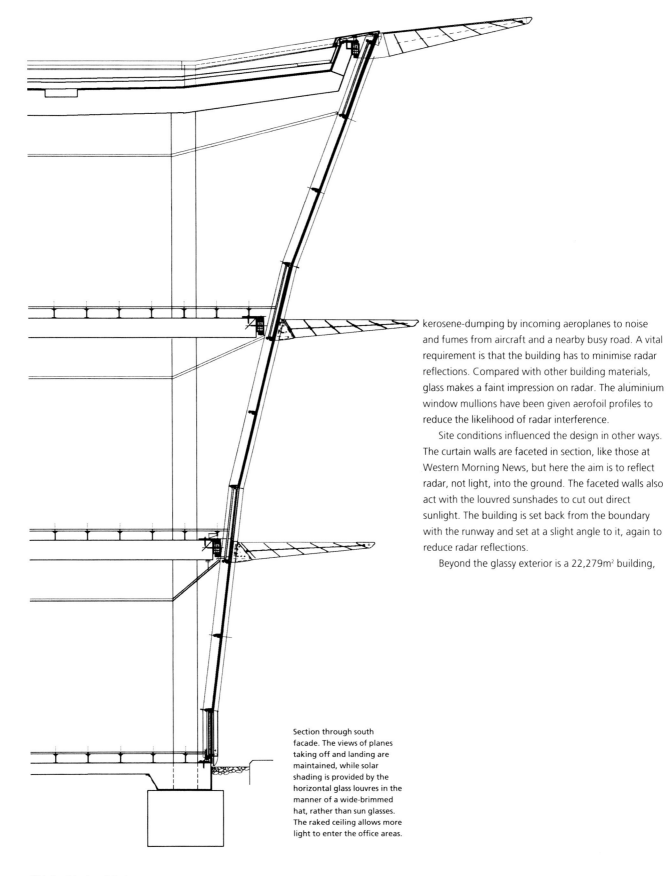

kerosene-dumping by incoming aeroplanes to noise and fumes from aircraft and a nearby busy road. A vital requirement is that the building has to minimise radar reflections. Compared with other building materials, glass makes a faint impression on radar. The aluminium window mullions have been given aerofoil profiles to reduce the likelihood of radar interference.

Site conditions influenced the design in other ways. The curtain walls are faceted in section, like those at Western Morning News, but here the aim is to reflect radar, not light, into the ground. The faceted walls also act with the louvred sunshades to cut out direct sunlight. The building is set back from the boundary with the runway and set at a slight angle to it, again to reduce radar reflections.

Beyond the glassy exterior is a 22,279m^2 building,

Section through south facade. The views of planes taking off and landing are maintained, while solar shading is provided by the horizontal glass louvres in the manner of a wide-brimmed hat, rather than sun glasses. The raked ceiling allows more light to enter the office areas.

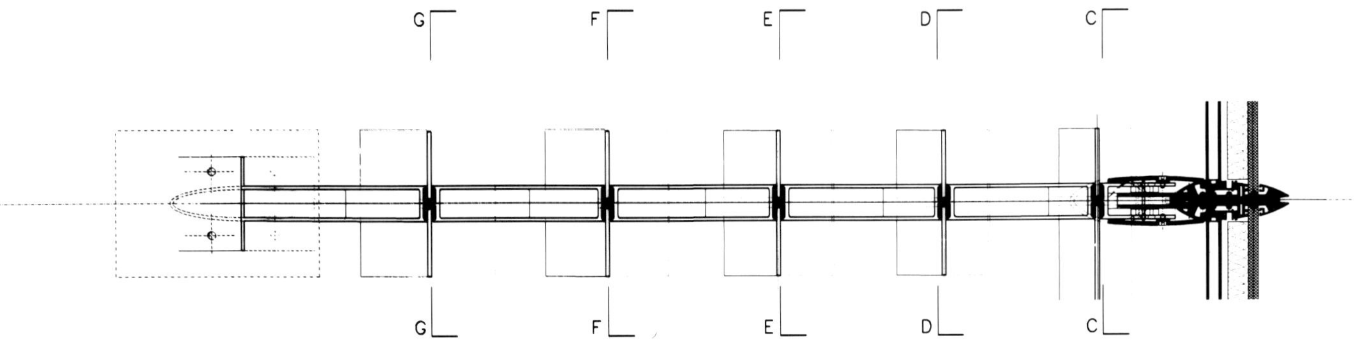

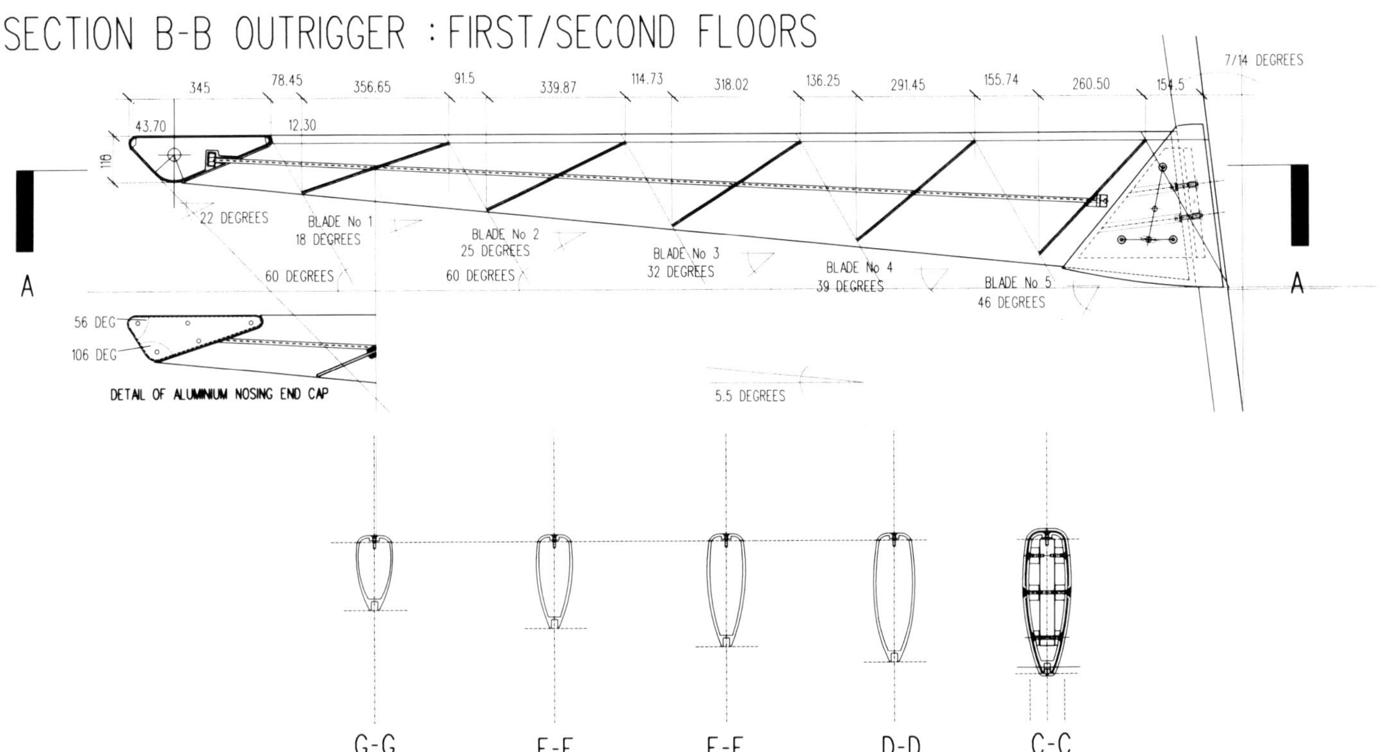

Sections through the louvre assembly of cast aluminium outriggers, extruded aluminium nosing and fritted, blue-glass, louvre blades.

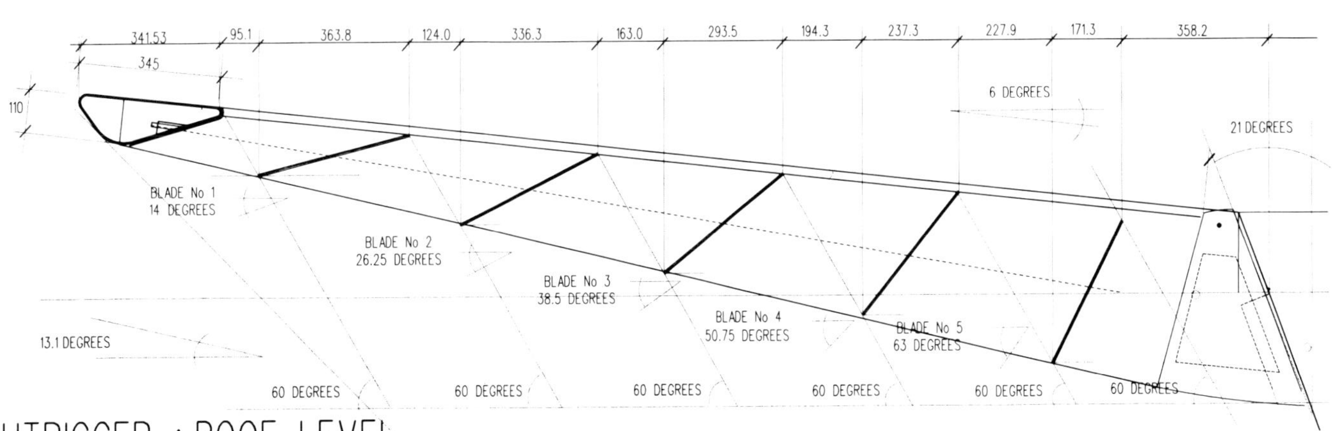

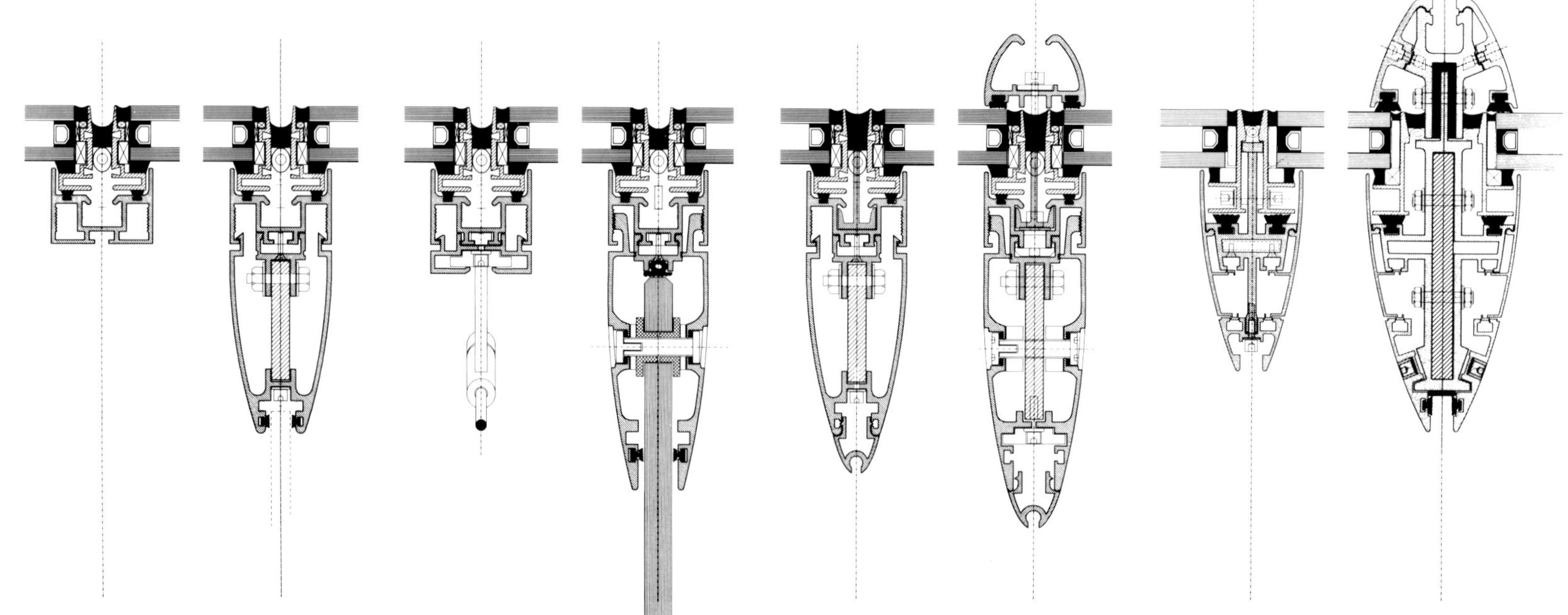

which is flexible enough to be let speculatively in the future, while physically accommodating the demanding technical requirements of British Airways. British Airways' flight and cabin crew business divisions will be accommodated in the structure, and its operations throughout the world will be monitored from this building. To allow for different letting patterns, the building is divided into three blocks, each with its own entrance and atrium, and it will be possible to let units as small as one-quarter of each floor plate.

Detailed section through the mullions and transoms of the four external glazing systems showing the family of component forms.

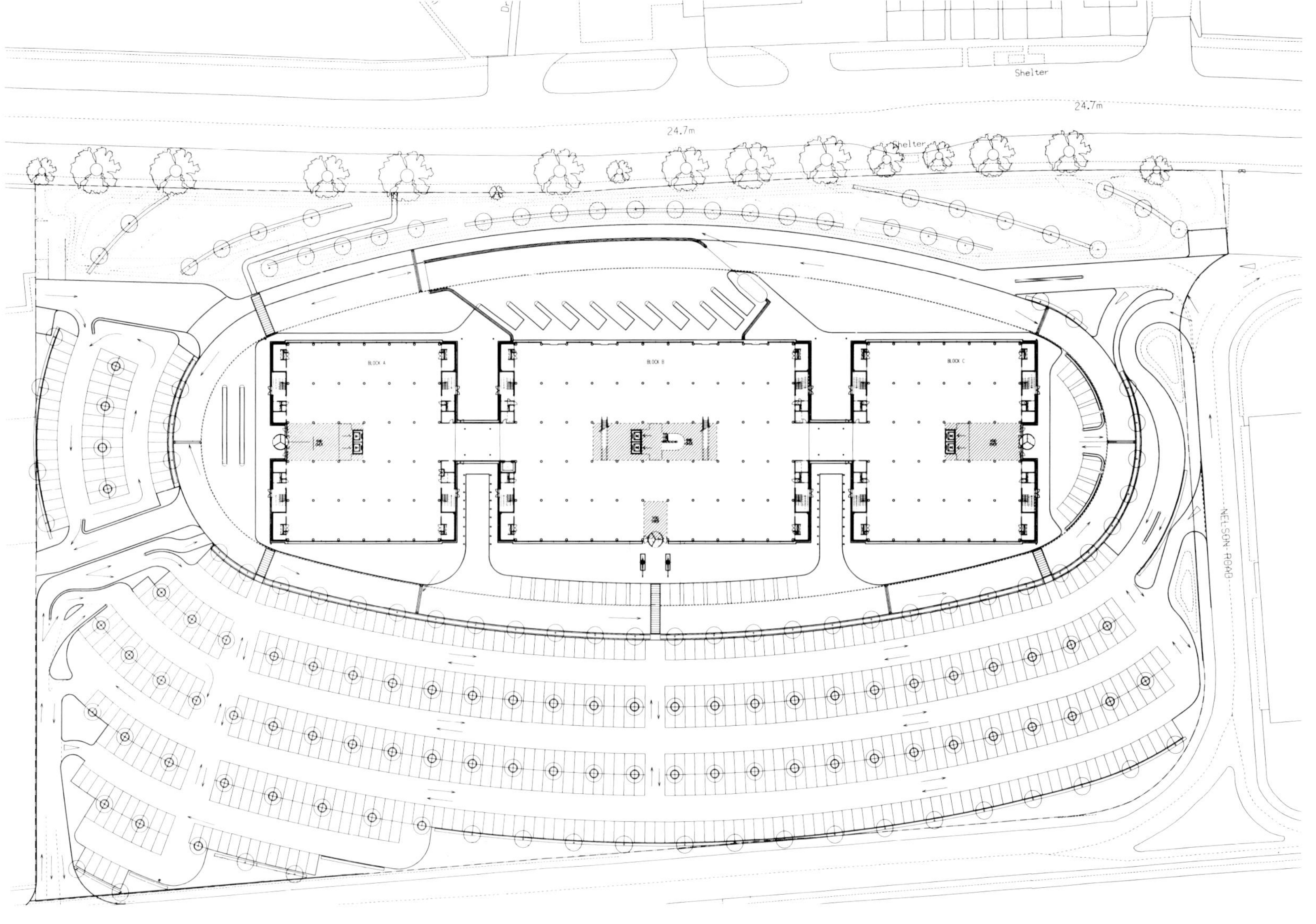

Overall site plan of the building surrounded by an elliptical road and car park. Heathrow's runway No 1 is located due south of the site, while the A4 runs along the north boundary.

Structure, Space and Skin

An edited transcript of the Lord Reilly Memorial Lecture given by Nick Grimshaw at the Design Museum in London on 15 October 1992

Three-masted schooner under construction.

Airship under construction.

Two beautiful structures: a boat under construction with massive oak ribs and its proud workforce standing beside it, and an airship built of materials that are as light as possible. This might not appear to have much to do with architecture, but then my work is not only about architecture. I am greatly interested in detail and the way things go together. I am interested in the human element of putting up structures, which is evident in construction photographs of Joseph Paxton's Great Stove (which he erected before the Crystal Palace), and in the trial bay of the Channel Tunnel Railway Terminal at Waterloo. This trial bay was erected in Yorkshire and then used on the building itself.

The title 'Structure, Space and Skin' is not meant to suggest that these are the only considerations in architecture – good workmanship, appropriate materials and economy are three others – but it is hard to think of a really good building in which these three elements do not figure prominently. To illustrate what I mean by these three elements: a horse skeleton is all structure, while the Omnimax theatre at La Villette in Paris is all skin; a bat's wing is definitely structure and skin. A shell combines all three in rather a beautiful unity: it has marvellous spatial qualities, its structure is extremely strong and it is a skin.

Many great buildings, which appear at first to be all structure, also have spatial qualities. The Eiffel Tower was erected as a temporary building with a licence for six months, and was widely disparaged at the time. It was thought to be a monstrosity, out of scale with its surroundings, but its licence continued to be renewed and now, of course, it is one of the most important symbols of Paris. It is worth noting the richness of detail. This was no mere piece of practical engineering. The shaping and sculptural quality of the steelwork is remarkable.

Even bridges are more than simple feats of engineering. They create space around and underneath themselves, and between the members; they lack only a skin. The same is true of the ferris-wheel in Vienna – an ephemeral-looking structure that hangs on cables from a central hub, just like a bicycle wheel. As with the Eiffel Tower, the scale is quite extraordinary and the effect is hugely powerful. These structures define space. They define an area. They become symbols.

In this country the great tradition of railway stations continued this theme, as well as greenhouses and other structures that the Victorians looked on as non-buildings. Buildings like Paddington Station or the Kibble Palace in Glasgow's botanical gardens had marvellously inventive and grand structures, but often also created cathedral-like spaces, and sometimes achieved extraordinary things with their skin.

All this comes together in the Crystal Palace, which is the most famous example of a building that has been rigorously thought through. It is one of the most significant buildings of the last two centuries. Yet it was almost accidental. An architectural competition was held and nobody was happy with the result. As a last resort Paxton was called in on the strength of his knowledge of greenhouse construction. He was asked simply to enclose the space, and get the job done at the last minute. Although it was all built by horse-power and manpower, it still holds the record for the maximum amount of space covered in the shortest amount of time.

The Crystal Palace project was analysed to the last detail, including the processes of building, such as the travelling gantries from which prefabricated elements and the glazing were installed. Most importantly, it is indisputably a piece of architecture. It certainly has the three elements. It has a very well-considered repetitive structure. It has grand spatial qualities, perhaps not in the way Le Corbusier created spaces, but in the same tradition as the medieval cathedral builders. As for the skin, it is still a model of prefabrication, dimensional co-ordination and of how to get things done. Most of this stems from the first conceptual sketches, which already show the central nave buttressed by aisles, which illustrates that you can create grand buildings if you get the concept right and pursue it with determination.

In contemporary architecture this tradition is continued by architects like Michael Hopkins, Sir Norman Foster or Ian Ritchie, whose work is often thought of as being only about structure. But buildings like Hopkins' Schlumberger Research Centre, near Cambridge, have all three elements in good measure. Seen from the surrounding countryside, it has a dramatic structure. It has skin, par excellence. It also has wonderful spatial qualities, with the cathedral-like, fabric-covered research hall in the centre, contrasted with the pure, almost Miesian offices and research laboratories, which form the aisles. It might be thought ephemeral but the fabric roof can last at least 25 years, which is a reasonable lifespan for a rapidly changing research laboratory, and can readily be replaced.

In Foster's Stansted airport terminal structure, space and skin are all beautifully achieved. The triumph of this building is what has been left out; how much of the normal mess and clutter of airports has been stripped away. One can contemplate the fine detailing of the skin, and the structure disciplines the whole space. It creates a daylit spatial quality that is unlike any other airport. In earlier schemes such as his Renault building at Swindon, Foster had shown how structure alone can define spaces.

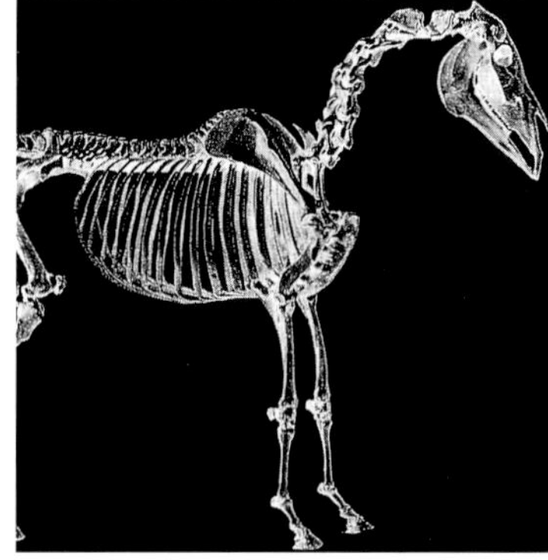

The Géode at Parc de la Villette, Paris.

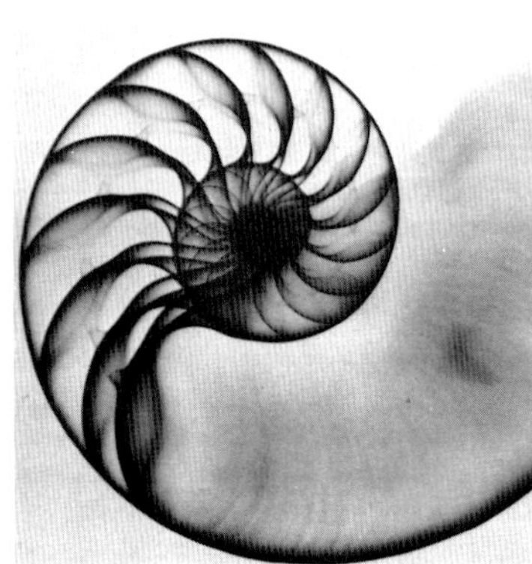

At the Pompidou Centre the gerberettes – the huge castings that act as levers to support the trusses – show the structural dynamics of the building in a way that anybody can understand. One can see how they hold the trusses, and how they are tied down on the outside with tension rods. At the same time they create internal spans of 50m, which give absolutely clear space inside to accommodate the building's different activities. Meanwhile, the architects have done marvellous things with the skin, which varies according to the functions inside and so gives great satisfaction to the outside observer.

Two designs with particularly fine skins are Ritchie's access towers for the Reina Sofia Museum in Madrid, and Foster's Willis Faber & Dumas building in Ipswich. On Ritchie's building, the skin is so transparent it's barely there. It reveals the structure holding the skin and offers a fascinating puzzle to the observer. Spatially, these towers contribute to the building to which they are attached; they allow access to it without spoiling the impact of its solid masonry construction. In Ipswich the skin does several different things: by day it reflects its surroundings but gives wonderful views from the inside; by night the glazed skin disappears altogether, and one can see through to the wonderful illumination of the slabs. Spatially this building was also innovative, in creating open floors and a grand route through the building along tiers of escalators.

In the work of my own office we apply these principles even to houses, where structure is seldom important. We gave our canal-side houses in Camden Town, London innovative and carefully considered skins, and raised the quality of the living space with the double-height living rooms. The structure is very simple, based on a system of party walls that meet the requirements of British building regulations, which have their origins in the Great Fire of London.

The Financial Times Print Works is the first of our projects in which structure and skin work together – the main structural columns that hold up the roof also support the building's skin with the help of cantilevered arms and plates to which the glass is fixed. But structure and skin also contribute to the space. We were greatly impressed by the massive printing presses, which are like the engines of a ship, so we created a great, clear space for them to occupy. The transparency of the skin gives dramatic night views of the printing presses. By day the glass gives very satisfactory reflections and marvellous intervening stages of translucency where one can see partly in and partly out. At dusk the fading daylight combines with the artificial lighting to create an effect reminiscent (though by different means) of the stained glass at Coventry Cathedral. This was done deliberately to lighten the lives of home-bound commuters on one of the busiest routes in London. From the inside the printing workers (who, in the past, would have been buried in the middle of industrial buildings) can see out.

In order to achieve all this the tolerances had to be worked out so that inaccuracies in the structure would not affect the fitting of the glazing. It is interesting perhaps to see how close my original sketch details are to the final shop drawing by Pilkington.

The influence of boats on our buildings has often been noted, but it is the detail and the practical thinking of boat construction that we apply to buildings rather than nautical imagery. At the Financial Times Print Works the steel masts, which hold up the glass skin, echo the masts and cross-trees of the *Cutty Sark* across the river, which are among the earliest steel masts ever used. By contrast with the FT, where steel rods give support to the glazing, the mast of a modern yacht is braced by stainless-steel tension cables. Detail is, of course, very important to us and, as with boats, the detail of the FT enables one almost physically to experience the dynamics of the structure: the way the arms project from the columns to hold the glass and the action of the rods holding the stainless-steel plates. One is acutely aware of how the stainless-steel plates hold the glass exactly in place.

On the building's towers we have used the skin in a quite different way. To contrast with the complex glazing structure we made the aluminium cladding of the towers as smooth and sleek as possible.

Such contrasts apply in many other of our buildings. When we won the competition to design the British Pavilion in Seville for Expo 92, we were very conscious of the great success of Paxton's 1851 Crystal Palace – the first great exposition building that anyone remembers. There have also been other good ones since, such as the Skylon and the Dome of Discovery at the Festival of Britain in 1951, which I can just remember.

The other key issues were climate and comfort because of the intense summer heat of Seville. Our site was in a key position, but the west side received the full force of the afternoon sun. The east side had a good orientation, facing what was called European Avenue, and to the north and south were other pavilions. We realised that the sun would fall on the east side for comparatively little time, added to which the Expo was only open from 10am. We therefore decided from the outset that water would be a theme of the pavilion and decided to make the east wall into a 'water-wall' with water running down to cool the building during the day. We considered using water alone

Victorian print of Crystal Palace.

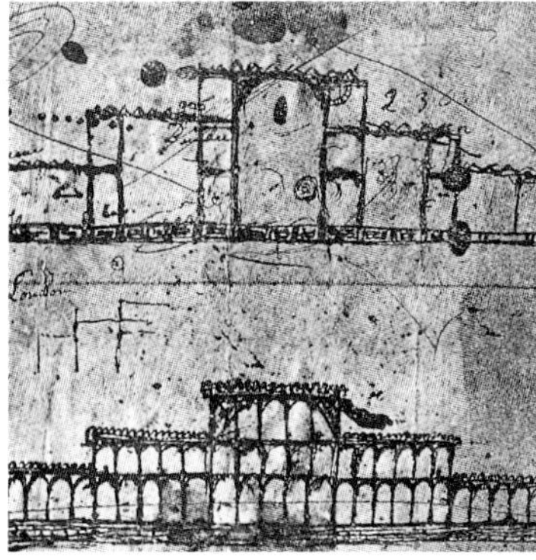

Joseph Paxton's design for Crystal Palace.

as a skin but strong thermal winds in the area would have made this impractical, as was shown by problems with some of the other water pieces on the Expo site. We planned from the outset to shade the south wall completely, which we eventually did with fabric. We also wanted to shield the surface of the roof from the sun with louvres, which would also allow cooling air to circulate between the louvres and the roof.

On the west side we decided to shield the internal space from the hammer-blow of the afternoon sun with water tanks. These had the same effect as a heavy masonry wall, which one normally finds in similar situations in Spain, but which would not have been appropriate for a temporary exhibition such as this. The water tanks retained the coolness of the building, as masonry would have done, and stabilised the swing of temperature during the cycle of day and night.

The Pompidou Centre in Paris.

Cast gerberettes for the Pompidou Centre.

A telling factor in winning the commission was to build a photomontage of the building using cardboard and lights, which conveyed the image we wanted to create, of a great water-wall, lit up at night, facing down European Avenue. We then built a more detailed model where one sees a similar effect by day.

The Expo pavilion also explores the three elements of structure, space and skin. The structure is highly legible and plays a leading role. One can see it in its skeletal form as a very simple clear-span structure, with tapered curved girders supporting the roof and cantilevered trusses coming up from the ground to hold them. At the ends masts support the sail-walls.

Spatially, I think we achieved the maximum. It is the same size as the nave and side aisles of Westminster Abbey, and I think people were genuinely awed by the space. We set out to give them different spatial experiences as they moved through the building: up the travelators for example, with views through the water-wall. The space just inside the sail-walls seemed to be particularly appreciated. There was always a queue outside the building and it proved to be one of the most popular pavilions.

In the skin the qualities of transparency, translucency and opacity were explored with care. We 'tuned' the water-wall with fascination to see what effects we could achieve. In the early morning sun one sees a marvellous, reflective sheen on the building and the water-wall is quite opaque. At night, by contrast, we took care not to shine light onto the running water to allow it to become semi-transparent. From the inside one experiences a dramatic range of light effects, depending on conditions outside. At night, one of the features of Seville was the proliferation of activities with different lighting effects, in which we played part, particularly during the evocative period when darkness is falling and the building is warming up and coming alive.

In terms of my own criteria the pavilion has an understandable structure, heroic space and a skin as highly developed as any at the Expo. And, although it was intended as a temporary building, its elements can be made to last for as long as anyone wants them to.

A more permanent example is the Channel Tunnel Railway Terminal at Waterloo, where the Channel Tunnel trains will arrive in London from the Continent. It comes close to fulfilling my criteria of structure, space and skin. It has structure on a grand scale. It has a complex skin, the design of which took tens of thousands of hours. And its spatial qualities will become apparent when it is opened.

The building's cross section shows how it works. The platforms are at an upper level, as they traditionally are in London: railways were built on viaducts so that traffic could pass underneath them. Below the platforms there is a departure lounge and an arrival concourse similar to those at airports, extensive catering arrangements for the trains, and car parking in the basement. This four-level operation is connected by some fascinating spatial links between the various levels. Ramps, stairs, lifts and travelators allow passengers to move between the spaces.

Waterloo is of a scale with the Parisian *grands projets*. It is 400m long and varies in width between 35m and 55m. The roof stretches from the existing Waterloo concourse to Westminster Bridge and, from its far end, one can see the Houses of Parliament. We developed the shape of the roof with computers and handmade models by some of the gifted modelmakers in our office, using a range of materials such as brass, which is easy to weld and solder. We then built our full-size mock-up of a bay in the middle of the Yorkshire countryside, which enabled subcontractors to check the details, and allowed us to develop the design of the skin and iron out problems in construction or design. We also developed the detailing with scale models of elements so as to resolve all the problems of the building off site: if the model does not work, then nor will the real thing.

Then, during construction, we had the opportunity to develop new details, which was one of the great joys of the project. One example was the giant casting that connects several elements coming together at one point and, repeated throughout the project, simplified the detailing immeasurably. Another was the stainless-steel lost-wax casting, which connects the main roof structure to the roof glazing structure. Again, this was repeated hundreds of times.

Main mast of the 'Cutty Sark'.

Glazing detail of Grimshaw's Financial Times Print Works.

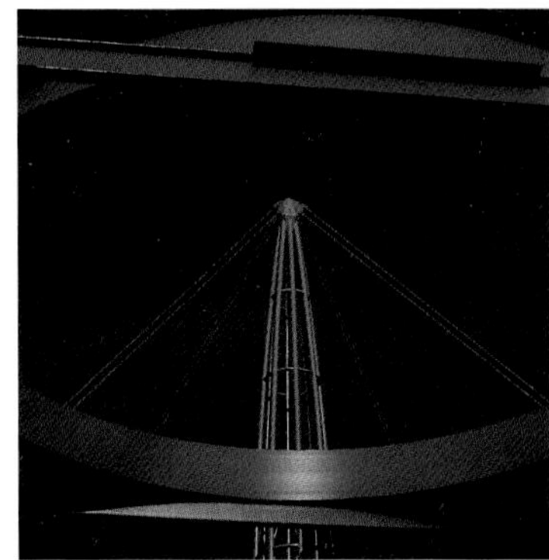
Grimshaw's Igus factory in Cologne.

Ferris-wheel in Vienna.

We wanted to create a roof structure with a heroic feel, a real railway station. We hope people will enjoy comprehending the way the roof works from looking at the details. The glazed wall at the end is one of the first to be braced against wind loadings with structure on both the inside and the outside. As for the skin, we explored it and its geometry almost to the ultimate degree. Where the platform narrows and the span of the trusses reduces, the glass panels had to change in size, which we accommodated by overlapping them like clay tiles on a roof. Where the building curved in plan we dealt with this with concertina gaskets between each roof panel, rather than cutting each one into a separate shape. The project is also built to last: the roof is mainly aluminium and stainless steel with stainless-steel sheeting; the finish on the steel is a long-lasting paint designed for use in the North Sea.

The same concern for structure and for detail guided the design of our factory for Igus. It is a plastics' factory of a type that would normally be a long, low processing plant. Since, however, we wanted to make the building highly visible from the motorway, we gave it a structure that uses pylons a little reminiscent of the Skylon at the Festival of Britain. They also serve a practical purpose as the roof is hung from them like an umbrella to achieve very large, uninterrupted spaces inside. This gives complete flexibility for the layout of the factory. The roof is set at a constant height so that all areas are equally suitable for both storage and manufacturing. The balance between them can be changed easily, which is a major consideration for modern factories. Even the offices are on free-standing platforms that can be moved around to suit changing needs.

Again, this building explores structure, space and skin. The structure is a dramatic one. The owner, who is a great enthusiast for the building, calls it 'his cathedral'. From my early sketches I was thinking of north-facing domed rooflights to give a pleasant quality of light inside and four large landscaped courtyards to improve the quality of light for the workforce in the depths of the building. Each courtyard represents a different season. The skin is the result of extensive and detailed consideration. It consists of pressed aluminium panels simply positioned and held in place by solid aluminium tabs. The panels and the glazing are interchangeable and the whole wall can easily be demounted so the building can be expanded.

At the *Western Morning News* building, the transparency of the skin is again of huge importance. The building is located on a north-facing hillside on one of the main approach roads into Plymouth. It houses a newspaper that sees itself as a major force in the city, and which wanted the building to be a prominent landmark. It might be thought to look like an aircraft carrier, which would not be inappropriate for Plymouth, but that was not the design intention. The shape comes from following the contours of the land, and from the walls of the building, which curve outwards to reduce reflections. We also found that, from a certain height above the ground, one could see Plymouth Sound, so we designed a meeting room and a special viewing platform on top of a lift and stair shaft. This, again unintentionally, recalls the bridge of a ship.

The structure and the skin develop the detailing of the Financial Times Print Works to a greater level of sophistication. The arms, instead of being fabricated, are one-piece castings. The columns follow the curve of the glass walls. The building is more sensual and organic: the curve of the glass, combined with the subtlety of the lighting at different times of day, will give it a really living skin. It also has some marvellous spaces such as the big stairwell in the middle with galleries round it, that permits maximum communication between departments. It has a highly legible structure. I believe that here we have started to raise the three elements of structure, space and skin to a new level.

This investigation is continuing with the design of the Berlin Stock Exchange. We want to generate interest in the streets of Berlin through transparency and translucency. At the moment the city's buildings tend to be monolithic: mainly of render with holes in the walls for windows. There is a flatness and a blandness about the street scene in Berlin, which I believe we can transform with the ideas we have developed with Western Morning News and the Financial Times Print Works.

I believe there is a great capacity for freedom in the design of buildings. They have an ability to change, adapt, become translucent or transparent, to change their skin and to respond to the activities and life they house. For me this can be represented by images that may not seem to have much to do with architecture, such as the view down the mast of a racing yacht or a group of sky-divers. I like buildings to respond in the way a boat responds to the wind. I like them to change in the way that sky-divers form a precise pattern at one moment and then change as they fall through the air. They are only in the sky for a few minutes before they are gone. We have to start thinking of buildings as things with life and vitality, as objects that can be used and changed, that can be made out of good materials if we want them to last, or out of cheaper materials if they are to be ephemeral. However long they last, they must be thoughtful, responsive mechanisms rather than dead, static monuments.

Interview

An edited transcript of a discussion between Nick Grimshaw and Hugh Pearman, broadcast on *Third Ear,* BBC Radio 3, 10 April 1992

HP *Nicholas Grimshaw is an architect who has, building by building since 1967, achieved an enviable reputation. While other architects leap to prominence with this short-lived style or that, Grimshaw prefers to work behind the scenes, gently refining his craft, steadily winning bigger and better commissions.*

Today he is the only architect I know to have had campaigners fighting to save one of his buildings from desecration before it was even built. That building is his rail terminal for Channel Tunnel trains at Waterloo in London, a great arching train shed of Victorian spirit in modern character, now being built at quite remarkable speed.

Already finished is his British Pavilion at Expo 92 in Seville, a technocratic show-stopper if ever there was one. Still to come is his competition-winning design for Berlin's new Stock Exchange – one of a number of commissions in greater Europe – and the Western Morning News *headquarters in Plymouth.*

You might think that a steadfast Modernist such as Nicholas Grimshaw would be having a rough time of it right now, but not so. In common with other exponents of that style, of that particular English technology-based architecture, he has never been busier – at home as well as overseas.

Nick Grimshaw, in your office you have an aluminium staircase supported on yacht masts. What does this tell us about your kind of architecture?

NG Well it's the sort of question a client might ask or might be concerned about in walking up it. And I enjoy explaining the stair. We used the yacht masts because they're very light and were easy to get into the office. We were all working there by that time. We used the groove that the sail slides in, to slide little brackets up to hold the treads of the staircase. We used yacht shroud cables to act as the side protection for the staircase, and we had our own aluminium castings done in London's East End for each end of it.

So it is a work of art from our point of view. We feel it demonstrates how one can use existing components and existing materials to create something. So it's a combination of using things that exist and inventing or creating things that don't exist, bringing them together to make something that really works.

Of course it had to work, you couldn't take clients up and down something that didn't work. But on the whole they're quite intrigued and enjoy it. I think they do see a careful approach, a caring attitude about the way things are done, which perhaps they would hope to see in their buildings if they were to commission one in the future.

HP *A lot of this approach is apparent in your British Pavilion at the Seville Expo. This is a kind of latter-day Crystal Palace, a rational but heroic composition of steel and glass. It has huge solar shades on top and a curtain of water perpetually running down the facade.*

Is this some kind of sly reference to the differences between the climates of Spain and Britain?

NG The whole essence of the design of the pavilion is to do with climatic control and energy-saving. We were aware that in past Expos many buildings had been exhibition boxes with very heavy air conditioning. We were also aware that Seville is the hottest city in Europe and that temperatures are often 45°C in summer. So the idea of controlling the climate by not using too much energy was really one of the key things behind the whole project.

We felt that people had lived in Seville very happily for hundreds of years in this climate. We wanted to analyse the way they did it and try to echo some of those ideas in our building. But of course we couldn't use the same form of construction because it was only a building theoretically designed for six months – to last six months, that is.

HP *So there's an energy-saving message there, a sort of green message as well as purely a glittering palace that will impress people?*

NG Absolutely, and the idea of putting the water-wall on the east side of the building was to cool the building down. And I think it's rather nice that the water-wall is run by solar cells on the roof. So you're actually using the heat of the sun to cool the building by transferring the energy from the sun to running the pumps that pump the water up for the water-wall.

HP *Now someone you've worked with out there on the water-wall is William Pye, the sculptor. How has that particular collaboration worked?*

NG After we had the idea of using the water-wall we realised that Bill had done work with water sculptures; there's a very fine one at Gatwick, which is a cone with water running down it. He's really got the knack of controlling water down to a fine art.

And so we thought it would be a very valuable collaboration. We wanted to work on the way the water would attach itself to the glass and run down the wall, and the different effects he could get with the water going down in waves, or splashing down, or whatever. And we went through a lot of experimentation with him. I've seen it working and I think it looks terrific.

HP *The Expo will be opening later this month. How do you feel now that the other nationalities have got their pavilions there, and they're up and they're running? How do we compare with Japan, say, or with France? Do we hold our heads up?*

NG I think so. I hope the British Pavilion will be seen as a serious piece of architecture, which also as a serious philosophical intent with the energy control and so on. And also I hope it will demonstrate an approach to the sort of quality of detailing that can be done that is, if you like, traditional in Great Britain.

HP *As an architect I think you would say you have a functionalist approach and yet architecture is an art as much as a science. Surely the Expo building is, as you are explaining, more than a box containing exhibits. Similarly, surely your Waterloo terminal is about the excitement of travel rather than merely sheltering trains? How would you describe the feel of your buildings rather than their everyday function?*

NG A building has to have atmosphere. It has to have appeal as you go into it. We talked, in the early days of Waterloo, about it being a sort of gateway to Europe but I think any building of that scale and size has to engender a degree of wonder as you go into it. You don't want to just hurry and scuffle into a train. You want to have some kind of feeling of wonder at being in the space. And that's what we've tried to achieve with the structure and with the lighting effects and so on.

HP *What will the experience be then for travellers arriving at your new Waterloo terminal in 1993?*

NG To come into the main railway station, past the Houses of Parliament and get a view of the river as you enter the station, must be a major plus factor for anyone coming from abroad. You then come into an arched structure that varies in span from 35m to 55m. Very wide-spanning, clear-spanning arches with no columns in the space at all. And at night-time, hopefully, it will be rather beautifully lit with uplighting instead of the usual kind of dim railway-station feel. And a nice light grey, whitish finish to the platform so you're not getting out onto tarmac.

HP *On Waterloo, particularly, the question arises that a building like that is an engineering as much as an architectural* tour de force. *How much of that building, say, is engineer Tony Hunt, and how much is architect Nicholas Grimshaw?*

NG I think you can only achieve what I hope we have achieved with the structure at Waterloo, through absolute collaboration, because the structure is completely integrated with the glazing and the stainless-steel roof covering. It's not a structure that you then apply finishes to. The finishes are linked and bolted onto the structure. We've been intensely involved in all the structural details. We've been up and down to the people doing the stainless-steel casting works, and also the huge steel castings, looking at the quality and finish of all those. And we've done it jointly in a total and happy collaboration with Tony Hunt.

HP *Take 19th-century examples, like Brunel and Digby Wyatt at Paddington Station, or perhaps Decimus Burton and Richard Turner at the Palm House at Kew. Which of those relationships would more describe yours with Tony Hunt, or is it a different thing these days?*

NG I think, it's very interesting, that the engineering has progressed very far in theoretical terms. For instance, we've got tapering tubes in the truss members, which look very elegant. When you're joining a thick member to a thinner member, to take the tube between the two of them is something which is very satisfactory to the eye...

HP *...Whereas the Victorians, you're implying, would merely fling girders across the whole thing.*

NG In lots of cases, of course, they achieved beautiful effects without actually being able to calculate them. But I think the science of engineering has moved on and can help us enormously in those kind of details.

HP *A big success of yours in recent years is the print works building for the* Financial Times *in London Docklands. I was with the fashion designer Jean Muir when she described it as an inlaid jewel box, and it's won all kinds of awards. Why go to all that trouble for what is fundamentally just a factory? There are no journalists in there, in fact journalists are rather worse served in their current headquarters.*

NG I don't think there should be a distinction between how much trouble you go to for one type of person rather than another. If anything you could say that the people working on a printing press, which is often quite repetitive work, should have a view of the outside world. To give them a chance to see out, to see traffic going by and to have a relationship with it, whether it's day or night, is, I think a really worthwhile achievement.

Every other printing press that's rebuilt itself in London (nearly all the main newspapers have done it) has just buried the press in the middle of the building like the engine room of a ship. The poor fellows working down there never see the light of day. So we thought we were doing a lot for the people working in the press. At the same time, perhaps, we were also doing quite a bit for people passing by the building in a sense that it was an exciting thing to see, and an exciting thing to pass by on one of the major routes out of London.

HP *Your building for the* Western Morning News *outside Plymouth is a child of the* Financial Times *building to some extent. But if the Financial Times Print Works was a jewel box, the Western Morning News with its curving glazed sides and its bridge on top is, to all who see it and who see the designs, a ship.*

What dictated the form of what some have seen as being a rather mannered building?

NG I was down there last week and I was very thrilled by standing in it. One of the prime things about the building is the site: it is a most beautiful site on a hillside with a valley full of big trees and a very nice stream with a dam across it, which we're going to use as a lake down just below it.

I was very affected by the site and also various things about the climate, such as the fact that the south-westerly winds are very strong there, coming straight in from the sea. We wanted to tuck the building below the brow of the hill. The curving shape started with the idea of following the contour of the hill directly. And so we had one curving side to the building. In the original design, the back of the building was flat but it didn't seem to look right. And so we made it symmetrical, so it had a curve each side, and then everyone started calling it a ship-like building. But it did evolve from the site and from the orientation more than anything else.

As far as the glazing's concerned, it was curved in the vertical plane because, when you view the building from down the hillside, you would have terrifically strong reflections otherwise. So it's rather like what they do with, say, a car instrument panel where you put the glass at an angle or curve it so you can see the instruments properly and cut out the reflections. We wanted people to be able to see into the building and see the press without reflecting the sky on the side of the building.

HP *In this case there are journalists in there as well as print workers. It's a complete headquarters building, I believe, isn't it?*

NG Yes, one of the really nice things, as an architect, is to get a building that's complete. So we're doing all the desks right down to the ink-blotters and the vase of flowers on the table before they move in. We've got the complete commission for Western Morning News, so I hope there will be a feeling of unity about the building and about the way it's designed.

HP *And what of your rather heroic conning-tower or bridge on top? What is that intended to do?*

NG The real thing behind that is that the newspaper is moving from the centre of Plymouth, where it is very much in touch with the sea, to a hillside four miles away. We discovered that at a certain height you could actually see Drake's Sound, you could see Plymouth Harbour from that hillside. So we thought it would be a marvellous idea to put a meeting room-cum-boardroom at that level so you could have panoramic views right across Dartmoor and across the sea. It's really an absolutely fantastic view up there.

And from being tucked under the brow of the hill to then go up in a lift and come out on this sort of viewing platform, rather like a lighthouse, on top is rather a nice experience, I think. It gives a different dimension to the building.

HP *This is 1992 and you're already doing work in mainland Europe. In fact, you've been doing work there for some time. But at the moment the Berlin Stock Exchange, of course, is on your drawing boards and a factory near Cologne. How do your European clients find you?*

NG With the factory for Cologne we had a marvellous experience because the client literally walked up to the front door of our office – it's the sort of commission an architect dreams of – and said, 'Mr Grimshaw, I have chosen you to be my architect'.

HP *He was from Cologne?*

NG Yes, and he'd been round looking at several of our buildings, particularly our industrial buildings in England, and he simply decided that was the kind of thing he liked, and that was what he wanted.

We had an enormous amount on at the time, and so I told him, 'I'm not sure we've got the time', (or something similar). And he said, 'but you must do it'. And I said 'well, you'd better come in and we'll talk about it'. That sort of thing is a marvellous experience as he wasn't concerned simply with the appearance of the building, he knew about the cultural background of what we were trying to do. He knew about repetitive panels and flexibility, and could talk about Charles Eames, and so on and so forth. He is a very cultured person and decided that the sort of building that was flexible and reflected really industrial design ideas was exactly what he wanted.

HP *Your Waterloo terminal with its great, jointed, arcing roof shows certain organic characteristics. It seems to me it's almost like dinosaur bones joined together. And your Berlin Stock Exchange also shows something of this more organic nature, something which perhaps your buildings haven't shown in the past. Exactly what are you giving Berlin with your new Stock Exchange?*

NG Berlin strikes me as quite a grey city. The buildings at the moment are all very flat-fronted; they're nearly all rendered, cement-faced buildings, with very little colour and hole-in-the-wall windows.

I felt very much that some kind of real drama and lift was needed on this site. The idea is to have expressed steel, a structure with a bony feeling and a terrific expanse of glazing on the street side, which would allow you to look into the building and down into the basement where we're going to have a design centre, and a lot of objects on display.

You would be able to look through to a pedestrian route, which passes right along the building, and see people walking along it. And across that route you can also see the enormous display board for the Stock Exchange. So literally standing in the street you can see right through the building and see the Stock Exchange prices clicking away on the board.

There are many other things going on there: three restaurants in the building, an energy-advice centre and so on. It will be very alive and a very light-seeming building, very transparent with marvellous lighting effects.

It will integrate itself with the street and give a dramatic feel to the street instead of this closed, blank feel you get normally walking around Berlin – often without shops present, as they bring windows with grilles or shutters right down to the street level. And so you can walk down a street where there's really almost nothing happening at all. So I think it will be a terrifically lively punctuation mark, if you like, in the street scene in Berlin.

HP *Has it become an object of affection to Berliners?*

NG Most new schemes get a rather difficult press in

Berlin and a nickname! There's a certain feel, at the moment, of holding onto the past.

We've had quite a good press. They seem to like the democratic feel of the building, the fact that it's not a point block; it's low, people can circulate through it, there are things in it that are interesting for the passer-by. All these have gone down quite well and it's now known as 'the reptile' because of its bony structure.

HP *Do you work in a different way to, say, a German architect or a French architect?*

NG There is a different tradition of working. In Europe the architect tends to be more the guy who does charcoal sketches and behaves more like the artist, and leaves it to other people to work out the details. In England, almost uniquely, I think, there is this tradition amongst a whole group of architects (I don't necessarily call them Modernists; I call them, in some ways, traditionalists who have emerged from the engineering tradition of Paxton and Brunel) who are really interested in the way things go together and in the way they're detailed. I think that is becoming more and more appreciated. People are getting fed up with wallpaper architecture and they want to see real details in the way they've appreciated them in the past. It's ageless in a way.

HP *Is this not the legacy of the Arts and Crafts tradition as much as anything? You mention the engineers but is there not the Arts and Crafts as well?*

NG Yes, there is. I think that putting things together beautifully and doing things beautifully was as much a part of the Arts and Crafts movement as it was a part of Victorian engineering.

HP *Since your first building in 1967, which was a helical tower of glass-fibre bathroom pods for students, you've done housing, sports halls, offices, factories, warehouses, transport buildings like Waterloo or your new airport pier at Heathrow. But is there a building type – it might be a theatre, concert hall, a church – that you're itching to do, if only someone would give you the chance?*

NG I think, I feel very drawn to the theatre. I've always been very interested in the theatre and I feel that we don't have a space in this country that can really deal with the sort of extremes of theatrical experience. We have a small place at the Riverside Studios in Hammersmith in London, which is quite nice. But I think a much larger version of that would be a marvellous thing to do, where people can really stretch their imaginations in terms of staging things and where designers could really work with the space and do very exciting things with seating and how they actually staged a performance.

HP *So rather than the orthodoxy, which is a black box theatre for experimental plays, you'd rather have radical architecture for radical theatre. Is that what you're saying?*

NG I don't think the architecture should impose too much. But one thing our pavilion from Seville could be used for would be exactly what I'm putting forward, in that it's a very large volume that could provide an excellent space for the arts.

HP *Well it's on the agenda, isn't it, just as a petition of critics and fellow architects was drawn up to successfully prevent your Waterloo terminal being engulfed by office blocks? So there are now voices calling for your Expo pavilion to be dismantled, like Crystal Palace, and brought back home to Blighty.*

Would you like to see that happen?

NG I don't want to be downhearted about what might possibly happen in Seville because, if the Spanish could turn the Expo site into a vibrant science park which really worked for them, I would be very happy for the building to stay there and to do some work on it to turn it into, say, a headquarters or conference centre for a company or whatever, or a training centre.

But if that does not happen, then I certainly would be very sad to see the building just dismantled and sold off for scrap, when it could probably be brought back to England and re-erected for perhaps only £5–6m compared with the £15m that it cost to build in the first place. So you're reusing a lot of the materials and bringing them back, re-erecting them. I think it would be a fascinating concept if one could find a site where it could be used as an arts building.

HP *Nicholas Grimshaw, thank you very much.*

Awards

Royal Institute of British Architects

1975 Warehouse, Citroën Cars, Runnymede (commendation)
1978 Assembly Plant, Herman Miller, Bath (principal award)
1980 Industrial Units, Winwick Quay, Warrington (principal award)
1980 BMW Headquarters, Bracknell (commendation)
1983 Castle Park, Nottingham (commendation)
1986 Warehouse, Herman Miller, Chippenham (commendation)
1989 Financial Times Print Works, London (national and regional awards)
1990 Rank Xerox Research and Development Facility, Welwyn Garden City (regional award)
1991 Heatwaves Leisure Pool, Stockbridge (commendation)

Financial Times Industrial Architecture Awards

1977 Assembly Plant, Herman Miller, Bath (principal award)
1977 Excel House, Reading (commendation)
1980 Winwick Quay, Warrington (commendation)
1980 Gillingham Business Park Phase One (commendation)

Structural Steel Design Awards

1969 Service Tower, International Students Club, London (principal award)
1977 Assembly Plant, Herman Miller, Bath (principal award)
1980 Gillingham Business Park Phase One (commendation)
1989 Financial Times Print Works, London (commendation)
1989 Homebase, Brentford (commendation)

Civic Trust Awards

1978 Excel House, Reading (commendation)
1978 Assembly Plant, Herman Miller, Bath (commendation)
1982 IBM Sports Hall, Hursley (commendation)
1989 Financial Times Print Works, London (national and regional awards)
1990 Rank Xerox Research and Development Facility, Welwyn Garden City (commendation)
1991 Heatwaves Leisure Pool, Stockbridge (commendation)

Architectural Design Awards

1974 Millman Street Redevelopment, London
1982 Industrial Nursery Units, Gillingham Business Park (commendation)
1983 Offices, Digital Equipment, Aztec West (bronze medal)

Department of the Environment Awards

1973 125 Park Road, London (commendation)

British Construction Industry Awards

1988 Homebase, Brentford (high commendation)
1989 Financial Times Print Works, London (high commendation)
1992 British Pavilion, Expo 92, Seville (high commendation and special commendation)

Royal Fine Art Commission/Sunday Times Building of the Year Award

1989 Financial Times Print Works, London (joint winner)

Other Awards

1977 Business and Industry Awards
Assembly Plant, Herman Miller, Bath (certificate of merit)
1980 Ambrose Congreve Award for Architecture
BMW Headquarters, Bracknell (commendation)
1981 European Award for Steel Structures
BMW Headquarters, Bracknell (commendation)
1987 BSC Structural Steel Classics 1906-1986
Assembly Plant, Herman Miller, Bath
1989 Illustrated London News Awards
Financial Times Print Works, London (winner – development category)
1990 European Award for Industrial Architecture
Financial Times Print Works, London (second prize)
1990 BBC Design Awards
Financial Times Print Works, London (finalist)

Project list

Public Buildings

British Rail Channel Tunnel Railway Terminal at Waterloo, London
British Rail Operations Centre at Waterloo, London
Department of Trade and Industry British Pavilion, Expo 92, Seville, Spain
Heathrow Airport Ltd Satellite and Pier, Heathrow Airport, London

Offices

Berlin Chamber of Commerce Berlin Stock Exchange and Communications Centre, Berlin, Germany
BMW (UK) Ltd Headquarters, Bracknell, Berkshire
Citroën UK Ltd UK parts headquarters at Runnymede, Surrey
Digital Equipment Co Ltd Offices at Aztec West, Bristol, Avon
Editions Van de Velde Offices at Tours, France
Grosvenor Developments Management centre at Gillingham Business Park, Kent
Igus GmbH Factory and headquarters, Cologne, Germany
Ladkarn (Haulage) Ltd Headquarters, offices and workshops in London Docklands
Standard Life Assurance Company Hartspring Business Park, Watford, Hertfordshire
Vitra GmbH Factory and central administrative offices near Basel, Switzerland
The Western Morning News Co Ltd Headquarters, editorial offices and printing press, Plymouth, Devon
Xerox Research UK Ltd Engineering facilities, offices and research centre, Welwyn Garden City, Hertfordshire
Lynton plc Combined Operations Centre for British Airways, London

Industrial / Warehousing

Electricity Supply Ltd Distribution centre at Castle Park, Nottingham, Nottinghamshire
Financial Times Ltd Printing plant, London Docklands
Grosvenor Developments Eight warehouses and manufacturing buildings at Gillingham Business Park, Kent
Herman Miller Ltd UK headquarters, manufacturing and assembly plant at Bath, Avon
Herman Miller Ltd UK central distribution centre at Chippenham, Wiltshire
Igus GmbH Headquarters and factory, Cologne, Germany
Ladkarn (Haulage) Ltd Vehicle maintenance and testing centre at London Docklands
Rotork Controls Manufacturing, storage and staff amenity building at Bath, Avon
Rotork Controls Manufacturing, storage and staff amenity building at Maryland, USA
J Sainsbury plc Industrial/workshop units, Camden Town, London
Slough Estates plc Three office/industrial buildings at Buckingham Avenue, Slough, Berkshire
Tambrands France S.A. New plant at Tours, France
Thames Water and Utilities Ltd, and London Docklands Development Corporation North Woolwich Pumping Station, London
Warrington and Runcorn Development Corporation Industrial buildings at Warrington New Town, Cheshire
The Western Morning News Co Ltd Headquarters, editorial offices and printing press, Plymouth, Devon
The Jet Stationery Co Ltd Proposed stationery print works, London Docklands

Communications

Wiltshire Radio Ltd Studios, offices and reception centre at Wootton Bassett, Swindon, Wiltshire
Yorkshire Television Feasibility study for a new studio at Leeds, Yorkshire

Sports and Leisure

IBM (UK) Ltd Multi-purpose sports hall at Winchester, Hampshire
Liverpool City Council Sports centre and leisure pool at Millbank, Liverpool, Merseyside
London Docklands Development Corporation Training and activity centre for sea scouts, London Docklands
Metropolitan Borough of Knowsley Leisure and communal facilities, Stockbridge, Liverpool, Merseyside
Oxford City Council Ice rink adjoining city centre, Oxford, Oxfordshire
Scottish Development Agency Feasibility study for Scottish National Aquarium in Glasgow, Strathclyde
Sports Council Twenty-four standardised sports halls nationwide
Willhire Ltd National Roller Skating Centre, Bury St Edmunds, Suffolk
Rush and Tompkins Leisure Proposed ice rink and entertainment centre at Basildon New Town, Essex

Interiors

Herman Miller Ltd Offices at Chippenham, Wiltshire
Herman Miller Ltd Prototype showroom facility at Bath, Avon
Igus GmbH Headquarters and factory interiors, Cologne, Germany
Vitra GmbH Office interior near Basel, Switzerland
Wiltshire Radio Ltd Studio interiors and reception area, Wootton Bassett, Swindon, Wiltshire

Planning

Electricity Supply Ltd Masterplan for 180-acre business park at Aztec West, Bath, Avon
English Industrial Estates Ltd Initial studies for a new technology park at Team Valley, Gateshead, Tyne and Wear
Greater London Enterprise Board Feasibility study for industrial area adjoining the Grand Union Canal, Islington, London
Grosvenor Developments Masterplan for 120-acre business park at Gillingham, Kent
Herman Miller Ltd Masterplan for 15-acre European headquarters at Chippenham, Wiltshire
London Docklands DevelopmentCorporation Alternative studies for land adjoining Docklands Light Railway, London
Standard Life Assurance Company Masterplan for Hartspring Business Park, Watford, Hertfordshire
Trafalgar House (Investments) Ltd Masterplan for 35-acre site at Bracknell, Berkshire

Retail / Showroom

Homebase Ltd Homebase retail centre, Brentford, Middlesex
MFI Ltd Showroom/sales centre at Gillingham Business Park, Kent
Port East Developments Proposed dockside retail/restaurant building, London Docklands
J Sainsbury plc Supermarket and underground car park in Camden, London
Southern Developments Ltd Proposed retail units at Basildon New Town, Essex
Vitra Ltd West End showroom, London

Residential

London Borough of Camden Eighty-three flats in Bloomsbury, London
Maunsell Housing Society Sixty flats in Wimbledon, London
Mercury Housing Society Forty flats adjoining Regents Park, London
J Sainsbury plc Eleven houses beside Grand Union Canal, Camden, London

Health and Welfare

University College London Student health centre, Camden, London
University College London Dental centre, Camden London

Industrial Design

Henderson Doors Ltd Insulated cladding panel system
Herman Miller Ltd Cladding system at Bath and Chippenham
International Students Club, London Prefabricated fibreglass bathroom units
Warrington and Runcorn Development Corporation Stainless-steel industrial toilet modules

Competitions

Anglo Japanese Consortium Kuala Lumpur International Airport
Bovis and Technical University of Brno Brno Technology Park
British Airports Authority Terminal Five, Heathrow Airport, London
British Olympic Bid Manchester 2000 Stadium and masterplan
Ministère de la Culture, de la Communication et des Grands Travaux, France Bibliothèque Nationale de France

Project Data

Channel Tunnel Railway Terminal at Waterloo, London, 1993
Overall dimensions approx. 400 x 48m (max) to 32m (min)
Structural dimensions 13m centres spanning 48m (max), 35m (min)
Contract value £130m
NGP design team Rowena Bate, Ingrid Bille, Conal Campbell, Garry Colligan, Geoff Crowe, Florian Eames, Alex Fergusson, Nick Grimshaw, Sarah Hare, Eric Jaffres, Ursula Heinemann, Doug Keys, David Kirkland, Chris Lee, Colin Leisk, Jan Mackie, Julian Maynard, Neven Sidor, Ulriche Seifutz, Will Stevens, George Stowell, Andrew Whalley, Robert Wood, Sara Yabsley, Richard Walker
NGP site office Paul Fear, Steve McGuckin
Client British Railways Board
Structural engineers YRM Anthony Hunt Associates (roofing and glazing); Cass Hayward & Partners with Tony Gee & Partners (terminal viaduct); British Rail Network Civil Engineer (approaches viaduct); Sir Alexander Gibb & Partners (basement and external works)
Fire consultant Ove Arup & Partners
Lighting consultant Lighting Design Partnership
Signage consultant Henrion Ludlow Schmidt
Quantity surveyor Davis Langdon & Everest
Flow-planning consultant Sir Alexander Gibb & Partners
M&E engineer J. Roger Preston & Partners
Planning consultant Montagu Evans
Construction manager Bovis Construction Ltd

North Woolwich Pumping Station, London, 1988
Overall dimensions 68 x 32m
Overall area 1,728m^2
Structural dimensions curved beams at 6m centres spanning 45m
Contract value £2m
NGP Paul Cook, Paul Grayshon, Nick Grimshaw, Christopher Nash, Mike Waddington
Clients Thames Water and Utilities Ltd; London Docklands Development Corporation
Structural engineer Sim William Halcrow and Partners Ltd
Quantity surveyor Bellamy & Wareham

British Pavilion, Expo 92, Seville, 1992
Overall dimensions 65m long x 40m wide x 24m high
Overall area 7,000m^2
Structural dimensions 7.2m centres spanning 32m
Contract value £15.8m
NGP Eion Billings, Paul Cook, Mark Fisher, Nick Grimshaw, Duncan Jackson, Andrew Hall, Rosemary Latter, John Martin, Christopher Nash, Julian Scanlan, Rob Watson
Client Department of Trade and Industry
Structural and environmental engineer Ove Arup & Partners
Quantity surveyor and construction cost consultant Davis Langdon & Everest
Water feature consultant William Pye Partnership
Management contractor Trafalgar House Construction Management Ltd

Operations Centre for British Rail at Waterloo, London, 1990
Overall dimensions phase one, 25 x 83m; phase one and two, 170 x 40m
Overall area phase one, 2,075m^2; phase one and two, 6,800m^2
Structural dimensions 3 x 6m (min) or 9m (max) grid
Contract value phase one, £7m
NGP Lindy Atkin, Stefan Camenzind, Nick Grimshaw, Matthew Keeler, Nicola MacDonald, Richard Walker
Client BRB Network SouthEast
Structural engineer Kenchington Little plc
Quantity surveyor Turner & Townsend
Services engineer J. Roger Preston
Management contractor Kyle Stewart Ltd

Shopping and Leisure Project, Port East, London, Docklands, 1989
Overall dimensions 20 x 144m
Overall area 6,913m^2
Structural bay dimensions 22.5 x 22.5m grid; roof spanning 16m
Contract value £5.2m
NGP Lindy Atkin, Mark Bryden, Rowena Fuller, Nick Grimshaw, Andrew Hall, Dana Karanjac, Julian King, Chrisopher Nash, Andrew Nicol, Bertholdt Pesch, Bob Tucker, Martin Wood
Client Port East Developments Ltd
Structural engineer Ove Arup & Partners
M&E engineer HH Angus & Associates (UK) Ltd
Cost consultants Mark Dunstone & Associares
Development manager Olympia & York (UK) Ltd
Construction manager Trafalgar Construction Management Ltd

Satellite and Piers, Heathrow Airport, London, 1993
Overall dimensions pier, 9m wide x 340m long x 3.5m high; CTA building, 36m diameter x 13.375m high; links one and three, 6.6m wide x 3m high; links two and four, 4m wide x 2.5m high; nose building, 61.5m long x 38m wide
Overall area pier, 3,060m^2; CTA building, 1,488m^2; links, 1,277m^2; nose building, 3,301m^2; Belfast lounge, 1,410m^2
Contract value £29.3m
NGP Nick Grimshaw, David Harriss, Susanna Isa, Jeremy King, Julian King, Brian la Fontaine, John Lee, Martin Hyams, Andrew Nicol, Michael Pross, David Radford, Marcus Springer, Hin Tan
Client Engineering Projects Group, Heathrow Airport Ltd
Structural, mechanical, electrical, electronic, building services engineer BAA Consultants Ltd
Quantity surveyor WT Partnership
Services consultant to NGP Loren Butt Consultancies
Construction manager AMEC Projects Ltd

Venice Biennale, 1991
Overall dimensions 450 x 312 x 40m high
Structural dimensions radiating column centres 55m (max) to 38m (min); roof span 75m (max)
NGP Christopher Campbell, Paul Grayshon, Nick Grimshaw, David Harriss, Michael Pross, Hin Tan, Simon Templeton

Nicholas Grimshaw & Partners' Offices, London, 1992
NGP Ingrid Bille, Nick Grimshaw, Neven Sidor, Simon Templeton
Staircase components Proctor Mast, Southampton
Contractor Brian Hannon, London

IGUS Headquarters and Factory, Cologne, 1992
Overall dimensions 102.5 x 68m
Overall area 7,400m^2
Structural dimensions 11.25 x 11.25m grid with 33.7m roof spans
Contract value DM19m
NGP Mark Bryden, Penny Collins, Nick Grimshaw, David Harriss, Dorothee Strauss
Client Igus GmbH
Bauleiter Michael Weiss
Structural and services engineer Whitby & Bird
Quantity surveyor Davis Langdon & Everest
Contractors Walter Bau-AG; Trafalgar House Construction Management Ltd

Bibliothèque Nationale de France, Competition, 1989
Overall dimensions 300 x 140 x 60m high
Overall area 158,000m^2
NGP Ingrid Bille, Jacque Ferrier, Nick Grimshaw, François Gruson, Matthew Keeler, Neven Sidor, Andrew Whalley
Client Ministère de la Culture, de la Communication et des Grands Travaux, France
Structural engineer Ove Arup & Partners

Hartspring Business Park, Watford, 1986–
Overall dimensions buildings one to five, 27 x 42 x 8m (two floors) or 12m (three floors)
Overall area 15,714m^2
Contract value £24m
NGP Chris Campbell, Robert Elliston, Nick Grimshaw, David Harriss, Julian King, John Lee, Colin Leisk, David Portman, Dorothee Strauss, Sarah Tweedie, Luz Vargas
Client Standard Life Assurance Company
Structural engineer Blyth & Blyth Associates (London)
Quantity surveyor Leonard Stace Partnership
Services engineer Blyth & Blyth (M&E)
Landscape architect RPS Clouston
Controls consultant JMC Partnership
Project manager Buro Four Project Services

Western Morning News, Plymouth, 1992
Overall dimensions 115m long x 51m wide at ground level
Overall area cross-floor areas 5,671m^2 (offices), 6,459m^2 (production areas)
Structural bay dimensions 6 x 6m grid
Contract value £14.9m
NGP Lindy Atkin, Eoin Bilings, Paul Grayshon, Nick Grimshaw, Andrew Hall, Duncan Jackson, Jonathan Leah, Nicola Macdonald, Christopher Nash, Julian Scanlan, Matthew Seabrook, Mike Waddington, Martin Wood
Client The Western Morning News Co Ltd
Structural engineer Ove Arup & Partners
Quantity surveyor Davis Langdon & Everest (Plymouth)
Services engineer Cundall Jonston & Partners
Contractor Bovis Construction Ltd

Berlin Stock Exchange and Communications Centre, 1991–1995
Overall dimensions 94.5 x 65m
Overall area 38,000m^2 gross
Structural dimensions 10.5 x 6m grid; arches spanning 20m (min) to 55m (max)
Contract value DM150m
NGP Stefan Camenzind, Nick Grimshaw, Matthew Keeler, Michael Pross, Neven Sidor, Dorothee Strauss
Clients Industrie-und Handelskammer zu Berlin (IHK); Verein Berliner Kaufleute und Industrieller (VBKI)
Structural engineer Whitby & Bird
Quantity surveyors Davis Langdon & Everest; Mott Green & Wall
Services consultant Whitby & Bird
Project managers Buro Four; Schofer– Marschal–Vedder

Combined Operations Centre for British Airways, Heathrow, London, 1993
Overall dimensions 188 x 27 x 12m high
Overall area 22,2858m^2
Structural dimensions 6 x 9m grid
Contract value £22m
NGP Stefan Camenzind, Penny Collins, Robert Elliston, Rowena Fuller, Nick Grimshaw, Andrew Hall, Julian King, Rosemary Latter, Jonathan Leah, John Lee, John Martin, Liz Parr, David Portman, David Radford, Luz Vargas, Martin Wood
Client Heathrow Airport Ltd
Agent Lynton plc
Structural engineer YRM Anthony Hunt Associates
Services engineer J Roger Preston & Partners
Quantity surveyor Davis Langdon & Everest
Radar consultant Dowty Signature Management Ltd
Acoustic consultant Ian H. Flindell & Associates
Construction manager Bovis Construction Ltd

Bibliography

General

Archigram 1965: 'Newcomer, Nick Grimshaw' (Nick Grimshaw's student thesis)

Atrium March, 1989: 'Talking to the Terrier'

Blueprint 23 July 1985: 'Urbane Spaceman', Martin Pawley (interview with Nick Grimshaw)

Building 23 July 1982: 'High-Tech with Zip', Colin Davies (interview with Nick Grimshaw)

Building 15 January 1988: 'Flight Path to Fame', Sutherland Lyall

Design October 1980: 'The Mobile Office', Deyan Sudjic (Nicholas Grimshaw & Partners' offices)

Deutsche Bauzeitung December 1988: 'Building with Steel' special issue, including 'When Structure Becomes Architecture' by Nick Grimshaw and 'Die Schwelle zur Architektur'

Experimental Architecture Peter Cook, Studio Vista, 1970

ICA Model Futures 1983, Bob Allies (on Nick Grimshaw's Architectural Association thesis)

Journal of the Royal Society of Arts December 1984: 'The Future of Industrial Building', Nick Grimshaw

Journal of the Royal Society of Arts September 1986: 'Reinventing the Factory', RSA–Cubitt Trust Panel (summary of a seminar held in October 1985)

National Structural Steel Association 1986 National Structural Steel Conference: 'The Changing World of Steel Construction'

RIBA Journal June 1968: 'Buckminster Fuller: Royal Gold Medallist, 1968', Nick Grimshaw

RIBA Journal October 1980: 'Energetic Architecture', Nick Grimshaw (benefits of mixed industrial/residential development)

RIBA Journal October 1992: 'Solar Powered Pavilion' – RIBA lecture on the British Pavilion, Expo 92, by Nick Grimshaw, Richard Haryott and Clyde Malby

Times 2 October 1991: 'Master whose Mettle is Galvanising', Marcus Binney

World Architecture No 14, 1991: 'White Knight of Technology', Martin Pawley

Channel Tunnel Railway Terminal at Waterloo
Architektur Actuell February 1992: 'London Tor zu Europa – Waterloo Terminal, London'
Architectural Review December 1989: 'Tale of Termini'
L'Arca September 1990: 'Un Tunnel sulla Stazione', Maurizio Vogliazzo
Building 31 August, 1990: 'Point of Departure', Denise Chevin
Building 8 May 1992: 'Joint Adventures: Waterloo Terminal', James McNeil
Building Design 18 March, 1988: 'Grimshaw Wins the Battle for Waterloo'
Building Design 30 March 1990: 'New Protest over Offices at Waterloo'
Building Design 8 June 1990: 'Waterloo Objections Dropped', Richard Keown
Building Design 2 November 1990: 'Grimshaw's Waterloo Terminal Gets the Go-ahead', Richard Keown
Construction Weekly 8 January 1992: 'Waterloo's West Side Story'
Guardian 23 April 1990: 'The New Battle of Waterloo'
Independent 9 December 1988: 'Waterloo at Heart of £589m Chunnel Plan'
Independent 24 June 1992: 'Light at the End of the Tunnel', Jonathan Glancey
Independent on Sunday 25 March 1990: 'New Age Spirit Meets its Waterloo', Jonathan Glancey
New Builder 1 October 1992: 'Snake Charm', Dave Parker
New Civil Engineer 6 September 1990: 'All Change', Andrew Bolton
New Civil Engineer 5 September 1991: 'Covering all Angles', David Hayward
New Civil Engineer 30 January 1992: 'Levels of Activity', Andrew Bolton
Observer 4 October, 1992: 'Snake in the Glass', Gillian Darley
Structural Engineer 3 December 1991: 'Testing the Roof'
Sunday Telegraph 15 April 1990: 'The Wrecking of a Masterpiece', Paul Finch
Sunday Telegraph 27 October 1991: 'The Chunnel Meets its Waterloo'
Times 12 October 1992: 'BR Offers Glimpse of a New Era in Rail Travel', Michael Dynes

North Woolwich Pumping Station
Architects' Journal 24 & 31 August, 1988: 'Docklands Submarine'

British Pavilion, Expo 92
L'Arca 59, 1992: 'Gran Bretagna: il Vessillo Techologico'
Arch + July 1990: Im Einklang mit den elementen', Philipp Oswalt
Architects' Journal 22 March 1989: 'No Strategy for Seville' and 'Grimshaw Wins, Losers Revolt'
Architects' Journal 22 & 29 August, 1990: 'Britain Versus Rest of the World', Callum Murray
Architectural Review June 1992: 'British Racing Green'
L'Architecture d'Aujord'hui September 1991: 'Britanniques à Seville'
Architecture Today April 1992: Expo 92
Blueprint December–January 1992: 'Seville '92 – The Making of the UK Pavilion'
Building 5 October 1990: 'The Gain in Spain', Denise Chevin
Building 16 April 1992: 'Expo '92, Seville', Martin Spring
Building Design 14 April 1989: 'Perspective: Winning Pavilion' , Paul Finch
Building Design 22 November 1991: 'Cool Quality', John Welsh
Building Design 17 April 1992: 'Expo 92'
Daily Telegraph 30 September 1989: 'Grimshaw: Back to the Future', Kenneth Powell
Financial Times 9 March 1992: 'British Pavilion Pulls it off', Colin Amery
Guardian 22 May 1991: 'Glass – with Care', John Hooper
Independent 27 September 1989: 'Pavilion Flows with Victorian Passion', Jonathan Glancey
Independent 29 March 1992: 'The Far Out Pavilions of Seville', Naomi Stungo
Informes de la Construccion January/February 1992: 'The British Pavilion in the Expo 92 World Fair in Seville'
New Civil Engineer 12 March 1992: 'Pavilions of Splendour'
Observer 10 October 1989: 'Standing in a Glass of its Own', Stephen Gardiner
Progressive Architecture May 1992: 'Seville's Expo 92 – Modernism on Stage', Philip Arcidi
Sunday Times 19 April 1992: 'The Far Out Pavilions', Hugh Pearman
Times 18 April 1992: 'Britain's Block Buster', Kenneth Pearson

Operations Centre for British Rail at Waterloo
Architecture Today 25, 1991: 'Detail: Nicholas Grimshaw & Partners Steel 'Trees' Span Waterloo's Tracks at the International Terminal'
Structural Engineer 17 September 1991: 'Cover Story: Waterloo Raft Development'

Satellite and Piers, Heathrow Airport
Building 22 May 1992: 'Pier Show'
Construction Weekly 8 January 1992: 'One Solution to Heathrow Headache'

Venice Biennale
Guardian 9 September 1991: 'The British Lions of Venice', Deyan Sudjic

Igus Headquarters and Factory
New Builder 26 March 1992: 'Steel Heart', Matthew Pettifer
Progressive Architecture 12, 1991: 'An Investment in High Tech – Production Plant, Cologne, Germany'
Structural Engineer 17 March 1992: 'Engineering and Architecture in Germany – Igus New Factory', Porz Lind, Mark Bryden and Mark Whitby

Western Morning News
Bovis Review 24 January 1992: 'Taking the Helm'
Building Design 3 May 1991: 'Western Morning News, Nicholas Grimshaw'
Evening Herald 17 March, 1990: "Top Architect for New Herald HQ'
Evening Herald 20 December 1991: 'Ship-building "Miracle" is Set air for Success', Ann Knight
Sou'wester (*RIBA Journal*, South West Region), September 1991: 'Hot off the Drawing Board: Grimshaw's Western Morning News Flagship'
Western Morning News 17 March 1990: 'Top Architect to Design new HQ'

Nicholas Grimshaw & Partners

The Team 1988–1993

Directors
Nick Grimshaw
David Harriss
Christopher Nash
Neven Sidor

Associates
Mark Fisher
Rowena Fuller
Paul Grayshon
Andrew Whalley

Yasmin Ahmad
Lindy Atkin
Stella Bartlett
Helena Barrett
Rowena Bate
Liz Bazalgette
Kim Bienefelt
Ingrid Bille
Eoin Billings
Mark Bryden
Stefan Camenzind
Christopher Campbell
Conal Campbell
Garry Colligan
Penny Collins
Paul Cook
Geoff Crowe
Robert Elliston
Florian Eames
Paul Fear
Alex Fergusson
Jacque Ferrier
Barbara Gould
François Gruson
Andrew Hall
Sarah Hare
Hannibal Hayes
Gill Hayes-Wogan
Susan Heathcote
Ursula Heinemann
Linda Hughes
Martin Hyams
Susanne Isa
Deborah Jackson
Duncan Jackson
Eric Jaffres
Dana Karanjac
Matthew Keeler
Doug Keys
Julian King
David Kirkland
Brian La Fontaine
Rosemary Latter
Jonathan Leah
Chris Lee
John Lee

Colin Leisk
Richard Levene
Henrietta Lynch
Nicola Macdonald
Jan Mackie
Michelle Macleod
Andrea Marlowe
John Martin
Julian Maynard
Andrew Nicol
Susi Nolte
Willie O'Brien
Rakesh Patel
Cheree Papprill
Berthold Pesch
Angus Pond
David Portman
Michael Pross
David Radford
Julian Scanlan
Matthew Seabrook
Caroline Smith
Alastair Snodgrass
Marcus Springer
Hayley Spurling
Jill Stanaway
Will Stevens
George Stowell
Dorothee Strauss
Hin Tan
Simon Templeton
Bob Tucker
Sarah Tweedie
Luz Vargas
Michael Waddington
Abby Walker
Richard Walker
Rob Watson
Patricia Williams
Sue Williamson
Martin Wood
Robert Wood
Dean Wylie
Sarah Yabsely
Soo Yau